T0320804

The Political Economy of Automotive
Industrialization in East Asia

The Political Economy of Automotive Industrialization in East Asia

Richard F. Doner, Gregory W. Noble,
and John Ravenhill

OXFORD
UNIVERSITY PRESS

OXFORD
UNIVERSITY PRESS

Oxford University Press is a department of the University of Oxford. It furthers
the University's objective of excellence in research, scholarship, and education
by publishing worldwide. Oxford is a registered trade mark of Oxford University
Press in the UK and certain other countries.

Published in the United States of America by Oxford University Press
198 Madison Avenue, New York, NY 10016, United States of America.

Library of Congress Cataloging-in-Publication Data
Names: Doner, Richard F., author. | Noble, Gregory W., author. | Ravenhill, John, author.
Title: The political economy of automotive industrialization in East Asia /
Richard F. Doner, Gregory W. Noble, and John Ravenhill.
Description: New York, NY : Oxford University Press, [2021] |
Includes bibliographical references and index.
Identifiers: LCCN 2020037151 (print) | LCCN 2020037152 (ebook) |
ISBN 9780197520253 (hardback) | ISBN 9780197520260 (paperback) |
ISBN 9780197520284 (epub)
Subjects: LCSH: Automobile industry and trade—East Asia. | Industrial policy—East Asia.
Classification: LCC HD9710.E272 D66 2021 (print) | LCC HD9710.E272 (ebook) |
DDC 338.4/7629222095—dc23
LC record available at https://lccn.loc.gov/2020037151
LC ebook record available at https://lccn.loc.gov/2020037152

DOI: 10.1093/oso/9780197520253.001.0001

1 3 5 7 9 8 6 4 2

Paperback printed by Marquis, Canada
Hardback printed by Bridgeport National Bindery, Inc., United States of America

Contents

Preface

All three of us have been studying the auto industry in East Asia for more than three decades. We began collaborating on research on the sector when the World Bank invited us to prepare a paper for its "post-East Asian Miracle" study (published as Doner, Noble, and Ravenhill 2004). Subsequently, we collaborated on other studies of the auto industry, including an article on the impact of accession to the WTO on China's auto industry (Noble, Ravenhill, and Doner 2005) and a background paper (by Doner and Ravenhill) for the World Bank's study of Malaysia and the middle-income trap (Yusuf and Nabeshima 2009). The present book is the culmination of the authors' long experience in studying the East Asian auto industries.

In the period since we began working on autos, the industry has changed dramatically. As evidence, one need look no further than under the hood of the contemporary vehicle. A quarter of a century ago, someone with a modest aptitude for mechanics could confidently replace key parts such as starter motors or carburetors. Today, most parts are hidden from sight (and easy access)—and sophisticated computer equipment is needed to perform a routine service on a vehicle.

When we began our collaboration, in the run-up to China's accession to the WTO in 2001, autos was the industrial sector in China that commentators identified most often as vulnerable to a loss of tariff protection (Harwit 1995; Lardy 2002). Predicted losses in employment in the industry ranged from half a million to close to 5 million jobs. Today, the Chinese auto industry is the largest in the world, producing more than 24 million passenger cars (up from 700,000 at the time of China's accession to the WTO) and close to 5 million commercial vehicles annually. It accounts for nearly 30% of worldwide vehicle production (Statista 2016).

While we continue to be fascinated by the car industry, researching it poses a number of challenges. With the ever-increasing use of electronic components in vehicles, the boundaries of the auto sector are less and less distinct. To some extent, there has always been a problem in isolating auto components in international trade. For instance, wing mirrors might be recorded by customs authorities under the more general tariff heading for glass mirrors; in a similar vein, GPS devices for autos are categorized under the rubric of "radar apparatus, radio navigational aid apparatus and radio remote control apparatus." The lack of specificity is often compounded by inconsistency in reporting by national customs authorities. At one point, we invested substantial time in drawing up a list of auto components and classifying them by level of complexity. When we attempted to make use of this classification, however, we found that some national customs authorities would, in one year, provide detailed breakdowns of auto component imports only, in the following year, to lump everything together under the heading of "automotive components not elsewhere specified."

We had hoped as far as possible to make use of standardized data from international organizations. But, because of incomplete and inconsistent reporting, this was frequently not available (and Taiwan's absence from most international organizations caused its own problems). Consequently, for some of our tables, we have had to compile data from a variety of national sources. The most useful sources varied from country to country—in some instances, national statistical yearbooks were helpful; in others, we relied very heavily on data collected by industry associations.

The analysis in this book rests on multiple research trips to our case study countries over the last three decades. On these trips, we conducted interviews with company managers, government officials, representatives of industry associations, auto research agencies and institutes, journalists specializing in the auto sector, and fellow academics. Between us, we had capacity to interview in most of the national languages—the exception was Korea, where we employed a translator. Because we were interested in answering the same research questions across all our cases, the interviews were semi-structured—but often wide-ranging when respondents were eager to go beyond our initial questions. As far as possible, we triangulated the responses across various sources—whether different interviewees or documentary materials. Obtaining access to the private sector is never easy—not least where researchers are regarded with suspicion (on one visit to Hyundai Motors, for instance, we were questioned why political scientists would be interested in the auto industry and whether, because one of us is affiliated with a Japanese university, we were working for Toyota!). Persistence pays off, however.

A grant from the Australian Research Council (DP0666673, "Responding to Globalization: Firms, the State and Upgrading in the Automotive Industry on the Western Pacific Rim") generously supported this project. This funding enabled the authors to make multiple field trips to our case study countries. It also facilitated meetings of the authors to discuss chapter drafts—in Thailand, in Berkeley, and at Stanford University. We are grateful to John Zysman, then Director of the Berkeley Roundtable on International Economics, and Don Emerson, then Director of the Walter H. Shorenstein Asia-Pacific Research

Center at Stanford University, for accommodating these meetings. The Australian Research Council funding supported a generation of PhD students in the Department of International Relations, Research School of Pacific and Asian Studies at the Australian National University—André Broome, Yang Jiang, Jikon Lai, Sang-bok Moon, Rongfang Pang, and Jeff Wilson—whose research assistance is gratefully acknowledged.

At Emory University, Elvin Ong and Andy Ratto collected data for some of the tables in the first three chapters; Katharine Tatum did a great job in formatting the first draft of the manuscript to OUP's requirements. A publications grant from the Balsillie School of International Affairs enabled us to employ Caleb Lauer, a PhD student at the School, to provide a final update to the figures and tables, and to compile the index. We appreciate both the grant and the outstanding work that Caleb did for us. Doner is grateful to Emory University's Department of Political Science and to the International Labour Organization for funding that supported his research. Several terms as Visiting Professor in the S. Rajaratnam School of International Studies at Nangyang Technological University in Singapore provided Ravenhill with an excellent base in Southeast Asia: he thanks the then Director of the School, Ambassador Barry Desker, for hosting him.

In Korea, Jung-Hyun Choi (최정현) was enormously helpful in setting up interviews for us and, where needed, providing simultaneous translation. Were it not for her persistence and powers of persuasion, we would have had far less success in gaining access to the seemingly impenetrable auto sector in Korea. We thank Hun Joo Park, of the KDI School of Public Policy and Management, for introducing us to Dr. Choi and for his other help on the Korean leg of this project. In Indonesia, we received substantial assistance from the late Thee Kian Wee, Ridwan Gunawan, and several former officials of the Astra Corporation. In Thailand, important insights into the evolution of the auto industry were provided by Boonharn Ou-Udomying, George Abonyi, Archanun Kopaiboon, Somsak Tambunlertchai, Achana Limpaiboon, Thavorn Chalassatien, Krisda Suchiva, Akira Suehiro, Adisak Kongwaree, Parithut Bhandubhanyong, Narong Varongkriengkrai, and Anittha Jutarosaga. Doner is especially grateful to Laurids Lauridsen for his exemplary scholarship and to Chayo Trangadisaikul, who has gone out of his way to provide an understanding of all levels of the industry in Thailand, from problem-solving on the factory floor, to business association initiatives, to ministerial debates and decisions. In Malaysia, Jean Law (MACPMA), Kevin Wai (JEBCO), Chow Siew Hon and Terence Chow (Yokohama Battery), Winston Hock (Nakagawa Rubber), Herman Leong (Tong Yong Rubber), and Paul Low (Malaysian Sheet Glass) all provided insights into the development of the industry and its contemporary challenges. Ravenhill is also grateful to officials from the Malaysian government and to senior executives at Proton, interviewed as part of the World Bank project.

For help with the China chapter, we would like to extend our thanks to Zhu Tianbiao, then at Beijing University, now at Zhejiang University; Kamiyama Kunio of Josai University, who took the lead in organizing several research trips to China; Shahid Yusuf, then at the World Bank, now at Georgetown University, for inviting us to conduct interviews at several innovative Chinese firms, including the leading privately-owned automotive parts firm Wanxiang; and last but not least to the University of Tokyo's Institute of Social Science for support with travel funds. In Taiwan, special thanks are due to Feng Chi-tai, then Taiwan's Representative to Japan; Yeh Kuang-shih, former Minister of Transportation; Hwang Wen-fang, then section chief of the Taiwan Transportation Vehicle Manufacturers Association (TTVMA); and Stephen Su, Jim Chung, Justine Cheng-mei Tung, and Chen Chih Yang of the Industrial Technology Research Institute (ITRI).

Finally, we are grateful to Kaoru Natsuda and John Thoburn for their advice and scholarship on the Southeast Asian auto industries, and thank the three readers for OUP who provided incisive comments and prompted us to clarify our arguments.

1

Introduction

Contrary to the expectations of convergence found in conventional growth theories, only a handful of countries have graduated from middle-income to high-income status in the last half century. Many developing economies appear to be mired in a "middle-income trap" in which they have been increasingly squeezed between the low-wage country competitors dominating mature industries and more developed country innovators dominating industries experiencing rapid technological change (Gill, Kharas, and Bhattasali 2007: 5). For most, the absolute gap between their per capita gross domestic product (GDP) and those of industrialized economies has increased (Kharas and Gill 2019). Lagging productivity is one, if not the fundamental, source of this gap (see, for example, Agénor and Canuto 2012: 3–4). Industrial upgrading is a key to closing this gap and thus a principal challenge facing developing countries.

Industrial upgrading, which we discuss in more detail in Chapter 3, occurs when domestic firms acquire the capabilities to move into higher value-added activities at global levels of efficiency. Our emphasis is on value added not simply through increases in the capital intensity of production (Krugman 1994) but rather as achieved by domestic firms producing at global levels of efficiency while absorbing advanced foreign technology and incorporating a widening range and higher level of local skills. This upgrading involves improvements in process, product, and functions, and in some cases shifts into new, related sectors (Barrientos, Gereffi, and Rossi 2011). If such changes are to occur in more than a few exceptional firms, they must involve what Lall (2000: 24) calls a "common national environment" that helps firms to develop new capabilities rather than merely doing more of the same thing or relying on foreign companies with advanced capabilities. In this book, our focus is on whether and how upgrading has occurred in the automobile industry in seven East Asian economies: China, Indonesia, Korea, Malaysia, the Philippines, Taiwan, and Thailand.

We are especially interested in going beyond what is usually labeled "industrialization," a concept that masks substantial differences in economic transformation. We distinguish between two stylized but analytically useful

The Political Economy of Automotive Industrialization in East Asia. Richard F. Doner, Gregory W. Noble and John Ravenhill, Oxford University Press (2021). © Oxford University Press. DOI: 10.1093/oso/9780197520253.003.0001

approaches to industrialization that lead to different levels of growth, each with their own challenges. In some countries, automotive industrialization involves *extensive growth*, consisting largely of vehicle and components assembly and, in some cases, exports, primarily under the aegis of foreign producers operating in global value chains. Extensive growth is principally characterized by economic diversification, i.e., changes in a country's economic structure through inter-sectoral shifts in the allocation of labor and other resources, which provide employment opportunities and generate foreign exchange earnings. But productivity gains from sectoral shifts typically do not on their own lead to increases in local value added based on inputs from national producers and on national technical capabilities (Waldner 1999; Amsden 2001; Doner 2009). Such increases are the key elements of upgrading, which for us is the essence of *intensive* growth.

Automotive "industrialization" in East Asia is striking for its variation in both strategy and performance (Table 1.1). As described in subsequent chapters, China, Korea and Taiwan have pursued various forms of intensive growth strategies with considerable success, whereas Thailand, by completely relying on foreign assemblers, has become a champion of extensive growth, manifesting impressive expansion of production, assembly, and exports. Although these achievements were part of a worldwide trend toward the transfer of automobile assembly to less developed economies where the major growth in global demand is occurring (discussed in Chapter 2), they were by no means inevitable. Indeed, auto production in many other developing countries, including some in East Asia, has been characterized by lags or stalls. Indonesia has achieved a degree of success at extensive auto industrialization only after decades of ineffective and expensive intensive growth efforts. In the Philippines, the site of the region's first automotive industrialization efforts, attempts to expand assembly and parts production through an extensive strategy under foreign auspices have largely stalled. Finally, Malaysia has persistently but ineffectively attempted to emulate Korea's strategy of

Table 1.1 Cross-National Variation in East Asian Automotive Industrialization

Performance	Strategy	
	Extensive	Intensive
Strong	Thailand	S. Korea, Taiwan, China
Weak	Indonesia (gradual improvement) Philippines	Malaysia

Note: Assessment based on performance data provided in Chapter 2.

intensive industrialization. Explaining this variance in both strategy and performance is the focus of this book. More specifically, through comparative case studies of automotive industrialization efforts, we highlight the impact of institutional and underlying political factors largely unaddressed by existing analyses.

The automobile industry is an obvious candidate for examining national upgrading efforts. For over a century, it has occupied a central position in the global economy. It has been a major source of employment and skill development in manufacturing, and one of the most important segments of international trade. The industry presents opportunities to local supporting industries by virtue of its myriad components and its powerful backward linkages to raw and intermediate materials such as steel, plastics, and rubber, as well as to machinery, computers, sensors and a wide range of capital equipment. In 2020, for example, the share of electronic components in the total cost of vehicles was estimated to be over 35%, nearly double its share at the turn of the century (Statista 2019a). The auto industry accounts for around 9% of the total revenues of the global semiconductor industry (Kendall 2018). It also creates substantial forward linkages to service industries such as sales, service and repairs, and insurance. And, outside of housing, cars are the biggest purchases most families ever make.

Given its economic significance, the automobile industry is also politically strategic. Not surprisingly, countries have long regarded success in the car industry as a cornerstone of industrialization and a symbol of national development. When the financial crisis of 2008–2009 hammered auto sales, governments across the world poured tens of billions of dollars into propping up local producers. More recently, the move toward hybrid and electric vehicles offers developing countries the prospect of "leapfrogging" to become pioneers in technologies that may sustain the next wave of industrial evolution.

Why then do the East Asian countries differ in their development trajectories in this crucial industry? Why, for example, has the Thai auto industry evolved largely toward extensive growth and done so with great success, whereas others have moved much more belatedly (Indonesia) or less successfully (Philippines) in this direction? Why have Malaysia, Korea, China, and Taiwan aimed at upgrading through intensive development, with Malaysia faring poorly compared to the latter three countries?

Resolving these puzzles requires us to ask questions such as: What kinds of national and sectoral capabilities are needed to help domestic firms develop the competencies required to manufacture and export vehicles or complex automotive components? How do such capabilities differ from those required where development is limited to auto assembly by foreign producers? What do local firms need if they are to develop the technological and managerial capacities to design as well as to manufacture automotive components? What kinds of difficulties are involved in generating such competencies? What kinds of organizational arrangements and institutions are required to overcome these difficulties? These questions are especially important given the failures inherent in technology markets (Lall and Teubal 1998). More specifically, to what extent do we find institutions, such as sectoral institutes, specialized training programs, and testing centers devoted to the diffusion and deepening of technologies new to domestic firms (Shapira et al. 2015)? And, most critically, under what conditions do political leaders, typically more interested in satisfying close supporters and reacting to immediate political concerns, opt to spend the time and resources required to build such institutions?

The answer we propose in this book engages major debates on development at two levels. First, our approach departs from the analysis in conventional, neoclassical economics. We argue that stable macroeconomic conditions, clear property rights, and free flows of productive factors are, on their own, far from sufficient to overcome the market failures and imperfections inherent in economic development, especially under conditions of rapid technological change. These include shortages of qualified personnel due to fear of poaching by competitors, lack of information about technologies appropriate to local firms, the need for and costs of experiential knowledge through active, hands-on "tinkering," long gestation periods with uncertain returns, a lack of complementary goods and services (e.g., physical infrastructure), and shortages of financing due to risk-averse lenders and imperfect financial markets.

By downplaying the significance of such challenges, mainstream economics accounts typically overlook the coordination and collective action challenges inherent in economic development, especially in upgrading. In doing so, they ignore institutions, whose function is precisely to overcome coordination problems by helping interdependent actors, especially firms, achieve joint gains (Hausmann and Rodrik 2002). As discussed in Chapter 3, development scholars' and practitioners' appreciation of institutions (beyond stable property rights) has grown significantly in the past few decades, as reflected in the emergence of "good governance," "national innovation systems," "developmental state," and "global value chain" frameworks. These institutionalist approaches represent significant advances in the understanding of the development process, and inform this book.

But we go beyond these frameworks. First, we emphasize and explore differences in development challenges, especially those inherent in intensive versus extensive growth. Second, we explore the institutional implications of challenges posed by these alternative strategies. We suggest that intensive development requires different kinds of institutions than those necessary to meet the challenges of extensive growth. Finally, we argue that institutions do not create themselves spontaneously simply because, in principle, they can promote efficiency gains among interdependent actors. Instead, we explore the conditions under which political leaders opt to support the development of such institutions. In sum, we propose a political economy explanation of the heterogeneity of East Asian auto industrialization as follows:

(1) Different forms of automotive industrialization require different kinds of competencies at both the macro (national or sectoral) level and micro (firm) level. These range from financial mobilization and basic infrastructure for extensive growth, to "quality infrastructure" such as testing and standards or technical training for the kinds of firm capacities required for intensive growth. The challenges of intensive growth (upgrading) are more demanding than those of extensive growth. Our arguments would be falsified if we found intensive growth, i.e., upgrading in national automotive sectors, in the absence of such competencies.

(2) The development of various competencies in turn poses different kinds of challenges and degrees of difficulty (reflected, for instance, in the amount and type of information and the number of actors whose participation is required). Addressing these challenges is a task for institutions that facilitate different kinds and degrees of exchanges among firms, officials, and workers. The precise, optimal design (e.g., degrees of decentralization or delegation) of such institutions depends on sectoral and national contexts. For our purposes, however, the key proposition is the idea of "goodness of fit" between institutions and development challenges. More specifically, we hypothesize that extensive growth will be associated with institutions that focus largely on mobilizing capital and labor, whereas intensive growth through upgrading will feature institutions that facilitate the absorption and development of technologies new to a country's firms.

(3) Politics—more specifically, pressures on leaders of political regimes—is key to institutional strength. Institutions with the capacities to promote upgrading will emerge to the degree that national regimes are compelled to address external threats and domestic unrest but lack easy access to resources enabling them to do so. Put more simply, tough conditions will, other things being equal, push leaders to deepen local industrialization through support of appropriate institutions despite

the vicissitudes of political and business cycles. They will be willing to make the hard choice of sacrificing current consumption to facilitate long-term development. We expect that only under such conditions will we find governments providing resources for upgrading institutions.

We introduce and assess our argument in the following steps: Chapter 2 begins by reviewing the lure and challenges of the global auto industry, and then establishes the book's core empirical puzzle: how to explain cross-national variation in response to these conditions within East Asia. We address this puzzle through a two-pronged comparative research design in Chapters 3–9. The first, covered in Chapter 3, consists of theoretically informed, cross-case analysis. In this "most-similar-different-outcome" design, we examine variation in the strategies and performance of seven countries pursuing automotive industrialization within the same region and the same producer-driven value chain. We systematically assess the strength of a number of existing explanations (e.g., population size, open trade and investment policies, "good governance" institutions, global value chains, national innovation systems), and find that none of these constitutes an adequate explanation for performance variation. We then assess our hypothesized explanation. We first track the strength of institutions for industrial coordination, learning, and diffusion, finding that such arrangements correspond closely to variations in performance. We then move back in the causal chain by exploring the factors that account for these variations in institutional strength; we find a close correspondence between constrained natural resource endowments, external threats, and domestic political pressures (what we label "vulnerability") on the one hand, and the strength of institutions for industrial diffusion and learning on the other.

Findings from such cross-case, "most-similar" comparisons are important for identifying variables that at first glance appear to be relevant but actually have little causal influence. For example, the fact that all seven of our countries have pursued automotive industrialization within the same global value chains and geographical regions suggests that these common factors are not relevant for explaining different outcomes. Similarly, the fact that both Indonesia and China have large populations and similar levels of per capita GDP but differ significantly in automotive industry performance suggests that population and income are far from determinant of industry performance.

On their own, such comparisons constitute an insufficient basis on which to draw strong causal conclusions because they typically require unrealistic and demanding assumptions to yield non-spurious conclusions. For our purposes, the key problem is the difficulty of assuming that we have identified each factor that contributed causally to automotive industry performance (Bennett 2004). More specifically, it is difficult if not impossible to exclude the possibility that other factors, besides or beyond the presence of certain kinds of institutions and pressures on political leaders, account for the superior performance of, say, South Korea, relative to Malaysia.

Such weaknesses in cross-case analysis typically lead researchers to a second strategy, within-case analysis, which we pursue in Chapters 4–9. To facilitate further cross-case analysis, we cluster the cases into "intensive" and "extensive" strategy groups, thus allowing a comparison between more and less successful cases within each group. Such an analysis cannot conclusively resolve what is, in effect, a problem of causal inference. Through more in-depth exploration of each national industry case, we provide a finer-grained assessment of performance and, most crucially, trace the temporal evolution of policies and especially institutions relative to such performance and the strength of our vulnerability variables.

2

The Lure and Challenges of the Automobile Industry

The automobile industry simultaneously entices and challenges developing countries. It is a leading employer and source of industrial output, a major trader, and a crucial integrator of manufacturing technologies. The industry has a wealth of backward and forward linkages. Autos also drive major financial and service sectors such as car loans, auto insurance, and networks of dealerships and repair shops. The industry holds unusual political and military significance, and serves as a marker of domestic and international prestige. Meeting the high requirements for quality and durability of automobile parts can help to raise the level of the entire manufacturing sector, including precision machining, multidimensional robots, computer-aided design and engineering, high-quality steel, injection molds, and other areas with important implications for the military-industrial complex. In this chapter we first briefly consider the significance of the automobile industry in global manufacturing and trade, discuss the challenges faced by firms in developing economies seeking to enter the industry, and then look at the evolution of production in the global industry and the specific performance of our case economies.

The automotive assembly and components industry employs more than 8 million people worldwide, more than 5% of the total global employment in manufacturing. In addition to these direct employees, the International Organization of Motor Vehicle Manufacturers estimates that about five times this number are employed indirectly in related manufacturing and service provision (http://www.oica.net/search/employment).

One reason for the attractiveness of the industry to developing economies is its role in international trade. Automotive products constituted 9% of total global trade in manufactures in 2018, trailing only office and telecom equipment, and chemicals: global exports of automotive products amounted to more than $1.5 trillion. The automotive industry also has a high positive income elasticity of demand: a 10% increase in income generates a 30% rise in demand for automobiles, a sharp contrast to most agricultural products,

The Political Economy of Automotive Industrialization in East Asia. Richard F. Doner, Gregory W. Noble and John Ravenhill, Oxford University Press (2021). © Oxford University Press. DOI: 10.1093/oso/9780197520253.003.0002

for which demand typically rises by only 2% with a 10% increase in income (McConnell and Brue 2005: 368). A country lacking a substantial domestic auto industry will face a drain on its balance of payments from increasing auto imports as per capita income rises. In the past, vehicle ownership has increased dramatically when annual per capita income reached approximately $3,000–5,000 (in constant year 2000 $US) and peaked around $10,000 (Wang, Teter, and Sperling 2011: 3298). China and Thailand crossed the $5,000 threshold at the end of the first decade of this century, and by 2016 Indonesia reached nearly $4,000.

The Challenges of the Contemporary Auto Industry

Despite the prominence and allure of automobiles, the car industry presents daunting obstacles to would-be new entrants in developing countries. Barriers to entry in assembly and production of the more sophisticated parts and components are extremely high. Besides the initial costs of investment, the challenges include the need for volume production to realize economies of scale, generating bargaining leverage in a market increasingly characterized by oligopsony, and (where appropriate) establishing a positive brand image.

New assembly plants typically require initial investments in the hundreds of millions if not billions of dollars, and require coordination of inputs from a vast array of suppliers. Large components require an even more substantial investment: the cost of developing a new family of engines is estimated at between $1.3 and $2.6 billion (Automotive News 2012). And emerging technologies are even more prohibitive: Hyundai announced in 2019, for instance, that it was investing $6.7 billion in the development of its hydrogen fuel system and a further $2 billion in autonomous driving technology (Song and White 2019; Song 2019).

New entrants also face the challenge of quickly ramping up output to reach efficient levels of production. For engines and transmissions, the conventional rule-of-thumb for minimum efficient scale was typically one million units per year; for foundry, pressing, and forging, it was two million plus. These figures are of such a magnitude that only a handful of manufacturers—General Motors (GM), Ford, Toyota, Nissan, Volkswagen (VW), Renault, and Groupe Peugeot Société Anonyme (PSA)—approximated the volumes required for minimum efficient scale for foundry activities in the 1990s. Early studies suggested that the penalty that manufacturers incur if producing at only 50% of minimum efficient scale (MES) is an increase in unit cost of approximately

6%. Hasan (1997) quotes data from Waverman and Murphy (1992) that suggest that this cost penalty rises to 20% when production is only 30% of MES, and to 34.5% at one-tenth of MES. Latecomers thus face a dilemma: maximizing cost competitiveness requires expensive investment in large plants, but if they are unable to sell all of that massive output, production will remain high-cost and inefficient.

The auto industry also presents imposing challenges of quality control and coordination. Unlike steel and commodity chemicals, where much of the technology is embedded in capital equipment available for purchase even by firms in developing countries, and the key to success is efficient use of production capacity, success in the auto industry requires integrating thousands of parts into an attractive and durable design. Market pressures and legal requirements for quality, durability, safety, comfort, drivability and performance, sound insulation, fuel efficiency, emissions controls, recyclability, and product liability are high and continue to increase. In 1998, American consumers surveyed by J. D. Power reported 176 problems per 100 vehicles. By 2009 the figure had fallen to 108, despite the increasing complexity and luxury of cars (J. D. Power and Associates 2010) (subsequently, the fall has been less dramatic, in part because of problems with more sophisticated electronics: in 2018, the industry average was 93 problems per 100 vehicles [J. D. Power and Associates 2018]).

Brand names matter in the auto industry, posing another barrier to entry. It is not just "petrol heads" that associate the name Aston Martin with luxury cars or that of Volvo with safe but rather staid vehicles. Moreover, it is far easier to damage a positive image than to overcome a negative brand image. Korea's Hyundai, for example, struggled for years to overcome the negative image that its early auto exports to North America generated. And, in the public mind, all exports from a particular country may become "tarred with the same brush" because of the problems of one manufacturer—hence the aversion to "Korean" cars in the late 1990s.

Production of vehicles and components has become increasingly consolidated in the hands of a few companies in the "global North." Very few countries have successfully launched and sustained a domestically owned assembly industry in the seven decades since the end of the Second World War; Japan was the first to do so, followed by Korea. Malaysia enjoyed some short-term success in exporting cars assembled by domestically owned companies but, as we discuss later in this volume, it failed to sustain its national champion assembler. Finally, China's independent companies, while still facing formidable challenges, seem to be on the verge of breaking into international markets as well as competing effectively within their domestic market, now the world's largest. But elsewhere around the globe, independent producers have disappeared or have been acquired by the major global players. Famous brands such as Volvo, Land Rover, MG, and Jaguar have all changed hands—some on several occasions. The liberalization of trade in auto products has enabled consumers to choose the advanced offerings of the global automakers and shun inferior local products.

As a prominent study concluded, the auto industry this century has been undergoing a "profound transition" from one historically based on exporting from home country–based exporters to a network-led industry organized around regional and global supply chains through which each major firm produces in all of the significant markets (Sturgeon and Lester 2004). This account slightly exaggerates—most global auto firms remain highly dependent on their home markets and at most one other region, and virtually none derives revenues evenly from around the world. Six of the top 10 auto components suppliers, for instance, all receive more than half of their revenue from sales in one regional market (Automotive News 2019). Nonetheless, it vividly summarizes important trends. Mergers and acquisitions have by no means uniformly succeeded, as Daimler's failed takeover of Chrysler and many other examples in the supply industry suggest, but the broad trend toward globalization and consolidation remains unchecked. The top eight global assemblers are estimated to have a 90% share of global revenues; the top 50 components companies command more than 80% of the global market (Automotive News 2017b).

Components

Whereas consumers usually think of the auto industry in terms of assembled cars, two-thirds or more of value-added in an automobile actually resides in the myriad parts that go into it. The annual value of auto components manufactured globally in 2018 exceeded $800 billion, based on the sum of global sales of the top 100 Original Equipment Manufacturers (OEM) parts suppliers (Automotive News 2019). Comtrade data indicate that the value of exports of auto components in 2018 approached $375 billions. The spread of lean production techniques has produced a reversal of the vertical integration so doggedly pursued by Henry Ford, and in a more moderate form by Alfred Sloan at GM. In order to increase flexibility, enhance transmission of price signals and market competition, and cut labor costs, assemblers spun off many of their parts divisions, led by Delphi (GM) and Visteon (Ford), which immediately became two of the largest parts firms in the world.

As with assembly, a major consolidation has occurred in the components industry in the last two decades. According to one study, auto parts manufacturers in North America numbered 30,000 in 1990, but had shrunk to 10,000 by 2000 and to 8,000 by 2004. By 2010, there were only 5,784 firms in the industry (Bureau of Labor Statistics 2011a). From 2014 to 2017, the combined value of supplier mergers and acquisitions averaged $50–60 billion; in 2018 it jumped to a record $97.5 billion, driven in part by a desire to enhance capabilities in technology for autonomous vehicles and connectivity (Automotive News 2019).

For many major parts, such as engine control systems or seats, a handful of global companies such as Bosch and Johnson Controls supply the vast majority of global demand. In order to facilitate just-in-time production, first-tier suppliers of modules and parts typically invest in facilities located near or even inside those of the final assembler. The components industry in East Asia has been deeply affected by these trends, particularly since the financial crises of 1997–1998 and 2008–2009. The entrance of Western assemblers, intensified competition for the region's growing markets, and shorter product cycles have pushed global automakers to expand parts manufacture in East Asia as part of increasingly integrated regional and global production networks.

Meeting the performance expectations of assemblers requires ongoing innovation by producers, another challenge faced by domestic companies in East Asia. Innovation in the auto industry is generally incremental and cumulative, based as much on tacit skills as formal research and development. Leapfrogging incumbents is much more difficult than in the many segments of the electronics industry that are periodically reshaped by radical innovations (although the move to electric vehicles may have a similar impact on the auto industry). Successful production of auto parts requires a combination of independence and tight linkages with suppliers. Some parts, such as tires, wheels, and batteries, are relatively independent of the design of the overall vehicle and from other parts, but most are tightly integrated. Auto assemblers, which might more accurately be termed system integrators, are enmeshed with component suppliers and lower-level parts producers in complex networks that balance cooperation and competition.

Several other developments within the global industry have further raised entry barriers to component producers that aspire to sell directly to assemblers. The most notable of these has been a move to common platforms (generally understood as a common underbody and suspension (with axles), although the term is often used freely in the industry). Since the mid-1990s, assemblers have increasingly produced a range of cars off the same product platform. In April 2012, for instance, VW announced that it intended to introduce a modular platform that would be used in 40 different models worldwide, involving a total production of 40 million units (Rogers 2012). The initial investment costs for developing these platforms are very high. But once established, platforms offer assemblers an opportunity to realize substantial economies of scale and scope as parts are standardized across a number of models. Korth (2003) cites the example of a major assembler that in 1995 used 45 different trunk lock mechanisms across its various vehicles. By 1999, it had reduced this total to 12. Assemblers have returned to the idea of producing "world cars" off a single platform. Ford's Fiesta, for example, is assembled in China, Germany, Mexico, Taiwan, Thailand, Venezuela, and Vietnam (http:// corporate.ford.com/company/operation-list.html#s1f30; accessed August 25, 2017).

For aspiring first-tier parts suppliers, the use of platforms poses several challenges. First, they have to work closely with the assemblers in the development of products that will function effectively across a range of vehicles. Second, they typically need to have a global presence to be able to supply to the various plants that are using the same platform. Third, they have to be able to produce in substantial volumes.

Related to the move to common platforms is a second trend, led by European carmakers: modularization. Instead of ordering and assembling all of the thousands of parts that go into an automobile, global automakers provide first-tier suppliers with rough specifications and then rely on the suppliers not only to produce the modules cheaply and reliably, but also to invest heavily in product innovation and to collaborate with them on the development of new vehicles. For the assemblers, this particular form of outsourcing reduces their capital requirements, forces others to share risks, and enables them to capitalize on expertise outside the firm. For parts producers, modularization can facilitate a move up the value chain and also enable them to develop technologies that can be applied across several manufacturers (realizing economies of scale and sometimes of scope). But it also involves very substantial investments. In 1996, parts firms devoted an average of 2.6% of revenues on research and development; by 2003 that figure had increased to 4.2%, nearly as high as that for the average global assembler (Misawa 2005).

Coupled with the downward price pressures that are endemic to the industry (in our interviews, we regularly heard stories of assemblers requiring at least an annual 5% reduction in price from component suppliers, and in some instances the figure was as high as 20%), the requirement for higher levels of capital outlays has encouraged a process of consolidation among first-tier suppliers similar to that among assemblers. All the largest first-tier suppliers— Robert Bosch (Germany), Denso (Japan), Magna (Canada), Continental

(Germany), ZF Friedrichshafen (Germany), and Aisin Seiki (Japan)—in 2018 had revenues above $30 billion (in comparison, the 2018 revenues for GM were $147 billion and for Ford $160 billion) (Automotive News 2019; General Motors 2019; Ford Motor Company 2019). Just as very few assemblers from developing economies have survived in this competitive industry, so very few parts companies from outside the industrialized world have grown to be major players. Of the top 100 global suppliers in 2019, only 18 companies came from outside the Triad of Europe, North America, and Japan (Table 2.1) (Automotive News 2019). Fourteen were from China and Korea. The smallest of these companies, Anhui Zhongding Sealing Parts, from China, had sales of $1.6 billion in 2019.

This failure to date of companies from other parts of Asia to grow into competitive global players stands in marked contrast to their success in electronics—although rapid growth by some Chinese suppliers may change this story.

Table 2.1 Component Suppliers from Outside the Triad in the World Top 100

Rank in Automotive News' Top 100 Supplier list	Supplier	Country
7	Hyundai Mobis	Korea
19	Yanfeng Automotive Trim Systems Co	China
22	Samvardhana Motherson Group	India
36	Hyundai-Transys Inc	Korea
37	Hyundai-WIA	Korea
42	Hanon Systems	Korea
49	Mando Corp.	Korea
57	BHAP	China
58	Nemak	Mexico
66	CITIC Dicastal Co	China
79	Johnson Electric Group	Hong Kong
80	Iochpe-Maxion	Brazil
86	Minth Group	China
88	Hyundai Kefico Corp	Korea
89	SL Corp	Korea
90	Wuling Industry	China
94	Seoyon E-wha	Korea
98	Anhui Zhongding Sealing Parts Co	China

Source: Automotive News, 29 June 2020 <https://www.nxtbook.com/nxtbooks/crain/an8097364512SITPF_supp/index.php#/p/SIntro> (accessed 31 October 2020)

In short, domestic companies in Asia face formidable challenges if they aspire to break into the ranks of leading first-tier component producers. Although the size of the industry provides scope for entry at lower tiers of the supply chain, the risk is that companies will be operating in a relatively low-technology segment where downward pressures on prices are most formidable. We turn now to the shifting range of policy instruments available to Asian governments seeking to navigate the challenges of the contemporary industry.

Constrained Policy Instruments

What policy instruments are available to Asian governments seeking to build their domestic capabilities in the automotive industry? Here we find a rapidly changing landscape. The trade and investment policy options available to governments are increasingly, but not entirely, constrained by commitments that they have entered into in bilateral, regional, and global trade regimes.

The automotive sector historically has been among the most heavily protected in manufacturing. Governments' desires to promote what has been regarded as a sector of strategic significance have led them to use the full panoply of protectionist instruments to attempt to develop local capabilities. The ongoing political sensitivity of the sector has had a powerful effect in shaping the emerging division of labor in the industry (Sturgeon and van Biesebroeck 2011).

Traditionally, most developing countries erected high barriers against imports of motor vehicles and components, including quotas, local content requirements, and extremely high tariffs, often exceeding 100%. They hoped that enticing investment, usually by global auto firms in local assembly operations, with promises of protection against imports, or by licensing technology from producers in advanced countries, would spur the creation of a local parts industry. Even after many rounds of trade liberalization under the World Trade Organization (WTO) and its predecessor, the General Agreement on Tariffs and Trade (GATT), regional agreements, and bilateral Preferential Trade Agreements (PTAs), autos and parts at the dawn of the 21st century attracted tariffs much higher than those in electronics or most other manufacturing sectors (Table 2.2). After acceding to the WTO in 2001 and completing a six-year transition period, China continued to levy a 25% tariff on imports of motor vehicles and 10% tariffs on auto parts. Even Thailand, famously accommodating toward foreign investment, imposed surprisingly

Table 2.2 2015 Tariffs on Assembled Vehicles and Auto Components

	Assembled Vehicles*	Auto Components**
Australia	5%	3%–5%
Canada	3%–6%	3%–6%
China	25%	9%–14%
Indonesia	27%–50%	5%–25%
Japan	0%	0%
Korea	8%	8%
Malaysia	15%–24%	13%–30%
Philippines	20%–30%	1%–16%
Taiwan	17.5%	0%–15%
Thailand	40%–77%	10%–30%

* Motor Vehicles listed under HS 8703 tariff heading.

** Auto Components listed under HS 8708 tariff heading.

Source: World Trade Organization Tariff Download Facility, http://tariffdata.wto.org/ (last accessed May 24, 2017). Data for Taiwan from Government of Taiwan, "Tariff Database Search," https://portal. sw.nat.gov.tw/APGQ/GC451 (last accessed October 20, 2019).

high tariffs on autos and their parts: as of 2013, tariffs on motor vehicles varied from 40% to 77%, while tariffs on auto parts ranged from 10% to 30%.

Non-tariff barriers and explicit or implicit local-contents requirements were also used extensively to protect the auto industry. Promotional measures included preferential allocation of financing, investments in research and development, and subsidies for testing, training, and technology diffusion. Even seemingly neutral (WTO-compliant) regulations often served to promote a particular policy or industry sector. In the case of Thailand, tax policy gave a huge preference to purchasers of one-ton pickups, thus encouraging consolidation within the pickup sector. Eventually Thailand became the world's second-largest producer and a major exporter of pickups, even while production and especially export of passenger cars at that time remained modest and heavily protected. In Japan, Korea, and Malaysia, differential rates of tax, dependent upon engine size, provided an advantage to domestic producers whose output traditionally was dominated by small cars.

Yet the trade regimes through which developing countries seek to promote their domestic auto industries have evolved, constraining the policy options that are available to them (Wade 2003). Most notable here are the WTO's Trade-Related Investment Measures (TRIMs) Agreement, and the proliferation of bilateral and minilateral preferential agreements. The TRIMs agreement, negotiated during the Uruguay Round of GATT talks, which concluded in 1994, marked the most extensive internationally agreed curtailment of industrial policy tools. The brevity of the agreement (six pages, including an Annex that illustrates the type of measures that are prohibited) belies its significance in outlawing many of the instruments that governments had previously used to promote local industries, including requirements for local content, trade balancing, and export performance measures. In subsequent cases that have come before WTO Dispute Settlement Panels, the agreement has been interpreted in an expansive way (and it is perhaps no coincidence that a majority of the cases considered by panels under TRIMs have involved the auto industry). Although developing economies were permitted to apply for an extension before they had to comply in full with the agreement, all TRIMs had to be removed by 2004. The Uruguay Round also saw the negotiation of the "Agreement on Subsidies and Countervailing Measures," which further limited the scope for governments to promote domestic industry in a discriminatory manner.

This is not to suggest that it is impossible for a creative government to devise ways to pressure foreign investors to comply with certain government objectives. But it is far more difficult for governments to impose formal requirements than in the past. China was obliged to amend its Policy on Development of Automotive Industry (Order No. 8 of the National Development and Reform Commission, May 21, 2004) following a WTO Dispute Panel finding that upheld complaints from Canada, the European Union, and the United States that the policy, which applied the tariff applicable to assembled vehicles to imported components if they exceeded a certain threshold value, violated the WTO's national treatment principle and obligations that China had accepted under its terms of accession. On the other hand, for countries with large domestic markets, various informal pressures can be brought to bear on foreign investors that have the effect of realizing the same goals sought through TRIMs—and this has certainly happened in China, where provincial governments have persuaded potential investors of the desirability of complying with specific local content targets that they have established. Even the smaller economies in the region have succeeded in carving out some "policy space" within the new WTO regime (on Malaysia and Thailand, see Natsuda and Thoburn 2014).

Most recently, the move toward bilateral and minilateral PTAs has subjected developing country governments to a new source of pressure for liberalizing their trade regimes. The heavy protection traditionally afforded the automotive sector has made it one of the principal targets in PTA negotiations. In East Asia, the main pressure on developing countries has come from the Japanese government, which has responded to calls from Japanese car makers not just to liberalize access to markets for assembled vehicles (including, for instance, removal of "luxury" car taxes), but also to make it easier for local subsidiaries of Japanese assemblers to import raw materials and components from Japan (see, for instance, Manger 2005). In bilateral trade agreements with Thailand and Malaysia, for instance, Japanese officials succeeded in negotiating a phased removal of the duties on car parts—over eight years in Thailand, and over three years in Malaysia. Sometimes these pressures were supported by local assemblers: in Malaysia, the national car companies, Proton and Perodua, shared an interest with assemblers of Japanese vehicles in unimpeded access to imported components. The (much smaller) domestic companies supplying components resisted. Duties on imported steel were to be phased out over a longer period. Neither Thailand nor Malaysia, however, made significant concessions on imports of *assembled* vehicles in these bilateral agreements.

Preferential trade agreements nonetheless provide opportunities as well as posing new challenges for countries that are able to establish themselves as regional export bases. A notable example is the agreement between Thailand and Australia, which allows (subject to local value-added requirements) duty-free access to the Australian market for vehicles assembled in Thailand and for components manufactured there. After the implementation of the agreement, Australian imports of assembled vehicles from Thailand tripled in value from $A1 billion in 2004 to $3.2 billion in 2007. Both Honda and Nissan switched their sourcing for vehicles imported into Australia from Japan to Thailand. As of 2019, thanks largely to the bilateral trade agreement, Australia remained Thailand's single largest market for vehicles, accounting for approximately one-quarter of total exports.

The implementation of the ASEAN Free Trade Area (AFTA) also had a profound impact on the industry in Southeast Asia. Although Indonesia and especially Malaysia had sought to exempt their auto industries from the liberalization of intra-regional trade, pressure from their ASEAN partners eventually prevailed. By 2008, even Malaysia lowered its tariffs on imports from its ASEAN partners in compliance with the AFTA agreement (see discussion in Chapter 7). As with agreements with extra-regional partners, assembled vehicles continued to enjoy protection through differential excise taxes and various non-tariff barriers, but trade in components was substantially freed up.

Recent developments outside of East Asia show how contemporary trade agreements can also provide new instruments for protection. The rules of origin in the recently negotiated revised NAFTA, the US-Mexico-Canada Trade Agreement, are a classic example. These not only increased the overall value-added requirement for vehicles to enjoy originating status (increasing from

66% for passenger vehicles in 2020 to 75% by 2023). They also added product-specific stipulations, including a requirement that by 2023 each vehicle should have a labor value content composed of at least 25% of high-wage material and manufacturing expenditures, and that at least 70% of the vehicle's steel be produced within North America (https://usmca.com/rules-of-origin-usmca/). Contemporary preferential trade agreements are more about creating rents than promoting trade liberalization (Ravenhill 2017). In the most advanced of regional schemes, the European Union, the single market does dismantle border barriers, but as Markiewicz (2019) argues, deep integration also makes new developmental tools available, not least through generous financing available through the bloc's Structural Funds.

New Opportunities for Developing Economies

If the trends toward consolidation and scale in the industry, coupled with the pressures for trade liberalization, present formidable barriers to entry for domestic companies into the global industry, the story is by no means uniformly bleak. Booming local markets for vehicles, coupled with vertical disintegration, have increased the opportunities for developing economies to insert themselves into regional and global supply chains, often securing substantial volumes of local assembly and associated component manufacturing, with positive effects on both exports and employment. In most instances, however, few local firms have participated extensively in the new domestic industries.

The vast majority of the increase in demand for autos globally is coming from developing economies, particularly in Asia, and is being met overwhelmingly from locally produced vehicles. In addition (although the overall effect is of a smaller magnitude), a substantial regionalization of production is occurring, with economies on the periphery of the main markets of Western Europe and North America emerging as significant bases to supply assembled vehicles to these markets. The consequence of these trends is a dramatic change over the first decade of the 21st century in the distribution of auto production. If we confine our focus for the moment to assembled vehicles, whereas Western Europe and North America accounted for 56% of global auto production in 1999, by 2016 their share had fallen to 24% (Japan's share in the same period fell from 20% to 11%) (data from http://www.oica.net). In other words, by 2016, developing and emerging economies accounted for more than one-half of global car production (of which China accounted for close to half). Whereas many industrialized economies experienced absolute declines in output of assembled vehicles, that in other parts of the world jumped substantially. The move of the industry toward developing economies is likely to continue as incomes rise: in China, under 3% of the population owns a car, in contrast to between 70% and 80% of the population in the United States (BBC News 2012).

Much of the recent success of some developing economies in the auto industry is a reflection of the fragmentation of production within the auto value chain. The relatively low value-weight ratio of components, coupled with the need for producers to be located close to assemblers and, in turn, the desire of assemblers to be in proximity to final markets, have caused "off-shoring" of production in autos to lag behind that of other sectors, most notably electronics. Nonetheless, fragmentation has afforded new opportunities. As Richard Baldwin (2014, 2016) notes, developing economies can now join existing supply chains rather than having to build them from scratch. Moreover, the transfer of know-how, capital equipment, and management have made it possible for advanced manufacturing plants to be created in developing economies in a remarkably short time period.

This potential for development through global and regional automotive supply chains contrasts with the 1960s or 1970s, when foreign direct investment (FDI) in auto production in developing countries typically led to a proliferation of inefficient, heavily protected import-substituting plants. Today, however, global assemblers and first-tier suppliers have made substantial investments, even in relatively low-income countries such as China and India. The resulting plants in these countries are capable of reaching world standards of efficiency and quality surprisingly quickly (Sutton 2004). Car assembly has become increasingly robotized, with a consequent reduction in labor inputs. The average car is estimated to require only 15–25 person hours for assembly (Zacks.com 2008).

Labor costs, including healthcare, pensions and other benefits, nonetheless, can still be a decisive factor in determining the location of assembly facilities. It is not just wages but indirect costs that have proved to be such a burden to the major manufacturers in advanced countries. According to the US Bureau of Labor Statistics (2011b), the hourly compensation for blue-collar workers in the US automotive industry in 2009 was composed of $22.19 in wages plus $14.79 in benefits plus $4.76 in healthcare—a total of close to $42 per hour. Then CEO of GM Rick Wagoner testified to Congress that healthcare costs added $1,525 to the cost of every GM vehicle produced in the United States, with the company spending more on healthcare than its expenditure on steel (US Department of Health and Human Services 2013). The significance of differences in labor costs even *within* the United States is seen in the migration of the industry to non-unionized locations in the South.

A 2005 report by the International Labour Organization (2005: 45) found that wages in the American manufacturing sector were 25 times higher than those in China, while wages in Germany (€47.8 or $US53 in 2018 [Statista 2019]) were 30 times higher. Wages in auto assembly in Mexico in 2002, even though 30% above the average wage in manufacturing, were estimated to be one-quarter of those in Canada, and one-sixth of those in the United States (Hufbauer and Schott 2005: Table 6.4, p. 377). The Bureau of Labor Statistics (2013) reported that the average hourly compensation (including wages, benefits, and social security) in the auto sector in India in 2010 amounted to less than $2.25. The Conference Board (2016) estimated that hourly compensation costs in manufacturing in China in 2013 were $4.12. Savings on labor costs apply not only in assembly, but comparable savings also occur in design and engineering. The costs of developing a car from the design stage in India are estimated to be $22.5–$50 million, in contrast to $400 million in Europe.

Although wages in developing countries have risen, and assemblers in some advanced economies (e.g., the US and UK) have moved plants to domestic locations where labor costs are lower, a significant gap remains. At least in standardized products, differences in productivity are insufficient to undermine the tremendous advantages in wages, benefits, and working hours enjoyed by less developed countries (Becker 2006). Raw materials, components, utilities, and capital equipment (a particularly important factor for China) are also less expensive in developing economies. Raw material costs in India are estimated to be 11% lower than those in Europe. Key inputs frequently enjoy implicit or explicit state subsidies.

The cost savings for assemblers may be substantial. Nissan's Executive Vice President Colin Dodge estimated, when announcing the company's decision in 2009 to establish a plant in India to manufacture small cars for the European market, that production on the subcontinent would reduce costs by at least 5% even on low-margin small vehicles: "Five percent saving is very significant. It's enormous money for us" (quoted in Nair 2009). Similarly, Carlos Tavares, the chief operating officer of Renault, testified before a French parliamentary commission that the costs of manufacturing a subcompact car in France were 1,300 euros more per vehicle than for the same car assembled in Turkey (Ciferri 2012).

The Changing Geography of Production in the Auto Industry

While the stunning growth of auto production in China, now by far the world's largest producer and consumer of cars, casts a shadow over the whole industry, it should not be permitted to obscure the very substantial gains in output made in other developing and transitional economies (Table 2.3). In terms of overall volume, the other impressive winner was India, with output increasing more than fivefold in the first decade and a half of this century to just over 5% of the global total. Output in two of our case studies, Indonesia and Thailand, roughly doubled during the period 2005–2018. Similarly impressive gains were made in some of the emerging economies of central and eastern Europe, particularly Serbia, Slovenia, and Slovakia (where the auto industry accounts for 50% of manufacturing output and more than 60% of exports of manufactures, led by the assembly operations of VW, PSA Peugeot Citroen, and Kia) (European Automobile Manufacturers' Association 2010). The experience of Slovakia is indicative of the emergence of significant supply bases for assembled vehicles on the fringes of the major markets of western Europe and North America. Turkey has also emerged as a favored production site for export to the European Union: Ford (primarily pickup trucks), Fiat, Renault, Hyundai, and Toyota all built substantial facilities there. In 2012, two-thirds of Turkey's domestic car production was exported; of this figure, nearly 80% went to EU markets (Republic of Turkey 2014). A comparable export ratio also applies to Mexico, with production overwhelmingly for the US market (The Economist Intelligence Unit 2014).

Of the countries on which we focus in this book, Malaysia and Taiwan are exceptions to this trend of substantial expansion in developing economies. The reasons for Malaysia's poor performance are detailed in Chapter 7; the decline in vehicle assembly in Taiwan reflects both stagnant sales in a densely populated market and the transfer of assembly operations to the mainland, one dimension of its increasingly tight economic integration with China (Chapter 9).

The significance of being located on the fringe of the world's largest auto markets is reflected in data on exports (Table 2.4). They point to the overwhelmingly regionalized nature of automobile trade. But Asia remains an exception to this rule. Historically, the strength of the Japanese industry, the backwardness of the industry in other parts of Asia, and the long-standing aversion of most Japanese consumers to imported cars long prevented the

Table 2.3 Domestic Vehicle Production 2019 and 2005

	World Ranking 2019	Cars 2019	Commercial Vehicles 2019	Total Vehicles 2019	Cars 2005	Commercial Vehicles 2005	Total Vehicles 2005	Ratio 2019 Total Vehicles to 2005 Total
World		67,149,196	24,637,665	91,786,861	47,046,368	19,673,151	66,719,519	137.5
China	1	**21,360,193**	**4,360,472**	**25,720,665**	**3,941,767**	**1,775,852**	**5,717,619**	**449.8**
USA	2	2,512,780	8,367,239	10,880,019	4,321,272	7,625,381	11,946,653	91.1
Japan	3	8,328,756	1,355,542	9,684,298	9,016,735	1,782,924	10,799,659	89.8
India	4	3,623,335	892,682	4,516,017	1,264,111	374,563	1,638,674	275.6
Germany	5	4,661,328	0	4,661,328	5,350,187	407,523	5,757,710	81
Mexico	6	1,382,714	2,604,080	3,986,794	846,048	838,190	1,684,238	236.7
South Korea	7	**3,612,587**	**338,030**	**3,950,617**	**3,357,094**	**342,256**	**3,699,350**	**106.8**
Brazil	8	2,448,490	496,498	2,944,988	2,011,817	519,023	2,530,840	116.4
Spain	9	2,248,019	574,336	2,822,355	2,098,168	654,332	2,752,500	102.5
France	10	1,675,198	527,262	2,202,460	3,112,961	436,047	3,549,008	62.1
Thailand	11	795,254	1,218,456	2,013,710	277,562	845,150	1,122,712	179.4
Canada	12	461,370	1,455,215	1,916,585	1,356,271	1,331,621	2,687,892	71.3
Russia	13	1,523,594	196,190	1,719,784	1,068,511	285,993	1,354,504	127
Turkey	14	982,642	478,602	1,461,244	453,663	425,789	879,452	166.2
Czech Rep.	15	1,427,563	6400	1,433,963	596,774	5,463	602,237	238.1
UK	16	1,303,135	78,270	1,381,405	1,596,356	206,753	1,803,109	76.6
Indonesia	17	**1,045,666**	**241,182**	**1,286,848**	**332,590**	**168,120**	**500,710**	**257**
Slovakia	18	1,100,000	0	1,100,000	218,349	0	218,349	503.8
Italy	19	542,007	373,298	915,305	725,528	312,824	1,038,352	88.1
Iran	20	770,000	51,060	821,060	923,800	153,390	1,077,190	76.2
Malaysia	23	**534,115**	**37,517**	**571,632**	**404,571**	**158,837**	**563,408**	**101.5**
Taiwan	31	189,549	61,755	251,304	323,819	122,526	446,345	56.3

Source: International Organization of Motor Vehicle Manufacturers, "Production Statistics", <http://www.oica.net/category/production-statistics/2019-statistics/> (Accessed 15 October 2020).

Our case study countries are in boldface.

Table 2.4 Leading Passenger Vehicle Exporters (Number of Vehicles)

	World Rank in 2019	2019	2005	Ratio of 2019 to 2005 (%)
Japan	1	5,391,763	5,595,420	96.4
Germany	2	4,515,806	6,436,649	70.2
Mexico	3	2,761,826	2,854,878	96.7
USA	4	2,690,804	2,239,879	120.1
Spain	5	2,534,667	2,027,430	125.0
Belgium	6	1,998,306	2,078,398	96.1
Canada	7	1,808,921	2,087,628	86.6
Rep. of Korea	8	1,808,570	2,026,389	89.3
China	9	1,524,576	307,336	496.1
Czech Republic	10	1,373,893	543,892	252.6
United Kingdom	11	1,328,368	1,233,132	107.7
France	12	1,326,530	2,746,030	48.3
India	13	1,223,288	238,912	512.0
Slovakia	14	1,163,929	174,190	668.2
Turkey	15	917,426	340,066	269.8
Poland	16	623,995	541,453	115.2
Romania	17	479,670	57,358	836.3
Thailand*	18	471,991	482,712	97.8
Netherlands	19	373,734	208,548	179.2
Slovenia	20	349,092	201,283	173.4
Austria	21	296,057	408,411	72.5
Indonesia	22	216,408	19,467	1,111.7
Taiwan**	30	30,512	1,093	2,791.6
Malaysia	33	18,445	15,015	122.8
Philippines		***	13,052	****

Source: UN Comtrade data accessed 17 October 2020. Data for Mexico are for 2006 and 2018. Data for France and Spain are for 2018.

Notes: All data (except Taiwan) are for HS Code 8703, motor cars and other motor vehicles principally designed for the transport of persons.

* HS Code 8703 does not include pickup trucks, which account for more than half of Thailand's exports of light vehicles.

** Data for Taiwan refer to Motor Vehicle Exports (ccc 3010) sourced from Taiwan, Ministry of Economic Affairs, Department of Statistics, <https://dmz26.moea.gov.tw/GMWeb/investigate/InvestigateDA.aspx?lang=E> accessed 10 December 2020.

*** 8703 exports from the Philippines in 2019 were valued at $3,601,679; quantity/unit data not available.

**** The ratio of the Philippines's 2019 (HS 8703) export value to its 2005 value ($169,893,663) is 2.1.

emergence of other Asian countries as supply bases for Asia's richest economy. To some extent, this situation is evolving with the growth of "reverse exports" from subsidiaries of Japanese companies located elsewhere in the region, most notably Thailand (although, as noted earlier, the most significant markets for Thai vehicles are outside of Asia). As for China, the cost advantages of producing domestically, coupled with the desire of assemblers to be close to consumers in what became their most profitable market, were reinforced by a strong desire on the part of central and provincial governments to ensure that the rapidly growing demand would be met from domestic sources. These factors will likely confine intra-regional trade in assembled autos in Asia to much lower levels than in Europe or the Americas.

The vast majority of output of vehicles assembled in Asia's developing economies consequently has been destined for consumption in their burgeoning domestic markets. The rapidly expanding domestic markets in China and India have weighed heavily on these figures. China's exports, however, are growing rapidly; in 2018 it exported just over 1 million assembled passenger cars, rapidly approaching the level of Thailand. This figure nonetheless represented only a small fraction of its total light vehicle production of just above 28 million. Indian production is more export-intensive (currently driven primarily by Hyundai and Suzuki), but nonetheless the ratio of exports to domestic production in 2018 was close to 30%, with exports of 1.2 million vehicles in a total production of more than 4 million cars. The contrast with Korea—where more than two-thirds of cars produced domestically are exported—could not be starker.

When we turn to exports of components (Table 2.5), the pattern is very different; the Chinese performance is particularly stunning. Over the period from 2005 to 2018, China's exports of auto components increased more than fivefold: the country was poised to overtake Japan as the world's third largest exporter. In contrast to the decline in Korea's exports of assembled vehicles over the period, those of components increased 250% (reflecting the relocation of Korean production to its major foreign markets—see Chapter 6). Similarly, Taiwan increased its components exports despite a fall in exports of assembled vehicles. Thailand also turned in an exceptional performance, increasing its components exports more than fourfold during the period (with Japan as its principal market). By the end of the period, Thailand's exports of components were twice the value of those of Taiwan: its world ranking in components exports (13th) was exactly the same as that for exports of assembled vehicles. Indonesia is also emerging as a significant exporter of components; only Malaysia and the Philippines continue to lag. This cross-national variation in exports of components is one feature of divergent

Table 2.5 World Rankings of Leading Auto Components Exporters

Exporters	World Rank in 2019	Exported value in 2019 ($thousands)	Exported value in 2005 ($ thousands)	2019/2005 (%)
World	–	393,521,058	226,063,589	174.1
Germany	1	61,796,400	33,061,475	187
USA	2	43,018,677	31,532,376	136.4
China	3	33,625,803	6,566,790	512.1
Japan	4	32,697,064	25,277,386	129.4
Mexico	5	30,659,940	9,788,222	313.2
Korea	6	18,981,682	7,718,957	245.9
Czech Republic	7	15,165,218	5,396,907	281
Italy	8	14,437,100	12,168,897	118.6
Poland	9	14,352,084	3,714,859	386.3
France	10	13,932,725	15,360,290	90.7
Canada	11	10,883,287	13,405,119	81.2
Spain	12	10,633,202	10,563,771	100.7
Thailand	13	8,039,565	2,120,010	379.2
Hungary	14	7,368,168	2,304,183	319.8
Romania	15	6,928,431	860,855	804.8
Belgium	16	6,491,356	6,218,676	104.4
UK	17	6,488,308	7,697,218	84.3
Sweden	18	5,203,258	3,929,859	132.4
India	19	5,032,374	1,022,013	492.4
Austria	20	4,733,079	3,148,904	150.3
Taiwan	22	3,910,370	2,698,258	145
Indonesia	28	1,705,438	757,862	225
Malaysia	29	1,069,429	372,913	286.8
Philippines	30	960,339	1,355,131	70.9

Source: International Trade Centre, Trade Map – International Trade Statistics, <https://www.trademap.org/tradestat/Country_SelProduct_TS.aspx?> (Accessed 17 October 2020) Auto Components defined as HS 8708, Parts and Accessories for Motor Vehicles

national responses to the opportunities and challenges of the auto industry, which we explore in detail in the next section.

Diverging Strategies

In the first chapter, we distinguished between countries in East Asia that have primarily pursued intensive growth strategies and those pursuing extensive growth strategies in the auto industry. As we discuss in greater detail in the following chapter, the institutional requirements to support these strategies are significantly different. But so, too, are the metrics to evaluate success in pursuing the two strategies.

The divergent national strategies pursued in our country case studies (Table 2.6) did not emerge full blown. They instead evolved as different responses to two features common to all our cases: the need for access to foreign technology controlled by foreign assemblers, and initial efforts to promote domestic (indigenous) producers, typically as part of an integrated industry.

Consider, first, the role of foreign producers. Automotive assembly is so complex that all latecomers to the industry have launched programs with assistance from one or more foreign partners. This was true of all of our country cases and even, in an earlier period, of Japan, when we consider the prewar investments by Ford and GM, and extensive postwar licensing from abroad. The initial strategy was to encourage domestic production to substitute for imports of assembled vehicles, usually through the local assembly of components produced by the foreign partner in the form of "completely knocked down" (CKD) kits. Import substitution on a small scale behind high protective tariffs typically made the locally produced vehicles more expensive than the imported models they replaced, particularly if protection inadvertently promoted a proliferation of inefficient assembly plants and excess capacity. In Thailand, for instance, by 1975 local assembly plants had the potential to produce six times the annual sales of domestic vehicles (Doner 1991: 195). To increase local value added and decrease the drain on scarce foreign exchange that nascent auto industries created, governments typically pressured assemblers to support local parts and components production by "deleting" specific components from the imported kit or by specifying local content targets (for instance, an exact share of output value) that assemblers were to meet.

But global automakers usually resisted the investments necessary to meet such localization requirements: they did not want to lose the opportunity to import vehicles and components from their global production networks; they did not trust the quality of domestically made components; and they feared being forced to share technology with locally based competitors. The early history of the auto industry in all of our countries was thus one of a tussle between governments eager to increase local value added (often strongly supported by domestic parts producers), and foreign partners reluctant to commit themselves to sourcing more components domestically.

Korea has been the most unswerving proponent of fostering national champions in the auto industry even when some local firms relied on foreign partners. China has consistently sought to foster domestic companies but has

Table 2.6 East Asian Automotive Strategies and Performance

Strategy	Country	Strategy and Performance
Intensive	Korea	**Strategy Change?** *No.* Consistent support for domestically owned assemblers (and parts producers) since 1960s.
		Performance: *Strong.* Global automakers with world-class engineering and design capabilities; highly successful independent brands (Hyundai-Kia); major vehicle and parts exports and overseas assembly but weakness among indigenous components producers except those spun off from Hyundai-Kia.
	China	**Strategy Change?** *Yes—partly.* After mid-1980s, significant opening to foreign investment; active export promotion. But consistent stress on integrated industry with significant indigenous participation.
		Performance: *Strong.* Increasingly competent Sino-foreign joint ventures; emerging independent firms with growing capacities (augmented by foreign design and engineering consultants), own brands, and some export capability; major parts exports; some vehicle exports.
	Taiwan	**Strategy Change?** *Yes.* From mid-1980s, gradually reduced efforts to promote domestic assembly base. But did not abandon local assembly entirely and continued promotion of domestic parts producers.
		Performance: *Strong.* Significant exports of replacement parts and modest exports of whole vehicles; some local original equipment parts production; some regional and even global expertise in electronics-related parts and electric vehicles (industry increasingly economically integrated with that of mainland China).
	Malaysia	**Strategy Change?** *Minimal until 2017* when the national champion, Proton, was sold to the Chinese company, Geely. Increased number of "national cars" and foreign involvement; slow trade liberalization under AFTA.
		Performance: *Weak.* Independent assembly capabilities (with substantial foreign help on R&D), but heavily reliant on protection and imported technology; limited exports of assembled vehicles; modest parts capacities, few parts exports.
Extensive	Thailand	**Strategy Change?** *Yes.* Significant move in 1990s away from localization based on protection and limits on numbers of brands and models toward assembly with minimal support for domestic producers.
		Performance: *Strong.* Assembly of volume models for local and regional markets; significant regional exports of parts; but foreign firms dominate; weak indigenous presence: little local engineering or design; few domestically owned upper tier suppliers.

Continued

Table 2.6 *Continued*

Strategy	Country	Strategy and Performance
	Indonesia	**Strategy Change?** *Yes*, but later than Thailand. Shift away from extensive protection of locally owned assembler and parts, especially after 1997 financial crisis.
		Performance: *Initially weak* but improving. Assembly of a few volume models primarily for local market; some local production of original equipment parts and modest exports.
	Philippines	**Strategy Change?** *Yes.* Shift away from protected localization, but new strategy still not clear.
		Performance: *Weak.* Minimal assembly for local market; parts exports to the region under multinational auspices originally through ASEAN's Brand-to-Brand Complementation scheme now under increasing competitive pressures.

been far more willing than Korea was at a similar stage of the local industry's development to rely on joint ventures with foreign assemblers; provincial governments have also adopted varying approaches toward the promotion of domestic companies (Thun 2006). China's auto industry policies have been marked by a persistent tension between the desire to promote domestic companies (including the local partners in joint ventures) and a recognition that foreign partners remain crucial suppliers of technology (and, increasingly, access to global production and sales networks). For Malaysia, the national car project based on the locally owned Proton brand became the defining feature not just of auto policy but of the Mahathir government's push for industrial deepening, which also had the objective of promoting ethnic Malay economic status. As discussed in Chapter 3, however, Malaysia's ambitious policy, unlike those of Korea and China, lacked the institutional strengthening necessary for upgrading. Despite very disappointing results, Malaysia's policy experienced only minimal changes until Proton was sold to the private Chinese company Geely in 2017.

Thailand, Indonesia, and the Philippines have all shifted toward an MNC (multinational corporation)–dominated assembly/export strategy, albeit at different speeds and with significantly varying results. Thailand's initial strategy involved promoting an indigenous supply base along with domestic participation in assembly through joint ventures with foreign partners (rather than a domestically owned "national champion" as in Malaysia). As part of this effort, Thailand attempted but later abandoned an effort to promote production of engine components by domestic firms. In the late 1980s–early 1990s, Thailand shifted focus to attempt to establish itself as the preferred assembly location in Southeast Asia for multinational assemblers and foreign components producers. This new approach involved not only providing appropriate infrastructure, export incentives, and support for the local production of one specific vehicle (one-ton pickup trucks), but also ending localization requirements and the limits previously imposed on the number of models and brands that had been designed to increase scale economies for local producers.

Indonesia's initial strategy involved the promotion of a domestic base in automotive components and intermediates with local participation in assembly through joint ventures. A Malaysia-like effort to promote a locally owned national car, the "Timor," in the last years of the Suharto regime, deteriorated into a rent-seeking farce. These localization efforts were abandoned during the 1997 financial crisis, after which the government allowed multinationals to take over the assembly industry. Although a latecomer, and lacking the infrastructure advantages of Thailand, Indonesia's strategic shift has resulted in significant growth in production and, to a lesser extent, in exports, especially in niches popular in the domestic market.

The Philippines case is one where the government has simply failed to adopt a consistent strategy. Political cronyism undermined an initial effort at gradual localization that emphasized the production of major functional components. It is interesting to note that this early emphasis on a limited range of specific components, as in the Thai case, mirrors aspects of Taiwan's eventual successful strategy. Later, hasty liberalization undermined efforts to promote a local industry. Nonetheless, early investments, combined with regional complementation schemes under the Association of Southeast Asian Nations (ASEAN), resulted in MNCs using the Philippines as an export base for a small number of components. But the country has been largely unable to build on that politically acquired base and remains heavily dependent on Toyota's complementation-related investments.

As with Thailand, Taiwan initially promoted a locally based assembly sector with local joint venture partners and, when confronted with overcapacity, allowed the gradual strengthening of multinational control over the joint ventures. But unlike Thailand's assembly-for-export focus, Taiwan has also provided incentives for the manufacture and export of components by domestic firms, while also providing low-key support to the one assembler committed to indigenization.

We analyze these strategic responses in greater detail in the case chapters. For now, we wish to emphasize not only variations in strategies but also in the *flexibility* with which countries adjusted to shifting constraints and opportunities. Explicitly abandoning costly efforts to foster protected, integrated industries, Thailand and Taiwan moved deliberately and successfully to pursue specific niches. Indonesia and the Philippines moved more gradually away from an integrated vision and have been slower and less successful at implementing an export strategy. Malaysia persisted with its costly effort to build protected "national champion" assemblers and local parts production, even as it failed to develop the institutional framework required to make this strategy successful. Conversely, Korea and China have largely succeeded with their original strategies of intensive development based in large part on domestically owned companies.

The comparative data in the previous section of this chapter show that the record of East Asian economies that have pursued extensive development strategies is by no means exceptional in the contemporary auto industry. Indeed, because the European industry has become more regionalized than its East Asian counterpart, the record of a number of countries on the periphery of the European Union has been superior to that of even our most successful case of extensive development, Thailand, measured by volumes of vehicle assembly and exports, jobs created, and foreign exchange earned (Table 2.7). These indicators are important both in themselves and because they reflect a core, dynamic component of economic growth: the efficient accumulation and mobilization of factors of production in the promotion of an industry new to the country. Promoting such structural change in itself involves numerous difficulties (discussed in Chapter 3).

But these indicators are not themselves sufficient to measure success in *intensive* development strategies: it is in the pursuit of these strategies that some of our cases distinguish themselves from developing economies elsewhere in the world. Extensive growth indicators tell only part of the development story. Consider the case of trade balances. In today's global value chains, parts often cross many national boundaries (and sometimes the same boundary several times) before the component or vehicle in which they are embedded reaches its final export market. Moreover, as we noted earlier in the chapter, "non-automotive" products, especially integrated circuits, constitute a significant and growing proportion of the value of assembled vehicles. Even positive "automotive" trade balances, measured by the conventional international trade category of auto parts, can conceal a lack of domestic value added, weaknesses in local technological capabilities, and the absence of indigenous firms. Put differently, even positive trade balances can mask a lack of intensive growth or upgrading—one reason why the multilateral economic organizations have begun focusing on trade in value added.

Table 2.7 Extensive Growth Indicators

	Year	Notes	China	Indonesia	South Korea	Malaysia	Philippines	Thailand	Taiwan
Vehicle Production (Total Units)	2019	1	25,720,665	1,286,848	3,950,617	571,632	116,868	2,013,710	251,304
Vehicle Production (Cars Only)	2019	1	21,360,193	1,045,666	3,612,587	534,115	45,853	795,254	189,549
Vehicle Production (Commercial Vehicles Only)	2019	1	4,360,472	241,182	338,030	37,517	71,015	1,218,456	61,755
Vehicle Export (Units)	2019	2, 3	1,524,576	216,408	1,808,570	18,445	33,757	471,991	32,482
Vehicle Import (Units)	2019*	2, 3	1,032,857	66,364	404,602	184,708	353,271	50,146	198,669
Vehicle Export (Value in USD thousands)	2019	2, 3	8,637,814	3,943,044	40,454,714	432,385	3,602	9,404,167	673,412
Vehicle Import (Value in USD thousands)	2019	2, 3	47,057,996	1,130,794	11,111,729	2,048,766	3,135,533	1,322,074	5,515,855
Vehicle Trade Balance (Value in USD thousands)	2019	5	–38,420,182	2,812,250	29,342,985	–1,616,381	–3,131,931	8,082,093	–4,840,920
Parts Export (Value in USD thousands)	2019	4	33,625,803	1,705,431	18,980,831	1,068,003	886,245	7,389,788	3,907,079
Parts Import (Value in USD thousands)	2019	4	25,220,956	3,381,517	3,866,563	2,647,375	600,441	6,134,832	1,520,895
Auto Parts Trade Balance (Value in USD thousands)	2019	5	8,404,847	–1,676,086	15,114,268	–1,579,372	285,804	1,254,956	2,386,184
Percentage Share of Auto Products in Export Trade	2019	6	1.7	3.3	11.0	0.6	1.3	7.2	1.4
Auto employment as % of manufacturing industry	2018	7	6.5	2.8	11.3	3.7	8.3	8.5	3.0
Value added as % of manufacturing industry	2018	8	5.2	10.4	9.9	5.0	7.7	13.7	2.6

Notes:

*China, Malaysia, and Taiwan are for 2019; Indonesia, Korea, and Thailand for 2018; Philippines for 2015.

(1) Source: International Organization of Motor Vehicle Manufacturers (http://www.oica.net/category/production-statistics/) Last accessed 31 October 2020. Data for the Philippines are for 2017.

(2) Data refers to HS8703: "Motor cars and other motor vehicles principally designed for the transport of persons". Source: UN Comtrade (https://comtrade.un.org/data/), Last accessed 31 October 2020.

(3) Data for Taiwan from Taiwan's Bureau of Foreign Trade Statistics (https://cuswebo.trade.gov.tw/FSCE020F/FSCE020F?menuURL=FSCE020F) for HS Code 8703. Last accessed 2 November 2020.

(4) Refers to HS 8708: "Parts and Accessories for Motor Vehicles." Source: Comtrade (https://comtrade.un.org/data/), Last accessed 31 October 2020. Taiwan from Bureau of Foreign Trade Statistics (https://cuswebo.trade.gov.tw/FSCE020F/FSCE020F?menuURL=FSCE020F) for HS Code 8708. Last accessed 2 November 2020.

(5) Negative number means a trade deficit.

(6) Source: UN Comtrade

(7) All data is for 2018 except Indonesia (2017). Source: UNIDO <https://www.unido.org/resources-statistics/statistical-country-briefs> accessed on 31 October 2020.

(8) All data is for 2018 except Indonesia and Taiwan (2017). Source: UNIDO <https://www.unido.org/resources-statistics/statistical-country-briefs> accessed on 31 October 2020.

The gap between extensive and intensive growth is reflected in the data in Table 2.8, especially in the case of Thailand. Although the Thai government likes to refer to its industry as the "Detroit of East Asia," other observers emphasize its risk of becoming the "maquiladora of Japan" because of the limited linkages between the foreign-dominated auto industry and the local economy, the lack of local-owned design and manufacturing capacity, and the absence of domestic firms in parts production. Thailand's performance in diversification far surpasses that of its Southeast Asian neighbors, but in upgrading of capabilities within the automotive sector, it lags not only South Korea but also China and Taiwan.

Particularly striking in this table is the clear gap between countries pursuing intensive and extensive strategies in the ratio of research and development to sales in the automotive industry. Moreover, countries pursuing an extensive strategy have not developed a domestic capital goods industry to support the automotive sector. Not surprisingly, they also lack the capacity to design and engineer whole vehicles. Only those countries that are pursuing intensive development in autos have domestically owned brands (and significant domestically owned components producers). In the next section we consider the potential advantages and disadvantages to reliance on foreign companies.

The Costs and Benefits of Relying on Foreign Assemblers

Foreign investment has increasingly been seen as affording a means of accessing global production networks (Moran 1998). Because foreign subsidiaries in developing economies are often now capable of producing efficiently by international standards and exporting to regional markets, they do not generate the drain on foreign exchange that the import-substituting plants caused in the 1970s and 1980s (although a careful analysis of the costs of imported raw materials, components, capital goods, and of royalty payments and profit repatriation would be required before any definitive judgment can be made of their net contribution to a country's balance of payments).

Foreign exchange consequences have traditionally been one of the major considerations in the debate over whether the "nationality" of firms matters: the developmental implications of ownership. This is one of those issues in the social sciences that can never be decided definitively because much depends on the counterfactual: What would the situation have been had the foreign investment not taken place? Would a competitive, domestically owned

Table 2.8 Intensive Growth Indicators

	China	Indonesia	Korea	Malaysia	Philippines	Thailand	Taiwan
Auto R&D/sales	1.82%	NA (Negligible)	2.17%	2% (assemblers) 0.14% (suppliers)	NA (Negligible)	0.3% (suppliers)	1.09%
Corporate R&D institutes	Yes	Minimal	Yes	Yes	No	Minimal	Yes
Ability to design and export new parts	Medium	Low	High	Low	Low	Low	High
Ability to design and engineer whole vehicles	Yes	No	Yes	Yes	No	No	Yes
Global center of excellence (independent or for an MNC)	Yes, for some "infotainment" parts	No	Yes	No	No	No	Yes, for a very few electronics parts (Ford)
Extensive use of domestic capital equipment	Yes	No	Yes	No	No	No	Yes
Major effort to develop EV/HV	Yes	No	Yes	Yes	No	No	Yes
Locally owned brands	Yes	No	Yes	Yes (Proton)	No	No	Yes (Yulon)
Overseas assembly	Yes	No	Yes	Yes (barely)	No	No	Yes
Outward FDI for parts	Yes	No	Yes	No	No	Yes (a bit)	Yes
Overseas R&D posts	Yes	No	Yes	Yes	No	No	Yes

Notes:

Authors' judgments based on materials in the case study chapters with the exception of:

—R&D/sales:

China: 2010 Yearbook, p. 530.

Taiwan: Data are for 2016. The category is "motor vehicle and parts manufacturing" under "III-2-31. Manufacturing Industry R&D Expenditure as a Percentage of Sales by Taiwan's Industrial Classification." Source: Ministry of Science and Technology, National Science and Technology Survey Indicators Index, http://was.most.gov.tw/WAS2/English/AsTechnologyE:DataIndex.aspx (last accessed July 23, 2018).

Korea: ContactKorea (2010).

Malaysia: Wad and Govindaraju (2011): 160.

Thailand: World Bank (2008): 62.

Indonesia and Philippines: No official data available.

company have emerged instead? Would it have been less reliant on imported technologies and components? Would it have established a denser network of relations with local suppliers? Would it have been capable of manufacturing a product that was attractive not only to domestic consumers but also to those in international markets?

Several sobering stylized facts have emerged, however, from studies of multinational corporations over several decades. As the debate over Chinese attempts to coerce American MNCs into sharing their technologies vividly illustrates, MNCs closely guard their intellectual property. They typically keep higher-value activities in their home countries, including most research and development activities (see, for example, Hirst and Thompson 2009). Sturgeon and van Biesebroeck (2011: 183) note the continued concentration in the Detroit region of high value-added activities in the auto industry: "Because of deep investments in capital equipment and skills, regional automotive clusters tend to be very long-lived." Multinationals sometimes withhold the latest technology from their foreign subsidiaries, fearing that it will leak to locally based competitors (Japanese and Korean companies operating in China often express these concerns). MNCs frequently dictate which markets can be supplied from a subsidiary, decisions that may conflict directly with a government's desire to promote exports, and which constrain the contributions that domestic production can make to a country's balance of payments. This was the case, for instance, with Daewoo in its first partnership with GM in Korea, and for the Australian subsidiaries of Ford and GM. It was also characteristic of MNC subsidiaries in the auto industry in Central and South America (Bennett and Sharpe 1985). Moreover, MNCs may engage in transfer-pricing activities that magnify the drain on the host country's balance of payments (in 2010, for example, the Australian Tax Office presented Toyota Australia with a bill for $A250 million for tax evasion undertaken through transfer pricing activities; Hagon 2010).

A reliance on MNCs can also have important implications for domestic politics and the prospects for upgrading domestic skills. Doner and Schneider (2016) argue that MNCs (because of their in-house capabilities and their potential mobility) are less likely to join coalitions in middle-income countries that push for the upgrading of local capabilities and skills. When facing difficulties, MNCs for obvious political reasons often close foreign subsidiaries before laying off workers at home (seen recently in Nissan's pulling production back to Japan following problems with its partnership with Renault).

Studies suggest that MNCs rely more heavily on imported components and on the local subsidiaries of other MNCs than do domestically owned companies and, consequently, their integration with local suppliers is shallower.

Strong support for this argument is found in a survey of auto assemblers in China conducted by Brandt and van Brieseboeck, who found that only 15% of the first-tier suppliers to "Western" (European and American) assemblers and only 5.5% of suppliers to "Asian" firms were domestic (Chinese) firms, whereas these constituted fully 61% of the first-tier suppliers to Chinese assemblers (Sturgeon and van Biesebroeck 2011: 194, Table 3). In Malaysia, the national car company, Proton, relied more heavily on locally owned component suppliers than did the assembly plants of its foreign competitors (Segawa, Natsuda, and Thoburn 2014). In China, the result was a steady increase in localization and an upgrading of competencies, which was reflected in a rapid increase in the share of domestic value-added in exports. This success stood in marked contrast to the Thai experience where the reliance on foreign firms led to little upgrading in the competencies of locally owned suppliers (Mao et al. forthcoming).

Studies of the auto industry have also confirmed a long-standing argument in the literature that differences exist not only between the behavior of domestically owned and foreign-owned companies but also within the category of MNC subsidiaries, depending on the nationality of the parent company. In particular, Japanese companies historically have been less inclined than American and European firms to localize management of their subsidiaries, to reduce their dependence on imported components, and to increase their integration with local companies (Ravenhill 1999). Such effects have been particularly pronounced in the auto industry, where Japanese "transplants" have been notorious for bringing a substantial part of their domestic supply chain with them (the close working relations between assemblers and suppliers in Japan's *keiretsu* networks often being seen as one of the principal sources of competitive advantage of the Japanese industry). Korean assemblers Hyundai and Kia have followed a similar pattern in their international operations.

It would be a mistake, however, to characterize such relationships as invariant. The incentives that drive company behavior change in response to evolving technology, cost structures, and trade regimes. As we have noted, with modularization and the globalization of platforms, all assemblers have increasingly forged close relationships with a limited number of first-tier suppliers—making it more difficult to gain entry to the top tiers of these networks, regardless of the nationality of the assembler. And, facing intensified competition and cost pressures in the 1990s, some Japanese assemblers increasingly opened up their sourcing networks (Noble 2001; Smitka 2002). But this move was not uniform (with Honda and Toyota maintaining their traditional supply networks), and even after some opening up, Japanese auto supply networks remained relatively closed in comparison with American auto networks or the supply networks of Japanese electronics companies (Solis 2003). Component producers we interviewed in Malaysia, for instance, noted that it was impossible for them to export to Japanese assemblers in Thailand because the Japanese automakers preferred to source from Japanese transplants. Moreover, the transplants in Thailand were also the preferred source of components for Japanese joint venture assembly operations in Malaysia itself (interviews, Malaysia, July 2008).

Has the advent of global supply chains made it impossible for developing countries to establish an integrated industry in the automotive sector? Richard Baldwin makes a strong argument that this is the case. He contends that the "second unbundling" generated by globalization, a reflection of the information and communication technology revolutions, "made it easy for rich-nation firms to combine the high technology they developed at home with low-wage workers abroad" (Baldwin 2011: 13). As a result, companies in developing economies are able to build world-competitive components for the supply chains with technology borrowed from abroad. Baldwin argues that it is actually now counterproductive for any developing economy to attempt to build an integrated domestic supply chain. To support this argument, Baldwin contrasts the success of Thailand's integration into regional production chains in the auto industry with the failure of Malaysia's "techno-nationalist" strategy of attempting to build an integrated industry.

We explore the contrast between the Malaysian and Thai experiences in detail in subsequent chapters and find that the story is more complicated than Baldwin allows. The limitations of alternative strategies may differ depending on the characteristics of the developing economy, and whether particular institutional configurations can help mitigate these limitations. Is the failure of Malaysia's intensive strategy inevitable in the auto industry in the current global environment? We suggest not. The Malaysian failure owes much to the institutional weaknesses that we document later in the book. In contrast, we have seen the emergence of independent producers in China that are largely following an "intensive" growth strategy.

The conventional wisdom—one that is largely persuasive—is that the barriers today to entry into assembly or first-tier supply that we discussed earlier in the chapter mean that for *most* developing countries, the question of whether to attempt to promote national champions or to rely on subsidiaries of transnationals is essentially moot. Only in rare cases—developing countries with very large internal markets and, despite low average levels of per capita incomes, substantial financial and human capital especially in engineering (with China and India as the obvious examples, and Brazil another candidate)—are there realistic possibilities for the emergence of independent assemblers or first-tier suppliers in the contemporary auto industry. Even then, the challenges are formidable—not least because of the demanding character of systems integration in auto assembly.

Although the difficulties in systems integration should not be underestimated, some developments within the global industry have been favorable for aspiring assemblers. The first is the trend toward modularization noted earlier that leaves the integration of various system elements primarily in the hands of first-tier suppliers. Given the presence of competition in the industry—there are typically three or four major international first-tier suppliers competing in each of the segments—the financial difficulties that the industry has experienced at all levels, and the rapid growth of the domestic market in some developing economies, first-tier suppliers have been very open to adapting and selling their latest technologies to any assembler capable of paying their price.

The growing availability of contract design and engineering services also is easing the entry of new assemblers and parts firms from developing countries. Design houses and engineering specialists are hardly new, of course, particularly in Europe. Even in the early 1970s, for example, Hyundai relied heavily on Italian design and English engineering and management to create its first export vehicle, the Pony. With improvements in telecommunications and computer-aided design, engineering, and manufacturing, a much higher degree of interaction between assemblers, designers, and suppliers is possible, facilitating more rapid design and introduction of new models than in the past. Whereas Hyundai produced the Pony virtually unmodified for six years, before introducing a new model of its own design, automakers in China, India, and other developing countries now contract out design and engineering for a whole series of new models and engines, and rapidly update them. Widespread participation by Chinese and Indian engineers makes it possible to cut costs for routine design and engineering, and for them to learn from the European experts responsible for project management and the most advanced areas of design and technology. The explosive growth of production in China and India, and the use of recurring projects, in turn, has convinced companies such as Pininfarina, Ricardo, and AVL to treat developing countries in Asia as crucial clients (Noble 2006).

In recent years we have seen some new assemblers enjoy surprising success in integrating key components into an apparently successful "whole" within remarkably short time frames. The independent Chinese producer, Chery, provides one example. Chery purchases engine design from AVL in Austria, and powertrains from the UK firm Ricardo (Sturgeon and van Biesebroeck 2011). Additional engineering work is outsourced to the (Proton-owned)

Lotus Engineering in the United Kingdom, and to Porsche Engineering in Germany. Other key parts are sourced from global first-tier suppliers including Valeo, Robert Bosch, and Johnson Controls. And firms with "deep pockets" from developing economies—notably China and India—have attempted to access cutting-edge technology by acquiring financially troubled assemblers or component producers in North America, Europe, and, more recently, Japan. They have also established design studios and engineering centers in Detroit, Milan, and other leading global automotive centers.

The availability of "designers for hire," coupled with often readily available capital—either because of high levels of domestic savings or through an increasingly globalized financial system—gives companies and governments in developing economies two of the elements of the package of benefits that foreign direct investment was traditionally identified as supplying. Whether the management skills of MNCs, often seen as another of their advantages, are actually superior to those available to domestic companies is something that is also increasingly open to question.

Nonetheless, the challenges of independent entry into the industry are formidable. As we will see from our case studies, national ownership is far from being a guarantee of success in the auto industry. Even with this unpacking of some of the components of the MNC package, domestic companies are still missing some key elements available to MNCs—most notably access to global distribution networks and a brand name. MNCs also benefit from their size when they are purchasing inputs: their procurement divisions use their volume purchases to secure raw materials at relatively low prices and pass these on not just to their own subsidiaries but also to their suppliers. And while even small and medium-sized enterprises are able to purchase sophisticated technology off the shelf (e.g., presses from Germany or Japan), it is only firms with deep pockets that can afford to engage the services of European design houses.

For smaller firms, the price for gaining access to assemblers' global production networks frequently is a loss of autonomy. Component producers we interviewed in Malaysia indicated that it was impossible to obtain a contract from a Japanese assembler unless the company entered into a technical agreement with a Japanese company—and the Japanese preference was often for a joint venture. A manager at one Malaysian components producer we interviewed in July 2009 said that if his company had entered into a licensing agreement with a Japanese company, then this would have required a royalty payment of 3% plus a 2% upfront fee—payments that would have reduced the company's profit margin by 70%. Japanese assemblers require their suppliers to open their books so that the assembler can scrutinize the suppliers' profit margins. With the assembler often selling the raw material to the supplier, the supplier is essentially entering into a profit-sharing arrangement in which the assembler dictates the terms.

We are not suggesting here that the relations between Japanese assemblers and their suppliers are uniquely unfavorable. Far from it. Component suppliers universally face downward price pressures. Assemblers have often commandeered the lion's share of supplier-initiated cost savings: GM acknowledged that when suppliers brought cost-saving ideas to it, GM kept 65% of the savings in the first year and 100% thereafter (Simon 2010). And Japanese assemblers, especially Toyota, are praised by many component suppliers for their willingness to provide training and technology to companies that enter into a technical agreement with them. In contrast, the relationship in Korea between a domestic assembler—Hyundai—and its domestic suppliers has traditionally been characterized as adversarial. Not only do suppliers face constant pressure to reduce costs, but it has only been relatively recently that Hyundai has put into place a wide-ranging program to work with suppliers to upgrade their skills (see the discussion in Chapter 6). All multinational firms increasingly concentrate on the most valuable parts of the value chain, relentlessly squeezing the profitability out of the remaining segments by outsourcing and pitting suppliers against each other and the "China price" (Kenney and Florida 2004).

It is not surprising, then, that experts advise developing countries to abandon aspirations to build national champions, and instead specialize in creating supply chains for a limited range of parts in which they possess or can develop comparative advantage, and then to develop the marketing skills to open up global markets rather than depending only on local sales (Sturgeon and Lester 2004). But merely producing to another's design deprives local companies of the opportunities for learning by doing, which is a prerequisite for developing the skills and knowledge that increasingly dominate the terms of competition in the global auto industry: "Without engaging in carrying out the design task, detailed component-specific knowledge will erode due to lack of opportunity for learning-by-doing. . . . When deciding on how to manage supplier relationships, managers have the classical, efficiency- and effectiveness-based product development objectives in mind. Knowledge-based objectives, such as learning, building up new knowledge bases, developing new skills, etc., often do not seem to occupy the minds of the managers who manage the new product development process" (Becker and Zirpoli 2005: 143).

Moreover, without initial scale it is difficult to compete on price or invest in operations overseas to support assembly clients. Outsourcing provides producers in developing countries opportunities to expand exports, particularly of labor-intensive goods, but it also exposes them to greater import competition. Even when exports expand, parts companies face unremitting pressure to cut costs and profit margins, and insistent demands to supply assemblers on a global basis—a tall order for most firms in developing countries. Assemblers enjoy enormous power in the market: in 2010, GM's procurement budget was estimated at $74 billion; its procurement division alone employed 6,700 people (Simon 2010). Dependence on foreign firms in the extensive model carries its own risks.

In the following chapter we look at alternative explanations and prescriptions for success in overcoming the challenges faced by economies pursuing economic upgrading. We elaborate our own explanation, which focuses on the development of institutions of industrial diffusion. We emphasize the importance of institutional fit: that different institutions are required dependent upon the strategy being pursued. We then turn to an examination of why some East Asian economies have pursued intensive strategies in the auto industry whereas others have favored extensive development.

3

Institutions, Politics, and Developmental Divergence

Simply talking about policy in the absence of institutions and underlying political alignments is unlikely to generate compelling explanations of—or prescriptions for—long-run growth.

—Haggard (2018: 60)

Add successively as many mail coaches as you please, you will never get a railway thereby.

—Schumpeter (1983: 62)

It is a great deal easier to find the capital for the construction of a modern industry than to run it.

—Hobsbawm (1968: 51, cited in Waldner 1999: 160)

In this chapter, we propose an explanation for the puzzles identified in Chapter 2: How do we account for cross-national variation in East Asian automotive development in the face of similar opportunities and constraints posed by the global automotive industry? How have Thailand and more recently Indonesia, but not the Philippines, succeeded in what we have labeled *extensive* development, i.e., in establishing vibrant, MNC-led assembly, but not in developing domestic capacities to design and produce parts and components, much less finished automobiles? How have Korea and to some extent China, but not Malaysia, succeeded at more *intensive* and independent automotive industrialization? How have they moved beyond assembly to upgrade the quality and sophistication of local products through improved design, engineering, and management? And why has Taiwan succeeded at a niche-based strategy of intensive development by focusing on components for the global replacement market? Put somewhat differently, how do we account for the ability of domestic firms in Korea, Taiwan, and China to *upgrade*, i.e.,

The Political Economy of Automotive Industrialization in East Asia. Richard F. Doner, Gregory W. Noble and John Ravenhill, Oxford University Press (2021). © Oxford University Press. DOI: 10.1093/oso/9780197520253.003.0003 to manufacture products with higher unit values, to move into related sectors, and to do all this at global levels of efficiency by adopting sophisticated processes, acquiring new functions, and by increasing backward linkages (Gereffi 2005; Humphrey and Schmitz 2002)?

The differences among the Southeast Asian cases suggest that extensive growth is far from easy, and that low labor costs are at best a necessary condition for such success. Beyond secure property rights and macroeconomic stability, successful extensive development requires what Waldner (1999) called a Gerschenkronian process of mobilizing funds and labor through, for example, investment incentives that support scale economies, infrastructure that facilitates exports and assembler-supplier linkages, and labor market arrangements that enable access to a flexible workforce.

As discussed in the following, implementing such measures constitutes sector- and even economy-wide coordination challenges. Coordination challenges refer to situations in which all actors prefer to coordinate (e.g., on standards) rather than acting unilaterally, but differ as to the specific way (e.g., the specific standards) on which to coordinate. Coordination problems differ from collective action problems in which unilateral action is the preferred outcome for some actors (e.g., free riders). Both problems are types of collective dilemmas, i.e., situations in which individual rationality does not result in an allocation of resources that maximizes social welfare (for an analysis of collective dilemmas in East Asia, see Noble 1998; Lall and Teubal 1998: 1371–1374 discuss market failures in technology absorption).

Because it involves the identification, absorption, and adaptation of new technologies *within* domestic firms, upgrading for intensive development is even more challenging. Improving products, processes, and functions depends not just on experience in assembling cars conceived, designed, and engineered by someone else, but also on the knowledge and capabilities that domestic firms glean from repeated opportunities to participate in the acquisition, creation, and integration of technology, often from foreign sources.

It is tempting to equate intensive growth with what is sometimes called "innovation-driven" as opposed to "investment-driven" growth, with the latter based on centralized coordination of investment and the former based on "inventing new technologies rather than . . . importing those invented elsewhere" and requiring, among other elements, a highly skilled workforce (Aghion, Guriev, and Jo 2019). But this formulation tends to conceive innovations only as technologies and practices *new to the world*. For our purposes, upgrading and intensive growth involves learning—identifying, absorbing, and adapting—technologies and practices *new to the firms*. And as endogenous growth theorists have argued, such a process is not a question of mechanically downloading some new codified, costless package of information and practices, but rather knowledge whose tacitness makes it tough to appropriate without existing technological capacity (Romer 1990; Cohen and Levinthal 1990). Such learning is difficult, involving its own coordination challenges both within the firm and market failures inherent in technology markets.[1]

Learning thus requires time, funds, qualified personnel, and knowledge beyond the reach of most domestic firms. For such firms, developing new competencies requires not only internal motivation (i.e., leadership), but also resources from a wide range of extra-firm actors.

Our argument can be divided into *what, how, and why* components. We first address *what* kinds of measures are required for different levels of industrial development. We contend that while both extensive and intensive development require extra-market policies, interventions required in the promotion of intensive development are different and, in many ways, harder to formulate than those for extensive development. We next observe that automotive industrialization policies are not self-implementing, which raises the question of *how* such measures are actually carried out. Our contention is that this process requires institutions capable of coordinating multiple agents that possess the required resources. For extensive growth, these actors and institutions include, among others, banks, investment boards, and relevant ministries (e.g., labor, transport, finance, industry). For intensive growth, the range of relevant actors widens further to include buyers, equipment suppliers, vocational schools, universities and polytechnics, testing centers, and research institutes. For intensive growth, the challenge is to coordinate this array of actors.

Consider attempts by government officials and automotive executives to nurture domestic capabilities through some form of local content requirements—whether in locally owned firms, foreign subsidiaries, or joint ventures. Such policies require the capacity to combine protection with productivity-enhancing pressure and resources. As seen in the cases of Korea, Taiwan, and, to some degree, China, success in such efforts required the institutional capacity to coordinate efforts by investment boards and ministries

[1] Market *failures* refer to situations in which rational action by market actors impedes efficient markets. Externalities, one type of market failure, involve spillovers—the unintended consequences of an individual's activities on others. In a negative externality, such as pollution, an individual's activities impose costs on others without the individual bearing the cost. In a positive externality (e.g., training by a firm), the individual generates benefits without the ability to capture them (e.g., due to poaching of employees). Public goods, a second type of market failure, are goods whose consumption by one does not reduce its supply to others or their opportunity to consume the good. Market *imperfections*, on the other hand, are situations in which the matching of buyers and sellers does not occur because key elements of efficient markets, especially the free flow of information and perfect competition, do not exist.

with those of technology-promoting agencies as well as with domestic firms. We shall see the problems resulting from a lack of such capacity—the low quality, high costs, and slow product delivery—in the cases of Malaysia and pre-liberalization Thailand and Indonesia. A striking illustration of the challenge involved is that Thailand's Board of Investments managed to adopt explicit incentives to promote technology spillovers from foreign producers only in 2017, after over four decades of empty claims that foreign direct investment (FDI) would help strengthen the domestic supplier base.

Even policies universally supported as necessary to increase firm competitiveness, such as technical-vocational education and training (TVET), require coordination among firms, investment boards, education and labor ministries, and educational institutions. The difficulties of such coordination, especially when educational ministries are politicized and faculty in educational institutions have few incentives to coordinate with the private sector, are reflected in the poorly developed technical training capacities in the extensive growth cases in our study. Our second core contention is thus that successful strategies require a "fit" between institutions and policy challenges of intensive vs. extensive strategies.

Finally, we move to the *why* question: Why have some countries had greater difficulty than others in developing appropriate institutions? Why, for example, has Malaysia's national car program largely failed to promote technological strength even in its domestic parts producers despite Malaysia's conscious emulation of and familiarity with the Korean experience? This question translates into a more political issue: under what conditions do political leaders develop and strengthen productivity-enhancing institutions? Our third contention is that political leaders will build such institutions only when confronted with a lack of easily accessible resources with which to counter domestic pressures and external threats.

This chapter assesses our arguments relative to contending explanations of variation in automotive industrialization in our seven countries. We begin with *firms*, the immediate actors in this industrial drama. What kinds of competencies are required by firms involved in extensive vs. intensive industrialization? We argue that neoclassical, market-based approaches fall short of accounting for performance variation, especially between extensive and intensive growth. By downplaying the market failures inherent in technology markets, they obscure the disequilibria inherent in the development process and the risks that firms face (Rosenstein-Rodan 1984). In so doing, they minimize the coordination challenges of development, especially in upgrading, and they downplay the potential benefits of market-friendly, sectoral interventions, i.e., industrial policies. We next address the potential benefits and the institutional challenges of industrial policies, especially those designed to strengthen firm technological capacities. The final section presents our frameworks and concludes by assessing other prominent institutional explanations, including those found in "good governance," global value chains, innovation systems, and developmental states approaches.

Firm Competencies in Extensive and Intensive Development: Coordination Problems

Extensive development is part of a broader process in which countries grow primarily through what McMillan and Rodrik (2011) label "structural change"—the movement from agriculture to industry, followed by diversification within manufacturing into sectors ranging from textiles to electronics to autos. Through a "Gerschenkronian" process, this involves mobilizing resources that are "hidden, scattered or badly utilized" for investments in non-traditional activities (Waldner 1999: 163). The shift has been central to the growth of many developing countries, including those covered in this book, where earnings from exports of manufactured goods have exceeded those of agricultural and other primary products since the mid-1980s. And, as noted earlier, successful extensive growth requires coordinating the provision of extra-firm resources with investment decisions.

Yet, with the partial exception of textiles and garments, most manufactured products are designed and engineered abroad and are highly reliant on imported inputs. Of course, diversification into more advanced sectors in countries such as Thailand, Malaysia, Indonesia, and the Philippines has included the production of higher value-added goods that include domestically supplied inputs. But as chronicled by research on Thailand (e.g., Warr 2011), Indonesia (e.g., Bland 2012), Malaysia (e.g., Yusuf and Nabeshima 2009), and the Philippines (e.g., Natsuda and Thoburn 2017), high-value added production in extensive growth countries has been largely a factor- and investment-driven process in which foreign producers have relied on low-wage labor, attractive investment incentives, adequate infrastructure, and foreign inputs to introduce products designed and engineered abroad, rather than incorporating domestic skills, inputs, and innovation (Porter 1998). In 2015, the most recent year for which data are available, in Thailand, 47% of value added in exports of motor vehicles came from outside the country (predominantly China and Japan); for Malaysia, despite decades of promoting and protecting producers, the figure was even higher at 56% (OECD, "Trade in

Value Added: Origin of Value Added in Gross Exports," https://stats.oecd,. org/index.aspx?DataSetCode=TIVA, 2018 C2, accessed November 15, 2019).

Indeed, with some variation, the Southeast Asian economies, including their auto industries, approach what Yoshihara (1988) termed "technologyless industrialization." As discussed later in this book, even Thailand, the region's most successful auto assembler and exporter, fares poorly on indicators such as the development and use of domestic capital equipment and intermediates (e.g., molds and dies, composites), and the capacity of local firms to design and export new parts, much less produce high-value parts and components. Similarly, the large volumes of wire harnesses exported from the Philippines, a country with an otherwise stalled automotive industry, are produced by multinationals with minimal domestic inputs.

If extensive growth emphasizes the mobilization of "hidden, scattered or badly utilized" resources for investments in non-traditional activities, *intensive* growth involves domestic companies accessing and absorbing technological (and related managerial) expertise new to the firms. Such expertise is critical to capabilities ranging from pre-investment analyses, to project execution, to process and product engineering, to industrial engineering, and establishing extra-firm linkages (Table 3.1).

But developing new capacities through the absorption and adaptation of "new" technology is fraught with market imperfections and failures. From the firm's (demand-side) perspective, these include imperfect information about the technology most appropriate to the firm; the long gestation periods, fixed costs, and uncertain returns in the development of tacit, experiential knowledge through trial-and-error tinkering; the lack of financing for risky new operations, especially in the imperfect credit and equity markets characteristic of developing countries; and the externalities, such as the potential leakage of new knowledge and skilled personnel to competitors (Lall 2000: 25; Hausmann and Rodrik 2002). Resolving such problems requires a range of specialized inputs, such as technical equipment, intermediate goods, skilled personnel, and market information. Yet problems exist on this supply side as well: these sophisticated inputs are imperfectly traded because sources such as vendors, consultants, and bankers incur significant costs in identifying and servicing the domestic firms, mostly small and inexperienced, that might be interested in moving into new products and processes (Shapira et al. 2015, p. 6).

The immediate actors in this industrial drama are thus individual firms. It is within firms that capacities noted earlier, such as preventive maintenance and equipment modification, must develop. As knowledge theories of the firm stress, an important mechanism through which this occurs is exchange of

Table 3.1 Illustrative Matrix of Technological Capabilities

	Pre-Investment	Project Execution	Process Engineering	Product Engineering	Industrial Engineering	Linkages
Simple Routine (experience based)	Feasibility studies, site selection	Civil construction, ancillary services	Debugging, quality control, preventive maintenance,	Assimilation of product design, minor adaptation to market needs	Work flow scheduling, time-motion studies, inventory control	Local procurement of goods and services, info exchange with and monitoring of suppliers
Adaptive, Duplicative (search based)	Search for technology source, contract negotiation	Equipment procurement, detailed engineering, training and recruitment of skilled personnel	Equipment stretching, process adaptation and cost saving, licensing new technology	Product quality improvement, licensing and assimilating new imported product technology	Monitoring productivity, improved coordination	Technology transfer of local suppliers, coordinated design, S&T links
Innovative, Risky (research based)		Basic process design, equipment design/supply	In-house process innovation, basic research	In-house product innovation, basic research		Turnkey capability, cooperative R&D, licensing own technology to others

Source: Adapted from Lall (1992: 167).

information among key actors within firms as social communities (Kogut and Zander 1992). But a firm-specific account alone is incomplete, especially when it comes to the technology absorption and development processes inherent in intensive growth in developing countries. Precisely owing to the challenges—the market imperfections and failures—involved in moving into new sectors and activities, the development of new capabilities within firms must occur in conjunction with a wide range of other actors, such as competitors, buyers, equipment suppliers, schools, testing centers, universities and research institutes. In other words, a firm's "capabilities are ultimately *relational*. . . . Its success depends substantially on its ability to coordinate effectively with a wide range of actors" (Hall and Soskice 2001: 6; Pietrobelli, Rasiah, and Lall 2012).

This coordination challenge is especially tough for intensive growth in developing countries, given the variety of inputs, actors, and information required by firms attempting to upgrade. The weight of the coordination problem facing firms thus requires that we extend our analysis to extra-firm institutions whose function is to address such dilemmas. And *it is because relevant institutions differ cross-nationally that variation in outcomes occurs primarily across countries rather than across firms* (Lall 2000: 24). Korea and Thailand provide a vivid and illustrative contrast. To be sure, Korea's Hyundai was far more successful than its compatriot Kia, which collapsed in the Asian financial crisis of the late 1990s before being absorbed by Hyundai, and Daewoo, which fell under the control of its former joint venture partner GM. Yet both—and even minor producers Samsung and Ssangyong—continue to produce and export vehicles conceived, designed, and/or engineered in Korea. Indeed, the facilities of Daewoo, once a basket case, have served as GM's global design and engineering center for small passenger vehicles.

In contrast, while many Japanese and Western automakers have made Thailand a base for assembly and even exports, none of their operations there does more than lightly adapt models conceived and engineered abroad. Thailand boasts no indigenous assemblers and very few domestic producers of high value-added parts or components. As we will argue, the success of Korean firms in the automotive sector rests on a complex of institutions and policies largely absent in Thailand. Such contrasts are seen more broadly: the Southeast Asian countries, unlike their Northeast Asian counterparts, have little involvement in upgrading and intensive growth in the automotive in-dustry. The major anomaly is Malaysia, which nominally followed the inten-sive development approach seen in Northeast Asia, but its limited success came only by retaining high levels of protection, and efficiency considerations were subordinated to identity politics, which ensured that the industry never became internationally competitive.

How might we assess the importance of extra-market institutions? In the next section of this chapter, we examine the dominant approach in mainstream economics, which largely ignores issues relating to market failures and coordination problems. We argue that the factors emphasized in explanations for development success in neoclassical economics fail to account for the divergent outcomes in our cases. Their weaknesses are especially notable with regard to the assumed benefits—positive spillovers—from FDI. This analysis leads us first to an appreciation of the potential benefits, as well as the institutional and political challenges, of various forms of sector-specific interventions, i.e., industrial policy. We then assess our own approach to these challenges: What kinds of institutions are required to carry out such interventions? What political conditions facilitate the development of such institutions?

Neoclassical Explanations

Market Size

Population alone does not determine the potential market for vehicles; per capita income is obviously also crucial, and market size itself is determined by several factors. The very concept of "market" is a social construction and thus requires careful specification. First, domestic demand can be influenced by a number of indirect and direct policy interventions such as improvement in roads and related infrastructure, as well as special excise and other tax incentives that can concentrate demand in a small number of market segments. Second, access to foreign markets increases opportunities for scale economies. For many years, the majority of Korea's domestic auto production has been exported. Exports have become a key dimension for Thai-based auto producers; and as noted earlier, Taiwan, a country with a population smaller than Malaysia's (23 million vs. 28 million), has demonstrated by its success in exporting standardized parts (e.g., bumpers and sheet metal) for use in aftermarket repair that successful niche strategies are possible even for countries with small domestic markets.

Finally, specific product and market-entry strategies can make it possible to attain scale economies even in limited domestic markets. For example, a key component in South Korea's automotive breakthrough in the early 1980s was achievement of scale economies by restricting production to just two firms and one engine size. Similarly, Thailand's decision to promote light commercial vehicles allowed it to become the world's largest production site for one-ton pickup trucks, and its recent move to attract "eco-car" production is based on hopes for similar benefits from specialization. Conversely, despite a population of over 80 million, Vietnam's auto efforts are hamstrung by a proliferation of close to 20 assemblers battling to produce a large number of models in a market where annual vehicle sales are under 250,000 (Economist Intelligence Unit 2010). But as Malaysia's experience demonstrates, limits on the number of producers and/or products are not a panacea: despite its promotion of just two national vehicle producers, poor vehicle quality and export weaknesses have prevented Malaysia from taking advantage of a domestic passenger car market accounting for nearly 40% of all new registrations in the Association of Southeast Asian Nations (ASEAN). Market size matters, but to a surprising degree it is a product of policy choices.

National Economic Growth → Sectoral Growth

An intuitively plausible argument is that overall economic expansion encourages development in sectors such as autos. The logic is that (GDP) growth, by stimulating savings, investment, and domestic demand, contributes both directly and indirectly to an expansion in automobile and auto parts production. Yet as Table 3.2 demonstrates, the link between annual GDP growth rates, at least since the 1990s, and national automotive performance is inconclusive. Malaysia, for example, enjoyed higher GDP growth in the quarter century after 1990 than its Thai neighbor but recorded a markedly inferior performance in the auto sector. Rather than economic growth,

Table 3.2 Annual GDP Growth (%)

	1970–1979	1980–1989	1990–1999	2000–2009	2010–2015	2016–2019
China	7.4	9.7	10.0	10.3	8.3	6.6
Indonesia	7.2	5.8	4.3	5.1	5.7	5.1
Korea	10.5	8.8	7.1	4.7	3.6	2.7
Malaysia	7.7	5.9	7.2	4.9	5.6	4.8
Philippines	5.8	2.0	2.7	4.5	6.2	6.5
Thailand	7.5	7.3	5.2	4.3	3.7	3.4
Taiwan	NA	NA	6.6	3.8	3.9	2.0

Sources: All data except Taiwan: Calculations from The World Bank World Development Indicators. Accessed at <https://data.worldbank.org/indicator/NY.GDP.MKTP.KD.ZG?view=chart≥ on 17 October 2020. Data for Taiwan is from "1-1a. Indicators of the Taiwan Economy: Economic Growth Rate at 2011 Prices (%)" from *Taiwan Statistical Databook* (2017, p.19 and 2019, p.1), accessed at: <https://www.ndc.gov.tw/en/News.aspx?n=607ED34345641980&sms=B8A915763E3684AC> on 17 October 2020; and Trading Economics: <https://tradingeconomics.com/taiwan/gdp> (Accessed 17 October 2020).

we might focus on levels of *per capita* income, since the income elasticity of demand for automobiles is high. But, again, this variable does not predict success in the automotive industry: Malaysia's per capita income is close to double that of Thailand. A focus on *per capita* incomes would also appear to be inappropriate in an era of regionalized value chains. The automotive world is no longer limited to self-contained national markets; countries with relatively low *per capita* incomes actually may be best placed to compete for some segments of the value chain.

"Sound Money/Free Markets"

If small domestic populations may be less of a limitation on automotive growth than is often assumed, some factors long emphasized by mainstream economists are clearly necessary for sustained growth: countries must provide adequate infrastructure, such as efficient ports and logistical capacities; the macro-economic climate must be reasonably stable and not biased against exports; firms must have access to capital, to modern technology, and to a competent, educated workforce (Haggard 2004). Our cases confirm the necessity of these conditions. Even as firms must be exposed to tough, competitive pressures, they must be able to count on modest inflation, stable exchange rates, and access to needed funds and knowledge. But the East Asian auto experiences, as well as the region's development experience more generally, also suggest qualifications to these core neoclassical contentions.

Monetary Stability and Fiscal Conservatism

While successful East Asian industrializers have managed to keep inflation fairly low by the standards of many developing economies, and exchange rates stable and realistic, they have, at times, deliberately "gotten prices wrong": they have provided loans at negative real interest rates (financial repression), distorted exchange rates, provided subsidies to select firms, and operated trade regimes whose complex, selective protections were inconsistent with neoclassical prescriptions, though the degree of variance from "correct" prices has generally shrunk over time (Amsden 1989). Nor are such measures limited to the East Asian Newly Industrialized Countries (NICs). As discussed later in this book, the growth of pickup truck production in Thailand would not have occurred without protection and targeted fiscal incentives. Meanwhile, Malaysia has had an enviable record of sound macroeconomic management, but this has not translated into success in the auto industry.

Trade Liberalization

Competition is an essential stimulus to efficiency, and free trade has the signal benefit of exposing domestic firms to competitive pressures. But the East Asian cases suggest several caveats to this truism. First, trade liberalization is not the only channel for competitive pressures. Government-imposed pressures to export, as seen in South Korea, can encourage the learning in domestic parts production as well as assembly that is so central to competitiveness. Domestic competition, as in China's inter-provincial rivalries, can replace or complement pressure from foreign products. Second, as discussed in the case chapters, trade liberalization in our successful cases of intensive development has, by and large, *followed* the achievement of competitiveness, not preceded it. Finally, regardless of its source, blanket exposure to market pressures is rarely sufficient to ensure the growth of a competitive domestic industry. The East Asian cases suggest that the benefits of liberalization and export promotion may depend on managerial and technological capacities built up *prior to or even simultaneously with* liberalization, even as exposure to market pressures can offset the inefficiency-generating consequences of protection and promotion. Exposure to pressure from established producers in the absence of internal managerial and technical know-how typically weakens rather than strengthens nascent auto producers.

Openness to FDI

Multinational parts producers and assemblers are an important potential source of automotive know-how. Access to such firms, especially through foreign direct investment, is often viewed as a necessary component for developing countries' industrial development (Moran 1998). But the purported benefits of FDI must be qualified. First, since FDI "will be pulled into countries already doing well, or expected to do well in the future," foreign investment is typically as much a consequence as a cause of growth (Temple 1999: 138; Haggard and Kim 1997). Second, the correlation between FDI volumes and the emergence of local technical capabilities is quite weak in East Asia. Although Singapore and Malaysia are both highly reliant on FDI as a percentage of gross domestic investment (Table 3.3), they differ significantly in terms of the development of national technical capacities. The pattern is similar in Thailand where, although aggregate FDI flows were substantially less than in Malaysia and Singapore at least through the mid-1990s, external finance has been key to the country's impressive growth performance (Jansen 1997b, 1997a). These funds have not, however, been associated with any significant deepening of local technical capacities, especially relative to the two East Asian countries with the lowest reliance on FDI, South Korea and Taiwan.

Table 3.3 Foreign Direct Investment (inward) as % of Gross Fixed Capital Formation (annual average)

	1984–89	1990–94	1995–2004	2005–2009	2010–2014	2015–2019
Korea	1.4	0.7	3.9	3.4	2.8	2.5
Taiwan	3.3	3.0	2.8	5.3	1.8	4.6
Indonesia	1.6	3.5	–0.3	5.5	6.6	4.7
Malaysia	8.8	22.4	12.4	13.2	14.5	10.8
Thailand	4.4	4.3	13.8	12.3	9.4	5.6
China	1.8	11.6	11.5	6.1	3.3	2.2
Philippines			6.5	8.3	5.3	8.2

Sources: Figures for 1984-1994 are % of Gross Domestic Investment, from UNCTAD, cited in Lall, (2000: 38). 1995-2015: UNCTAD *World Investment Report 2017* Annex Table 5. Accessed at <http://unctad.org/Sections/dite_dir/docs/WIR2017/WIR17_tab05.xlsx> on July 23, 2018.

2017-2019 except China and Taiwan calculated from "Gross fixed capital formation (constant 2010 US$)" accessed at: <https://data.worldbank.org/indicator/NE.GDI.FTOT.KD> on 18 October 2020 and UNCTAD WIR 2020 "FDI [inward] flows, by region and economy, 2014-2019" Annex table 1: <https://unctad.org/system/files/official-document/wir2020_en.pdf>

China GFCF from <https://www.oecd-ilibrary.org/economics/investment-gfcf/indicator/english_b6793677-en> accessed on 21 October 2020.

Taiwan GFCF from *Taiwan Statistical Data Book* 2019, p.10: <https://www.ndc.gov.tw/en/News.aspx?n=607ED34345641980&sms=B8A915763E3684AC> accessed on 21 October 2020. $NT at 2011 prices converted to USD at a rate of 30.5:1 (rough average of 2011 annual exchange rate).

The gap between foreign investment flows and technological upgrading reflects the fact that attracting foreign producers is not the same thing as promoting and benefiting from spillovers from them (Narula and Dunning 2012: 39). Our cases embody these differences: The combination of extensive FDI inflows and technological weaknesses led a World Bank study to label Malaysian and Thai development strategies "passive FDI-dependent learning," as opposed to the more "active FDI-dependent learning" seen in the East Asian NICs (Yusuf and Nabeshima 2009: Chapter 7). Here, "passive" refers to liberalizing FDI policies without evaluating the kinds of externalities that may result; without considering whether and how domestic actors can internalize them; and without developing broader, non-firm assets to support firms' absorptive capacities (Narula and Dunning 2012: 38). Such "passive" strategies may be appropriate and sufficient for extensive (i.e., investment-driven) growth. But cases of successful intensive growth have adopted an active stance toward FDI: They have "sought to attract . . . [FDI] . . . but have also built up domestic absorptive capacities in tandem" (Narula and Dunning 2012: 38).

Moreover, it is worth noting how the potential contributions of FDI to host countries' development have increasingly become "unpackaged." As we discussed in Chapter 2, those firms in developing economies with sufficiently deep pockets have increasingly been able to purchase technology—whether components or design capabilities—from specialist suppliers. Similarly, managerial and other specialists who embody "tacit technology" can be recruited internationally, and the integration of international capital markets has made it much easier for firms in developing economies to raise capital internationally. In other words, countries no longer necessarily need FDI to access technology, capital, and managerial skills. But most developing-country firms do not have such deep pockets. And even accessing these resources is not the same as effectively absorbing them. As we explain later in this chapter, the transfer of "new" practices from outside actors such as global producers is highly complex and context-dependent (McDermott and Pietrobelli 2017). The countries that have succeeded in promoting technology spillovers to local firms have done so through various types of government interventions designed to promote specific economic sectors and activities over others, also known as industrial policies (Hevia et al. 2017).

The Case for New Industrial Policy

Although many analysts in the neoclassical tradition allowed for the possibility of market failures, their retort was that attempts by the state to intervene to ameliorate them would result in a welfare loss: government failures were likely to be more costly than market failures. Deepak Lal (1983: 103–106), for instance, concluded that there were only two "feasible alternatives"—"a necessarily imperfect planning mechanism" and "a necessarily imperfect market mechanism"—and "the latter is likely to perform better in practice." These arguments received a boost from the poor performance of state-led import-substitution industrialization in Africa and Latin America, which contributed to their debt crises in the 1970s and 1980s. The "Washington Consensus," with its raft of policy prescriptions for reducing the role of the state, represented the reassertion of neoclassical orthodoxy at the end of the 1980s.

Skepticism about the efficacy of industrial policies extended to discussions of the East Asian "Miracle." Economists working in the neoclassical tradition emphasized that the success of East Asian newly industrializing economies was founded on countries pursuing sound macroeconomic policies, that it frequently rested on the application of additional inputs rather than on a growth in productivity, that policies to promote specific sectors risked encouraging rampant rent-seeking similar to the Latin American experience, and that many new firms thrived without state support (in a huge literature see, for example, Industry Commission 1990 on the importance of market-conforming policies; Young 1994 on total factor productivity; and Callon 1995 on the failures of industrial policy in Japan in the 1980s). The Asian financial crises of 1997–1998, particularly the failure of many of Korea's heavily indebted and over-extended chaebol (Noble and Ravenhill 2000), provided further grist to the neoclassical mill.

For neoclassical economists and the major international economic organizations, the lessons were clear. Their advice was to avoid "vertical" policies that targeted particular firms or sectors. Instead, they advocated more "functional" measures designed to improve factor markets without favoring particular activities (Lall and Teubal 1998: 1369). The objective was to address only the most generic market failures through policies such as general worker training and education, openness to foreign technology, physical and regulatory infrastructure, and non-targeted incentives for R&D. Under these kinds of policies, firm practices and performances would presumably improve through competitive emulation (Pack 2000). Further support for such generic measures has come from multilateral economic institutions who see them as key to taking advantage of growth opportunities afforded by participation in global value chains (Taglioni and Winkler 2016).

Few today would advocate (even if it were possible under contemporary global rules on trade and investment) the kind of heavy-handed intervention seen in the 1960s and 1970s, which included complete protection against imports, heavy restrictions on FDI, and lavish (often unconditional) provision of preferential finance. But the 2008–2009 global financial crisis demonstrated that "markets were not necessarily efficient," leading the World Bank's Chief Economist to recognize the limits of passive participation in global value chains and the fact that industrial policy "has come out of the cold" (Lin 2010).

For one thing, the effects of "old industrial policy" continue to cast a long shadow. Tariffs, subsidized credit, and other industrial policy tools remain significant in the auto industry, as can be seen from the examples of China, Taiwan, Thailand, India, and other countries. Strategic tax policy still plays a role in Thailand, with its small pickup trucks, and even in Japan, where special tax rates protect *kei* minicars. However, on balance, and increasingly over the last couple of decades, the new industrial policy goes beyond the rather blunt instruments of the 1980s, such as heavily subsidized credit, and draws on what may be termed the "best practices" of the East Asian experience, including close coordination between the state and private sector actors.

In addition, more differentiated and nuanced conceptions of industrial policy have emerged in light of a deeper understanding of the industrialization strategies of the NICs (e.g., Wade 1990, 2014), the apparent success of industrial policies in China, and the bases for sector-specific successes within otherwise non-industrialized countries, including electronics in Penang (e.g., Hutchinson 2008), wine in Argentina (McDermott 2007), and aquaculture in Chile (World Bank 2014). Picking winners was not always successful in East Asia, but there was persuasive evidence of effective state intervention in a number of countries to enhance technological upgrading by domestic companies.

Alongside persistent efforts such as local content promotion, in contemporary industrial strategies we see a greater emphasis on policies that promote the technological and managerial capabilities of firms. In contrast to factor-driven, "Gerschenkronian" policies focusing on capital accumulation, Waldner (1999) labels these technology-promoting measures "Kaldorian," after the British economist's emphasis on manufacturing *productivity* (Kaldor 1957). This distinction has the advantage of leading us back to a focus on firm capabilities. The "new intellectual consensus" (Stiglitz and Lin 2013) on the potential for industrial policy reflects a deeper understanding of the political economy of learning and innovation. It builds on the contention in development economics that markets alone will not optimally provide those goods, such as knowledge, that are characterized by significant public good elements and externalities (Greenwald and Stiglitz 2012). Moreover, markets are typically unable to resolve many of the coordination problems hindering development unless upstream and downstream investments are made simultaneously.

The new industrial policies consequently start from the importance of developing appropriate institutions to foster the creation, distribution, and assimilation of knowledge. They emphasize the importance of measures that strengthen private agents through discovery and diffusion of learning (Kuznetsov and Sabel 2011). We thus see fewer policies aimed at specific firms (i.e., the promotion of "national champions") and more measures oriented toward competencies that are applicable more broadly. For example, as reflected in recent training programs in Thailand (Technology Promotion Association [Thailand-Japan] 2019), competencies in flexible automation technologies such as robotic welding, mechatronics, and computer numerical control (CNC) machining are important to both advanced manufacturing in general *and* to the automotive industry in particular.

In acknowledging the importance of competency-strengthening policies, this new approach to industrial policies complements and goes beyond theories of the firm as knowledge integrators (e.g., Grant 1996). It highlights the ways in which such learning is a social process whereby firms' capacity for upgrading is strongly influenced by extra-firm sources of information. This understanding of firm capabilities as relational, noted earlier in this chapter, has led to a renewed appreciation of the broader institutional environment in which firms operate, especially the public-private linkages that can promote the diffusion of industry-wide goods (Kuznetsov and Sabel 2011; Haggard 2018: 3; Johnson 1982). Institutions to enhance information collection, monitoring, signaling, and industrial coordination and diffusion are a critical part of the context in which firms learn.

This new and evolving understanding of industrial policy informs our core arguments. The rough distinction between Gerschenkronian capital accumulation and Kaldorian technology promotion policies provides a basis for our contention that cross-national variation in performance is in large part a reflection of the industrial policies adopted and the institutions that (attempt to) formulate and implement them. It enables us to evaluate the contention that policies aimed at upgrading pose particularly difficult sets of challenges. Meeting such challenges requires specialized institutions that are themselves not easy to establish. This argument is consistent with an understanding of the need to go beyond the assertion that "institutions matter." We need to specify the kinds of challenges involved in effective industrial policies (e.g., Schneider 2015).

Policies and Challenges: The *What* Question

As seen in Table 3.4, the East Asian countries varied in both their industrial policy choices and their capacities to implement them. Relative to the extensive cases, the successful intensive cases—China, Korea, and Taiwan—were both active and relatively effective with regard to measures designed to promote local firms' technological capacities. These included, among others, offering FDI incentives conditional on technological spillovers, investing in sector-relevant technical and vocational training, and promoting what is known as "quality infrastructure." The latter refers to the complex of public, private, and mixed institutions that help firms meet quality, safety, and environmental standards (which was one of the keys to Japan's early industrial development; see Shapira 1992). They do this in large part through services focusing on accreditation and conformity assessment in MSTQ—metrology, standards, testing-evaluation, and quality (World Bank 2018a). Our unsuccessful intensive growth case helps demonstrate the importance of such measures: Malaysia has been passive with regard to testing and standards and unsuccessful in implementing automotive-specific measures to promote technological spillovers and improve workforce quality.

Table 3.4 Industrial Policy: Choice, Effectiveness, Flexibility

Industrial Policy Types	Intensive Cases			Extensive Cases			
	China	Taiwan	Korea	Malaysia	Indonesia	Philippines	Thailand
Functional							
Property rights: general	Mixed (only gradual increase in IPR protection)	Yes	Yes	Yes	Yes, but variation	Yes/but only partially effective (smuggling)	Yes
Macroeconomic stability	High (except 1985–1996)	High	High	High	Low-medium	Medium-high	High
Education: basic	Strong	Strong	Strong	Moderate	Weak	Weak	Weak
Infrastructure: basic physical	Strong	Moderate	Strong	Strong	Weak	Weak-moderate	Strong
Ease of labor flow	High	High	High	High	High	High	High
Gerschenkronian (Capital Accumulation / Mobilization)							
Trade measures: Tariffs and/or Qualitative Restrictions (e.g., quotas)	Moderate after WTO entry in late 2000	Moderate after WTO entry in 2002	Moderate-high	High (national car) until AFTA	High until 2000s	Low	High for selected products
Fiscal incentives (e.g., excise taxes)	Widespread at provincial level	Low	Low: Not a significant instrument	High (excise taxes for national car)	n.a.	Low	High (pickups, EVs)
Subsidized credit for capital-intensive investments	Widespread at provincial level	Low	High	High	High (e.g., steel) until 2000s	Low	Low

FDI: promote for auto/ no strings	No: FDI encouraged but only in joint ventures for assembly	No: restrictions until mid-1990s	No: FDI restricted before OECD entry	Moderate; depends on niche	Varies; now high	High	High until 2017
FDI: restrict-promote local capacities	Yes	No: restrictions until mid-1990s.	Yes	Yes	Varies; now low	Yes, until	No
Infrastructure: physical (e.g., indust. estates)	Yes	Yes	Yes	Strong	Weak	Moderate	Strong
Market promotion (e.g., FTAs, complementation, export info)	Strong	Strong	Strong	Moderate	Weak but strengthening	Weak	Moderate
Kaldorian (Technology Promotion)							
Trade measures: tariffs coordination between up-downstream	Yes	Yes	Yes	Yes	Medium	Weak	Medium
Support local enterprise R&D	Yes/ effective	Yes/ effective	Yes/ effective	Yes but effective only in electronics	No	No	Yes/ineffective
FDI: promote w/ spillover incentives	Yes/ effective	Not after mid-1990s	Yes/ effective	Yes/ineffective	No	Yes/ ineffective	Yes/ineffective
Promote tech transfer to local firms via assembler-supplier schemes	Yes/ effective	Yes/ effective	Yes	Yes/ ineffective	No	Yes/ ineffective in 1970s; No at present	Yes/ineffective

Continued

Table 3.4 *Continued*

Industrial Policy Types	Intensive Cases			Extensive Cases			
	China	Taiwan	Korea	Malaysia	Indonesia	Philippines	Thailand
Infrastructure: Quality /MSTQ	Strong	Strong	Strong	Weak	Weak	Weak	Weak, but recently strengthening
Education/ training: advanced mfg (e.g., robotic welding, CNC)	Strong	Strong	Strong	Strong only in electronics	Weak	Weak	Weak but strengthening
Support pre-competitive consortia	Yes	Yes	Yes	No	No	No	No
Strategic flexibility	Mixed (insistence on support for SOEs and reluctance to drop the 50% cap on foreign ownership of assembly)	Yes (slow but steady liberalization after mid-1980s)	Yes—but only after post Asian Financial Crisis consolidation of the industry	Low-medium (slowly, partially)	Low-medium (but slowly, partially)	Low-medium (slowly)	High: shift to EOI and focus on pickup trucks in 1980s

Key: CNC: Computer Numerical Control.
Source: Authors' judgment based on case chapter material.

Our extensive cases were either inactive with regard to measures such as investing in quality infrastructure or specialized training, or ineffective on others, such as efforts to support local firms through assembler-supplier schemes. Yet even successful extensive growth strategies have required more than functional measures. The most successful extensive case, Thailand, has been distinguished by its active and effective use of targeted trade, fiscal, foreign investment, and infrastructural measures.

In the following, we highlight the policy differences associated with alternative approaches to automotive development because they pose different types and degrees of challenges. These differences in turn help to identify the kinds of institutions required for intensive vs. extensive automotive development.

Information

Encouraging investment in new sectors for extensive growth requires knowledge about issues such as the size of labor force required by new producers, the nature of new infrastructure required by export-oriented production, and the fiscal measures that most affect consumer behavior. But to a significant degree, this information is relatively codified and easy to gather. Collective action dilemmas become more difficult where the solution demands information that is highly technical, or specific to particular times and places, or where no clear template exists. These conditions are especially relevant for intensive growth. Identifying and making use of technology new to the firm and its particular locale is a risky, technical, and tacit process for which most developing-country firms have neither clear templates nor experience. Consider, for example, the need for developing-country firms to meet global product and process standards through MSTQ capacities. MSTQ-related information is constantly changing with market shifts, and it varies across products: because no one size fits all, "a tailor-made approach is necessary" (UNIDO 2016; Kellerman 2019). Similarly, reforming education and developing training programs requires extensive information about firm and sectoral needs, as well as about the varying locales in which education institutions operate. The long history of failed education reform and vocational training initiatives, even in otherwise successful cases such as Thailand (Chapter 4), attests to the lack of easily transferable templates in these areas (Grindle 2004). Calibrating tariff rates in order to promote linkages among producers and users (i.e., final assemblers, parts producers, and supporting industry producers of capital equipment and intermediates) requires extensive information to determine, for example, which products need to be counted as intermediate inputs versus finished products. Effective promotion of technology spillovers from FDI requires incentives based on knowledge of MNC needs and of local firms' capacities, as well as the capacity to monitor post-investment activities by MNCs.

Length and Complexity of Implementation Chain

Industrial development promotion typically involves coordinating the actions of multiple actors. In the case of extensive growth, encouraging firms to invest in automotive assembly or parts production, for example, requires orchestration of investment boards responsible for incentives, industry ministries responsible for issuing factory licenses, transport ministries responsible for roads and ports, utilities responsible for electricity hookups, and finance ministries responsible for tariff levels, exchange rates, and customs administration. The fact that, as described later in this book, Indonesia and the Philippines were rarely successful in these measures indicates that reconciling the interests and actions of multiple agencies and their stakeholders does not occur automatically.

But these measures pose fewer challenges than intensive growth policies that aim at changes in firm practices with the focus not so much on what they produce but on how they produce. Unlike, say, exchange rate policies that can, with some qualification, be formulated and implemented with the "stroke of a pen," helping individual small and medium-sized firms meet stringent product and process standards through MSTQ, despite significant variation in the scale, experience, and expertise of the local firms, requires the participation of certification bodies, inspection agencies, testing facilities, and calibration laboratories, all of which are under the jurisdiction of national standards bodies and ministries (Hsieh 2015).

And whereas extensive growth does not necessarily require linkages with domestic producers, the process of upgrading at the heart of intensive growth involves fostering dynamic complementarities that require, for example, coordinating tariff and related policies among customs officials, trade ministries, and business associations representing different parts of the automotive value chain. Similarly, effective technical training requires the coordinated involvement of industry specialists, curriculum developers, and instructors, as well as university or polytechnic administrators and education ministries. Opposition, abstention, and/or free riding by individual parties can thwart the policy (Noble 1998: 21).

Winners and Losers

Development tasks are more challenging when losses are felt more quickly than benefits and when the losers are more organized and powerful than the winners. Distributional problems certainly occur even in extensive development, for example when governments attempt to consolidate final producers in order to achieve scale economies and reduce waste of resources on inefficient firms. Governments need to let weak firms die out or be absorbed by more efficient rivals, whether through market competition, policy pressures, or some combination of the two. Given the lobbying power of auto firms, especially assemblers, such rationalization is often contested.

Promoting potential linkages in intensive growth can also impose losses on some players. The process of rent transfer from finished-goods producers to inefficient upstream suppliers that has characterized most protected automobile industries in the developing world is inconsistent with the efficient provision of local inputs. Efforts to reduce the flow of rents are likely to encounter resistance from the current beneficiaries. The costly, unsuccessful effort to promote domestic steel production for use in the Indonesian auto industry, as documented in Chapter 5, is a telling example. Similarly, achieving an efficient supplier base typically requires not just technology support for domestic suppliers, but also the capacity to bear the political costs of rationalizing weaker firms out of the market.

Visibility and Intertemporality

Policy achievements are often composed of bricks and mortar that can serve as a source of rents and are relatively easy for both constituents and industry participants to monitor. School construction and factory openings, along with employment rates, export volumes, and foreign exchange earnings will therefore tend to garner more political support than less visible measures such as vocational curriculum development or product improvement by mold and die producers resulting from their participation in public testing facilities. Development measures also differ with regard to the time required for implementation and the emergence of visible results. An extensive literature concludes that "short-term outcomes dominate long-term outcomes in voters'—and therefore, in politicians'—calculations" (Jacobs 2011: 16). The "time inconsistency" problem, in which policy shifts or even reverses due to factors such as changes in coalitions, the removal of a "policy champion," or payoffs to government officials, undermines governments' willingness to invest resources in line with prior agreements. This policy instability poses significant obstacles for intensive growth-promoting efforts, such as R&D and skills development, whose implementation and resulting benefits take time (Doner and Ricks 2017).

A useful example of policy-specific challenges involves FDI promotion. Going beyond attracting FDI for employment and foreign exchange generation to promote technology spillovers requires site-specific information with regard to the technological properties of various industries, the strategic concerns of foreign producers, as well as the evolving capacities of domestic firms. It requires the ability to work with multiple domestic actors capable of supporting domestic firms. It requires the ability to withstand pressures from domestic firms that cannot meet new standards. And, in light of the gradual nature of such spillovers, it requires the capacity to monitor policy outcomes over a long period of time (Felker and Jomo 2003).

Institutions: The *How* Question

Building on the preceding paragraphs, Table 3.5 highlights the particular challenges associated with policies pursued by the countries adopting intensive automotive growth strategies. As policies do not implement themselves, it is important to identify the types of institutions that can formulate and carry out the policy challenges of different development trajectories. In the following, we argue that bureaucratic strength, broadly defined, does not capture the performance variation among our cases, especially the differences between extensive and intensive growth cases. And while education and research are strongly correlated with the overall upgrading of an economy, it is unclear how such qualities relate to specific sectors such as the auto industry.

Bureaucratic Capacity

Comparing the effectiveness of bureaucratic institutions in promoting industrial upgrading is a daunting challenge. As a first cut, we examine the "good governance" approach pioneered by the World Bank (Burki and Perry 1998; Kaufmann, Kraay, and Mastruzzi 2010). The Bank, along with Transparency International and other international agencies, provides copious data, mostly compiled from surveys of international business executives, on an annual basis going back to the 1990s. These indices are genuinely comparative and relatively objective. Because they are not produced by any one government

Table 3.5 Extensive–Intensive Growth Policy Difficulties

Policies	Extensive	Intensive	Difficulties
Property rights protection (property, profits)	✓	✓	Low: small number of actors; low information; visible
Macroeconomic stability to stabilize costs of capital: monetary, fiscal, exchange rate policy	✓	✓	Medium: distributional costs main challenge
FDI: attract investment for jobs and to gain access to foreign exchange through tax exemptions, export subsidies etc.	✓	✓	Medium: relatively low technical info; multiple actors; visible results
Trade: ensure access to imports and facilitate exports through tariffs, customs	✓	✓	Medium: need to coordinate trade administration bodies; distributional costs may be important (smuggling)
Labor: access to unskilled and semi-skilled through basic education, reduced barriers to rural➜urban movement	✓	✓	Low
Market development and access through trade agreements, rationalization, fiscal measures (e.g., excise taxes) for domestic consumption and scale economies	✓	✓	Medium: market-specific information; multiple agencies involved in fiscal policy; distributional costs from rationalization
Infrastructure (physical) through roads, electricity, IT	✓	✓	Medium: technical information required; possible distributional challenges (e.g., eminent domain)
FDI: promote technology and related spillovers through special investment incentives		✓	High: technical information; monitoring by multiple actors; not highly visible; length of implementation
R&D by domestic firms		✓	High: technical information; multiple agencies and firms; length of implementation
Labor: access to skilled, specialized workforce through technical-vocational education		✓	High: technical and sector-specific information; multiple actors; not highly visible
MSTQ to facilitate product acceptance		✓	High: technical information tailored to firms, sectors; multiple actors; lengthy implementation process

or industry association, the indices are a useful first approximation of bureaucratic capacity. In the first decade of this century, our case countries fell into three groups on the World Bank's "government effectiveness" indicator (World Bank 2018c). Korea, Taiwan, and Malaysia were closely bunched at or just over the 80th percentile. Thailand and China were ranked about the 60th percentile, while Indonesia and the Philippines were around the 50th. From 1996 (the earliest data available) to 2009, the relative rankings were quite stable. Most countries improved over time, but progress was particularly notable in Korea, China, and Indonesia. Since 2010, China has continued to improve its position while Malaysia has fallen back, so the gap between them has narrowed substantially. On the more specific measure of "regulatory quality," the countries fall into the same three groups. "Control of corruption" and "rule of law" yield similar rankings, though Thailand fares a little better and China somewhat worse on these other indicators of government effectiveness. The World Economic Forum's survey of perceptions of the quality of physical infrastructure such as transport, telecommunications, and energy yields similar outcomes, though Thailand and especially Malaysia score a little higher (Schwab 2010: 388).

In sum, these broad measures of institutional quality produce results consistent with each other and approximating our automotive outcomes. Some significant anomalies remain, however. Malaysia's automotive accomplishments are not as impressive as its rankings on surveys of institutional quality would predict, while China is an "overachiever." In addition, the "good governance" framework has some deeper flaws, which we address later in this chapter.

Bureaucratic Quality and Autonomy

A second measure of bureaucratic capacity looks specifically at the quality of the officials staffing government institutions. A prominent survey by Evans and Rauch (1999) of the "Weberianness" of bureaucracies—the degree to which bureaucratic agencies rely on meritocratic recruitment and provide rewarding, long-term careers for their officials—produces results largely consistent with other measures of government effectiveness and with the success of our countries in pursuing intensive development (Table 3.6).

Evans and Rauch's survey covers only five of our seven countries (no data are provided on China and Indonesia). Tjiptoherijanto (2010) however, asserts that the Indonesian civil service trails that of its neighbors. Meanwhile, Rothstein (2015) dubs the contrast between the apparently weak "Weberianness" of China's party-dominated system and its impressive policy outputs "the China paradox." He attributes this paradox to a non-Weberian but potent form of "cadre" or mission organization in which civil servants are not neutral implementers of rational-legal orders, but are motivated by ideology and incentives set by, and systematically monitored by, the ruling party. These

Table 3.6 Weberianness of Bureaucracy

Country	Weberianness (meritocratic recruitment; rewarding, long-term careers) From 0 (lowest) to 14
Korea	13
Taiwan	12
China	NA (Fairly high)
Malaysia	10.5
Thailand	8
Indonesia	NA (Low)
Philippines	6

Sources: Evans and Rauch (1999: 763). China: Rothstein (2015); Yang (2004); Indonesia: Choi (2009).

results indicate that the key factor determining the contribution of institutions to upgrading is not necessarily the power of the state, as developmental state theorists would have it, nor transparency, openness, and neutrality, as the World Bank and foreign business executives would like to believe, but the organizational integrity and long-term orientation of institutions.

Bureaucratic Capacity: Outcomes in Education, Science, and Technology

As a third approach, we can infer bureaucratic capacity from a relevant outcome: measures of attainment in education, science, and technology. Access to primary education largely mirrors our national automotive performance: attendance has improved in all countries, but China is closer to Korea and Taiwan, while the Southeast Asian countries lag slightly, especially when it comes to educating girls.

Data on academic performance are sketchier—none of the major comparative studies, such as TIMSS (Trends in International Mathematics and Science Study) and the OECD's PISA (Programme for International Student Assessment), includes data for all of our case countries on the same variables. Collectively, however, they suggest a sharp divide between Northeast and Southeast Asia, and thus between countries successfully pursing an intensive growth strategy based on upgrading, and countries depending on extensive growth. Korea and Taiwan are star performers, even compared with the most advanced industrial democracies; in contrast, test scores are low in Indonesia, where many students drop out before completing junior high school, and rank at the very bottom in the Philippines, where scores are low even for those who stay in school. Once again, Malaysia is in an intermediate position, with below average scores in science and mathematics (both declined from 1999 to 2007 but recovered somewhat after that). An official survey in Malaysia [NEAC 2010: 5] noted the "stagnant contribution by total factor productivity and education to output growth". Neither TIMSS nor PISA has conducted a national examination in China. Test runs of PISA in 2012, 2015, and 2018 in the country's most developed areas (Beijing, Shanghai, Jiangsu, and Guangdong in the first two rounds, with Zhejiang replacing Guangdong in 2018) generated results suggesting extraordinary excellence in mathematics and science and to a lesser extent reading (OECD 2016), though some knowledgeable critics raised doubts about the representativeness of the test populations (Strauss 2019).

The gap between the Northeast Asian countries, which have aggressively pursued upgrading, and the Southeast Asian countries is even clearer when it comes to higher education and research and development activities (Table 3.7). Attendance alone does not tell the story: Korea and Taiwan, where virtually all young people advance to some form of tertiary learning, far outstrip the other countries, but Thailand is also surprisingly high, with a 45% attendance rate, much higher than Malaysia (36%) or China (25%). Key to

Table 3.7 Science and Technology Activities

	R&D researchers per million population, 2018	R&D as share of GDP, 2010-2018	S&T Journal Articles, 2016	Patent Applications filed: residents, 2018	Patent Applications filed: non-residents, 2018
Korea	7,980	4.14%	63,063	162,561	47,431
China	1,307	1.95%	426,165	1,393,815	148,187
Taiwan	6,100	2.79%	27,385	39,604 (2019)	35,048 (2019)
Malaysia	2,397	1.24% (2010–2016)	20,332	1,116	6,179
Thailand	1,350 (2017)	0.68% (2011–2017)	9,581	904	7,245
Indonesia	216	0.24% (2016–2018)	7,729	1,407	8,347
Philippines	106 (2015)	0.14% (2011–2015)	916 (2014)	529	3,771

Sources: World Bank, *World Development Indicators Databank* accessed 18 October 2020; National Science Board *Science and Engineering Indicators 2018* at <https://www.nsf.gov/statistics/2018/nsb20181/> on 18 October 2020; World Intellectual Property Organization at <https://www.wipo.int/ipstats/en/statistics/country_profile/> on 18 October 2020; Taiwan Intellectual Property Office, Annual Statistics 2019 at <https://www.tipo.gov.tw/en/lp-303-2.html> on 18 October 2020.

explaining this anomaly of high participation rates but low achievement is the relatively poor *quality* of Thai education (see, e.g., Somchai 2013).

In the 2020 Times Higher Education survey of leading world universities, China placed 22 schools (not including six others in Hong Kong) in the top 500, Korea 10, and Taiwan five (Times Higher Education 2020). Of our Southeast Asian countries, only two universities made the top 500, Malaysia's University of Malaya, in the "351–400" class, and the University of the Philippines, ranked between 401 and 500. Of the 50 top universities in mechanical and aerospace engineering, China had five entries, Korea had three, and Hong Kong two; no other university from our case countries made the list. Four other leading middle-income auto producers, had only five universities in total in the top 500 (Brazil (2), the Czech Republic (1), Mexico, and Turkey (2)), and none in the top 50 for mechanical and aerospace engineering.

Research and development spending, patenting activity, and publications in international scientific and technological journals all show a yawning gap between the Northeast Asian countries, including China, and their counterparts in Southeast Asia (Noble 2017). Also striking is the relatively weak performance of Malaysia, which spends far more than Thailand on research and development, but records virtually no more patents and produces fewer than half as many science and technology publications as its Southeast Asian neighbor. Indonesia, which is doing well at extensive growth, and the Philippines, which is not, trail far behind all the others.

Education and research prowess, then, are reasonable predictors of success in upgrading, but there are also some significant anomalies. Nor are education and research completely exogenous to industrial institutions and policies. As with bureaucratic quality, we need to see how these accomplishments actually are applied to the auto industry. A full assessment of the quality of institutions directly related to industrial promotion and the automobile industry requires detailed case studies, such as those in subsequent chapters in this volume. Here, we provide a brief comparative analysis of national automotive institutes in our case studies.

National Automotive Institutes

Industry or sectoral institutes are a type of "intermediary organization" designed to improve firm performance by linking users of "new" technology, i.e., firms, with providers and channels of this knowledge, such as business associations, research technology organizations, cooperative training programs, and public testing and research centers (Intarakumnerd and

Charoenporn 2013b). As components of quality infrastructure noted earlier, automotive institutes can contribute to sectoral strengthening by providing advice and information on issues such as MSTQ, brokering transactions between two or more parties, and helping to secure access to material support for collaborative innovation through activities such as:

- helping create and disseminate national and international standards for safety, emissions, quality, and recyclability;
- testing and certifying vehicles and parts, including evaluation of crashworthiness and quality of fuels and emissions control equipment;
- providing engineering troubleshooting and technical guidance for firms learning to meet product and process standards;
- diffusing information and technology new to member firms;
- undertaking research and development of new automotive technologies;
- coordinating training in sector-required skills.

The specific functions and relative significance of the institutes may vary. But in all countries, the services provided by automotive institutes are especially important for components suppliers, particularly smaller and locally owned parts suppliers (assemblers and local subsidiaries of major global suppliers can rely on the home company or their own efforts).

Funding for and design of automotive institutes tend to follow a common pattern of public-private engagement. Central governments generally provide the initial capital investment for land, buildings, test equipment, and proving grounds. Operating expenses typically come from a combination of government subsidies, research contracts from government agencies, and fees paid by private firms for services such as testing, certification, and engineering support. Beyond funding, the private sector plays critical roles in identifying needs and information sources as well as helping to design and staff these organizations.

Evaluating and comparing the institutes' significance and effectiveness is crucial for our study, but it is a difficult task, not least because each national economic environment is different. We focus first on relatively observable factors such as timing of establishment and abundance of resources, particularly personnel. Timing and resources reveal a clear tripartite division of our case countries. Governments in Korea, China, and Taiwan established large and impressive automotive institutes relatively early. In Thailand and Malaysia, automotive institutes appeared later—well after the move toward trade policy liberalization—and remain far less developed. Finally, institutions capable of filling even a small number of the functions noted here have yet to appear in Indonesia or the Philippines (Table 3.8).

Table 3.8 National Automotive Institutes

	Institute	Year Established	Staff	Functions	Related / Support Organizations
Korea	Korea Automotive Technology Institute (KATECH)	1990	500	Testing/assessment Research	KAMA; KOTRA; KIST; various economic research organizations; associations
	Korea Automobile Testing and Research Institute (KATRI)	1987	300	Forecast/planning Training	
China	China Automotive Technology and Research Center (CATARC)	1985	4,570	Testing/assessment Research Forecast/Planning Training	SOE research institutes; National Passenger Car Quality Supervision and Inspection Center, etc.; associations
Taiwan	Automotive Research & Testing Center (ARTC)	1990	440	Testing/assessment Research Forecast/Planning Training	ITRI (technology; economic research); CSIST; MIRDC; associations
Thailand	Thailand Automotive Institute (TAI)	1998	100	Forecast/planning Training Testing (minimal)	Thai Automotive Parts Assoc.
Malaysia	Malaysia Automotive, Robotics and IoT Institute (MARii) — formerly known as the Malaysia Automotive Institute (MAI)	2010	65	Forecast/planning Training	Malaysia Auto Parts and Components Mfgs. Assoc.
Indonesia	none	—	—		
Philippines	none	—	—		

Key:

KAMA: Korea Automobile Manufacturers Association

KOTRA: Korea Trade Promotion Corporation

KIST: Korea Institute of Science and Technology

Source: Author field visits and personal communications; institute web sites and pamphlets

Web sites (English versions):

Korea: KATECH—http://www.katech.re.kr/eng/open_contents/sub01/0101.html; KATRI—http://eng.kotsa.or.kr/katri/katri_01.jsp

China: CATARC—http://www.catarc.ac.cn/ac_en/index.htm

Taiwan: ARTC—http://www.artc.org.tw/index_en.aspx; ITRI—http://www.itri.org.tw/eng/; CSIST—http://cs.mnd.gov.tw/English/index.aspx;

MIRDC—http://www.mirdc.org.tw/english/

Thailand: TAI—http://www.thaiauto.or.th/index_eng.asp

Malaysia: MAI—http://www.marii.my/

To evaluate effectiveness, we look partly at the opinions expressed by executives of local auto firms, both local and globally owned, in interviews we conducted. Relying on business opinion alone, however, can be misleading, especially when trying to compare across countries. Executives of private companies tend to praise projects that benefit them directly and ignore or denigrate those that do not. They often criticize the government and its institutions but, at least in Asia, are rarely libertarian: they do not want the government to refrain from intervening, but want it to intervene more effectively, at lower expense, and in ways that help the competitive position of their firms. Accordingly, we place particular weight in our evaluation on the interest local firms show in utilizing automotive institutions and participating in projects or consortia organized by them. By these criteria, we arrive at a ranking that is highly consistent with, though not exactly the same, as ordering the institutes by abundance of resources. We discuss national automotive institutions in detail in the country chapters that follow. Here, we provide a brief sketch to support our argument that successful intensive approaches to automotive development have been associated with the development of capable sectoral-specific institutions.

Taiwan combines effective institutions in a compact package that is relatively easy to coordinate. Taiwan's Automotive Research and Testing Center (ARTC) provides extensive test equipment and several large test tracks. Participation in its activities is widespread. The organization also receives support from three other government-affiliated technology institutions that cover but are not focused solely on the automotive industry. In Korea, similar functions are handled by two separate institutions, one of which specializes in safety testing. Together, they control extensive physical facilities and have 800 employees, about twice as many as Taiwan's ARTC, to serve a population and economy twice as large. The two Korean institutes were established about the same time as the ARTC.

China deploys enormous resources in support of industrial upgrading in general and the auto industry in particular, but it also has significant problems in bringing them to bear, partly because of the huge size and diversity of China's industrial base. The China Automotive Technology and Research Center, established in 1985 when China first opened its auto industry to joint ventures with foreign firms, has grown rapidly and employs a staff of over 4,000, by far the largest of the automotive institutes in our case countries. It is a major player in international standard-setting, and works on numerous reverse engineering projects to help local firms master advanced technologies. As discussed in Chapter 8, however, doubts have arisen with regard to issues such as the transparency of the center's crash-testing procedures and its neutrality, due to its creation of "new energy" subsidiaries that compete with client firms.

If China's supportive institutions are powerful but sometimes ill-coordinated, automotive institutes in Southeast Asia are closer to "too little, too late." Thailand did not establish an automotive institute until 1998, just as the Asian financial crisis pushed most Thai parts suppliers into bankruptcy or forced them to sell out to global parts giants. For most of its life, the Institute has lacked facilities, such as a dedicated building and test track. The staff of 100 has spent much of its time on industry planning, a task that the automotive institutes in Northeast Asia leave largely to specialists in industrial economics, although in the past five years the Thai institute has devoted significant attention to the development of an industry training program. All these limitations are magnified in Malaysia, even more surprisingly given the country's aspirations to pursue an intensive development strategy in the sector. Malaysia only established an automotive institute in 2010, staffed by just 20 personnel, most of whom specialize in industrial economics rather than auto technology. Until recently, its only role was to provide training courses, but in 2017 it added a design center and an emissions testing center. In 2018, it was reorganized into the Malaysia Automotive, Robotics and IoT Institute (MARii). With a staff of only 65 to cover an expanded range of activities running from "big data analytics" to commercialization of a biochip sensor to detect Covid-19, it showed severe signs of overstretch and PR gamesmanship (Aziz 2020; MARii 2020). Finally, as of 2019, Indonesia and the Philippines had yet to establish automotive institutes.

Institutional Ecologies

Rather than operating in isolation, automotive institutes reflect, influence, and even overlap with a broader set of institutions including, among others, sectoral business associations, deliberative councils, training providers, and public testing and research agencies. Owing to the challenges of technology absorption and linkage development, these institutions are especially important for the strengthening of local firms so critical to intensive growth. Indeed, as the "varieties of capitalism" literature has argued, institutions tend to be "complementary" with each other (Hall and Soskice 2001). That is, the effectiveness of one institution is often a function of the performance of others. For example, because their creation is itself a collective action challenge, automotive institutes emerge and thrive in part through the collective efforts of firms in sectoral associations. The public sector is of course part of this ecology: fragmented public agencies such as investment boards and industry ministries will, other things being equal, tend to be mirrored by weak associations and institutes. Table 3.9 provides preliminary evidence, drawn

Table 3.9 Capacity of Sectoral Institutions

Institutions	Korea	Taiwan	China	Malaysia	Thailand	Indonesia	Philippines
Investment boards	High	High	High	Medium	Medium	Low	Low
Automotive institutes	High	High	High	Low	Low	Low	Low
Business associations	Medium	High	Medium	Low	Low	Low	Low
Public testing–research institutes	High	High	Medium	Low	Low	Low	Low
Standards agencies	High	High	High	Low	Low	Low	Low
Tech-Vocat education and training	High	High	Medium	Low	Low	Low	Low
University–industry linkages	High	Medium	High	Low	Low	Low	Low
Resistance to clientelism	High	High	Medium	Low	Low	Low	Low

Source: Case chapters.

from our case studies, of the argument that effective automotive development institutions are associated with the presence of supporting institutions, which, in turn correlates closely with automotive industrial performance. One example of the importance of institutional complementarities is that during the high-growth period Japanese and Korean firms gained access to foreign technology on terms controlled or at least overseen by the government (e.g., Mason 1992; Kim 1997; Misawa 2005).

Political Origins of Institutions for Upgrading: The *Why* Question

Even if national leaders are aware of the kinds of institutions and complementarities required to build strong automotive industries and observe their success elsewhere, replicating effective institutional packages is extremely difficult. As Rodrik (2007: Ch. 1) has argued, institutional innovations do not travel easily. Part of the problem is the context-dependency of effective institutions and the need for iterative experimentation (Andrews 2013). But why would leaders ever promote and reward such experimentation? Why would leaders, who typically focus on maintaining power by channeling largesse to narrow constituencies and claiming credit for protecting or saving political clients, instead defer consumption and invest scarce resources to provide the kinds of public and quasi-public goods necessary to build and sustain economic competitiveness?

Take the case of strong, encompassing business associations—institutions generally assumed to be good for growth. If such institutions "typically do not arise automatically out of the business community but are rather promoted by state actions" (Schneider 2010: 57), why would state leaders promote such potentially threatening groups? To pose the question differently, why did Ferdinand Marcos craft business associations in the automotive industry for the enrichment of himself and a small group of cronies (Doner 1991: Ch. 7), whereas Park Chung-Hee, as noted earlier, promoted efficiency-oriented automotive institutions insulated from corruption in other sectors (Kang 2002)?

An argument popular in the early developmental state literature was that the Park administration enjoyed autonomy to promote institutional strengthening and thus growth, whereas Marcos did not. But Marcos's ability to impose martial law for 14 years (1972–1984) suggests that he was far from a puppet of private interests. The autonomy argument begs the question of why some administrations enjoyed and made constructive use of autonomy and others did not.

We propose an explanation that highlights variations in the pressures that leaders face. Diverse institutional capacities reflect first and foremost differences in the interplay of external security threats, popular pressures for welfare improvement, and resource endowments. Our argument is that the stronger the claims on resources, due to ongoing, endemic external threats or popular pressures, and the more scarce the resources available to satisfy such claims, the higher is the likelihood that political elites will invest in institutions to promote industrial upgrading (Doner, Ritchie, and Slater 2005). In the rest of this section, we provide preliminary evidence that our argument accounts for significant differences in automotive performance between Northeast and Southeast Asia as well as certain intra-regional differences.

Some qualifications to our argument merit note. We recognize the dynamic nature of our variables even as we emphasize the tendencies for path dependence. Consider, for example, the impact of shifting reliance on natural resource exports. From the mid-1980s onward, the composition of exports in all of our Southeast Asian cases changed dramatically, with manufactures substantially displacing primary commodities as the principal source of export earnings. By then, however, political configurations were entrenched: what we see across the region, by and large, is the "stickiness" of institutional configurations and the importance of the particular configurations that were in place at the time when economic policy paths were originally taken (Noble 2017). Similar arguments apply in the consideration of security threats. This stickiness is best understood, however, as a set of constraints within which limited pockets or pulses of institutional innovation can occur in times of financial difficulty, as seen in the short-lived surge of industrial restructuring efforts in Thailand on the heels of the Asian Financial Crisis.

Security Threats

The nature and magnitude of the external threat, and/or how it was perceived by political elites, provide the most fundamental distinction between our Northeast Asian cases, where threats were intense and viewed as endemic, and Southeast Asian cases, where threats were more moderate and episodic. Korea was torn apart by a war that directly involved China and the United States (and the Soviet Union indirectly); the South has had to live for more than half a century with an erratic and heavily armed neighbor with which it has yet to sign a peace treaty. The People's Republic of China (PRC) regards Taiwan as a renegade province and has repeatedly stated that it will use force should the island attempt to assert de jure independence from the mainland.

Meanwhile, China has lived with fears that it would be attacked either by the West or (at times) by the then Soviet Union; these fears drew China into the Korean conflict and two wars involving Vietnam.

Although Korea and Taiwan were, after Israel, the most significant beneficiaries of US economic and military assistance in the postwar period, governments in neither country had confidence that they could rely on these resources in the medium to long term. This was particularly the case in Taiwan, where economic aid ended in 1965. The opening to China in the 1970s caused alarm about the reliability of the US security guarantee. Similarly, in Korea, US linkage of the provision of resources to demands for economic reform (and, in the 1970s, for voluntary export restraints) created uncertainty about US intentions and reinforced an unwillingness to rely on external resources.

In all three countries, the external security threat fostered a reluctance to depend on uncertain alliances and diplomatic links, and led to the adoption in the 1960s through the 1980s of "techno-nationalist" strategies (Keller and Samuels 2003) characterized by the belief that a country can only be secure if it exerts substantial control over the generation of knowledge and the standards for design and manufacture rather than depending on investment or licensing from abroad. Although we have seen variation over time in how assertively the three countries pursued techno-nationalist strategies, and differences across them in how they seek to develop domestic capabilities (with Taiwan and China more open to foreign direct investment than was Korea during its drive for heavy industrialization), all three countries have shown a greater and more persistent inclination toward techno-nationalism than any of our Southeast Asian cases, as seen most recently, for example, in China's controversial "Made in China 2025" plan.

Unlike their Northeast Asian counterparts, Southeast Asian countries have not been exposed to existential external threats. Although Thailand shares borders with states that have for most of the last 50 years either been hostile to the Thai government or the source of cross-border conflicts, the external danger has never been as endemic or of the same magnitude as those faced by the Northeast Asian countries. Malaysia endured a short military confrontation with Indonesia immediately after gaining independence, but subsequently has not faced a significant external security threat. Neither Indonesia nor the Philippines faced significant external threats. One consequence is that Southeast Asian countries have been able to devote proportionally fewer resources to military expenditure than did either Korea or Taiwan (see Figure 3.1, which contains comparative data for 1989, the first year for which SIPRI provides such information). Nor have the large Southeast Asian states, unlike their counterparts to the north,

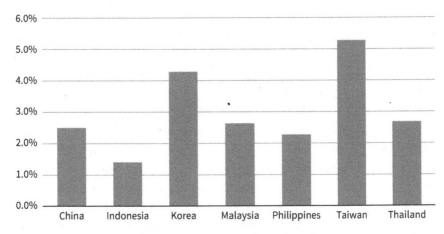

Figure 3.1 Military expenditure as a percentage of GDP (1989).

Source: Stockholm International Peace Research Institute, *SIPRI Military Expenditure Database* (https://www.sipri.org/databases/milex).

instituted universal and lengthy military conscription for males, arguably an important experience both in developing national identity and for inculcating notions of national vulnerability.

Rather than external threats, the primary source of insecurity in our Southeast Asian cases over the last half century has been internal, involving racial, religious, regional, and, less often, class rivalries (Slater 2010). These have not, however, stimulated the levels of popular mobilization and resistance seen in Northeast Asia. This is consistent with recent quantitative findings that ethno-nationalist secessionist challenges, such as those seen in Southeast Asia, pose a more limited threat to elites than broad-based communist insurgencies linked to Cold War dynamics (Han and Thies 2019). And where domestic mobilization against the state has occurred, Southeast Asian leaders have made effective use of their more extensive natural resource endowments to address it, while avoiding the difficult challenge of industrial promotion.

Resource Endowments

Both Korea and Taiwan, particularly in comparison with our Southeast Asian cases, are extremely land-poor (Figure 3.2). Although agricultural productivity significantly improved following the land reforms and agricultural investment that began under US occupation, neither country had land endowments sufficient to provide a foundation for substantial earnings from

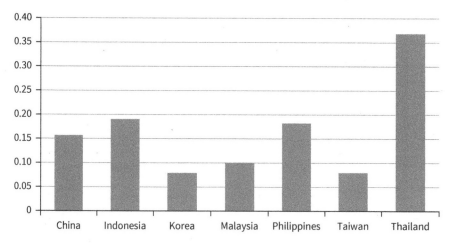

Figure 3.2 Cultivatable land per capita in 1960 (hectares).
Source: World Bank, *World Development Indicators*, except for Taiwan (Republic of China, *Taiwan Statistical Data Book* 2007).

agricultural exports. Moreover, Taiwan and Korea were largely dependent on imports for the raw materials and energy required for industrialization (Figure 3.3).

Consequently, Korea and Taiwan could only sustain growth by promoting exports of manufactures. Efficient industrial deepening was a situational imperative. Political elites had powerful incentives to defer consumption and to make investments in the institutions required for industrial upgrading. Simultaneously, Korea and Taiwan attempted to improve prospects for the rural population through promoting productivity improvements and educational opportunities. As Doner, Ritchie, and Slater (2005: 342–343) note, "these side payments were fiscally affordable, yet institutionally challenging" in that they required a substantial building of institutions to upgrade agricultural output, e.g., through the construction of a network of extension services. By the mid-1960s, more than half of the merchandise export earnings of both countries were derived from manufactures (*two decades* before our other cases reached that level); by the end of the 1960s, the figure had climbed to 80% (Figure 3.4). In contrast, China was able to sustain a prolonged period of autarkic industrialization, driven by its security concerns, because of its relatively abundant natural resources. Through the early 1990s, China was actually a net exporter of energy. However, the export-oriented growth strategy that turned China into the world's assembly plant also eventually transformed China into the world's largest importer of several raw materials, and a major importer of oil.

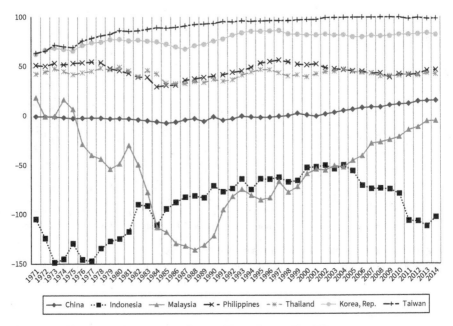

Figure 3.3 Net Energy Imports as a Share of Total Energy Use (%)
(negative figures reflect net energy exports)

Source: World Bank <https://data.worldbank.org/indicator/EG.IMP.CONS.ZS?end=2015&name_desc=false&start=1960>

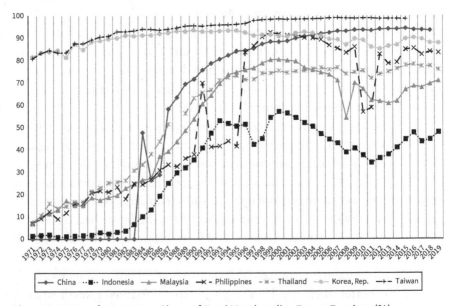

Figure 3.4 Manufactures as a Share of Total Merchandise Export Earnings (%).

Source: World Bank, *World Development Indicators Databank* except for Taiwan (Republic of China, *Taiwan Statistical Data Book* 1992, 2002, 2007, 2011, 2016, and 2019). Last accessed at <https://www.ndc.gov.tw/en/News.aspx?n=607ED34345641980&sms=B8A915763E3684AC> on 20 October 2020.

The relative abundance of natural resources in Southeast Asia produced a very different political economy of development. Galvanized by race riots in 1969, Malaysia used (and developed) its natural resources (e.g., rubber) to improve the welfare of politically important rural Malays (Kuhonta 2011) and to subsidize otherwise inefficient manufacturing. The emphasis, starkly visible in the Malaysian auto industry, has been on ethnic equity rather than on economic efficiency. Thus, one of the key motivating factors behind the creation of the national car in Malaysia was to provide compensation for Malays who had not shared in the benefits from the country's high rates of economic growth in the 1960s. Similarly, on coming to power in Indonesia, Suharto's New Order faced not only long-standing communal and regional tensions but, above all, the specter of widespread communist mobilization. Suharto's government engaged not just in macroeconomic stabilization, but also in effective measures to improve agricultural development, education, and family planning. As in Malaysia, however, the government devoted little of the oil revenue windfall to the creation of institutions for industrial diffusion and upgrading. Instead, the New Order government "wasted a good proportion of Indonesia's newfound oil wealth on unproductive and inefficient hi-technology and capital intensive industrial products" (Rosser 2004: 17). And whereas in Northeast Asia, initially inefficient industries were exposed to external competition, Indonesia's oil revenues generally allowed the state to continue supporting industries such as autos, steel, and aerospace through the provision of extensive protection and subsidies.

Until recently, Thailand has experienced neither the ethnic tensions of Malaysia nor the large-scale, class-based mobilization of Indonesia. Moreover, until the late 1970s, the availability of additional land for cultivation relieved political pressures and discouraged agricultural innovation, allowing the rural sector to function as a "labor sink" to absorb unemployed or underemployed workers (Siriprachai 2012). In the Philippines, popular discontent, as in the case of the Hukbalahap and the New People's Army, was often violent. But conflict remained sufficiently localized to be contained through local side payments, electoral mobilization, and repression. The impetus to build institutions for industrial diffusion remained weak in Southeast Asia.

Southeast Asia's experience is consistent with arguments that a "resource curse" can hinder economic growth and transformation (Auty 1994: 11; cf. also Sachs and Warner 1995). Resource abundance fosters protected, inefficient domestic producers (who, along with those linked to natural resource sectors, constitute entrenched coalitions), dampens pressures for industrial maturation, and discourages sustained efforts to improve technical skills and industrial linkages (Ross 1999; Coxhead and Li 2008). Although the export composition of these economies was transformed in the 1980s, it was largely through a process of extensive development through their insertion into the lowest level of global value chains (such as the assembly of electronic components in the Philippines).

If revenue inflows reduced pressure on the Southeast Asian countries to upgrade, we should expect cuts in such inflows to encourage policy and institutional reforms. Painting with a broad brush, we can trace how such changes have indeed occurred on occasion, most obviously in response to the collapse of commodity prices in the first half of the 1980s and to the 1997 Asian Financial Crisis. But as suggested earlier, such reforms have been limited and short-lived, reflecting how relatively weak the pressures actually were, and the weight of established institutions. A well-known example of this pattern is "Sadli's law" in Indonesia, i.e., the tendency for "tough times," characterized by declines in oil revenues and thus government revenues, to generate "good policy" involving cautious macroeconomic policy, and liberalization of trade and investment. This pattern captures much of Indonesia's economic reform dynamic (Fane and Warr 2008: 144). As described in the case chapters, a similar pattern of greater policy openness and the promotion of manufactured exports in the face of decline in revenue from commodity exports holds for Malaysia and Thailand.

Drops in revenue, however, did not lead to sustained efforts in automotive upgrading-related areas such as testing or skills development. One reason was uncertainty about future flows of revenues from commodities. Another factor is the "sticky" consequences of earlier resource flows in their shaping of key political institutions. As Smith (2012: 208) notes, despite the striking increase in Indonesia's manufactured exports, "What did not (and generally does not) vanish overnight were the long-term political and economic ramifications of Indonesia's decades of serious oil export dependence." In Indonesia and Malaysia, continued substantial petroleum revenues in the 1990s underwrote inefficient auto industries. A third factor is that countries enjoyed continued access to FDI. In Thailand, attracting Japanese assembly operations and more generally relying on FDI in the auto industry was a "soft option" that required minimal reform of and investment in domestic institutions.

Alternative Approaches

Our approach is, of course, not the only one addressing variation in industrial performance. Indeed, our arguments are consistent with and partly overlap with other prominent frameworks. But as discussed in the following, none of these captures what we consider to be the components of a full explanation of variation in industry performance: policy-specific challenges, the importance of technology-promoting institutions, and the political origins of these institutions.

In this section we focus on three approaches that have emphasized the role of institutions in promoting rapid economic growth in East Asia: as shorthand, we label these "good governance," "national innovation systems," and the "developmental state."

Good Governance

As noted previously in our discussion of bureaucratic capacity, clean, transparent government administration bears a fairly strong association with successful automotive development. Yet the good governance explanation has a number of limits. First, it provides little insight into differences between success in extensive vs. intensive growth. Second and more problematic is the potential endogeneity of good governance. Rather than good governance promoting growth, it may be that growth leads to good governance, *or* both governance and growth might be a function of still a third variable. The fact that most assessments of bureaucratic capacity tend to be *post hoc* adds to such concerns.

Particularly problematic is the possibility that respondents at least partially inferred the quality of the institutions in the countries in which they work from the success of the firms in those countries. In fact, Kurtz and Schrank (2007) find that World Bank indices are subject to significant "halo effects"— countries that have grown in the recent past receive higher scores. Moreover, expatriate foreign business executives, a key source of good governance assessments, are likely to assess institutions at least partly by the degree to which they facilitate the activities of foreign firms rather than, or even at the expense of, those of local firms. Finally, it is far from clear that foreign business executives have sufficient local experience to assess accurately, say, the range of a country's initiatives to upgrade education and skills, and whether the scores they report on that country can be compared reliably to those produced by expatriates in other countries.

A second problem is the risk of assuming that some general measure of administrative capacity necessarily translates into equivalent capacity to promote the automotive sector. As discussed earlier, this is a particular problem for Malaysia, whose rankings on surveys of institutional quality far exceed its performance in developing institutions required to support intensive development in autos. The stark difference in institutional quality and performance between Malaysia's struggling auto industry and its dynamic rubber sector highlights the significance of cross-sectoral variation (Doner 2016). Thailand presents a somewhat similar puzzle: The country's institutional strength in macroeconomic policy and FDI investment promotion has not translated into effective upgrading-related policies (Doner 2009). There is no *ex ante* reason to assume that a state agency successful in attracting employment- and export-generating foreign investment through tax exemptions will necessarily succeed in promoting industry-relevant competencies such as skills, or testing and measurement, or technical training.

A third and related problem lies in the danger of neglecting the likelihood that effective institutions will vary with local conditions as well as policy objectives. Thus, China's experience suggests that a key component in effective state industrial promotion is the willingness and capacity to experiment with policies and institutional mechanisms. Indeed, some argue that the most successful administrations "work to promote experimentation, aggressively replicate(s) successful results, and actively seek to improve on them" (Whittaker et al. 2010: 461; see also Whittaker et al. 2020). The institutions through which such experimentation occurs often exceed or even violate "good governance" prescriptions (Kurtz and Schrank 2007).

A fourth and related problem is the possibility that, in specific contexts, "dirty" administration might be developmentally benign, even useful. Thus, many observers assumed that a meritocratic, "clean" administration was a key part of the Korean miracle. Yet as David Kang (2002: 20) has argued, Korea, like the Philippines "had extensive corruption that permeated the normal politics of elections, economic policy making, taxation, and the day-to-day running of the country. . . ." The Korean case suggests that a degree of corruption is not necessarily incompatible with bureaucratic capacity, particularly for governments capable of protecting pockets of bureaucratic excellence (Roll 2014).

Finally, the good governance literature tends to neglect politics or, more specifically, a political economy analysis of cross-national variation, "beyond genuflection to the fact that . . . [some countries] avoided the insidious effects of rent-seeking" (Haggard 2018: 26). Indeed, a 2016 World Bank review concluded that while politics is at the heart of governance failures, "it has been a subject that the Bank has danced around" (Lateef 2016: 28). The significance of politics is seen in this book's Korean and Philippines cases, where the value of such governance characteristics as bureaucratic expertise and meritocratic recruitment depends on what political leaders do with them. As discussed in Chapter 5, President Marcos and his cronies undermined well-trained and committed Philippine officials who had developed one of East Asia's earliest and most sophisticated auto industrialization policies. Conversely, Park

Chung-Hee hived off the country's extensive corruption, allowing him "to meet his patronage requirements and still seek economic efficiency" (Kang 2002: 64; Roll 2014). Engaging in significant corruption was certainly a prerequisite for firms in the Korean auto industry to gain access to the massive rents generated by a highly protected domestic market and subsidized loans: nonetheless, ongoing access to these rents depended on firms not just continuing to supply funds to governments but also, in a pattern Amsden (1989) described as "reciprocity," on complying with the performance targets negotiated with them in exchange for state protection and subsidies.

National Innovation Systems

The national innovation systems (NIS) framework usefully highlights the significance of institutional ecologies discussed earlier in this chapter. By focusing on the interactions of factors such as industrial development banks, public-private councils, R&D organizations, and university-industry linkages, the innovation systems framework helps to identify the networks "that produce knowledge within national borders" (Intarakumnerd 2018: 5; Nelson 1993). Yet while highlighting the importance of developing specific firm capabilities, work in this tradition pays little attention to the specific capabilities and institutional arrangements appropriate for different levels or types of innovation. How, for example, might different tasks require different degrees and types of coordination among key actors? Although authors working in this tradition note differences in firm performance across sectors (e.g., Patel 1994), few authors focus on how the institutional environment for promoting innovation varies from one sector to another (Malerba 2002 is an exception). This gap relates to a second limitation of the NIS approach—namely, the lack of attention to the importance of private-sector institutions and their design, e.g., degree of delegation, and incentives for participation (Schneider 2004). Finally, the cross-national (and even cross-sectoral) variation among NIS-related institutions suggests the importance of political influences on these arrangements. Yet, with few exceptions (e.g., Breznitz 2007; Wong 2011a), this issue is relegated to a residual category of "political will."

Global Value Chains

Global value chains (GVC) scholars have made important contributions to our understanding of development by analyzing the cross-national, intra- and inter-firm networks through which developing country firms might upgrade (e.g. Gereffi 2014, 2005). By learning from global buyers and components producers, developing country firms can build on their competitive advantage to develop specialized capacities (Kummritz, Taglioni, and Winkler 2017: 1). Of particular relevance to this book are the opportunities, as well as challenges, inherent in producer-driven networks, including global and regional automotive production (e.g. Sturgeon et al. 2016).[2]

Yet by focusing on within-value chain opportunities, that is, primarily on relations among firms, the GVC framework provides only a partial sense of the factors influencing firm upgrading. Recent work, including studies by the World Bank, has emphasized the ways in which local gains from GVCs depend on specific government policies, especially those, as stressed in this book, that strengthen skills development and help firms meet standards (Kummritz, Taglioni, and Winkler 2017: 4). Similarly, and consistent with our argument that policies do not implement themselves, an extensive review of GVC case studies concludes that a crucial element in firms' ability to upgrade within GVCs is the local institutional environment and, more specifically, "the capacity of the state" and "public-private collaborative engagement" (Pipkin and Fuentes 2017: 547, 549). The absence of effective local institutions designed to promote spillovers from foreign producers will result in weak technological capacities on the part of local firms and, as a result, fragile linkages between them and foreign lead firms (Ravenhill 2014). Such expectations are consistent with our cases, as well as with recent findings in the auto industries of central Europe of "weak, dependent, and . . . detrimental linkages [that] contribute to limited knowledge transfer from FDI to domestic economies" (Pavlinek 2018: 160).

Such findings about the contingent nature of local benefits from GVCs are consistent with our previous discussion of the obstacles to spillovers from foreign producers to local firms. They also reflect the fact that the advantage an MNC derives from internalizing and transferring proprietary knowledge to its subsidiaries can block its ability or even desire to transfer such knowledge to suppliers, especially less developed ones. To upgrade through collaboration with MNCs in sophisticated supply chains "demands that suppliers maintain a minimum level of capabilities or absorptive capacities (McDermott and Pietrobelli 2017: 322).

---

[2] In producer-driven chains, such as autos, large, typically global manufacturers coordinate the value chain, including backward and forward linkages. In buyer-driven chains, as in garments and footwear, producers operate in response to buyers' decisions with regard to design and marketing. Entry barriers are typically higher in the producer chains that are characteristic of the auto industry.

Some authors argue that GVCs provide a solution to collective action problems. Waldner (1999: 239), in noting that GVCs act as conduits for the transfer of new products and technologies, and provide access to international markets, asserts that GVCs "are the institutionalized expression of past solutions to collective dilemmas." Consequently, he concludes, "state intervention to resolve collective dilemmas is less critical. . . ." While we agree that GVCs can help address some collective action dilemmas, they actually create others. The role of the state may have evolved—but it is as critical as ever, not just in addressing collective action dilemmas, but also in attempting to ensure that local economies maximize their benefits from participation in GVCs.

Developmental States

Of the approaches covered in this section, the developmental state framework is closest to our own arguments. First, the more sophisticated work in this tradition emphasizes development as a set of coordination problems, including those involving the transfer and adoption of innovation and technology (Noble 1998). Second, it is profoundly institutionalist, highlighting not only the importance of "strong" (cohesive, autonomous) states, but also the need for deep, systematic public-private engagement, as elaborated in Evans's (1995) concept of "embedded autonomy." Third, the methodological approach of most developmental state scholars, i.e., the comparative historical analysis of cases, sheds light on the diversity and context-specificity of institutional approaches to coordination problems. Such diversity is evident among, for example, the cases of successful intensive growth covered in this book.

However, in this book we highlight some areas to which developmental state scholars have paid less attention. One is the distinction among tasks and among relevant institutions. With partial exceptions, such as the identification of different but quite broad state roles in development (Evans 1995; Wade 1990), the literature contains little analysis of how specific policies might respond to particular challenges of technology development and absorption (Kim and Kwon 2017 provide a recent partial exception on Korea). A second gap is the lack of specificity regarding the political underpinnings of strong institutions. This gap is, to an extent, the result of the framework's emphasis on the importance of the autonomy or insulation of government leaders from rent-seeking interests (Haggard 2018: 3), an emphasis which has led some authors to criticize the "thin politics" of the developmental state framework (Wade 1992: 307).

We contend that the argument presented in this book remedies this neglect of politics and other gaps in the developmental state and other prominent approaches.

Conclusion

We seek to explain how and why some countries have pursued extensive development in the automotive sector (comprising domestic assembly of vehicles and, to some degree, parts conceived, designed, and engineered abroad), whereas others have adopted intensive development (including not just assembly but upgrading of local capacities to plan, design, and engineer vehicles and to produce sophisticated local parts for them). We also seek to account for intriguing differences within each of these dramatically contrasting approaches, such as the greater success in extensive development of Thailand and (more recently) Indonesia compared to continual laggard Philippines, and the anomalous position of Malaysia, which has adopted industrial policies somewhat similar to those in Northeast Asia, but with much less institutional support and market success.

Our argument is that both the distinction between extensive and intensive development and the variations within them reflect differences in the development of a wide range of institutions to support the creation and diffusion of automotive-related skills. Those institutions appeared earlier and have developed much more fully in Northeast Asia—Korea, China, and Taiwan—than in Southeast Asia. Differences in institutional development, in turn, reflect a powerful political logic: governments facing external security threats or internal political threats that they cannot buy off with abundant resources are far more likely to make significant human and financial investments in a long-term program to build institutional capacity (cf. Taylor (2016)). The balance of threats and resources was especially crucial in the transition from the import-substitution policies that had prevailed through the 1970s, to the liberalization that accelerated in the 1980s and 1990s.

Our initial support for this argument has been correlational. We find a broad correspondence between automotive outcomes and standard indicators of governance quality produced by the World Bank and other organizations, but note that these indicators alone may be insufficient or even misleading when explaining contrasting developmental trajectories. Consequently, we have introduced a number of more specific measures. We find that the quality of administration as measured by the "Weberianness" of bureaucratic careers correlates closely with the outcomes in the automotive industries in our case studies. Tellingly, strong institutions more specific to industrial development, such as those in the fields of education, training, research and development, and industrial outreach, match very closely with economic outcomes in the auto industry. To explain why institutional configurations differ so markedly across our cases, we have examined political pressures on government leaders and found a rough congruence between these and the levels of investment in institutions required for industrial deepening. To supplement these correlational arguments, our within-case analyses in Chapters 4–9 follow a "causes of effects" design (Mahoney and Goertz 2006) in which we begin by examining shifts in industry performance and then trace the evolution of policies, institutions of industrial diffusion, and their political origins.

4

Thailand

Early Opening and Export Success

> Whether the Thai automotive industry will become an export ori-
> ented industry supported by competitive parts suppliers, or just re-
> main . . . an export base for assemblers who rely on . . . global suppliers
> and imported parts, will be decided within five years.
>
> —UNICO (1999: 3-1-189)

Thailand is our primary case of successful *extensive* development. The impressive volume of Thai-based automotive assembly and vehicle and parts exports,
the largest in the ASEAN region, reflects a highly efficient assembly base, dominated by foreign assemblers and component producers and driven largely by
growth of capital stock rather than by indigenous productivity. This trajectory has been the result of deliberate policy interventions to achieve efficient
scale economies and expand exports. These policies have been formulated
and implemented by relatively cohesive institutional networks motivated by
broader economic concerns, especially foreign exchange problems. Yet those
same factors have not resulted in what we have labeled *intensive* growth: a
manufacturing complex based at least in part on domestic firms producing
parts and components, providing intermediate and capital goods, improving
processes, and participating in product design. Further, the industry's very
expansion, and the interests benefiting from it, have weakened pressure for
more intensive growth. Finally, concerns over Thailand's political stability,
combined with Indonesia's emergence as a large market and alternative target
for automotive foreign direct investment (FDI) (see Chapter 5 in this volume),
raise questions as to the sustainability of Thai automotive growth.

As with other case chapters, this analysis of Thailand begins with an assessment of the country's automotive performance, proceeds to an analysis of the
relevant policies and institutions, explores the political origins of institutional
capacities, and concludes with a summary of major points.

The Political Economy of Automotive Industrialization in East Asia. Richard F. Doner, Gregory W. Noble and John Ravenhill, Oxford
University Press (2021). © Oxford University Press. DOI: 10.1093/oso/9780197520253.003.0004

Thailand's Uneven Automotive Performance

In 2017, Thailand accounted for almost half of ASEAN's total vehicle production, ranking 12th in global production and becoming the world's sixth largest commercial vehicle producer as a result of its "product champion" strategy of emphasizing the production of one-ton pickup trucks. These have accounted for roughly 50% of Thai production and around two-thirds of exports (Limpaitoon 2013: 29). Vehicle production rose from roughly 500,000 in 2000 to just under 2 million in 2017 (Figure 4.1; and Board of Investments Thailand 2015), while vehicle exports rose from virtually nothing to roughly half of total production (Figure 4.2). Although vehicles have dominated Thai auto exports, auto components have accounted for close to one third of the total (Figure 4.3).

Successful extensive growth has resulted in the industry becoming a key component of Thailand's economy, accounting for nearly 12% of GDP, and roughly 650,000 jobs (Chalassatien 2016: 115; ASEAN Briefing 2017). With its high export ratio, the Thai auto industry has become a significant foreign exchange earner: By 2016, automobiles and parts constituted Thailand's third largest source of export revenues, with a total value of about $27.2 billion (https://tradingeconomics.com/thailand/exports-by-category). Further, a large percentage of vehicle parts and components come from Thai-based (but not Thai-owned) firms.

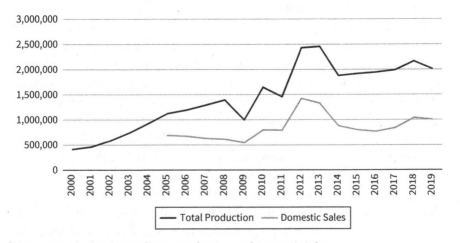

Figure 4.1 Thailand's Total Auto Production and Domestic Sales.

Source: International Organization of Motor Vehicle Manufacturers at <http://www.oica.net/production-statistics/> and <http://www.oica.net/category/sales-statistics/> accessed 31 October 2020.

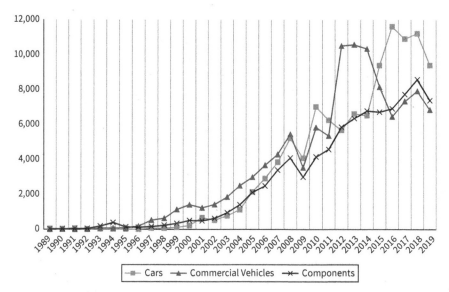

Figure 4.2 Thailand Exports of Vehicles and Components ($m).

Source: UN Comtrade data, except for 2016 exports: https://tradingeconomics.com/thailand/exports-by-category.

Local content growth reflects the extensive participation of foreign produ-cers. Prior to the 1990s, automotive multinationals (MNCs) were attracted by an extensive domestic supplier base that was nurtured by local contents regulations and compatible with MNC strategies of establishing independent,

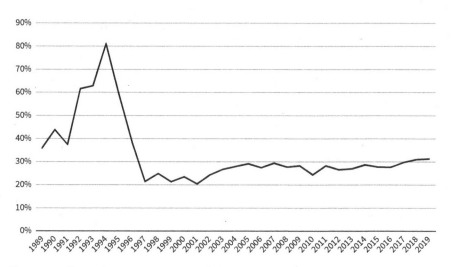

Figure 4.3 Share of Components in Total Thai Auto Exports (%).

Source: UN Comtrade.

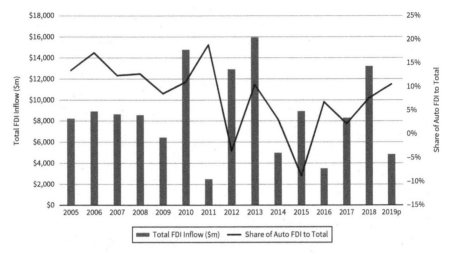

Figure 4.4 Thailand FDI Inflows and Share of Auto FDI ($m)

Source: EC_XT_059 Foreign Direct Investment Classified by Business Sector of Thai Enterprises (US$) at <https://www.bot.or.th/App/BTWS_STAT/statistics/ReportPage.aspx?reportID=656&language=eng> accessed 30 October 2020.

protected national production sites. By the mid-1990s, and especially after the 1997 Asian financial crisis, Thailand's shift away from protection to export promotion both encouraged and benefited from the assemblers' move to a new division of labor in which countries specialized in particular products as parts of regional and global value chains (see Chapter 2). The result (Figure 4.4) was a significant rise in automotive FDI beginning in the late 1990s. This growth was led by Japanese firms (and affiliated suppliers) whose brands account for well over three-quarters of vehicles produced in Thailand. By 2008, there were roughly 500 Japanese suppliers operating in Thailand, compared to 160 in Indonesia, 100 in Malaysia, and fewer than 15 in Vietnam (Yamamoto 2012). From 2005 through 2016, the automotive sector accounted for an annual average of over 12% of all net FDI (Figure 4.4). Western firms—GM, VW, Ford, and BMW—and affiliated suppliers followed in the early 2000s, contributing to Thailand's position as a key component of the automotive division of labor in Southeast Asia (UNCTAD 2014).

Weakening of Thai Firms

Yet along with this extensive growth came a drastic decline of the *indigenous* automotive supply base. The shift to exports following the 1997 Asian financial crisis, the end of local contents requirements in 2000, and the lifting of the 49% foreign ownership ceiling in 1999 drastically reduced the indigenous automotive presence, a process subsequently described as "a silent policy decision to permit transnationalization of manufacturing" (Phongpaichit and Baker 2008: 270). The disappearance of Thai-owned assemblers is not surprising in light of the scale economies and quality levels required to compete in the liberalized economy. Less anticipated was the deterioration of Thai supplier and support industry firms, since one factor attracting foreign automakers to Thailand in the 1970s and 1980s was the country's large number of local suppliers.

When the assemblers shifted to a full-blown export strategy after the 1997 Asian financial crisis, few if any domestic first-tier supplier had developed design and engineering capacities to support the modular production strategies required by global supply chains, and the assemblers had lost interest in supporting lower-tier suppliers (Lauridsen 2008: 730). Many local producers either went out of business or were effectively taken over by foreign "follow source" suppliers (Kohpaiboon 2006: 237–240). Almost all Thai-owned and managed firms are found among the roughly 1,700 second- and third-tier companies making simple products such as plastic and rubber parts and metal stampings for sale to first-tier suppliers (Limpaitoon 2013: 37). By the early 2000s, Thai-owned, first-tier firms constituted only 10–15 suppliers (Lauridsen 2008: 719).

Export Growth

Automotive export growth in Thailand is largely a multinational affair. The country has maintained a positive automotive trade balance since 1997, initially fueled by exports of vehicles produced by multinational assemblers. Exports of parts also continued to rise, most of which also came from foreign producers, such as Visteon and Delphi (Figure 4.3; and Kohpaiboon and Jongwanich 2013: 220). Indeed, over 60 of the 100 world's largest auto part suppliers operate in Thailand (Board of Investments Thailand 2015: 5).

The ASEAN region is the largest export market for Thai auto parts ($6.01 billion in 2018), followed by the U.S. ($3.83 billion), Japan ($2.97 billion) and China ($1.68 billion) ("TAFTA Propels Automotive Exports" 2019).

Local Content

Levels of local content for pickup trucks, officially estimated at 80%–90%, are probably closer to 60%, since products coded as locally produced often consist primarily of imported inputs. Further, most "local" content is actually produced by the subsidiaries of multinationals. One scholar estimates that local Thai firms contribute no more than 10% of the parts purchased by most assemblers (Yamamoto 2012; see also UNCTAD 2013: 137–138).

The performance of domestic firms is disappointing even in products that one might have expected to show significant growth via access to relevant raw materials, long production experience, and low entry barriers. **Stamping parts** lead the Thai industry in both sales and number of employees due to the sector's scale economies, low value-to-weight ratio, and long years of experience. Yet stamped parts are normally designed by the assemblers. As the world's largest producer and exporter of natural rubber, it is not surprising that Thailand is the largest **rubber auto parts** exporter in Southeast Asia. Yet most of these exports come from 30 foreign, largely Japanese, suppliers, including Yokohama Rubber and other tire producers and auto parts manufacturers such as Nishikawa Rubber, for which Thailand constitutes the most important investment site in ASEAN (Yamamoto 2011). Finally, stimulated by demand from the electronics and automotive sectors, Thailand has a large number of **mold and die** producers. These products, especially molds, have a decisive influence on the development of prototypes and thus the nature and manufacture of a final product. As such, they serve as the bridge between localization of production based on foreign inputs and what Ito et al. (2018) label "localization of development" (17) or "real localization" (59). Not surprisingly, then, officials have been eager to promote Thailand as a regional hub for mold production (Awawachintachit 2012). But less than 5% of the country's roughly 1,110 mold and die operations have the personnel and equipment necessary to meet the industry's export-level requirements; and most of these are a handful of Japanese firms or joint ventures whose aggregate investment exceeds all other members combined. The shortage of precision engineering capacity and high costs for raw materials and skilled labor are reflected in a deficit in mold and die trade that grew significantly with the expansion of vehicle exports (Federation of Asian Die and Mold Associations [FADMA] 2007: 11; Limpaitoon 2013: 12). Highlighting these problems, a 2018 study of Nissan's supply chain described the technological levels of large molds and dies produced in Thailand as still at "an immature level," forcing automakers to rely on in-house production at local facilities or imports from Japan (Itoh et al. 2018). The picture with regard to local capacity to produce capital equipment is even gloomier (Jeenanunta, Kasemsontitum, and Techakanont 2012).

Most domestically owned suppliers have failed to expand and deepen capacities across the spectrum from simple-routine operations management, to the duplicative-imitative skills required for effective use and modification of process technology, to capacities for product modification and development (Kondo 2012).

There are, to be sure, some partial exceptions to this grim picture. First-tier firms such as the Somboon Group, Aapico, Sammitr Motor Mfg., Summit Auto Body, the Summit Group, and Thai Sammit do conduct some R&D, although it seems mainly limited to process engineering, testing, and minor product modifications (interviews, July 2010, July 2012, November 2017). However, owing to the assemblers' global sourcing strategies, to our knowledge *none* of the domestic firms acts as a "sub-system integrator." That is, they do not coordinate the production and assembly of parts from second- and third-tier firms. And much of their production is of a second-tier nature that follows the designs of global integrators, such as Japan's Denso. Some also produce for the local replacement market (REM). But the benefits of REM exports are often limited by licensing conditions imposed by foreign technology owners regarding quantity, price, territory, duration, and field of use. As a result, the overwhelming majority of Thai suppliers lack a regional footprint, much less the global presence required for full participation in assemblers' value chains (Yamamoto 2012: 43).

These weaknesses run counter to arguments that extensive growth will lead naturally into intensive development or that best practices by one firm will diffuse to others through competitive emulation (Pack 2000: 86). They also challenge assumptions that the presence of MNCs on its own will generate technological and managerial spillovers to local firms through demonstration effects, labor mobility, technological licensing, subcontracting, and/or "R&D" centers (Fan 2002). As discussed in Chapter 3, effective promotion of spillovers requires active complementary policy interventions, and requisite institutions, to strengthen local firms' capacity for learning. But owing to poorly formulated and implemented policies to strengthen local firms (discussed in the following section), Thailand has been a *passive* FDI-dependent learning country (Yusuf and Nabeshima 2009: 159) rather than an active one (interviews with officials from Thai Automotive Institute, Toyota Tsusho Electronics, Technology Promotion Association (Thai-Japan), and Toyota Motor Asia-Pacific Engineering and Mfg. Co.).

Policies

Thailand's automotive strategy shifted from classic import substitution in the 1960s to a hybrid strategy combining trade and investment liberalization with interventionist features designed to promote the production and export of particular products. This strategy aimed to (1) increase employment and foreign exchange earnings, and (2) help local firms to become more competitive through decades of localization-inspired production experience, greater scale economies, competitive pressures induced by liberalization, and spillovers from foreign producers. The country has succeeded in the first of these goals—extensive growth—but not in the second, intensive growth. In the following, we review key policy measures that help to explain these mixed results.

Trade and Related Investment Measures

Rather than a sudden reversal, Thai trade policy underwent a gradual evolution from measures designed to protect local producers toward a de facto FDI promotion strategy with only superficial support for local producers (Doner 2009; Natsuda and Thoburn 2013: 417–418). During the 1960s, the approach was one of general import substitution, pursued through raising tariffs on both completely-built-up vehicles (CBUs) and completely-knocked-down (CKD) kits. Despite some tariff cuts on specific items, as late as the 1980s the auto sector was the most protected segment of Thai manufacturing, with tariffs of 150% and 80% on CBU and CKD passenger motor vehicles respectively. This strategy of protection *cum* increased FDI promotion also involved tax exemptions on capital goods imports, temporary corporate tax exemptions, and relaxation of limits on foreign ownership of land, resulting in an influx of Japanese assemblers and significant growth in the volume of locally assembled vehicles.

However, by the 1970s, the growth of local vehicle assembly encountered two problems: limited scale economies due to a proliferation of makes and models, and balance of payments problems caused by rising imports of CKD parts. The government responded with efforts to make localization more efficient. This involved limits on makes and models, minimum investment requirements for new entrants, and local content (LC) requirements backed up by special tax incentives for the production of particular parts. Production volumes increased, but model limits and minimum scale requirements proved difficult to implement, and enforcement of LC requirements was undermined by a formula that allowed assemblers to inflate the value of locally sourced parts. Automotive trade deficits continued to grow.

In response, Thai officials further intensified efforts to boost localization. They raised local content requirements but based them on a formula that prioritized parts and components whose potential for standardization and scale economies increased learning opportunities for local firms, but whose technical features were within those firms' capacities (Doner 2009). To focus on localizing a small number of major components, in 1978 the government initiated a collaborative project to produce diesel engines for pickup trucks. This was the vehicle Thai officials targeted as the country's first "product champion" because of its export potential and its domestic market appeal, especially in rural areas, where farmers typically relied on the same vehicle for transporting goods and people. After several years of bargaining, in 1987 three Japanese assemblers agreed to specialize in one component each, to exchange these components, and to involve a major Thai engineering firm, Siam Nawaloha (a member of the giant Siam Cement Group), in the production of each component.

The hoped-for collaboration fell apart, however, as each MNC pursued its own production of major components, the government failed to support technology diffusion, and Siam Nawaloha dropped out of the project and was eventually taken over by a Japanese firm (http://www.attg.co.th/index.php?p=Milestone). Lacking technological support, the auto industry remained reliant on protection. Indeed, it remained the most heavily protected sector in the Thai economy.

But the project's emphasis on scale economies through a "product champion" strategy and its ability, at least initially, to draw in MNCs as key players signaled the beginning of a broader shift: away from reliance on protection and LC requirements toward a willingness to support the move of MNCs from fragmented, national strategies to more coordinated, regional approaches. Thailand began to build on its existing supplier base, which encouraged Mitsubishi to use Thailand as an export base for regional and global value chains, a move that triggered interest by its Japanese rivals (Doner 2009: 249). This shift was further encouraged by a more general shift toward export promotion, fueled by an influx of export-oriented investment due to the 1984 devaluation of the Thai baht and the strength of the Japanese yen after the Plaza Accord of 1985.

This shift toward exports by multinational automakers intensified in the following decade. In the early 1990s, Thailand began to reduce local content requirements, lift bans on CBU imports, end restrictions on series and models, reduce tariffs on CKDs, and actively promote regional trade agreements, notably the ASEAN Free Trade Area, an agreement that opened up regional markets for vehicles produced in Thailand. Increased competition and newly liberalized CBU imports squeezed prices and profit margins. Enhanced competition pushed assemblers to increase exports and provided new opportunities for local firms to make up for the reduction in localization requirements. The strategy proved remarkably successful in enticing investment and exports. From 1994 to 1997 the value of investments in auto assembly and parts production quadrupled compared with the previous four-year period (Paopongsakorn 1999: 7–8).

The 1997 Asian financial crisis pushed Thailand to a full-blown, foreign-led export strategy. The collapse of domestic demand compelled the assemblers to use exports as an outlet for excess capacity, a development that benefited from the further depreciation of the Thai baht. Thailand revised its trade and related policies to take advantage of these new conditions, abandoning local content requirements in 2000 and making good on a 1993 commitment to end restrictions on foreign ownership. The Thai government cut duties on imported machinery and materials and reduced vehicle excise taxes (Kohpaiboon and Warr 2017).

Thailand became the first developing country member of the WTO to end foreign ownership restrictions in 1999 and to abolish local content requirements (2000). Regionally, Thailand had been an active supporter of the Japanese-inspired Brand-to-Brand Complementation (BBC; 1988–1995) regional scheme promoting trade in parts and components among member countries within the same brand; it subsequently supported the ASEAN Industrial Cooperation Scheme (AICO; 1995), a more generalized version of the BBC extending liberalization to trade among different brands; the ASEAN Free Trade Area (AFTA; signed 1992) noted previously; and a series of bilateral FTAs, including with Australia (2005) and Japan (2007). However, these trade measures have focused solely on market opening; none has involved active efforts, such as workforce development, to improve the competitive position of domestic firms (Pongsudhirak 2012; Niyomsilpa 2008: 80–81).

Tax Policy

The shift from reliance on local content requirements to the use of fiscal policy has been key to attaining scale economies through promotion of product champions. Thai officials combined tariff concessions with excise taxes to concentrate market demand on the first product champion—one-ton pickup trucks (Doner 2009; Natsuda and Thoburn 2013). Beginning in 2007, (Natsuda and Thoburn 2013: 21), the government adopted a similarly pragmatic, and far from neutral, approach to structuring automotive markets in an effort to nurture a second would-be product champion—the Eco Car, a vehicle intended to meet stringent emissions standards and sell in sufficient quantities to attain economies of scale. Demand for the vehicles has been stimulated by special excise taxes and large tax rebates for first-time car buyers.

Physical Infrastructure and Cluster Promotion

Since the early 1990s, Thailand has successfully facilitated the siting of assemblers and their suppliers in proximity to one another, so important to the automotive modularization strategies discussed in Chapter 2. It has done so through the development of the Eastern Seaboard economic corridor under the jurisdiction of the Industrial Estates Authority (IEA) of Thailand. The IEA encouraged privately financed and operated estates within which firms enjoy easy profit repatriation, full property rights over land (to be used to secure local financing), financial services, exemptions on corporate income taxes and tariffs on capital goods and raw materials, and access to on-site power, logistical support, and deep-water ports (Aveline-Dubach 2010). In 2017, the government initiated an even more ambitious infrastructure program, the Eastern Economic Corridor (EEC): a $43 billion project that aims to turn three southeastern provinces into "a hub for technological manufacturing and services," including next-generation vehicles, with strong links to Thailand's ASEAN neighbors (Dunseith 2018; interviews with Science-Technology Innovation Policy Institute officials and with advisor to the EEC Office, Bangkok, May 22–28, 2018)

Limits to Learning under Extensive Growth

Local Content Legacies

By the end of the 1980s, Thailand's tariffs and local content requirements had stimulated the growth of the largest indigenous supply base in ASEAN. This approach, however, encouraged linkages based on policy rather than market logic. Thai suppliers earned excess profits—rents—on goods produced at "local market," i.e., minimally acceptable, quality (Kohpaiboon 2006: Ch. 8). Local firms faced few incentives to improve technological capacity and entered the phase of export promotion lacking the kinds of competencies required to take full advantage of the new opportunities.

Trade Regime Beneficiaries

In principle, the post-1997 adjustments in the trade regime favored local producers. The increase in CKD tariffs gave them greater protection, while reduced import duties for inputs in principle allowed them greater access to high-quality inputs. But as implemented, these changes did less to strengthen Thai suppliers than to encourage a foreign-dominated value chain in Thailand. CKD tariffs protected not just Thai suppliers but also foreign "follow source" firms serving MNC-affiliated assemblers.

A second problem was Thailand's "dualistic" trade regime of protection with selective exemptions. On the one hand, because Thailand was reluctant to totally forego tariff revenues, import duties on inputs—capital equipment and materials—were lowered, rather than eliminated. On the other hand, to minimize the impact of remaining tariffs on the export sector, the government offered exemptions and rebate schemes. These did little for indigenous suppliers since (1) foreign-owned firms often preferred imported inputs; (2) only direct exporters, typically foreign-owned firms capable of meeting export requirements, qualified for the exemptions and subsidies; (3) indigenous firms often lacked information about the schemes and the managerial capacities to work through Board of Investment (BOI) requirements (author interview, executive director, Thai-German Institute, Bangkok, November 20, 2013).

Cluster Spillovers

In 2003, after visiting Thailand at the invitation of Prime Minister Thaksin, Harvard Business School professor Michael Porter suggested clusters as mechanisms to help Thailand move beyond factor-driven, low-wage, low-skill development (Suehiro 2010: 160–161). In autos, Thailand needed to transform industrial estates into mechanisms to facilitate assembler-supplier linkages, technology transfer, and skills development. The Thai government agreed in principle, but the World Bank (2010: 12) concluded that the estates remained largely *logistical* arrangements, and more recent findings "do not support the notion that the entry of foreign input suppliers after 1997 had positive spill-over effects on domestic suppliers" (Kohpaiboon and Warr 2017: 20). This is less to deny the presence of several important component producers, such as those in the Summit group noted earlier, than to highlight that these cases are the exceptions. Confirming this view is the fact that, in value terms, around 80% of the parts Denso purchases in Thailand are from Japanese suppliers, with the remaining 20% procured mostly from Thai, as well as Indian and Taiwanese, suppliers (Itoh et al. 2018: 71–72). Protection and flawed localization policies certainly bear some responsibility for these disappointing results. But equally important are weaknesses in measures to promote local innovation. Many observers fear that the new Eastern Economic Corridor will follow this pattern of extensive growth with limited local linkages and few spillovers to spur productivity (Bruton 2017).

Innovation Support

A close observer of Thai development has argued that Thailand is a case of *"mismanaging innovation systems"* (Intarakumnerd 2018: 14). Thai officials have emphasized R&D rather than improving skills and meeting standards for local firms whose main challenges involve *incremental* process improvement and technology absorption; they have assumed that active efforts to generate spillovers by multinationals are useless if not counterproductive; and they have argued that sector-specific policies are market distorting and should be avoided. These perspectives have translated into weak policies in several key areas. Even in R&D and related policies, such as intellectual property protection, Thai performance has been weaker than its ASEAN peers (World Bank 2018b).

Testing and Standards
Local parts firms pushed for a fully equipped local testing facility since 2002, efforts that intensified with the desire to qualify products for the Eco Car program (interviews, Bangkok 2010, 2012, 2013, 2015). These efforts seemed to pay off when the government agreed to establish an R&D center by 2008 to certify products in areas such as emissions, lighting equipment, and braking. But the project bogged down as the private sector and government disagreed over sharing the cost of over $100 million (Panthong 2012). Similarly, in 2013, an effort to create a vehicle testing center spearheaded by the Office of Industrial Economics stalled in the face of disputes about funding and competition from a race track–oriented center proposed by a well-known politician (March 8, 2013, "Detroit of Asia," *The Nation*, March 8, 2013). After over a decade of efforts by private auto parts firms, a single testing facility was finally approved in 2017—for tires.

Education and Technical Training
Shortages of technical personnel have become a major theme in assessments of Thai economic growth prospects, especially as Thai firms face increasing competition from lower-cost neighbors (UNCTAD 2015). These problems have been especially serious in the automotive industry (World Bank 2012b: 11). In 2015, as demand for engineers surged, only 7,880 out of 26,031

engineering graduates applying for employment qualified for actual employment (Patthana 2017).

Thai officials and firms have made sporadic but largely ineffective attempts to address these problems through technical and vocational training and education (TVET). As part of its effort to lure GM to Thailand rather than the Philippines in the mid-1990s, the Thai government committed itself to building a $15 million automotive training institute (Bradsher 1996), but the institute never appeared. Other efforts included university-based automotive degree programs and related innovation-promotion schemes, which analysts describe as poorly financed, designed, and implemented (Intarakumnerd and Charoenporn 2013a). The impact of these programs, especially TVET, has been limited by their relatively small scale, a neglect of process, as opposed to product-related R&D, insufficient incentives for engineers to focus on technology rather than management and administration, and a lack of industry-relevant curricula (Brimble and Doner 2006; Doner, Intarakumnerd, and Ritchie 2010). Indeed, it appears that the principal mechanism for improving the competitiveness of local suppliers comes from Japanese assembler and first-tier producers' suppliers associations, such as Denso's *hishokai* (Itoh et al. 2018: Ch. 5).

More recently, public and private officials have launched a number of training initiatives. Led by the Thai Automotive Institute, one of the public-private bodies established in the wake of the Asian financial crisis, and the Federation of Thai Industries, these include:

- a Skill Certification System for the Automotive Industry;
- an Automotive Human Resources Development Program (2006–2011) designed to expand the supply of trained personnel in competencies based on particular areas of expertise of Toyota, Honda, Nissan, and Denso;
- an Automotive Human Resources Institute Project (2012) to expand the number of trainers in areas such as materials testing and production preparation;
- an Automotive Human Resources Development Academy (AHRDA) modeled on the German dual vocational training system;
- strengthening of TVET institutions linked to the Eastern Economic Corridor.

Although it is too early to assess the results of these initiatives, they do show potential for improving the quantity of technical personnel and productivity of Thai suppliers, especially since they have emerged in part from a more assertive Thai private sector represented by the Federation of Thai Industries (Chalassatien 2016). There are, nevertheless, reasons for caution, if not skepticism, as to the value of these programs for Thai firms. First, the dominant implementation role of Japanese firms suggests that the programs will strengthen Japanese suppliers, further contributing to the enclave nature of the auto industry. There are also concerns as to the impact of migration and subcontracting on motivations for training. Although precise data are difficult to obtain, the AHRDA's founder estimated that of the automotive industry's roughly 650,000 workers in 2014, around 120,000 (over 18%) were migrants "with low or non-existent levels of skill" (Chalassatien 2014: 115). Most of these migrants are part of the large subcontracted automotive workforce that has grown as firms seek to cut costs in the face of rising wage rates and to ensure flexibility in the face of volatile demand, a fact illustrated by the industry's laying off 30,000 subcontracted auto workers in 2014 in response to an industry slowdown (Jittapong 2014). Few if any subcontracted workers join the roughly 18,000 members of the 114 fragmented automotive unions (Asia Monitor Resource Center 2015). The result of migration and informality is a lack of pressure for higher wages that would in turn require and stimulate greater investments by employers in training to raise productivity (Economic Intelligence Center 2015: 11).

Financing
The use of tax incentives, loans, grants, and equity financing to support innovation by local firms has been inflexible and isolated from the industrial promotion efforts of the Ministry of Industry (Intarakumnerd 2018: 51–52). As a result, Thai resources devoted to innovation have been quite low, even as measured by overall R&D expenditures (0.25% of GDP in 2005, compared to 0.64% in Malaysia and 2.61% in Singapore), by number of R&D personnel, and by private sector R&D expenses (UNCTAD 2015).

Linkage and Supplier Development
The Board of Investment launched a series of supplier development efforts, including the BOI Unit for Industrial Linkage Development (1991), a National Supplier Development Programme (1994), and a Master Plan for the Development of Supporting Industries (1995). These, along with a Japanese effort to modernize local tool and die firms through a dedicated Metal Industries Development Institute, have had minimal success (Lauridsen 2008: 726; interview, director, Thai-German Institute, November 13, 2017). Only in 2017 did the BOI introduce a "merit-based" investment promotion plan to capture spillovers through non-R&D technology upgrading, collaboration with local

universities, and local supplier development (Intarakumnerd 2018: 14; author interview, BOI official, May 23, 2018).

Institutions

Underlying the performance and policies reviewed in the previous sections is an uneven set of institutional arrangements: a fairly strong but narrow network focused on developing and implementing the product champion policy; a much weaker and more fragmented set of actors responsible for upgrading; and a recent, belated effort to promote coordination.

Institutional Context: 1970s–late 1990s

The first three decades of Thai automotive growth occurred under a public-private coordinating body, the Automobile Development Committee (ADC). Within the ADC, Ministry of Industry (MOI) officials worked with representatives of other ministries, especially the agencies responsible for tariff and tax incentives, the Board of Investment, and Ministry of Finance (Doner 2009: Ch 7).

The ADC's effective coordination and consultation helped it to reconcile the preferences of local auto parts and input producers. These firms, frustrated with the resistance of assemblers to increases in local contents requirements, in 1978 established an independent group—the Thai Automotive Parts Manufacturers' Association (TAPMA). Although most TAPMA members were relatively small firms, the association included the large Thai producer Siam Nawaloha. With backing from a nationalist minister of industry, TAPMA was a strong voice for localization into the 1980s. Technocrats operating largely within the MOI's Office of Industrial Economics took what might be called a "soft nationalist" position, combining a commitment to localization and backward linkages with sensitivity to foreign exchange constraints and the need for scale economies. The technocrats ensured that localization was not overly costly by incrementally narrowing local content rules and related incentives to focus on a smaller and more realistic range of components and on pickup trucks.

The mid-1980s debt crisis and auto market downturn began to weaken the ADC-led coalition of efficiency and localization proponents. As emphasis shifted to addressing foreign exchange constraints by tapping into demand beyond the domestic market, the local content-supporting minister of industry was replaced by a technocrat more oriented to short-term efficiency. This weakened the voice of local parts producers in automotive policy, resulting in an MOI "master plan on car exports" and commitments to end local content requirements and foreign ownership restrictions (Haraguchi 2010: 4). The concern for earning foreign exchange also strengthened the Industrial Estates Authority, which became responsible for developing the Eastern Seaboard into a locus of foreign direct investment and industrial activity (Techakanont 2011: 199–201).

A Restructuring Committee, established in 1984 and chaired by the National Economic and Social Development Board (NESDB), conducted numerous sectoral studies aimed at improving sectoral productivity, including in autos. But the effort "foundered in every case" (Muscat 1994: 199). This failing was in part due to a reduction in overall pressures for reform due to a 1984 devaluation that boosted exports and led to an influx of Northeast Asian FDI searching for a low-wage export base. But also important were conflicts over tariffs between the Industry and Finance Ministries and between assemblers and upstream suppliers. In addition, there was no evidence of significant input by agencies responsible for supplier development, vocational training, and R&D.

The Asian financial crisis pushed government policy toward full deregulation (Haraguchi 2010: 21). With the end to limits on foreign ownership in 1999, the organizational voice of domestic producers "largely disappeared" (Niyomsilpa 2008: 77). Following the end of LC requirements in 2000, the Automobile Development Committee was disbanded. As a senior Ministry of Industry official noted, there was no longer a "proprietor" (*chao paap*) of automotive policy (author interview, Bangkok, July 13, 2010).

Institutional Context: 2000–present

Since the ADC's demise, no single institution has overseen Thai automotive development. Instead, the auto-related trade, investment, fiscal, and infrastructural measures contributing to the industry's extensive growth have been crafted by a network of institutions whose leading component has been the MOI's Office of Industrial Economics (OIE) (interviews with officials of Thai Automotive Institute, Thai-German Institute, Thai-Japan Institute, Rubber-Based Products Club, Thai Auto Parts Manufacturers Association). Three institutional developments complemented the OIE: the efforts of the Thailand Automotive Institute to help plan, coordinate, and implement new initiatives for the industry in response to the 1997 crisis; a strengthening of the Industrial

Estate Authority; and a 2002 decision to move the BOI from the Office of the Prime Minister into the MOI to facilitate overall coordination between the bodies responsible for investment promotion and those involved in industrial planning (Lauridsen 2008: 664).

The mixed results of the country's move into environmentally sustainable vehicle production illustrate the network's strengths and weaknesses. The move began in 2007 with Phase 1 of the Eco Car, touted as the country's second "product champion." This was a well-considered effort to address the emerging demand, especially in the ASEAN region, for energy-efficient vehicles and to ensure efficient scale economies in the process. (Phase 1 Eco Cars were gas-powered vehicles of 1.3 liters or below, or diesel-powered cars of 1.4 liters or below, that conformed to Euro IV emission standards with fuel consumption of no more than five liters per 100 kilometers. On the role of the OIE, see https://www.bangkokpost.com/auto/1668000/the-man-behind-thai-auto-policy.) Using generous incentives (tax holidays, duty-free machinery imports, reduced excise taxes) in exchange for assembler commitments to produce at least 100,000 vehicles a year, Thai officials were sufficiently cohesive to push several foreign assemblers to produce 1.64 million Eco Cars despite resistance from some of the more powerful Japanese firms, and Finance Ministry concerns over lost tax revenues from Eco Car incentives (Niyomsilpa 2008: 81). Institutionally, the effort was led and coordinated by the Ministry of Industry's Office of Industrial Economics.

But the Eco Car project ran into some significant challenges. The network struggled to attract investments by *all* the assemblers, some of which, unlike in the case of pickup trucks, already had other production sites in the region for fuel-efficient vehicles. In fact, of the five would-be participants, only two honored their commitments (Maikaew 2017). Second, officials misjudged the size of the domestic demand for Eco Cars: Under pressure to deal with an overcapacity problem (production in 2015 was almost 2 million vehicles out of total production capacity of over 3.5 million), the government was compelled to support market-distorting, first-time buyer subsidies. Buyers overextended themselves, resulting in large numbers of defaults, forcing the government to draw on the national budget to compensate losses from the excise tax cuts (IHS Markit 2015). Finally, the network failed to anticipate the growing attractiveness of electric, as opposed to fuel-efficient internal combustion engine (ICE), vehicles. These problems led to a second phase of the Eco Car program in 2013, involving a greater emphasis on exports and vehicles with greater fuel efficiency requirements. These included even smaller CO_2 emissions, better fuel consumption, and smaller diesel engines than Phase 1 vehicles, as well as the ability to meet EURO 5 (vs. 4) emission standards (thaiauto.or.th/2012/news/news-detail.asp?newsid=3172). The effort enjoyed some success, at least in the short term. By early 2017, exports of Eco Cars amounted to some 934,000 units compared to roughly 700,000 domestic sales of these vehicles, and by 2018, the country had produced over 2.4 million Eco Cars, which accounted for half of domestic passenger car sales (Bangkok Post 2019b).

But domestic sales of Eco Cars remained dwarfed by traditional vehicles, especially pickup trucks (Thai Kasikorn Bank 2019). Especially concerning was growing competition in the Eco Car market from within the region, especially Indonesia's low-cost-green-car program, as well as pressures to meet increasingly stringent EU emission standards and to address Thailand's dire smog problem (the head of the OIE estimated that, with 11 million Bangkok residents, the annual market value for protective masks was over 200 billion baht; Bangkok Post 2019b). These challenges triggered a fairly abrupt shift to an emphasis on electric vehicle (EV) development (Larkin 2017). Beginning in 2017, the BOI began offering promotional privileges (tax holidays and tariff exemptions) for vehicle and parts production related to three types of energy-saving vehicles: hybrids, plug-in hybrids, and battery electric vehicles (13 producers were granted privileges; Arisitniran 2019), with the expectation that Thailand's EV market would reach 600,000 vehicles by 2030 (Thailand Automotive Institute [TAI] 2012).

This review of Thailand's move into low-emissions vehicles reveals both positive and negative features of the country's institutional arrangements. On the positive side, key organizations, led by the OIE and including the BOI and MOI, formulated a fairly aggressive, cohesive and nimble Eco Car strategy. The agility of the strategy, including the pivot to EVs, also reflects the country's impressive sensitivity to external challenges—from regional rivals and from broader market demand for stricter emission standards. The move to battery EVs has been gradual, especially as the local supply chain and infrastructure are far from sufficient to support the development of battery EVs (Bangkok Post 2019a). On the negative side, the country's middle-income status has limited the actual domestic demand for new vehicles, forcing reliance on exports and unsustainable government subsidies for domestic purchases. In addition, the move to EVs lacked clear coordination. Almost two years after the BOI began offering promotional privileges to producers, the private sector was pushing the government to establish a National New Generation Vehicle committee in light of the fact that "*current EV policies have no committee taking responsibility or following up, while the three ministries . . . [Industry, Energy and Transport] . . . have no power to make decisions or take action*" (emphasis added; Arisitniran 2019). The fact that the BOI was moved back to the Prime Minister's Office in 2014, after having been shifted to the MOI some 10 years earlier, could not have facilitated coordination. Finally, the whole focus of these efforts has been on attracting investment, especially by foreign producers, i.e., on extensive growth. Attention to the intensive growth consequences, such as the impact of new vehicles on the health of domestic firms, has been secondary at best—despite the strong concerns expressed by rubber product producers (interviews, Thai Polymer Society meeting, November 12, 13, 2018).

Institutions for *Intensive* Development without Continuity or Coordination

The preceding discussion reinforces the broader picture of largely ineffectual productivity-promoting institutions in Thailand. The Thai Automotive Institute, involving public and private sectors, produced a number of "master plans" to make Thailand Asia's high value-added automotive hub with a strong parts industry. These plans included proposals to improve productivity, human resources, engineering, and to create linkages with specific foci such as auto electronics, all supported by appropriate institutions such as "knowledge sharing centers (Thailand Automotive Institute [TAI] 2012: 3–15). Yet the efforts of the TAI and related bodies have not been effective, as reflected in the continuing weakness of local firms. The problem has not been a *lack* of institutions (Table 4.1) but rather time inconsistency and fragmentation.

Time Inconsistency

The Industrial Restructuring Programme (IRP), the productivity promotion effort initiated in response to the 1997 Asian financial crisis, illustrates the politically induced fragility of Thai institutions for industrial diffusion and upgrading. Led by a respected technocrat, the IRP aimed in part to provide technical assistance to Thai firms through measures such as equipment modernization and skills development. Drawing on thousands of hours of business-government consultation, the IRP generated 24 projects to be coordinated by newly established public-private "institutions," including the Thailand Automotive Institute.

A combination of electoral politics and devaluation-induced export growth aborted this effort (Doner 2009: 28–29). Thaksin, then in opposition, made SME (small to medium-sized enterprise) promotion a key element of his party's program in anticipation of upcoming elections. Not to be outflanked by Thaksin, the existing government's Industry Minister Suwat Lippatapanlop

Table 4.1 Upgrading-Related Institutions: Thai Automotive Industry

Private Sector	Public Sector	Educational Institutions	Public–Private Intermediaries	Projects/Initiatives
FTI: Federation of Thai Industries	MOI: Ministry of Industry (Office of Industrial Economics, Dept. Indust. Promotion)	Chulalongkorn University	TAI: Thailand Automotive Institute	AHRDP/AHRDA: Automotive Human Resources Development Program/Academy (FTI, TAI, Japanese firms)
TAPMA: Thailand Auto Parts Mfg. Assoc. (FTI)	BOI: Board of Investments	KMUTT: King Mongkut's University of Technology—various campuses)	MIDI: Metal Industries Development Institute	Graduate programs in automotive engineering (Chulalongkorn, KMUTT TNI)
TAIA: Thai Automotive Industry Assoc. (FTI)	IEA: Industrial Estates Authority of Thailand	KMUTL: King Mongut's University of Technology, Lad Krabang	TPI: Thailand Plastics Institute	Consulting services (TPA and Dept. of Indust. Promotion)
RPIC: Rubber Products Industry Club (FTI)	MOL: Ministry of Labor (Dept. of Skills Formation)	RTEC: Rubber Technology Center	TSI: Thailand Steel Institute	Collaborative research (KMUT campuses/ Suzuki; TRF/RTEC)
TATMA: Thai Automotive Tire Mfgs. Assoc.	NSTDA: National Science and Technology Development Agency	Prince of Songkla University		
TGI: Thai German Institute	STIPI: Science, Technology and Innovation Policy Institute	TNI: Thai-Nichi Institute of Technology		
TP: Technology Promotion Association (Thai-Japan)	TRF: Thailand Research Fund			
	Rubber Research Institute of Thailand			

made equally forceful appeals to SMEs. The result was a shift from the IRP's focus on *technical assistance* to *financial support* for SMEs. Throwing money at the problem rather than helping firms to identify and address specific competitive weaknesses produced "traditional behavior of rent seeking among SME owners" (Suehiro 2010: 154–155). Further, on taking office in 2001 with a devaluation-fueled growth in exports, Thaksin dropped any effort to upgrade SMEs and replaced the IRP with a National Competitiveness Committee (Lauridsen 2008: Ch. 19). More than a name change, this shift marginalized much of the existing automotive network.

As part of a more general effort to centralize control over sectoral policy, Thaksin encouraged firms to work directly through the BOI rather than the official industry coordinator, the TAI. This meant that the "main projects in the development of the automobile industry . . . [including the AHRDP skill development initiative] . . . were . . . transferred from the TAI to Japanese assemblers" (Suehiro 2010: 164). It also implied a further weakening of the voice of Thai parts producers that the TAI considered to be a prime constituency.

Frequent cabinet changes, part of a quota system of ministerial allocations required for coalition maintenance (McCargo 2002), further undermined the TAI, since the Ministry of Industry, the TAI's "parent" agency, was a frequent target of these changes (interviews with executive director, TGI; former head of the TAI; and head of Rubber Products Industry Club).

The long-serving administrative head of the TAI had to work with and educate 14 industry ministers in 11 years. Agency shifts also undermined policy stability. A Japanese-supported Metal Industries Development Institute was replaced by an independent, German-supported foundation which, despite its real contribution to the development of tool and die–related expertise, has been affected by frequent ministerial changes in the MOI, including the BOI's departure to the Prime Minister's Office in 2014 (interview with former director, TGI).

Political influence extended beyond ministerial appointments, as evidenced by the case of Suwat, a prominent politician who, in addition to being minister of industry from 1998 to 2000, held other ministerial posts (transport, university affairs, labor, justice) in various governments from 1994 until 2007, when he was banned from politics for five years due to alleged corruption. Suwat reportedly had little if any automotive-related expertise and, despite leaving the Industry Ministry in 2000, retained a major voice in determining leadership of the TAI and sub-ministerial appointments within the Industry Ministry. Suwat was also allegedly involved in the MOI's regulation of used car imports. The legality of these imports was unclear; and the required environmental checks overwhelmed the MOI's inspection capacity and undermined its ability to develop advanced testing services (interviews with TGI director; and official, Office of Industrial Economics).

Fragmentation, Lack of Expertise, and Conflicting Incentives
Government Agencies
Apart from the Office of Industrial Economics (OIE), the Ministry of Industry has not been effective in automotive industrial promotion since the end of the ADC. The Industry Ministry traditionally focused largely on local content. Since the end of these requirements in 2000, a central activity of the ministry has been inspection and license renewal by its Department of Factories (Krom Rongan), an activity that has contributed little if anything to the competitiveness of local firms. One Thai association leader concluded that apart from OIE staff, MOI officials had little sense of the auto industry's competitive position (author interview, November 11, 2013).

The position of the BOI—the agency responsible for investor incentives—has been somewhat tenuous. As noted, the Board was housed in the Prime Minister's Office until it was moved to the MOI in 2002, only to be shifted back to the Prime Minister's Office in 2014. Nor has the BOI staff had the opportunity to develop much technical expertise, since until recently, the Board has focused on promoting FDI with few explicit efforts to encourage spillovers to domestic firms. Only in May 2017, after over three decades of promotional incentives, did the BOI come out with an explicit set of incentives to promote spillovers under a "National Competitiveness Enhancement Policy" aimed at, among others, the "next generational automotive" sector. Yet these incentives account for a minute percentage of foreign investments. Moreover, given the vagueness of the incentives and the fact that they previously came under the purview of the Finance Ministry, the Board itself is not clear how to implement them (author interview, BOI official, May 23, 2018).

The Board's contribution to upstream linkages has also been minimized by the fact that its policy of tariff and tax deductions tended to favor imports of machinery (Lauridsen 2008: 860). All of this has resulted in weak ties between the BOI and the smaller local producers; indeed, a BOI official acknowledged that the BOI traditionally focused on large firms, whereas mostly SMEs came under the purview of the Ministry of Industry's Department of Industrial Promotion (interview, May 23, 2018). These weak linkages with local producers are reflected in the statement of the president of the main local parts association—TAPMA—that the BOI did not consult with the association in crafting the Eco Car incentives (interview, Bangkok, November 13, 2013). Coordination theoretically improved with the transfer of BOI into the Industry Ministry in 2002, but, as noted, this move was reversed a decade later.

The ways in which inter-ministerial fragmentation has undermined intrasectoral linkage development is illustrated in the case of rubber-based auto parts. Divisions among the Industry, Agriculture, and Commerce ministries have, until very recently, resulted in the absence of overall coordination to strengthen the production of rubber-based auto parts, especially by local firms (Abonyi and Doner 2013). In 2015 a "Thailand Rubber Authority" was finally established, but this body is dominated by upstream (farmer) interests, and soon became mired in controversy over efforts to bolster prices of natural rubber at the expense of local rubber consumers such as the auto industry (Seetong 2017; interviews with rubber product industry club officials, November 22, 2017, May 24, 2018).

Finally, there has been little integration of technology with industrial and export promotion. As late as 2016, the Ministry of Science and Technology was not categorized as an economic ministry and had few ties with the MOI or domestic firms (Intarakumnerd 2018: 15). Nor has there been effective coordination between economic development agencies and a highly fractured education and skill development network. Indeed, a World Bank report (2012b: 34) described the formal education system, run by the Ministry of Education, as plagued by "overlaps and fragmentation in planning, financing, monitoring, evaluation and other functions . . . [that] . . . generate functional incoherence and inefficiency." Similar problems characterize the training system led by the perennially weak Ministry of Labor: its Skills Development Department lacked the resources to coordinate various technical ministries and private training providers (UNCTAD 2015).

In addition, unlike the East Asian NICs, Japan, and even Malaysia, Thailand has no integrated agency—no "Ministry of International Trade and Industry"—designed to strengthen the value added and linkages of Thai exports. Only after the 1997 crisis was a combined trade-and-industry ministry considered, only to be dropped, along with the IRP, as exports rebounded after the baht devalued (Doner 2009: 122). Nor does the agency responsible for tariffs—the Finance Ministry—have much experience in industry and industrial restructuring (Intarakumnerd 2018: 15). Further, negotiations over free trade agreements have usually been led by the Ministry of Commerce, whose "key performance indicators" emphasized number of treaties signed, not domestic linkages (Niyomsilpa 2008: 80).

Private Sector Organizations

The strengthening of domestic linkages requires some form of collective input from indigenous producers, but two cleavages have weakened the voices of local firms since 1999. One, between foreign and indigenous producers, has plagued TAPMA, the primary representative of indigenous Thai firms, with roughly 500 members. Although its formal goals include strengthening the technological competencies of its members, from 1997 until around 2013, TAPMA fought a rearguard effort to protect *markets* for local firms largely by lobbying on trade and investment incentives (interviews with director of Thai Automotive Institute, Bangkok, July 12, 2010; with former TAPMA officer, Bangkok, July 21, 2011; and with chair of Rubber Parts Industry Club/FTI, Bangkok, August 8, 2015).

Since the end of local content requirements, the absence of focus on upgrading also reflects the weak associational presence of the industry's main drivers and sources of technology—foreign producers. Although TAPMA members include first-tier parts producers, the number of indigenous first-tier firms is small, while the technology-related activities of foreign producers have largely taken place either in-house or in conjunction with associated firms, or are not carried out in Thailand at all. Further, efforts by foreign firms to influence policy often occur through direct contacts with officials rather than through the much messier but more comprehensive process of working out common policy positions that benefit domestic as well as foreign firms (Suehiro 2010: 166).

Domestic parts firms are also represented by product-specific "clubs" within the peak Federation of Thai Industries such as the Rubber Products Industry Club, a highly active representative for Thai-owned and -managed Thai producers of rubber products such as tires (interviews with officers of Rubber Products Industry Club).

But the Club's policy influence and capacity to aid members do not match its level of activity. This is in part due to the lack of engagement of multinational tire producers in productivity-related issues and their decision to split off and form a separate group—the Thai Automotive Tire Manufacturers' Association. It also reflects the dominance of the upstream-oriented Ministry of Agriculture and the lack of support for downstream producers by the Ministry of Industry. The result is that the MOI has had little sense of the needs of downstream producers (interview, Bangkok, November 11, 2013).

Public-Private Organizations

An indication of Thai policymakers' *awareness* of the need for upgrading was the establishment of "intermediary" or public-private organizations designed to address collective action problems in areas such as skilling and technology acquisition. In autos, two are especially important: the TAI and the Thai-German Institute (TGI) (interviews, TPA executive director, Bangkok, July 17, 2010, August 11, 2012). As noted, the TAI has been active in developing "master plans" with key players. It has also provided consulting and testing services to the Automotive Human Resource Academy (Table 4.2). The TAI has roughly 100 employees, of whom only 10% have master's degrees. Thirty of the staff are engineers and 20 are technicians with vocational degrees. The TAI's impact has been limited by the fact that its public sector funding has been short-term and conditional while support from larger firms has been lukewarm. As a result, the TAI has had to rely on short-term consulting contracts (interview with vice president of TAI, Bangkok, November 12, 2013; material on the TAI also draws from Intarakumnerd, Gerdsri, and Teekasap 2012: 91; Intarakumnerd and Charoenporn 2013a: 104–105; and interview with executive director of Technology Promotion Association in Bangkok, July 17, 2010).

The TGI, a joint initiative by the Thai and German governments, began operations in 1995, partly in response to the perceived weaknesses of the earlier efforts at support for local tool and die makers. This institute focuses on upgrading of SME manufacturing capacities through training courses and industrial services in areas such as machine design, tool and die manufacturing, and material testing. With roughly 100 staff members and several regional branches, TGI has reportedly trained some 4,000 students a year in various courses. As with the TAI, funding has been a problem. Financing from Germany ended in 2004–2005 when the German government decided that with Thailand's move into middle-income status the institute ought to be self-funded and led by Thais under MOI supervision. The result is that, with frequent ministerial turnover, the TGI has often been compelled to bid for short-term, money-generating projects that undermine the longer-term objectives of technology dissemination and R&D (interview with two former executive directors of TGI,). Weak links with the private sector have been a problem, owing in part to a tradition of reliance on MOI funding and the reluctance of SMEs to pay for training (KFW Entwicklungsbank 2005). However, the TGI's central role in recent robotics development efforts (noted below) may provide it with opportunities for more stable growth.

These problems have made it difficult to implement long-term development initiatives. Thailand's automotive landscape is full of master plans that are at best aspirational and at worst pleasant dreams. Indeed, Thai firm managers often talk about their country doing a lot of plan . . . *ning*, with *ning* being the Thai word for "quiet," as in "nothing happens" (interviews, director of Rubber

Technology Center). All of this confirms Suehiro's broader conclusion about Thailand, consistent with this book's core argument: "limitations in institutional capacity may be the most important element for the poor outcomes in the sectoral policies in Thailand" (Suehiro 2010: 166–167).

A New Direction?

In light of these past weaknesses, recent attempts at institutional strengthening (Table 4.2) stand out, beginning with the previous (2014–2018) military government's establishment of a high-level committee on scientific and technological workforce development and extending to a wide range of sector- and capacity-specific initiatives involving the Federation of Thai Industries. The FTI has strengthened ties with the Ministry of Labor's Department of Skills Development and has established almost a dozen "institutes," including those devoted to "research development for industry" and "human capacity building" (see https://www.fti.or.th/2016/eng/ftiinstitute.aspx, accessed December 12, 2017). Each of these institutes, such as the Center for Robotics Excellence, presumes strong stakeholder collaboration (Chalassatien 2016; Thai German Institute [TGI] 2018). More recently, the BOI established an

Table 4.2 Recent Innovation-Related Initiatives

(1) 13 newly established government committees; focus includes development of "a scientific and technological workforce for sustainable national development" (Patthana 2017).

(2) High-level working group meetings to "Develop Technology Roadmap to Drive National Research and Innovation System" organized by National Science and Technology Development Agency (author interviews and participation, November 2017).

(3) Science, Technology and Innovation Policy Institute (STIPI), established by NSTDA as source of proposals on human resource development and sectoral strategies (including next-generation vehicles) to escape middle-income trap. Linked to Eastern Economic Corridor www.kmutt.ac.th/stipi/main/en/

(4) Center for Robotics Excellence (CoRE). Partnership between Thai-German Institute and numerous public institutions. To develop automation-related human resources in support of technology transfer and integration of robotics and automation with AI, smart sensors, etc. (Thai German Institute [TGI] 2018).

(5) Thai Research Fund partnership with several Thai universities to foster innovation in support of local tire producers (author interview, Rubber Products Industry Club official, November 5, 2017).

(6) Automotive Human Resource Academy, created 2015, to develop curricula for each level of automotive employee backed up by national certification framework; based on German dual vocational education system (Chalassathien 2016a; author interview with Chalassathien, November 2017)

(7) Automotive Testing and Research Center.

(8) BOI merit-based incentive scheme to promote closer links between MNCs and local firms (Intarakumnerd 2018: 19).

agreement with Thailand's leading universities to improve links between the manufacturing and educational sectors (https://finance.yahoo.com/news/ thailand-boi-university-network-spur-101400298.html). And finally, the Eastern Economic Corridor (discussed in the following), the previous military government's $43 billion initiative designed to move Thailand out of middle income, will include "next-generation" automotive production (including electric vehicles) as one of its first five sectoral components (Sunseth 2018).

It is too early to say whether these new arrangements will prove more durable and effective than their predecessors. The past performance of Thai institutions suggests that caution is in order. As one long-time observer and participant has noted, for all its many initiatives in sectoral economic policy, Thailand is weak in implementation, coordination, and follow-up (interview, professor and government consultant, Thammasat University). These weaknesses may well persist in what, as of 2020, remains a volatile political and institutional environment. The military-dominated government, which came to power through highly contested elections and questionable electoral arrangements, remains fragile. The need to satisfy coalition partners has led to games of "coalitional chess" in which politically based ministerial appointments are likely to undermine the stability, cohesion, and expertise of key government agencies (https://www.bangkokpost.com/thailand/politics/ 1731819/a-game-of-coalition-chess).

Political Origins of Institutional Weaknesses

The weakness of Thailand's automotive institutions in sponsoring intensive growth is not due to ignorance. As we have seen, Thai agencies have undertaken multiple efforts at strengthening local firm productivity through skills development and industrial linkages. Yet all their programs have been fragmented and short-lived. Our explanation involves "politics" as both proximate and longer-term, structural pressures on Thai political leaders, as discussed in Chapter 3. The impact of proximate politics on upgrading-related institutions is evident in the deleterious impact of cabinet and ministerial changes on the operations of the Thailand Automotive Institute, of electoral competition and government change on the IRP, of Thaksin's populist strategy on consultative mechanisms at the national as well as auto sectoral levels, as well as shifting coalitional dynamics under the military, whether as direct ruler (2014–2019) or dominant player in an elected government (2019–present).

The fact that these pressures did not undermine the Thai institutions so effective at *extensive* growth reflects the country's intermediate position along the continuum of vulnerability presented in Chapter 3. Thailand is relatively but not extremely sensitive to resource constraints, even as it has a fairly easy time with regard to external and internal claims on its resources. Viewed comparatively, Thailand has confronted conditions more challenging than those facing Malaysia, Indonesia, and the Philippines, but much less threatening than those confronting Korea, Taiwan, and China.

With regard to resources, Thai political leaders have been consistently sensitive to the need for foreign exchange. Indeed, the intensity of Thailand's institutional initiatives has varied inversely with access to foreign exchange revenues. The ongoing efforts at industry rationalization, including the "product champion" strategy, reflected leaders' concerns about the industry's drain on foreign exchange. The attempted liberalization of the mid-1980s was prompted by the need to resolve the country's debt crisis. Prime Minister Anand's successful tariff liberalization in 1991–1992 reflected his belief in the need to prepare Thai firms for the potential loss of foreign investment to NAFTA participants and pressures from looming WTO membership (Niyomsilpa 2008: 82). The more recent push into a second product champion—the Eco Car—reflected the belief among top MOI officials that Thailand was facing growing competition, especially from Indonesia, and that the auto industry could not sustain growth based only on the dwindling market for pickups. As the director of the OIE noted, Thailand needed the Eco Car because the country could not afford to put all its eggs in one basket (interview, August 10, 2012).

But each of these crises was relatively mild and short-lived due to Thailand's ability to earn and attract foreign exchange. The country's diversified export basket, bolstered by devaluations in the 1980s and after the AFC (Doner 2009), eased pressures on the Thai baht. Equally important were external funds: the flood of East Asian investment during the 1980s, and the $1.5 billion in development aid from Japan's "Miyazawa Fund" and $300 million from the Asian Development Bank in the wake of the Asian financial crisis of 1997–1998 (Doner 2015b). Still a further safety valve has been the availability, particularly since the Asian financial crisis, of a large, informal labor force, including subcontracted workers (many of whom are among the estimated 2–4 million migrants working in Thailand).

Nor has Thailand faced significant pressures from abroad or below. Thailand has not experienced foreign threats since the end of the Vietnam conflict in 1975 (Doner, Ritchie, and Slater 2005; Chapter 3 of this volume). Popular sectors have been organizationally weak, reflecting the existence of a large land frontier until the 1980s, an agricultural sector that continues to function as a labor "sink," and levels of informality as high as 40%–60% of the workforce

(Phongpaichit and Baker 2008; Hewison and Tularak 2013). Civil society organizations have been fragmented and fragile (Unger and Mahakanjana 2016: Ch. 6). Protests by Thai farmers, who still account for over a third of the population, occur frequently but tend to be specific to particular products and themes, especially commodity prices. Industrial labor is, if anything, even weaker politically, owing to internal fragmentation, state repression, and the high levels of informality noted earlier (Brown 2016; Charoenloet 2015).

These weaknesses contribute to the absence of broader peak associations able to articulate, mobilize, and reconcile the interests of Thailand's popular sectors, even in the face of persistently high levels of income inequality after 1997 (Phongpaichit and Benyaapikul 2014: 7–8). Coming full circle back to proximate political factors, this anemic interest articulation is further reflected in the country's feeble party system, composed of political parties described as faction-ridden, unstable, largely uninterested in policy, and generally detached from broad societal groups (Unger and Mahakanjana 2016: Ch. 6). The exception was, of course, Thaksin's Thai Rak Thai party, whose electoral successes from 2001 owed much to its espousal of policies aimed at improving popular welfare, including accessible healthcare, village financing, and loan forgiveness. But the Thai Rak Thai party, personalized and faction-ridden, largely ignored labor as well as small business, and in practice emphasized populist rather than upgrading-related measures (Doner 2009).

What then accounts for the recent upsurge in upgrading-promoting programs and institutions discussed earlier (Table 4.2)? The core motivation seems to be a growing awareness of the limits of Thailand's existing growth strategy, in which productivity gains have been driven largely by the movement of labor from low-productivity agriculture to high-productivity manufacturing (World Bank 2018b: 36). According to interviews conducted in late 2017, local industry, represented by the FTI, has become increasingly aware of (1) growing competition from lower-wage neighbors, especially Indonesia; (2) looming labor shortages due to an aging population and limits on the supply of migrant workers, currently critical to Thai industry; and (3) the need for active efforts to attract and retain FDI.

The innovation-related responses to these problems have been subsumed under the broader goal of "Thailand 4.0," a project that refers broadly to the modernization of every sector in preparation for the digital era. For manufacturers such as automotive producers, the goal is "smart factories" that integrate sensors, real-time data transfer, and advanced robotics (Hayworth 2017). The Eastern Economic Corridor is a key component of Thailand 4.0. And while it has clear potential for positive spillovers, in practice the EEC initiative seems to focus primarily on the mobilization and allocation of capital.

This is especially important as net capital inflows and FDI—required for the public sector projects critical to Thailand's economic recovery—have been stagnant or negative since the Asian financial crisis (World Bank 2018b: 26, 30).

There is thus the danger that the focus on attracting capital and generating foreign exchange will crowd out the longer-term and institutionally more difficult efforts at diffusion and innovation. Indeed, there are good reasons to anticipate that investment promotion à la EEC will be part of a shorter-term, distributional strategy of clientelism or populism for Thais alongside public (or club) goods infrastructure for foreign producers. This was especially the case for Thailand's military regime, which faced no external security threats but significant pressures to manage the economy, hold elections, and address still simmering frustration by rural and low-income citizens vulnerable to populist appeals. For such a regime, capital inflows constitute a safety valve, if not a mini-resource curse that facilitates satisfying popular pressures.

It is thus not surprising that the government has put pressure on already fragmented agencies to come up with "quick wins" (interviews with participants in government-sponsored technology roadmap exercise, November 18, 2018). This short-term perspective was also reflected in and reinforced by frequent cabinet shifts, even under a military regime: in November 2017, the government announced its *fifth* cabinet reshuffle since the 2014 coup, which replaced the sitting Minister of Science and Technology with a marketing expert. And finally, with 2019 elections looming, the leader of the military government began the shift from dictator to clientelist politician by wooing old-guard politicians and even appointing two sons of a provincial "godfather" as cabinet-level advisors (AFP 2018).

For the auto industry, all of this points to Thailand expanding its function as a hub for somewhat more diversified and higher value-added operations, but mostly under foreign auspices. Vehicles will still be overwhelmingly conceived, designed, and engineered abroad—with few linkages to Thai firms. Successfully attracting foreign capital through, for example, the EEC is no mean feat, and it could be undermined by persistent political instability. But attracting foreign capital requires much less institutional capacity than pursuing an active learning approach to FDI policy that promotes spillovers to and upgrading by domestic producers.

Conclusion

As our primary case of successful extensive growth with relatively little progress in upgrading and linkages with domestic firms, Thailand confirms key elements of the explanatory framework introduced in Chapter 3. Becoming the leading automotive producer and exporter in ASEAN as well as one of the world's largest vehicle exporters required mobilizing capital for modern, non-traditional activities. Far from a "natural," free-market process, this involved (1) creating a market for products with large scale economies; (2) attracting investment, mostly from foreign assemblers and suppliers; and (3) encouraging exports of these products. These occurred through deliberate and targeted policies formulated and implemented by specific institutions that were in turn motivated by particular sets of pressures on decision-makers.

Tax and infrastructure policies were particularly effective. The government made effective use of excise taxes to encourage production of pickup trucks, a vehicle with significant domestic and export demand, as well as one without competing regional production sites. These were combined with measures to attract foreign producers that included tax exemptions, input tariff reductions and export rebates, and infrastructure development that significantly facilitated both exports and interaction between assemblers and their follow-source suppliers. These policies were developed by a loose but effective set of institutions centered on the Office of Industrial Economics in coordination with the BOI, Ministry of Finance, and Thailand Automotive Institute. These policies and institutions in turn reflected the sensitivity of political leaders to foreign exchange and market access. This is seen in the shift from import substitution to export promotion in the 1980s, leading to the end of local content requirements by the year 2000; the product champion strategies; support for industrial estates; and the initiation of a public-private sector consultative process (IRP) devoted to upgrading in the wake of the 1997 Asian financial crisis.

But if sensitivity to economic constraints encouraged policies and institutions devoted to extensive development, the relatively moderate and short-lived nature of these pressures also helps to explain what did *not* happen. Despite persistent statements about the importance of strengthening the domestic supply base, the government paid little effective attention to developing institutions promoting domestic upgrading. The 1997–1998 Industrial Restructuring Program's public-private sector consultative process, for example, was disbanded after a devaluation spurred renewed exports. Long-proposed testing centers were delayed and watered down. With the exception of the OIE, the Ministry of Industry failed to develop automotive expertise or to forge linkages with export and science and technology agencies. The Thai Automotive Institute and Thai-German Institute suffered from unstable government support. Associations were relatively weak and, until quite recently, focused on lobbying rather than workforce development. The BUILD program to promote assembler linkages with local firms was never implemented.

And only after over 30 years of automotive industrial promotion did the BOI take vague steps to link FDI incentives to domestic spillovers.

A comparative perspective helps to clarify the achievements and limitations of Thailand's automotive trajectory. The alacrity and effectiveness of Thailand's move to export promotion based on scale economies, the effectiveness of relevant institutions, and the country's sensitivity to economic pressures vividly contrast with the much longer commitment to inefficient import substitution, the lack of cohesive institutions, and the easier access to resources of Indonesia, Malaysia, and the Philippines.

But successful extensive development was institutionally less demanding than the intensive growth seen in our Northeast Asian cases. Thailand has succeeded where information requirements are limited to identifying promising products from existing lineups already developed in advanced countries, and fashioning incentives and complementary infrastructure to attract foreign firms. By contrast, strengthening domestic firms and encouraging assembler-supplier linkages would have required a deeper understanding of the needs of local firms, especially the requirements for technology absorption and incremental innovation. In addition, Thai success was based on the coordination of the relatively small number of actors required to implement tax and infrastructure policies. In fact, with the partial exception of the industrial estates, privately operated but overseen by the Industrial Estates Authority, the government's role largely ends with "stroke of a pen" decisions about incentives. Monitoring to ensure that firms meet investment, production, employment, and export levels is thus relatively easy. In contrast, the intensive growth seen in the Korean, Chinese, and, to a lesser extent, Taiwanese cases required the coordination of much larger numbers of actors, including associations, public-private sector consultative groups, sectoral institutes, testing centers, and government agencies devoted to R&D, investment screening, export support, and project financing.

Finally, Thailand has arguably had a relatively easy time in managing the distributional outcomes of its strategy. The main winners have been the powerful foreign assemblers and parts producers. Thailand's export orientation and pickup truck strategy have helped to resolve the assemblers' excess capacity and scale economy problems while conforming to their global value chain strategies. The achievements of the Eco Car and EV projects remain to be seen. What is clear is that the major losers have been the majority of local parts firms whose voices were diminished with the lifting of foreign ownership requirements (Phongpaichit and Baker 2008: 270) and the increasingly demanding product and process standards required for participation in global value chains.

5

The Philippines and Indonesia

Extensive Development Arrested and Delayed

The Philippines and Indonesia initiated serious efforts at automotive in-dustrialization in the 1970s. The Philippines aimed to combine local sup-plier upgrading with MNC-linked exports, whereas the Indonesian strategy was a more straightforward intensive development strategy through import substitution. Neither country succeeded in these initial efforts. Permissive conditions—weak external threats, limited popular pressure, and relatively easy access to foreign exchange—undermined policy stability and hindered efforts at developing institutions capable of strengthening local firms and linkages. Moves to more extensive development came only with the tight-ening of economic pressures, and then resulted in significantly different levels of progress. This chapter addresses similarities across the two countries—why neither succeeded in upgrading or in matching Thailand's successful move to large-volume, MNC-based assembly and exports—and their differences: why Indonesia has begun to rival Thailand as an MNC assembly base, whereas the Philippines has not.

The Philippines: Policy Instability and Divided Institutions

In 2008, a prominent Philippine scholar described its auto industry as a case of "arrested development" (Ofreneo 2008). As evidence, he pointed to the industry's limited scale of production, its low capacity utilization, the dis-appearance of most of the original producers of car parts, and feeble parts exports. A more recent study, emphasizing the industry's outdated produc-tion processes, high raw material prices, and incomplete automotive supply chain, confirmed that the situation did not change much in the following decade (Sturgeon et al. 2016).

This outcome is puzzling in light of the fact that, in the 1960s, the Philippines was the region's "automotive pioneer" (Sturgeon et al. 2016: 23).

The Political Economy of Automotive Industrialization in East Asia. Richard F. Doner, Gregory W. Noble and John Ravenhill, Oxford University Press (2021). © Oxford University Press. DOI: 10.1093/oso/9780197520253.003.0005

As the country's Automotive Industry Workers' Association lamented, "In the 1960s we were second to Japan in Asia in . . . vehicle assembly. In the 1970s, we were overtaken by South Korea; in the 1980s, by Malaysia; and in the 1990s by Indonesia and Thailand. Today Vietnam might overtake us" (cited in Ofreneo 2008: 76).

Key to the industry's hard times, consistent with the theme of this book, has been a lack of political support for the development of institutions required to formulate and implement automotive industrial policy and industrial diffusion. Domestic political instability and a related economic crisis undermined key industrial development institutions in the early 1970s. The result was the collapse of the Progressive Car Manufacturing Project (PCMP), a sophisticated strategy, officially launched in 1971, combining import substitution with explicit incentives for automotive exports. The ensuing liberalization process was much more abrupt than in Thailand or even Indonesia, leaving producers unprepared for new competition. Subsequent auto industrialization efforts have been plagued by inconsistent fiscal and trade policies. Technology-promotion measures have been nearly nonexistent, as have coordinating institutions, none of which rivals even the relatively weak Thai Automotive Institute.

Philippine Automotive Performance

The Philippine assembly industry has two striking characteristics (Figure 5.1). One is its small scale and erratic character. The country produced only 112,000 vehicles in 2015, barely more than the total two decades earlier, despite a large population (103 million) and a per capita income roughly equal to that of Indonesia (production totals rose to 141,252 in 2017, and then fell to just 79,763 in 2018). The country remains ASEAN's worst performer in vehicle production (Desiderio 2019). The other important feature is an unusually large gap, filled by imported vehicles, between production and sales (Figure 5.1) (Desiderio 2019).

Over 60% of assembly output consists of commercial vehicles—light commercial vehicles and "Asian utility vehicles"—rather than sedans, a mix similar to that found in most developing countries. The number of assemblers has fluctuated wildly over the years, ranging from two to more than a dozen. As in other Southeast Asian countries, subsidiaries of Japanese assemblers dominate: Toyota has a large and increasing share of over 40%, while Mitsubishi runs a distant second (Philippines News Agency 2016). In 2015, the largest assemblers, Toyota and Mitsubishi, generated 49,000 and 5,000 total vehicles

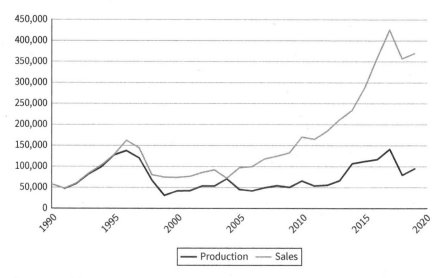

Figure 5.1 Philippines Vehicle Production and Sales.

Source: Production & Sales 1998-2016 <https://OICA.net>

(some years are estimates; not always consistent from year to year. Sales include commercial vehicles). Sales 1990-2004: Aldaba (2008: 14). Production 1991-1998: Quimba and Rosellon (2011: 9). Production and Sales 2016-19, ASEAN Automotive Federation, <http://asean-autofed.com/statistics. html≥ (accessed 12 April 2020)

of two models, respectively (Sturgeon et al. 2016: 26). Toyota's capacity utilization rate of only 60% in 2008 was the highest of the major car assemblers (Ofreneo 2008: 73). The absence of economies of scale is one reason why it costs 70% more to produce vehicles in the Philippines than in Thailand (Sturgeon et al. 2016: 26, 40).

After 2014, rapid economic growth pushed per capita incomes into the "sweet zone" for consumption of automobiles, leading to a major upswing in sales and ambitious plans for extensive (but not intensive) production. But increased imports of regular and "gray" vehicles swallowed most of the new demand.

Parts production, too, is of only modest scale. Actual local content of assembled vehicles is only 10%–15%. As of 2014, the Philippine components industry produced only about 330 parts, of which only 92 appeared in whole vehicle assembly; between 1996 and 2014 the total number of parts suppliers increased by only 16 to a total of 256 (Sturgeon et al. 2016: 27, 39; Raymundo 2005: 9–11). Roughly 132 parts producers are first-tier suppliers, largely MNC-owned "follow sources" producing wire harnesses, transmissions, stamped parts, suspension systems, and large-injection molding. The roughly 126 second- and third-tier suppliers are largely small, Filipino-owned operations producing simple metal parts. Rubber and plastic account for another quarter, while electric and electronic parts constitute only 8% (Motor Vehicle Parts Manufacturers Association of the Philippines [MVPMAP] 2013).

Parts exports, which significantly exceed imports (Figure 5.2), are modest compared to those of Korea, Thailand, or even Taiwan. The industry imports few parts because it assembles few vehicles.

The Philippines does show surprising strength in three areas: transmissions, wire harnesses, and (to a lesser extent) brake parts. It is puzzling that a poor country with a weak industrial base exports hundreds of millions of dollars a year in transmissions. Production of transmissions is capital intensive and requires assembly of a large number of precise and durable parts. Philippine industrial economists optimistically but implausibly attribute the country's success in production of transmissions to a comparative advantage in skilled labor (Ofreneo 2016: 56–57). In fact, their research inadvertently suggests a complementary but more policy-dependent explanation. Mitsubishi and other foreign firms first began exporting transmissions from the Philippines in the 1970s as a quid pro quo for the right to participate in the PCMP. In the 1990s they built on this experience and expanded exports of transmissions as part of the Philippines' contribution to the multilateral BBC (brand-to-brand complementation) and AICO (ASEAN Industrial Cooperation) schemes designed to overcome the limitations of ASEAN's then small and isolated domestic markets (Raymundo 2005: 60–61; Ofreneo 2016: 54–58). Export of transmissions is thus not an indication of increasing industrial sophistication

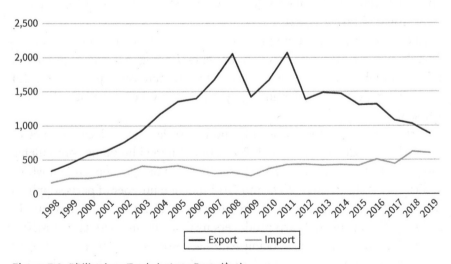

Figure 5.2 Philippines Trade in Auto Parts ($m).
Source: UN Comtrade.

or the merits of participating in global value chains, but rather an idiosyncratic legacy of import substitution and ASEAN policy initiatives.

Wire harnesses, in contrast, are highly labor intensive, so it is not surprising that a poor country like the Philippines would have a natural advantage in their production. Yazaki of Japan invested in 1974 and the resulting joint venture grew to employ 10,000 workers, dwarfing all other firms in the automotive sector. Virtually all employees worked on the assembly floor as manual laborers. A few smaller wire harness firms prospered as well. Yet wire harnesses depend on inputs of high-quality copper, all of which had to be imported. Nor did Yazaki-Torres engage in any design or engineering.

As with production of transmissions, exports of wire harnesses grew out of earlier regimes of protection and promotion. Until overall ASEAN liberalization in 2004, wire harnesses were protected by relatively high tariffs of 30% (15% on a most-favored-nation basis). More modest but still relatively high tariffs (20%; 10%) protected domestic production of brake parts, another successful export area (Ofreneo 2016: 56; Aldaba 2007: 10–13, 19).

As with other original equipment manufacturer (OEM) components, production of these high-volume export components is highly import dependent: In addition to high-quality copper, wire harness producers import key parts such as terminals and electrical switches, while transmission producers depend on China for forged parts and on India for polished metal parts (Sturgeon et al. 2016: 39; Aldaba 2008: 19). Thus, the industry's robust exports of a small number of import-dependent components is consistent with its strikingly thin supply chain. Aldaba (2008: 23) found that imported raw materials accounted for 61% of automotive production costs in the Philippines vs. only 20% in Thailand. The Philippines has failed at extensive development of both assembly and parts production.

Philippine Automotive Policies

Challenges of Rationalization, Trade, and Investment

Philippine automotive policies have been haphazard, incoherent, and inconsistent. This is the result less of unusually unrealistic goals than of faulty implementation and design, weaknesses that in turn reflect institutional fragmentation and political short sightedness. From the PCMP in the early 1970s to the most recent CARS (Comprehensive Automotive Resurgence Strategy) program (Table 5.1), Philippine policymakers have consistently declared their intention to build up an indigenous supply base by drawing in foreign assemblers rather than establishing a national champion firm as in

Table 5.1 Evolution of Philippine Automotive Policies

Policy; Presidential Administration	Years	Features
Importation	1916–1950	CBU importation from United States.
Import-substitution industrialization	1951–1972	Ban on auto imports. CKD assembly by Ford, Chrysler and GM.
Progressive Car Manufacturing Program (PCMP); Marcos	1972–1986	Ban vehicle imports. Increase local content (15%–>80%). Participants to establish parts plants and finance CKD imports through own foreign exchange earnings. Limit assemblers (5).
Car Development Program (CDP); Corazon Aquino	1987–2001	Local content 38%–>51%. Participants to develop at least one major component accounting for at least 9% of local content and generate 50% of own foreign exchange requirements through direct or indirect parts exports. Rationalization: initially only three participants but gradual opening resulted in 11 car assemblers by 1994. Removal of import quotas. Sharp tariff reduction: CBU: 70%, 1981; 50%, 1982; 30%, 2001. Parts: 30%, 1980s; 20%, 1993; 10%, 1995; 3%, 1996.
Motor Vehicle Development Program (MDVP); Macapagal, Benigno Aquino	2002–2015	Tariff cuts for imports of parts and raw materials. Incentives for CBU and parts exporters.
Comprehensive Automotive Resurgence Strategy (CARS); Benigno Aquino, Duterte	2015–	Incentives—not requirements—for assemblers sourcing 50% of body weight domestically and generating 200,000 units of one model over six years. Investment in parts and/or shared testing facilities encouraged. Limited to three companies (three models).

Sources: Sturgeon et al. (2016: 25); Ofreneo (2016: 50–56); Aldaba (2016a).

Malaysia. They have attempted to do so by requiring foreign assemblers to invest in local parts production and by trying to attain scale economies through incentives to limit the numbers of participants, models, and components. In sum, the Philippines strategy has consistently aimed at building a regional manufacturing hub—a strong, efficient, local supply base integrated with foreign assemblers and, more recently, global supply chains (Aldaba 2016a).

Yet poor implementation of rationalization efforts and inconsistency between industrial promotion and trade policy have repeatedly frustrated efforts to reach economies of scale. Both are rooted in institutional weaknesses. The rationalization failure is seen most strikingly in the PCMP, a relatively well-conceived plan developed by technocrats in the Board of Investment (BOI). The BOI, the industrial development and investment promotion arm of the Department of Trade and Industry (DTI), announced it would select at least two but no more than four assemblers (Doner 2015a: 40–46).

Institutional fragmentation and intervention by President Marcos combined to torpedo BOI's efforts to limit the number of participants (Doner 2015b: 165–169). The National Economic Council opposed the BOI's limits and pushed to raise the number of participants from three to four; Marcos, pressured by Ford and GM, raised the number even higher; and the industry's key business group, the Philippines Automotive Association, shifted from supporting the BOI to espousing an every-firm-for-itself policy of lifting limits entirely. The number of passenger vehicle assemblers never went below five and for much of the 1970s stayed at eight (Ofreneo 2008). Capacity utilization hovered around 40%. The number of domestic parts firms did rise from only 32 in 1974 to between 150 and 200 by the end of the 1970s (Doner 1991: 43), but actual local content levels remained low, local parts firms were plagued by high failure rates, and little technology transfer took place (Ofreneo 2016: 69).

The oil shock, the explosion of the debt crisis, the corrosive influence of Marcos cronies, and the political turmoil of the last Marcos years crippled efforts to deepen automotive industrialization. The domestic market shrank and the government proved unable to monitor, much less enforce, local contents compliance. The PCMP eventually collapsed, with only two participants left by 1984 (Ofreneo 2008: 70).

Policy incoherence—especially tensions between industrial promotion and trade policy—continued after the end of the PCMP. The Car Development Program's (1987–2001) stipulation that local content increase to 40% by 1990 was undermined by the Structural Adjustment Program that technocrats in the Marcos government signed with the International Monetary Fund (IMF) in 1979–1980. Tariffs on CKDs were cut from 30% in 1981 to 3% in 1996, while tariffs on parts and components ranged from 10% to 35% (Aldaba 2014: 35–36). Domestic parts and components producers rightly complained that this tariff structure encouraged the importation of CKD kits and parts over locally produced parts (Aldaba 2007: 8). Despite later adjustments, Philippine tariffs remained low compared to those of other Asian producers, resulting in a flood of imports. (Ofreneo 2008: 73).

The actual tariff liberalization process was also problematic. Unlike Vietnam, China, and even Thailand, which undertook trade liberalization in a relatively calibrated way, the Philippines' liberalization was broad brush. Local producers "were caught with their pants down because they were neither informed nor consulted on the schedule and scale of the liberalization measures" (Ofreneo 2017). This put the Philippines at a disadvantage vis-à-vis its major competitor, Thailand, which always kept its tariffs higher than in the Philippines. Also problematic was the increasing complexity and instability of tariff rates (Maquito 2008: 36).

The goal of promoting local assembly and parts production has also been seriously undermined by imports of secondhand vehicles priced 30%–50% lower than their new counterparts, along with "surplus" (often secondhand) parts. Lack of expertise and enforcement capacity at the Land Transport Office and the Bureau of Customs have allowed imports with falsified papers to flow through the country's free ports and special economic zones (Sturgeon et al. 2016: 26; Aldaba 2008: 26–27). As late as 2009 they still accounted for 27% of new registrations (Aldaba 2013: 3).

Finally, scale economies were undermined by a 2003 decision to impose a uniform value-added tax on *both* locally assembled and imported vehicles. Unlike in Thailand, where lower excise taxes helped focus demand on the popular one-ton pickup trucks, the Philippine strategy of not distinguishing local from foreign products, or taxing one or two promising segments at lower rates, weakened the market for the most promising product—the Asian utility vehicle, a potential "product champion" for which the Philippines developed expertise in design and assembly (Aldaba 2007: 15). This was a crucial difference from the strategic tax policies adopted in both Thailand and the Northeast Asian powerhouses.

Technological Upgrading

Automotive industrialization strategies have been largely devoid of specific policies and institutional capacity designed to improve the technological levels of local producers. The government controls entry, but after that, conducts "practically no regular follow-up . . . and monitoring." Policy has also been highly "assembler-centric," leaving auto parts manufacturers to fend for themselves (Maquito 2008: 36–37). A survey of parts and components producers reported poor government support for R&D and little help in negotiating with assemblers on industry linkages and technical assistance. These limitations are evident in the 2015 CARS program, whose principal components were fiscal incentives for volume production and minor regulatory reforms such as streamlining of registration and business-matching activities (Natsuda and Thoburn 2017: 21). Although industry participants, especially local parts firms, have long called for the creation of testing facilities, only in 2015 did the Department of Science and Technology launch a decidedly modest Auto-Parts Testing Facility (Department of Science and Technology 2015).

Attention to another crucial component of technological capacity—skills formation—has also been in short supply, both in the economy overall, where labor productivity has been weak both in the economy overall, rising only 1.6% annually between 2001 and 2010 (Bitonio 2012: 6), and in the automotive sector more specifically (Aldaba 2008: 28). The instability of the workforce discourages firms and workers from investing in skills formation. Philippine laws require firms to change the status of contract workers to *regular* employees after six months. Given the cyclical nature of the industry and the volatility of automotive policymaking, firms avoid this requirement by laying off contracted workers before the six-month period expires and hiring a new batch. The resulting labor turnover and informality (estimated at between 40% and 60% of the employed workforce [Ofreneo 2016, 122]) discourages long-term investments in skills (Aldaba 2007: 41).

Nor has organized labor been active in promoting technical and vocational training. The Automotive Industry Workers Association (AIWA), an alliance of 15 union affiliates whose 20,000 members comprise 27% of the industry's approximately 75,000 workers (Department of Trade and Industry and Board of Investments n.d.), has focused on strikes, the smuggling problem, and tariffs rather than skill development. Mitsubishi's transmission operation faced union strikes every three years during the 1980s, and in 1998 and 2000 Mitsubishi and Toyota assembly affiliates also experienced debilitating strikes protesting layoffs following the Asian financial crisis (Ofreneo 2008: 76; Aldaba 2007: 26). In 2001, an alliance of the AIWA and unions aimed at protecting jobs by reducing smuggling and opposing tariff reductions on completely-built-up vehicles (CBUs) under AFTA resulted in the creation of a Tripartite Industry Council for the Automotive Industry in cooperation with the Department of Labor and Employment (DOLE) (Fashoyin 2003: 23; Ofreneo 2008: 76). The Council was active during the term of President Arroyo in the early 2000s, but it had little to say about skills or productivity, and soon fell dormant (personal communication from Prof. Rene Ofreneo, May 17, 2017). This experience follows a general Filipino pattern in which collective bargaining routinely ignores questions of productivity enhancement (Bitonio 2012: 32; Fashoyin 2003: 35).

Infrastructure

The emphasis of the auto industry's 2016 road map on improving infrastructure reflects major gaps in the Philippines' roads, ports, airports, and water and energy supply (Aldaba 2016b). The World Economic Forum's *Global Competitiveness Report 2016–2017* ranked the Philippines a lowly 95 out of 138 countries surveyed for physical infrastructure, and 91 for quality of institutions. On both measures, the Philippines trailed not only Malaysia, Thailand, and Indonesia, but even developmental latecomer Vietnam (Schwab 2016: 46–47, 297). The state of "soft" infrastructure is equally poor. The country lags not only Malaysia and Thailand, but also Vietnam and in some cases Indonesia, on measures such as ICT access, numbers of researchers, R&D expenditures as percentage of GDP, university-industry collaboration, quality of scientific research institutions, and company spending on R&D (Quimba and Rosellon 2011: 20; Symaco 2013: 189–192).

Philippine Institutions

Ill-conceived and inconsistent policies in the Philippine auto industry reflect serious institutional weaknesses. Fragmentation was not apparent, however, in the earliest automotive development program (Doner 1991: Ch. 7). The Board of Investment officials designing the PCMP program were technically well-informed in their formulation of policies aimed at combining efficient localization with export promotion. The political situation also seemed propitious, at least for implementation. When President Marcos proclaimed martial law in 1972, the Philippines seemed like an emerging "developmental state": the BOI, autonomous from recalcitrant local economic interests, could "rule" as Marcos "reigned." In practice, however, the efforts of technocrats to implement core features of the PCMP were stymied not only by the inter-agency divisions and the ambivalence of the main automotive association noted earlier, but also by Marcos's intervention on behalf of a crony who owned the local Toyota assembly operation.

An interval of institutional reinvigoration followed the collapse of the PCMP. The Department of Trade and Industry and the Board of Investment assumed leadership. The Philippine Institute of Development Studies accumulated important industry-specific knowledge, as reflected in a series of high-quality discussion papers on automotive development (e.g., Aldaba 2007, 2008).

Yet institutional fragmentation soon reasserted itself. First, the conflicts between the BOI and the macroeconomic agencies focusing on immediate revenue collections have continued, as have inter-agency tensions over smuggled vehicles. Second, the minimal role of the Department of Science and Technology and weak coordination among existing R&D and educational institutions have undermined efforts at industrial diffusion (Quimba and Rosellon 2011: 63). In line with strict neoclassical assumptions, the country has proceeded as if opening the economy would raise the technological base of the country automatically (Ofreneo 2017; 2015: 119). Similarly, the Department of Labor and Employment (DOLE) has focused more on wages than productivity (Doner 2015b). Tellingly, the Labor Department agency devoted to skill formation, the Technical Education and Skills Development Authority (TESDA), has no ongoing linkages with the DTI's recently established Auto Parts Testing Facility (personal communication from TESDA official, Qualifications and Standards Office, June 14, 2017).

Private sector divisions at both national and (automotive) sectoral levels have mirrored and reinforced bureaucratic fragmentation. In the early 1990s, support for trade liberalization by the country's major peak business association, the Philippines Chamber of Commerce and Industry, triggered the creation of a rival association, the Federation of Philippine Industries (FPI). Led by a prominent domestic auto parts producer, the FPI worked to promote the interests of domestic industries by fighting against smuggling and criticizing liberal economic policies as favoring foreign capital (Mikamo 2013: 17). But local parts firms lacked the leverage of the key pro-liberalization groups, especially those dominated by foreign firms or their local partners. The Chamber of Auto Manufacturers of the Philippines (CAMPI), the Motor Vehicle Parts Manufacturers Association of the Philippines (MVPMAP), and the Philippine Automotive Competitiveness Council Inc. (PACCI) focused on liberalizing trade to facilitate entry into regional and global value chains. Importers, represented by the Association of Vehicle Importers and Distributors (AVID), also favored liberalization. Not surprisingly, this fragmentation within the private sector also impeded the creation of sector-wide, public-private coordinating institutions like Thailand's Automotive Institute (Aldaba 2007: 34).

Government officials, facing the prospect of increased economic integration in ASEAN, attempted to address the problems of institutional fragmentation by introducing the Manufacturing Resurgence Program (MRP) in 2012 and the Industrial Priorities Plan (IPP) in 2014 (Raquiza 2015: Ch. 3). The automotive-specific CARS program grew out of close consultation between the DTI, the Philippine Institute of Development Studies, and an at least nominally consolidated private sector under the aegis of the foreign-dominated PACCI. The CARS program was the most developed of the 29 industrial road maps submitted to the DTI as of June 2015 (Mangulabnan 2015: 1; Raquiza 2015: 20).

Two crucial actors have been only minimally involved in this nascent corporatist effort, however: parts producers and labor. Local parts firms were not listed as participants in the public-private team responsible for the CARS program, and only a few firms linked to MNCs have qualified for participation in the program itself (Canivel 2017). Organized labor is also conspicuous by its absence. The analysis of human resource development planning cited in the industry road maps makes no mention of organized labor, even as it explicitly notes the positive, productivity-enhancing roles of unions in Singapore (Mangulabnan 2015; see also Fashoyin 2003: 35).

Moreover, divisions within the state soon began to undermine the implementation of the MRP and CARS. According to one DTI official, the former was closer to a "hodge-podge of programs from various agencies" than a comprehensive industrial policy (Raquiza 2015: 25). The whole effort was initiated by a small number of DTI officials, but the department lacked the resources to function as a lead agency for such an ambitious effort. Further, DTI's efforts have run up against widespread skepticism in the Department of Finance and elsewhere about even a deliberately market-conforming industrial policy. As one economist noted, "industrial policy" has bad connotations in the Philippines, both because of its link to crony capitalism under Marcos and because the state has historically been so inefficient: ". . . if government can't even collect garbage well, how can they do industrial policy?" (cited in Raquiza 2015: 30).

Despite these obstacles, the CARS program marked the most advanced effort to date to promote manufacturing. In part, it reflected pressure from global automakers to create the minimal measures necessary to incorporate Philippine operations into regional production networks. But even the best-case scenario for the CARS program—an assembly-led sector with even less local participation than in Thailand—is questionable in light of the overall weakness of the Philippine state, even compared to Thailand. In late 2019, one observer warned that the CARS program was headed for an "epic fail" as the government's tax reform increased government revenues but weakened domestic demand (Gamboa 2019).

Philippine Politics

External Security

The Philippines is an archipelago and faces no external threats that would require a strong military backed by a robust industrial base. That is not to say that the country has never faced security crises. The colonial struggle, first against Spain and then against the United States (1898–1902), the invasion by Japan in World War II, threats from the Soviet Union during the Cold War, and pressure from China in the South China Sea all impressed upon Filipino leaders an indelible lesson: no feasible military buildup would enable the Philippines to withstand the might of industrialized powers such as Japan,

Russia, or China. However, as long as Manila went along with the dominant power, the United States, the country was safe. Thus, in 1951 Manila signed a security treaty that allowed the United States to maintain major air and naval facilities in the Philippines. Natural disasters and popular dissatisfaction forced the United States out in the early 1990s, but the security guarantee remained intact, and by 2012 concern over pressure from China led to a partial reopening of the Subic Bay Naval Base and Clark Air Base to US forces.

Even after a minor buildup under President Benigno Aquino III (2010–2016) in response to the perceived threat from China and greater spending in other ASEAN countries, the military effort of the Philippines remains distinctly modest at about 1.3% of GDP (World Bank). The Philippines has not felt the need to create a significant military-industrial complex that might catalyze the auto industry.

Resource Revenues

Agriculture constituted an important source of foreign exchange and government revenues for much of the 20th century, with sugar accounting for roughly one-fourth of the country's total exports from the late 1940s until 1974 (Doner 2009: 171). As late as 2015, primary commodity exports such as ores and metals, agricultural raw materials, food, and fuel exports amounted to 15.1% of total merchandise exports (World Bank 2018c). Other non-trade-related inflows complemented natural resource revenues: "As long as the system was being lubricated by external funds," especially foreign loans and aid from the United States, and revenues from US bases, "there was no need to make any hard decisions regarding contending economic paths" (Hutchcroft 1991: 426).

The bases closed in the early 1990s, but remittances from overseas Filipino workers (OFW) took their place to become "the economic life-raft that inhibits sustained efforts toward the emergence of a more coherent economic development strategy" (Blank 2014: 284). The "manpower export" effort began in the mid-1970s as a stopgap employment program to provide opportunities for those unemployed owing to the stunted growth of manufacturing. Manufacturing's share of employment fell from 11.9% in 1970 to 8.4% in 2010, while agriculture's share remained high at 33% (Ofreneo 2015: 115). This temporary solution, however, has become a key feature of the Philippine economy: an estimated 10 million Filipinos were working abroad as of 2013, accounting for roughly 18% of the working-age population (Fund 2015: 16). Remittances rose from 1.9% of GDP in 1980 to a high of 13.3% in 2005, before declining to over 9% in 2015, still far more than in most other lower middle-income countries (Burgess and Vikram 2005: 5).

The impact of remittances on overall Philippine growth is inconclusive (Burgess and Vikram 2005), but from the perspective of industrial diffusion, reliance on remittance revenues is pernicious. They have allowed the government to avoid difficult poverty-reduction tasks and have reduced citizens' incentives to hold the government accountable (Barajas et al. 2016: 41). In the absence of a public institution devoted to channeling remittances into developmental activities such as the expansion of manufactured exports, as was the case in South Korea (Stahl 1986: 921), they have served mainly to boost the consumer-oriented informal economy. Only recently, under the Duterte administration, has the government initiated a migrant labor bank devoted to harnessing the remittances that now go through the informal financial system (personal message from official in Philippines' Office of the President, August 22, 2020). Remittances have also contributed to real currency appreciation, which reduces export competitiveness. Remittances have also helped stabilize capital flows (Fund 2015: 22), thus reducing the balance of payments pressures that have spurred leaders in Thailand (and, to a lesser extent, Indonesia) to invest in efficient export manufacturing. The continuous increase in remittances did contribute to the surge in buying power that in turn inspired the CARS program (Ramboa 2019). But remittances also moderated pressure to address the program's weaknesses noted earlier, not to speak of the country's minimal efforts to increase automotive-related skills.

Domestic Political Pressures: The Persistence of Clans and Clientelism

Philippine elites have not been pressured by contentious domestic politics to invest in broader growth-promoting institutions. The country has confronted prolonged regional insurgencies, including the communist "Huk" rebellion from the 1940s until 1965 and the Moro insurgency by Muslim rebels in Mindanao and related southern islands, especially since 1969. But the Huks never exerted a strong impact outside their central Luzon heartland. The Muslim resistance consists mainly of small-scale activities such as kidnappings and bombings that do not require and cannot be solved by a mechanized military response (Slater 2010). The 2017 uprising by the Islamic State–backed Maute group in Marawi, Mindanao, was a shocking exception, but it actually drew the government, traditional Muslim activists, and neighboring Muslim-dominant states closer together, and reinforced the central roles of dialogue and diplomacy rather than military force in combating the insurgency (Cook 2017).

This lack of broad-based, contentious politics, reinforced by the availability of labor remittances, has resulted in "the absence of any national programme-based organisations—i.e. either political movements or parties—that might link the actions of politicians to a specific national agenda" (Medalla, Fabella, and de Dios 2014: 14). Indeed, Montinola (1999: 135) describes Philippine parties as "merely temporary electoral and legislative alliances designed to maximize the election chances of individual politicians." Unusual features of the Philippine budgetary process further discourage stable, programmatic parties (Abinales and Amoroso 2017: 315–316; Montinola 1999: 136). Congressmen and senators each receive individual development allocations that support particularistic rather than broad, programmatic initiatives. Further, the president wields sole control over large swaths of the national budget, including a Presidential Social Fund supplemented by revenues from sources such as the state-owned gambling facility and joint ventures with multinational oil companies. This system of "pork as governance" provides the president with great leverage over members of Congress, who typically switch to the president's party after elections. The result is non-programmatic, personalistic, or clan-based clientelistic parties, dominated by persistently powerful landed interests (e.g., Goodman 2019). Short time horizons sabotage the time-consuming efforts required to create durable institutions, such as business-government consultative groups or sectoral testing centers (Noble 2017). Free from major external threats and dominated by clientelism, Philippine politics has repeatedly foiled efforts to coordinate policy, look to the long term, and develop public-private institutions for industrial diffusion. Hutchcroft's mid-1990s summary of the importance of external support remains true today: "while plundered internally . . . [the Philippine state] . . . is repeatedly rescued externally" (Hutchcroft 1994: 226; Abinales and Amoroso 2017).

Indonesia: Toward Extensive Development

After a long series of failed efforts at more "intensive" automotive production, Indonesia has become more successful than the Philippines at emulating Thailand's strategy of attaining scale economies by liberalizing trade and encouraging investment by MNCs. Yet, the industry really opened up only after the Asian financial crisis, over a decade after Thailand began shifting to export promotion. Indonesia's wrenching policy shift responded to calamitous domestic economic collapse and resulted in an even weaker indigenous automotive presence than in Thailand.

Indonesian Automotive Performance

Two articles published 15 years apart in the same journal capture the evolution of the country's auto industry. In 2000, the authors of "How Not to Industrialize? Indonesia's Automotive Industry" described the industry as a "classic case of an infant industry which has failed to grow up." The industry suffered from serious market fragmentation and exported barely 1% of its production, the lowest share in the region (Aswicahyono, Basri, and Hill 2000). Fifteen years later, Natsuda, Otsuka, and Thoburn (2015) more optimistically asked whether the industry's trajectory might represent a "Dawn of Industrialization" by virtue of rising vehicle and parts production, growing FDI, and potential for local upgrading within joint ventures.

Indeed, the country's vehicle production rose from under 100,000 in the mid-1970s to over 389,000 units in 1997. After diving to only 58,000 in the wake of the 1998 Asian financial crisis, production rebounded to over a million vehicles by 2017 (Figure 5.3) (Natsuda, Otsuka, and Thoburn 2015; Gaikindo [Association of Indonesian Automotive Industry] 2019, #963; ASEAN Automotive Federation 2019). The industry contributed some $5 billion in exports and employed around 1.5 million people in 2018 (Gaikindo 2019; Awiscahyono et al. 2018: 145). Multipurpose passenger vehicles

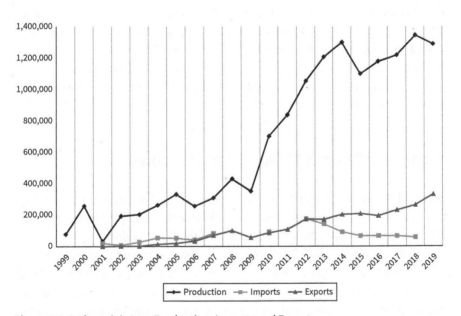

Figure 5.3 Indonesia's Auto Production, Imports and Exports.
Sources: Gaikindo (Association of Indonesia Automotive Industries), <https://www.gaikindo.or.id/> and UN Comtrade data.

(MPVs), also known as "people carriers," dominate the industry, accounting for two-thirds of production, followed by pickup trucks (Thoburn and Natsuda 2017). The country's major assemblers are almost all affiliated with Japanese companies: affiliates of Daihatsu (a subsidiary of Toyota specializing in small cars) have the largest production capacity (530,000 vehicles), followed by Suzuki (270,000), Nissan and Toyota (250,000 each), and Honda (200,000) (Investments 2018).

Despite its impressive growth, the industry reveals some important weaknesses. Capacity utilization has been relatively low, at 62% of installed capacity of 2 million vehicles (Aswicahyono, Christian, and Faur 2018). In addition, the trade deficit has mushroomed alongside the industry's expansion— from $487 million in 2017 to $1.3 billion in 2018—(Gaikindo [Association of Indonesian Automotive Industry] 2019). The problem is not with vehicles, but rather with parts and components. Vehicle exports increased from 56,000 in 2009 to close to 200,000 in 2017: the dollar value of exports rose from $2.8 billion in 2014 to $3.2 billion in 2018 vs. imports of $2.1 billion in 2014 to $2.8 billion in 2018 (Investments 2018).

Low levels of imported vehicles may reflect the launch of better quality (Japanese) vehicles assembled in and exported from Indonesia, but probably more important are two factors that made imports more expensive: inflation (driven by increased fuel costs due in turn to cuts in fuel subsidies) and a weakened rupiah (Investments 2018). The chief source of the automotive trade deficit lies in the country's reliance on parts imports. From only $59 million just prior to the Asian financial crisis, parts exports reached $1.01 billion in 2008, but, despite government efforts to promote the country as a vehicle and parts manufacturing hub, fell to just $45.2 million in 2010 following the global financial crisis (EIBN [EU-Indonesia Business Network] 2015: 12) and, after rebounding fell again after 2012 (Figure 5.4). Export totals then rose to $1.6 billion in 2014 and $2.1 billion in 2018, but imports totaled $2.9 billion in 2014 and rose to $3.8 billion in 2018 (Gaikindo 2019).

Increasing FDI, especially from Japan, has been key to the industry's expansion. As of 2013, Toyota and its subsidiary Daihatsu accounted for 55% of auto output, Suzuki 15%, and Mitsubishi 11% (Gaikindo 2014). Automotive investments increased tenfold over the 2009–2013 period to $3.7 billion, involving over 570 project proposals from foreign investors and 57 from domestic interests (BDO 2014).

This FDI was attracted largely by Indonesia's present and potential market size. The country has a population of 264 million and has sustained an average economic growth rate of over 5% per year since 2000. Indonesian car ownership in the early 2010s was only 80 per 1,000 people, compared with 123

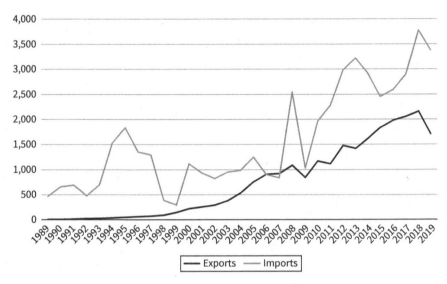

Figure 5.4 Indonesia: Trade in auto components (US$ millions).
Source: Production data from Oica.net; imports and exports from UN Comtrade database.

in Thailand and 300 in Malaysia (EIBN [EU-Indonesia Business Network] 2015). FDI has also been attracted by Indonesia's participation in regional production networks. Indonesia is Toyota's regional production site for gasoline engines and one of four global supply bases for its IMV (Innovative International Multi-Purpose Vehicle) program (Takii 2004: 26).

The industry suffers from severe weaknesses. As the industry has expanded, the role of local firms has shrunk (Takii 2004: 4). Three large local firms, including Astra, at one point the most promising local manufacturer, have exited production of OEM parts to focus on distribution and sales (Natsuda, Otsuka, and Thoburn 2015; Abimanyu 1997). A firm in the Astra group does produce spare parts (Indonesia-investmetns.com/business/Indonesian-companies/astra-otoparts/item930), but overall, local producers have operated at "the lowest position in the value chain ladder."

Indonesian Automotive Policies, Institutions, and Politics

In addition to building on increased demand fueled by political stability and prudent macro policies (EIBN [EU-Indonesia Business Network] 2015: 15), Indonesia's recent success in pursuing an extensive growth strategy reflects sector-specific policy shifts. In this section, we identify these changes, their institutional corollaries, and the broader political factors influencing these shifts.

Indonesian Policies
Trade and Investment
In the 1990s, Indonesian automotive policy shifted from heavy protection, predicated on enhancing "national resilience," to broad liberalization (Doner 2009: 260–266). The protectionist stage, which ran from the early 1960s to the mid-1990s, began with a localization effort promoting ethnic Indonesian (*pribumi*) entrepreneurs via tariffs on CBU imports, and then shifted to a combination of CBU import bans and targeted mandatory deletion measures. The government eventually focused on locally produced axles, engines, and transmissions to promote links between foreign assemblers and local components firms. These ambitious plans were predicated on growing domestic demand and access to government subsidies, both dependent on revenues produced by the oil boom of the late 1970s and early 1980s.

The collapse of oil prices from 1986 compelled policymakers to focus on short-term efficiency. They replaced the mandatory, item-by-item localization strategy with a more market-based incentive policy in 1993 (Thee 2012: 278) and abolished limits on foreign ownership in automotive manufacturing, which stimulated expansion of local production by Japanese subcontractors in Indonesia (KPMG 2014: 4). Tariff reductions also stimulated local parts and components firms making low-technology accessories, but only a few local parts firms could efficiently produce OEM products, and even then, only by assembling imported parts for the domestic market (Thee 2012: 278–280).

In 1996, buoyed by a temporary upswing in oil prices, the government attempted a last-gasp effort to sponsor an integrated auto industry based on Indonesian producers (Aminullah and Adnan 2011). As with Malaysia's Proton, Indonesia's "national car" program granted hefty tax and tariff exemptions to automakers producing cars bearing Indonesian brand names and supposedly developed with domestic engineering and designs. In the event, the benefits went only to the "Timor," a compact car to be produced by President Suharto's youngest son in a joint venture with Korea's Kia (Chalmers 1998). Unlike the Proton, however, the Timor died a quick death during the Asian financial crisis owing to protests from rival producers, a ruling that Indonesia had violated the WTO's Agreement on Subsidies and Countervailing Measures, and the country's acceptance of an IMF structural adjustment program requiring it to end local content requirements and to remove tariff and non-tariff barriers.

The failure of the national car scheme, the last gasp of significant protectionism, triggered significant liberalization. In 1999, the government introduced a simpler, more liberal tariff system. Beginning in 2006, the government abolished import tariffs on car components and spare parts for exported units, exempted raw materials for components, harmonized tariffs, ended restrictions on imports of whole vehicles, eased foreign ownership limits, and began participating in regional trade agreements andcomplementation schemes (KPMG 2014; EIBN [EU-Indonesia Business Network] 2015).

Rationalization, Scale Economies, and Efficient Localization

Previous efforts at rationalization had fallen victim to politics. Through the early 1990s, Indonesian politics was marked by patrimonial arrangements involving myriad interests in and out of government that feasted on state contracts. The national oil company, Pertamina, purchased a large number of local vehicles and provided key funds for upstream industries, including the inefficient, state-owned Krakatau Steel, which was intended to supply steel for the local production of automotive parts (Chalmers 1994: 23, 162). As a result, the auto industry "probably attracted more rent seeking activity than any other major manufacturing activity in the country" (Aswicahyono and Feridhanusetyawan 2004: 17).

Market fragmentation also resulted from the structure of the Indonesian private sector. Each major domestic business group established a "Trademark Holding Sole Agent" controlling several automakers, each of which typically produced more than one foreign brand and was anxious to maintain its separate sales network. The original hope was that this arrangement would facilitate the technology transfer process. In fact, it led to a proliferation of brands that undermined standardization and impeded formation of close links between foreign firms and local partners (Aswicahyono 2000: 219, 33).

The post-AFC reforms included a number of measures designed to promote localization through greater scale economies. First, the government encouraged a reduction in the number of brands and models by transforming Indonesian Trademark Holders from assemblers into mere distributors (Indonesian Commercial Newsletter 2004). Second, in 2009 the government began identifying promising vehicle types. The policy was crystallized in the 2013 introduction of incentives and tax breaks to producers of low-cost green cars (EIBN [EU-Indonesia Business Network] 2015: 13–14), sales of which rose from 51,180 in 2013 to 234,554 in 2017 (Investments 2018). In addition, the government introduced an "incomplete knocked-down" policy (Natsuda, Otsuka, and Thoburn 2015: 57). By imposing lower tariff rates on subcomponents than on CKD parts, the government aims to promote the local assembly of CKD parts by, for example, importing and assembling engine parts rather than importing engines. The hope is that moving upstream in assembly will encourage greater transfer of technology and know-how from foreign firms.

Technological Upgrading

Despite several decades of promotion and foreign engagement, Indonesian parts firms have suffered from poor productivity and a general inability to meet OEM standards (Thee 2012: 292–294). Indonesian firms have failed to keep up with global industry standards even in the production of labor-intensive, low-tech parts. Industry sources reported that of the original 900 or so independent body parts producers, only 10 survived as of 2007, and those worked only on specialty parts, especially for buses (interviews with Thee Kian Wie, July 12, 2007, and with head of Giamm, July 11, 2007, Jakarta). Local firms are especially weak at assessing and acquiring technology, particularly now that the large manufacturing conglomerates are no longer involved in auto production. The few surviving local suppliers focus largely on replacement parts, but unlike the export-oriented Taiwanese firms, the Indonesians have been limited to the *local* aftermarket (Thee 2012: 292).

These problems reflect weak and inconsistent government technology policies. Most local parts firms lack "links with global, regional, or even local R&D institutes" (Thee 2007: 44). This weakness is especially striking in light of a grandiose technology promotion effort led by B. J. Habibie, a German-trained aerospace engineer and future president, called home by President Suharto in 1976 to head the well-funded Agency for Assessment and Application of Technology (Badan Pengkajian dan Penerapan Teknologi BPPT) (McKendrick 1992). Habibie focused on the development of an Indonesian aviation industry, but there is no evidence that Habibie's efforts led to technology spillovers for economy as a whole, much less for the automotive industry. Nor did these high-tech efforts trigger any general increase in R&D or skills development. As of 2013, the country's R&D spending amounted to only around 0.08% of GDP, far lower than the 0.21% in Thailand (2007), 1.13% in Malaysia (2012), and 4.03% in South Korea (2012) (World Bank).

There is also no evidence of strong technology support services in metrology, standards, testing, and quality support (MSTQ). The Asian financial crisis reduced the already minimal funds available for standards and testing, and the situation has not improved since then. With only one laboratory qualified to test all component parameters, domestic certification remains expensive and time-consuming for smaller domestic firms (Tijaja and Faisal 2014: 11; EIBN [EU-Indonesia Business Network] 2015: 39–40). Automotive testing is thus largely in the hands of foreign firms who are focused on reducing delays in certifying imported products for the local market rather than facilitating technology upgrading by local producers.

Infrastructure

Poor roads, railroads, and ports stifle progress toward extensive development. An acute shortage of good roads, especially in the Jakarta area, has impeded the capacity of companies to ship products along the supply chain (EIBN [EU-Indonesia Business Network] 2015). Weaknesses in infrastructure are especially problematic for smaller, local firms, which face high shipping costs and bureaucratic delays (Pasha and Setiati 2011). Infrastructure development has been plagued by a lack of financing due to a tax collection rate so low that it trails even those of Cambodia and the Philippines (Kim 2017), inter-ministerial conflicts, and clashes between central government officials and newly empowered localities. Road building has become a long and complex political problem (Davidson 2015).

Indonesian Institutions

Policies for the automotive sector have been plagued by deficiencies in expertise, coordination, and monitoring, presenting numerous rent-seeking opportunities to domestic political interests. These policy deficiencies have ceded key decision-making to the multinationals, and have undermined measures to strengthen the technological capacities of local parts firms.

Localization efforts in the early 1970s were led by the Ministry of Industry's Directorate for Basic Industries. Allied with Pertamina, supported by the assemblers and parts associations, and leading an Inter-Departmental Permanent Committee on the auto industry, the Directorate appeared to be in a strong position to implement the 1976 policy governing mandatory deletions from imported kits. But over the next 15 years, bureaucratic effectiveness was undermined by conflicts between Industry ministers and leaders of the Directorate, between the Ministry and the Capital Investment Coordinating Board (BKPM), which wielded enormous discretionary power (Lewis 1994: 8), and between the Directorate's willingness to cooperate with foreign producers and the more techno-nationalist approaches of Habibie's Agency for Assessment and Application of Technology (BPPT). The role of foreign producers became especially important in the early 1980s as the second oil price rise triggered an effort to encourage MNCs to support localization of engine components by local firms. Both the Ministry and the BKPM, however, lacked the capacity and will to monitor the foreign firms. As the official responsible for negotiations with the foreign auto firms noted, "the private sector wanted to invest in engine production, so the government pulled right out. Why should we worry?" (Chalmers 1994: 30). Left to their own devices, few local firms were in a position to negotiate with the giant multinationals for enhanced access to technology.

By the late 1980s, declining oil revenues pushed the Industry Ministry to pursue a more efficiency-based strategy, culminating in the 1993 "incentive" policy. The level of concertation in this effort, described by Chalmers (1998: 2) was striking: the "Department of Industry came to rely on business for policy suggestions. The automotive producers' associations . . . were centrally involved in drafting new decrees." The parts producers' association, Giamm, was particularly active in working out the details of the incentive program (author interview, former Giamm director, July 11, 2007, Jakarta). Consistent with our argument, this higher level of public-private engagement developed under the pressure of temporary resource constraints.

Unlike in Taiwan, Korea, and eventually China, however, Indonesia's resource shortage was episodic, not endemic. Nor did it occur in the context of an external security threat. As a result, this incipient corporatist arrangement was short-lived. The runup to the Asian financial crisis witnessed not only Tommy Suharto's infamous "national car," but also a merger of the Ministries of Industry and Commerce in 1995 that weakened the resulting Ministry of Trade and Industry, not least because President Suharto named an infamously corrupt crony, Bob Hasan, as minister of the new agency (interviews with Astra managers and association officials, July 9–12, 2007, Jakarta). Technocrats emphasizing the need for macroeconomic stability and the benefits of reliance on multinationals clashed with the highly subsidized push for self-reliant technological development by Habibie, and with those who used nationalism, as in the case of the "national car," as a cover for simple rent-seeking.

Since Suharto's ousting, the Industry Ministry (again separated from Commerce in 2004) has been hobbled by a lack of coordination among its numerous and frequently rotating directors general, most of whom are selected by new ministers and have little expertise. According to an official in the Ministry of Industry interviewed in 2007, the agency had almost 40 directors general, one for each sector. Combined with intense inter-party competition in a strengthened legislature, instability and fragmentation caused auto import licensing to become a source of corruption (interview, July 9, 2007). In addition, the Ministries of Industry and Trade have clashed on issues ranging from tariffs on auto parts to the identity and number of sectors marked off limits to foreign investors (Patunru and Rahardja 2015). The Ministry of Industry itself has lacked stable, technocratic leadership. These complex institutional arrangements reflect a persistent "broad spectrum" policy, one that combines pragmatic, technocratic perspectives in some areas, such as greater openness to automotive MNCs, with a statist-nationalist ideology in others, as in continuing automotive tariffs. Tariff relief is possible, but the process, which was transferred from the Finance to the Industry Ministry, is lengthy and therefore costly, especially for smaller domestic firms. Indeed, tariff relief and the procurement of environmental approval and standards certification constitute significant "unnecessary regulatory burdens" (Aswicahyono et al. 2018). These increase costs for all firms, but one can assume that the burdens are especially heavy for smaller domestic producers.

Finally, technology support services have been weak. Thee (2006) highlighted the low level of MSTQ services and the general disconnect between already weak public-sector research institutes and industry, as well as the problem of ministerial fragmentation (Aswicahyono et al. 2011: 32). This set of problems impeded even the limited spillovers potentially available from arrangements such as the Indonesia-Japan Economic Partnership Agreement (IJEPA) (Pasha and Setiati 2011: 141).

Policymakers have not been oblivious to the need for development planning, not least in the automotive sector. But efforts have been unimpressive. In 2011, the government announced a Master Plan for Acceleration and Expansion of Indonesia Economic Development (MP3EI). The plan focuses on 15 subsectors, of which one is automotive components and accessories. But an Asian Development Bank (ADB) analysis highlighted the plan's institutional weaknesses, especially limited coordination among stakeholders and lack of enforcement (Tijaja and Faisal 2014: 16). Similarly, in 2013 the government proposed an Indonesian Automotive Research and Development Institute (INARD) to support local firms, with a focus on low-cost green cars (Indrawanto 2013). However, this initiative operates under the Ministry of Education and Culture, and there is no indication that it has accomplished anything. Finally, a 2015 National Industry Development Plan designed to promote the production of new products, including electric vehicles, stipulates the need for technology development in areas such as new materials for batteries but makes no mention of related testing and research facilities or technical training programs (Gaikindo 2019).

Indonesian Politics
External Security
Indonesia has not faced conventional external threats to national security (Campbell 2012: 49). Since Suharto became president and *Konfrontasi* against Malaysia ended, the country has enjoyed a benign regional and global order.

Its closest neighbors—Singapore and Malaysia—are small and militarily in-significant. Territorial disputes are trivial. As part of island Southeast Asia, Indonesia was insulated from the Indochina conflicts on the mainland. All of this translated into a pragmatic, low-profile foreign policy, the smallest mili-tary budget in Asia (never over 1% of GDP), and a military focused only on internal threats (Nehru 2015). It also translated into a striking lack of pres-sure to integrate industrial technology efforts, such as Habibie's, noted ear-lier, with the country's national security structures (McKendrick 1992: 62–63; Campbell 2012: 48).

Resource Revenues

Natural resources have been a consistent albeit volatile component of the Indonesian economy (Thee 2006: 345–346). As of 2015 the broad category of "energy and natural resources" still accounted for 24% of the country's GDP, and coal was the country's most valuable export (Dutu 2015: 7, 23). The relative importance of oil and gas industries has declined since the boom years of the early 1980s. In fact, with stagnating domestic oil production and rising consumption, Indonesia now depends on *imports* for almost half of its oil consumption. But volatility is not limited to oil. Prices of coal and crude palm oil, which now dominate the country's exports (contributing one-third of total exports), are also unstable and are strongly influenced by oil, as falling oil prices have led to falling coal and palm oil prices (Thee 2006: 345–346).

The volume and volatility of resource revenues have swayed the evolution of Indonesian automotive policy and related institutions (e.g., Aswicahyono 2000). Facing economic chaos and high levels of debt in 1965, Suharto followed "Sadli's law" by deferring to pressure from neoclassical economists to drastically reduce state intervention. But the quadrupling of world oil prices in the early 1970s generated a tsunami of revenue and triggered au-tomotive localization movements, especially the 1976 and 1983 efforts to use mandatory deletion to raise local contents. The dramatic increase in oil prices simultaneously attracted foreign automakers anxious to benefit from Indonesia's oil-fed prosperity (Chalmers 1994: 18) and fueled Indonesian eco-nomic nationalism. In 1974, riots targeted Toyota and its local partner, Astra, prompting Astra to show its nationalist credentials by supporting the 1976 and 1983 localization programs (Chalmers 1994: 25). State-owned Pertamina bolstered this strategy. Until 1976, the company's director ran *eight* auto as-sembly, import, and distribution operations (Doner 1991: 249). Oil rents also financed state-owned enterprises in automotive-related upstream industries, including the steel producer Krakatau (Tijaja and Faisal 2014: 7). Overall, oil provided a "cushion" that permitted inefficient industrial expansion, as illustrated in the mandatory deletion programs (Lewis 1994: 9).

That cushion proved unreliable. The collapse of oil prices in early 1986, combined with the obvious inefficiencies of the mandatory deletion program, led to the more market-oriented 1993 incentive policy. The result was a dual-track strategy, with competing ministries backing rival strategies (Thee 2006: 344–345; 2012: 103). Along with the limits on localization measures imposed by the IMF and WTO in the wake of the Asian financial crisis, the lack of *stable* resource rents has exerted strong pressure to abandon the protectionist track and pursue an export-led, extensive automotive strategy, albeit one laced with strains of protectionism.

Domestic Political Pressures

Early Indonesian automotive policy was heavily influenced by a concern for *pribumi* entrepreneurs and, subsequently, domestic firms in general. Unlike in Malaysia, however, such pressures have dissipated. Outbreaks of ethnic and religious violence, although more frequent in recent years, have been limited. Further, Indonesia has no equivalent of Malaysia's UMNO (i.e., an ethnic- and religious-based organization dominating national politics), although in recent years the influence of political Islam has increased in a number of parties. Further, the general trend of Indonesian politics has been toward more distributive than programmatic political parties. Such parties have formed "cartels"—coalitions of parties sharing power and spoils through control of specific ministries, despite having opposed each other in elections (Slater 2018). The result is to encourage short-term gains while discouraging clear policy positions and weakening efforts to create effective institutions for activities with long-term payoffs, such as industrial diffusion.

Conclusion

The weaknesses of the Philippines and Indonesian auto industries—the absence of strong local firms with robust linkages to assemblers, the unsystematic way in which each country liberalized toward a more extensive development strategy, and the persistence of protectionism and rent-seeking in automotive policies—are unsurprising in light of the relatively moderate challenges each faced relative to the Northeast Asian cases and even Thailand. Neither has faced serious external threats, the Philippines owing to US protection along with geographical location, Indonesia owing to its size and location. Both have had access to resource-related funds beyond even those available to Thailand, while neither has faced pressing claims on these finances. The Philippines enjoyed extensive foreign aid, loans, and military spending into the mid-1980s and has subsequently had access to both commodity export revenues and remittances that still account for roughly 10% of GDP. Indonesia has had access to various types of mineral revenues which, despite the declining significance of oil and gas, still account for almost a quarter of GDP. Finally, popular pressures that would require significant resources have been largely episodic and place specific. In both cases, these conditions have translated into institutional weaknesses in areas such as technology support, trade policy, and infrastructure development most starkly different not only from the Northeast Asian cases, but also from the institutions supporting Thailand's fairly consistent shift to extensive growth beginning in the early 1980s.

Finally, how do we account for the differences between the two cases? How do we explain the Philippines' weak assembly, thin supplier base, and high imports—what Ofreneo (2008) labeled "arrested development"—versus what we might call Indonesia's "delayed development," in which the country gradually but more effectively liberalized and promoted a sizable expansion of domestic automotive assembly?

At one level, the explanation lies in institutions. Although Indonesia's ministries have exhibited inter-agency conflicts and suffer from a lack of expertise, they have coalesced around a minimum set of liberalization policies, including loosened foreign ownership limits and tariff reforms. Similar reforms in the Philippines have been undermined by more intense inter-agency differences, such as between the Department of Trade and Industry and the Land Transport Office, that have resulted in significant numbers of imported vehicles, and by strong divisions among private sector automotive interests.

The more critical question has to do with the origins of institutional differences. Economic constraints fueling a push toward overall reform, including more efficient extensive development in the auto sector, were weaker in the Philippines than in Indonesia. Remittances constituted a more consistent source of revenue for the Philippines than highly fluctuating oil and palm oil revenues did for Indonesia. Moreover, the 1997 Asian Financial Crises exerted different impacts on the two countries. The Philippines' limited exposure and fairly effective response to the crisis ironically undermined pressure for further reforms (Hicken 2008: 207). By contrast, Indonesia's leaders learned from the crisis and its painful, humbling aftermath the importance of stabilizing and restoring confidence in the financial sector. This was done not only through monitoring the balance sheets of financial institutions, but also by keeping a tight rein on the balance of payments. Concern for foreign exchange tilted the policy calculus toward relaxing restrictions on foreign ownership of assembly and parts operations.

6

Korea

Successful Intensive Industrialization

[T]here would be no next Japan, even if a developing country created a lean-production industry that could match the product quality and labor productivity of the best lean producers.

—Womack, Jones, and Roos (1991: 262)

[I]t is easy to forget how close [the Korean] auto industry came to being stillborn, a victim of mismanagement, inconsistent government policy, corruption, and lack of technology, capital and managerial know-how.

—Clifford (1998: 254)

[I]t is unlikely that Hyundai Motor Company can become a major world producer of automobiles. Indeed, most forward-looking analysis of this sector suggests that the world industry will become increasingly dominated by a handful of firms, maybe as few as six but no more than eight. No analyst believes that Hyundai will be one of them.

—Graham (2003: 143–144)

VW's greatest fear isn't Toyota, it's Hyundai.

—Headline in *Automotive News Europe* (July 13, 2010)

Despite the pessimism expressed at the turn of the century, Korea is the only country since Japan to become a major exporter in the auto industry primarily through the activities of domestically owned companies. In 2017, Korea was the sixth largest producer of passenger cars in the world, trailing only China, the United States, Japan, Germany, and India. Remarkably, more than two-thirds of these vehicles were exported (Figure 6.1). Exports of vehicles in 2019 numbered more than 2.4 million (down from the peak of

The Political Economy of Automotive Industrialization in East Asia. Richard F. Doner, Gregory W. Noble and John Ravenhill, Oxford University Press (2021). © Oxford University Press. DOI: 10.1093/oso/9780197520253.003.0006

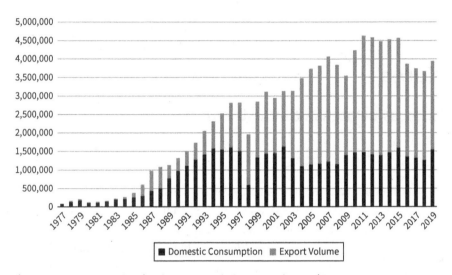

Figure 6.1 Korea: Car Production, Domestic Consumption and Exports.

Source: KAMA Annual Reports; KAICA website <http://www.kaica.or.kr/bbs/content.php?co_id=statics> Accessed on 21 October 2020.

3 million in 2012), and were worth $41 billion, fully 7.5% of the country's total merchandise exports. To complement vehicle exports, component exports amounted to $19 billion (data from <https://comtrade.un.org/data and https://www-statista-com/statistics/947324/south-korea-automotive-export-value/>. Many of these components were destined for assembly in the overseas plants of Hyundai and Kia, which produce an additional 4 million vehicles a year.

Korea's success in the automotive industry provides robust support for our argument that strong institutions are necessary for the success of a domestic auto industry. Korea has often been portrayed as the archetypical developmental state, more unified even than "Japan Inc." However, as more accounts of the policymaking process became available, particularly those contributed by Korean authors, it has become increasingly clear that characterizing Korea as an ideal-type developmental state was at best incomplete and often downright misleading. The institutional structure of policymaking was very different from that in Japan. Struggles between competing bureaucracies led to frequent U-turns on policy. Corruption occurred, often on a massive scale. Yet from the 1970s through to the present day (when, with the increasing share of imported cars in the domestic market, state agencies have targeted foreign companies for "price collusion"), one thing has remained constant (although not always uncontested): the desire to promote an integrated domestic auto industry. And, consistent with the overall argument of this book,

Korea's wealth of auto-related institutions, as well as those that provide technical education, have provided crucial support for the industry's rise to global prominence.

The early 1970s were a turning point for the industry, marking a move away from rent-seeking toward efforts to encourage an internationally competitive industry. Security considerations lay at the heart of this change. Increasing doubts about the reliability of the US security guarantee prompted the government to pursue the Heavy and Chemical Industry (HCI) initiative, in which autos figured prominently. Various policy instruments, whose relative importance has varied over time, have been used to support the state's goals for the industry. These included sealing off the domestic market from imports, providing subsidized loans for preferred companies and tax breaks for R&D, and the creation of a dense network of institutions that provided support for industry in general and the automotive sector in particular.

Policies, Industry Development, and Performance

As in all our countries in this study, the Korean industry began through import-substituting efforts that afforded opportunities for rent-seeking. Unlike most of its counterparts in the region, Korea moved quickly to an export-oriented industry based on intensive development.

State efforts to develop a local auto industry began in 1962 with the adoption of a Five-Year Plan for the Promotion of the Automobile Industry and the Law for the Protection of the Automobile Industry. The Law, ostensibly modeled on Japan's 1936 Automobile Industry Act (Kim 2000: 36), prohibited the import of assembled vehicles, barred imports of parts and components except for assembly, and exempted parts imported for use in local assembly from taxes and tariffs. The Ministry of Commerce and Industry (MCI) was given the power to license entrants into the industry and to inspect their quality of production.

The government initially designated the Saenara Automobile Company as the sole producer of small vehicles, the intention being to foster economies of scale. Saenara was able to capitalize on its monopoly to sell assembled Nissan Bluebirds for close to double the price it paid for the kits (Lee 2011a: 302). The company collapsed in July 1963, having assembled only 2,773 vehicles, when the government, facing a severe foreign exchange shortage, banned imported car kits (Bent n.d.). After a struggle between rival factions in the military regime, the government allowed Shinjin to take over the Saenara Plant, but local content was a dismal 21% (Lee 2011a: 304). Attracted by the rents accruing to

Shinjin, and supported by local component manufacturers, the newly founded Hyundai Motors (HMC) and Asia Motors petitioned the government to be permitted to enter the industry, a request that was granted in 1967 for HMC and the following year for Asia—on condition that the companies negotiate an alliance with a producer from a developed economy. HMC entered a joint venture with Ford; Asia assembled cars and buses through tie-up with Fiat. Output remained minuscule: in the mid-1960s, the assembly of CKDs amounted to only 3,430—only slightly more than the number of vehicles "manufactured" through rebuilding used cars (Kim and Lee 1983: 296).

The tariff-free access given to imported components provided local assemblers with no incentive to increase domestic value added. Competition between the companies occurred primarily through a proliferation of models, which limited opportunities for standardizing components. The industry's output was minuscule because of the limited domestic market: in 1971, annual production was under 30,000 vehicles; there were only 100,000 registered cars for a population of nearly 30 million; per capita income at this time was only $300 (Chung and Kim 2014: 3). Moreover, because multinational vendors imposed restrictions on the export of assembled kits, the industry generated a substantial drain on foreign exchange.

Concerns over the nascent industry's contribution to Korea's trade problems, following the failure to reach the target of 90% local content by 1967 (Lew 1992: 142), prompted the MCI to draw up the 1969 Plan for the Comprehensive Promotion of the Auto Industry, which aimed for full localization of the industry. The plan provided schedules for localization of content for each passenger model: assemblers were required to achieve 100% local content by 1973, and to reach output levels that would make the industry internationally competitive by 1976. Companies that complied with the schedules were promised privileged access to domestic and international loans. The MCI also announced plans to designate one company as the sole producer of engines—plans that were thwarted by rivalries among the companies, by instability in their international links, and by political upheavals at home.

These initial import-substituting efforts came to an abrupt end with the economic and political upheavals that began in 1971. The devaluation of the US dollar in August 1971 was accompanied by American restrictions on imports, which hit Korea's main export, textiles. The withdrawal of one-third of the US troops stationed in Korea exacerbated foreign exchange difficulties (a loss of $100 million in payments), as did the return of Korean troops from Vietnam. In response to Korea's deteriorating external balance, the IMF ordered a ceiling placed on loans from commercial sources. Economic problems interacted with domestic political unrest to precipitate a crisis environment that led President Park first to declare a state of emergency after his re-election in 1971, and then to dissolve the National Assembly and suspend the constitution in October 1972. A new constitution, the "Yushin" (rejuvenation) constitution, was approved in a rigged referendum the following month, which gave the president the power to rule by decree and to appoint one-third of the members of the National Assembly. Just three months after its proclamation, the government announced its Heavy and Chemical Industry drive.

The HCI used many of the same policy instruments that the state had marshaled in previous five-year plans but differed in being more directive, in tying finance to performance, and in how the strategy was formulated and executed. Whereas the Economic Planning Board (EPB), created in June 1961, had played the leading role in the first two five-year plans, which covered the period 1962–1971 (Jones 1975: 49–51), the HCI initiative was driven by the president himself and his staff in the president's executive office and residence, the Blue House (Soh 1997: 105). The EPB (dominated by economists skeptical of the ambitious targets of the HCI) was bypassed in a process initiated jointly by private firms, relevant ministries, usually the MCI, and the president's Planning Council (Choi 1991: 106).

The key change in policies toward the auto sector, embodied in the Long-Term Plan for the Promotion of the Auto Industry announced by MCI in April 1973, was the insistence that auto companies develop a "citizen car" with an engine capacity of less than 1.5 liters. For a relatively young industry with experience only of assembling imported kits—and on a very modest scale—the plan was enormously demanding. To support the fledgling industry, the full panoply of state instruments was brought to bear:

- *Protection of the domestic market*: All imports of assembled vehicles were prohibited, a ban not lifted until 1986 (a prohibition on imports of small cars from Japan was maintained until 1999). Even after imports were liberalized, the state used other methods to dissuade consumption of foreign cars: it was frequently rumored that anyone driving an imported vehicle would likely be subject to a tax audit. Differential rates of taxation were imposed, determined by engine capacity. Although legitimate under the GATT/WTO because the measure did not discriminate between vehicles depending on their country of origin, its effect over the years was to favor domestically produced vehicles, which typically had small engines. Standards required of assembled vehicles were often thought to be drawn up in conjunction with and tended to favor Hyundai, the dominant domestic producer (an allegation we heard from a senior GM Korea manager). And such was the level of nationalism that, at least until the first decade of this century, the purchase of a foreign-brand car was disdained, no matter how inferior the local product (a situation completely different from that in Malaysia, as we discuss in Chapter 7). These combined pressures ensured that in 2000, more than a decade after access to the Korean market had been liberalized, of total registrations of 1.44 million, only 11,000 were foreign-made vehicles (Ravenhill 2003: 116).

- *Allocation of capital*: subsidized loans and credit were made available to preferred producers. This was the essence of the strategy that Alice Amsden (1989: 139–155) termed "getting relative prices wrong." The state acted as guarantor for foreign loans, whose interest rates were lower than those available in the domestic market: over 70% of Hyundai's investments in the 1970s were financed from foreign sources (Kim 2000: 48). The interest rates on bank loans to targeted sectors were almost always below the inflation rate: for the period 1974–1980, the average real interest rate was calculated to be minus 6.7% (Woo 1991: 159; Guillén 2001: Figure 7.1, p. 188). Access to international loans enabled companies to undertake massive investments without depending on foreign direct investment (FDI) (Mardon 1990). Preferred firms also received tax breaks on investment and on research and development expenditures.

- *Repression of labor*: Korea's auto industry was built on a Fordist model, in which the availability of relatively low-cost labor was an essential feature. Hyundai banned trade unions and unilaterally determined wages. Lansbury, So, and Kwon (2007: 66) estimated that 30%–40% of the average monthly earnings of $456 of Hyundai's production workers in 1983 were derived from overtime and bonus payments: workers had no option but to work overtime to earn a living wage. The state backed Hyundai's management by violently suppressing labor unrest.

- *Government limitations on entry to the industry*: Although the state on several occasions failed to implement plans to consolidate the industry, for two decades it limited the number of domestic producers—in 1989, for instance, denying a proposed Samsung-Chrysler joint venture permission to enter the market (Green 1992: 420).

- *Dissemination of information on technology*: a dense network of state research institutes supported the auto industry in particular and science and technology R&D more generally (discussed in the following).

The relationship between state and private sector was more complex than is often portrayed. Because the vision of President Park Chung-Hee for creating an autonomous Korean auto industry was initially shared enthusiastically within the sector only by Hyundai's founder, Chung Chu-yong, Hyundai had a privileged position in the formulation and implementation of policies in the first two decades of the industry. This was a coincidence of interests in pursuit of a common goal. Even though corruption was rife—corporations were estimated to have paid "voluntary contributions" to the government that averaged 22% of their net profits (Woo 1991: 9)—the high debt-equity ratios of corporations (double those in Taiwan) enabled the state to discipline them for failure to meet stipulated targets—at least until the 1980s, when corporations became less dependent on state-approved sources of finance (Choi 1991) and some became "too big to fail" (Kim 1988).

Hyundai was the only company to embrace the state's conception of a domestically manufactured citizen's car. In 1976, it introduced Korea's first domestic model, the Pony. The success in doing so was impressive for a company with less than a decade's experience in the auto industry, even though it was heavily dependent on imported components, capital, and expertise. Hyundai dramatically increased its share of the domestic market from 19% in 1970 to 39% in 1973 and, with the introduction of the Pony, to 58% in 1977 (Lansbury, So, and Kwon 2007: 52). The other two companies in the industry—General Motors, which had entered into a joint venture with Shinjin in 1972 (General Motors Korea, GMK), and Kia, formerly a producer of bicycles and motorcycles, which began car production in 1973—did not want to take the risk of developing a genuinely Korean car. GMK, in particular, suffered from its parent company's pursuit of a world car strategy, where models would be produced at multiple locations. It chose for its citizen's car the Chevrolet 1700, a rebadged Holden LJ Torana, which failed miserably in the Korean market because of its heavy fuel consumption and outmoded looks (from 1972–1978 only eight thousand were manufactured). Kia, meanwhile, was content to produce local variants of foreign cars: it manufactured a version of the Mazda Familia for its citizen's car and also assembled models under license from Fiat and Peugeot.

Production costs in the Korean industry remained internationally uncompetitive because of the expense of importing components and the limited size of the domestic market. In 1979, the peak year before the second oil shock, the industry's total production was only 113,600 vehicles, spread across eight domestic models. In 1979 the MCI estimated that despite low wage rates, Hyundai's production cost for the Pony was $3,972 compared with an estimated cost for Toyota's Corolla of $2,300 (Altshuler et al. 1984: 42–43). Limited exports failed to offset the cost of imported components. Hyundai began exports in 1976, when six cars were sent to Ecuador in exchange for bananas (Green 1992: 414). By 1979, exports of the Pony reached about 19,000, but these were sold at a considerable loss in international markets (Altshuler et al. 1984: 43). Exports from GMK and Kia were negligible given the restrictions imposed by technology licenses.

The Long-Term Plan succeeded in its goal of generating a genuine domestic car. It also pushed the local content ratio up to above 90%, albeit with relatively high-priced components that often fell short of international quality standards. The industry at the end of the 1970s, however, was producing at well below minimum efficient scale and lacked international competitiveness. In 1980 the domestic demand for autos declined 50% following the imposition of austerity measures in the aftermath of the second oil price crisis: capacity utilization fell to 26% (Green 1992: 415). The new round of economic and political instability following the assassination of Park Chung-Hee in October 1979 precipitated a struggle over future policies toward the auto industry. The "liberalizers" in the EPB, the Ministry of Finance, and the Bank of Korea argued that the experience of the Long-Term Plan demonstrated that Korea could not be an internationally competitive producer of assembled vehicles but that it should instead focus on producing components, a position backed by the World Bank and the International Monetary Fund. The "statists," concentrated in the Blue House and MCI, believed that protection should be continued to enable the industry to overcome temporary problems and to gain international competitiveness.

The outcome was an uneasy compromise in which even greater *dirigisme*—attempts to force mergers in the industry—was justified in the name of building a competitive industry. The government proposed to tackle the surplus capacity issue by forcing a merger between General Motors and either Daewoo or Hyundai, with the intention of producing a sole domestic producer of autos that would have a powerful foreign partner. Kia would be forced out of automobiles into the production of light commercial vehicles, where it would enjoy a monopoly. Daewoo and Hyundai were given the choice of specializing in either autos or electricity generation, ceding their production capacity in the other sector to their business rival. Hyundai initially resisted the plan, but when forced to choose opted against the wishes of the government for the passenger car industry. In August 1980, Hyundai acquired Daewoo's share in Saehan Motors in exchange for its electricity generator business. But merger negotiations between Hyundai and GM over the next two months broke down over the sharing of equity in the new joint venture and over management rights. This masked a deeper division over whether Korea's future sole player in passenger vehicles would be merely one cog in the global GM operation, with the option to export only through GM networks, or whether it would be an autonomous company free to choose its own models and export markets. Following a prolonged stalemate, the MCI decided to nullify the merger agreement between Hyundai and Saehan, and abandoned the idea of limiting auto production to a single producer (Lee 2011a: 316–318). Daewoo rejoined a joint venture with GM in 1982 (taking the name Daewoo Motor Corp.). Hyundai continued to produce as an autonomous company. And in 1986, Kia was permitted to re-enter passenger vehicle production.

The forced merger attempt marked the high tide of *dirigisme* in the Korean auto market. Its abandonment was testimony both to differences within the bureaucracy on how best to establish an internationally competitive industry and to the waning of state power relative to that of the chaebol. It did, however, succeed in temporarily creating a duopoly that enabled the realization of economies of scale. Policymakers came to realize, however, that substantial exports would be required to create a competitive industry—and that only markets in advanced economies were of sufficient size to offer significant sales opportunities. In turn, this led to a new focus on upgrading quality, initially through a deepening of links with foreign partners.

Hyundai forged closer ties with its recent partner, Mitsubishi, which in 1982 took a 10% shareholding in Hyundai (raised to 14.7% in 1985). Assistance from Mitsubishi was critical in the introduction of Japanese-style quality management techniques, which quickly brought substantial savings in production costs (Lansbury, So, and Kwon 2007: 58). In 1983, Mazda acquired 10% of Kia; in 1986, when Kia re-entered auto production, Ford acquired a further 10%. Although Kia maintained management autonomy, Mazda provided the vehicles and technology, Ford the international marketing. GM increased its investment in Daewoo to expand the annual production potential of its existing plant to 400,000 vehicles. Although Daewoo nominally had managerial control of the joint venture, GM retained half of the seats on the board, whose approval was necessary for all major decisions (Lew 1992: 42).

The 1980s were the first golden period for the Korean industry. The investments at the start of the decade led to a substantial rise in domestic production capacity. The foreign partnerships also paid dividends through technology transfer. Domestic demand recovered quickly after 1981. The Korean industry also benefited from an enormous lucky break, the imposition by Japan's Ministry of Trade and Industry in May 1981 of "voluntary restraints" on auto exports to the United States following pressure from the White House and Congress. The restraints were not removed until 1994: because they were measured in number rather than value of vehicles, Japanese producers moved exports up-market, thereby opening up an opportunity for the Korean industry to compete for the low end of the market.

By 1986, auto output exceeded 600,000 vehicles, more than four times the level at the start of the decade. Even more impressive was the share of exports, which in that year surpassed domestic consumption for the first time. By 1988, Korean producers were selling more than half a million cars in the US market, giving them a 4% share of total sales (Womack, Jones, and Roos 1991: 262). The early stage at which the Korean industry gained significant penetration of advanced economies' markets was unprecedented. Capacity continued to be added rapidly: by 1988, output topped the one million mark for the first time. In that year, the government permitted another entrant to the industry, the specialist SUV producer, Ssangyong, which later entered into a strategic alliance with Daimler-Benz.

Hyundai continued to lead the industry in the 1980s. It remained the only manufacturer in Korea that produced a genuinely Korean car rather than a variant of a model built by foreign partners. The *Excel*, the company's first front wheel drive car, became the company's first export to the United States. Thanks to a bargain price of $4,995 and the scarcity of Japanese competition, it set US records for a first-year import by selling 168,882 units, which soared to 264,000 in 1987 and to 405,000 in the following year. But then a combination of factors led to a collapse in the US market (Sexton 2010: 1). The Excel acquired an appalling reputation for quality and reliability, becoming the butt of jokes on late night television. Quality concerns arose at a time when a combination of domestic and international factors caused severe problems for the industry. Democratization led to an explosion of labor unrest and wage demands. Hyundai's labor costs doubled over a three-year period (Sexton 2010: 1). The Korean won meanwhile appreciated significantly against the yen. And Korean cars faced new competition in the US market: Japanese companies had responded to the voluntary export restraints by building plants in low-wage states in the United States to produce competitive small cars. An attempt by Hyundai to circumvent US protectionism and the high won by opening a $400 million assembly plant in Bromont, Quebec, Canada, proved an expensive disaster: production at the 100,000 capacity plant peaked in 1991 at 28,201: the plant was closed in August 1993 after only 14,243 vehicles were manufactured that year (Thorpe 2005).

In contrast to the previous crisis in the industry, the state's response to that at the end of the 1980s was muted. The fundamental reasons were changes in the domestic and international contexts, and in the balance of power between the chaebol and the state. With democratization and economic liberalization (required if Korea's aspirations to join the OECD were to be realized), the instruments available to the state were much reduced. It was impossible to insulate the domestic market from international forces. Labor repression was largely a thing of the past. The principal policy instrument the state retained was to control which companies were permitted to enter the industry—which kept Samsung out of auto production until 1994. The state's role essentially had been transformed from one of directing the industry to one of providing support.

The response to the crisis consequently was in the industry's own hands. Rather than retrenching, the industry invested in further capacity. Production continued to expand into the early 1990s, although the volume of exports did not recover to the previous peak reached in 1988 until 1993 (Figure 6.1). In a response to the poor reputation that Korean cars had acquired in markets in advanced economies, the industry turned its attention to developing economy markets, which grew rapidly in the 1990s. Hyundai increased the number of markets to which it was exporting from 65 in 1986 to 141 in 1994 (Lansbury, So, and Kwon 2007: 53). Frustrated by GM blocking its efforts to sell into Eastern Europe, the traditional preserve of GM's European subsidiary Opel, Daewoo acquired GM's share of its joint venture for $170 million in 1992. Daewoo then gained GM's approval to export to developing countries in 1993, and to North America and Europe in 1995 (McDermott 1997: 500). Meanwhile, the government of Kim Young-Sam risked creating further excess capacity by permitting Samsung to enter the industry after Samsung promised to situate its $1 billion plant (with a capacity of 500,000 cars annually) in Kim's hometown of Busan (Kang 2002: 165).

Korean companies not only expanded domestically, but also used their deep pockets to establish or acquire design centers in Europe and the United States to tap into foreign engineering expertise: Daewoo established a center in Worthing, UK, in 1994; Samsung acquired the Huntington Beach facilities of International Automotive Design West Coast, Inc. Both Kia and Hyundai had design centers in California. They also rapidly expanded their international assembly operations. Daewoo attempted to buy its way into Eastern Europe by acquiring Poland's FSO from GM, and took a 50% stake in Oltcit, Romania's second largest producer. In all, Daewoo purchased 13 plants in 10 countries, including India, Iran, Ukraine, and Uzbekistan. Daewoo also built new overseas production facilities in Uzbekistan and Poland. Between 1993 and 1998, Daewoo added overseas production capacity of close to one million passenger cars (Kim 2009: 280).

By 1996, the industry appeared to be in good health once more: total output reached a record 2.8 million vehicles (more than double the level at the start of the decade), with exports constituting a record 1.3 million units (a fourfold increase from 1990). But then calamity struck the industry again in the form of the Asian financial crisis. The scramble in the 1990s to create new capacity had come at a high price. The debt burden of Korean auto companies escalated rapidly in the 1990s as they took advantage of the easy access to loans afforded by financial liberalization. The average debt ratio for auto producers increased from 416% in 1995 to 530% in the following year, substantially above the already high average of 300% for all manufacturing companies (*Korea Herald*, May 10, 1997). Ssangyong, which had invested more than $2.5 billion in new production lines and component plants following the initialization of its alliance with Daimler-Benz in 1992, had a mind-boggling ratio of 10,496%. Overinvestment caused the capacity utilization rate to slump to 70% by the middle of the decade.

Even before the financial crisis caused a collapse in domestic demand in 1998, Korean auto companies were in trouble. Ssangyong and Kia were reported to have made no profits in their auto operations throughout the 1990s. Some analysts suggested that Daewoo Motors had never made a profit. Kim (2009: 277) cites company reports that indicate small net profits were made from 1995 through 1998. But whether these were accurate is questionable. The lack of financial transparency within the chaebol pre-crisis and the practice of cross-subsidization of subsidiaries make an accurate judgment on such issues impossible, but the government's Financial Supervisory Committee's investigation of Daewoo uncovered some evidence of the scale of the chaebol's economic problems and unorthodox financial management. It found 23 trillion won (US$18 billion) in accounting errors on Daewoo's books (*Korea Times*, July 21, 2000).

Kia— the country's seventh largest chaebol and one of the few chaebol that was professionally managed rather than under family control—had to seek a bailout from creditors in July 1997. Although it had diversified into 11 industrial sectors, vehicle manufacture remained its core business. It had the second largest production capacity after Hyundai Motors (1.2 million cars annually) and was a significant exporter (over 250,000 units each year). Together with its heavy vehicles subsidiary, Asia Motors, it had close to 7,500 subcontractors with a total of more than 600,000 employees (*Korea Herald*, July 22, 1997). By most accounts, the Kia Group had been comparatively well managed until the early 1990s. Its subsequent efforts to diversify into construction and steel, coupled with the overcapacity problems in the auto industry, became its undoing. By July 1997, the Kia group had accumulated debts in excess of $10.7 billion.

Contending views within the bureaucracy as to how to respond to Kia's bankruptcy and to that of several other chaebol outside the auto sector, produced paralysis. Liberalizers argued that the market should determine the outcome and be permitted to deliver its own restructuring of Korean industry. Statists saw the problems of the corporate sector as at least temporarily reversing the secular shift in the balance of power between the government and the private sector, and an opportunity for the state to force rationalization in key industries and to promote stronger national champions (Ravenhill 2003). While the government dallied in its response to Kia's problems, Ssangyong Motors went bankrupt. Here a swift (nationalist) solution was forthcoming: Daewoo took over its rival by assuming a 53.5% stake in the company. The price, however, was a further 2 trillion won ($1.8 billion) in debt for Daewoo, which was to contribute to its own failure the following year.

After several months of indecision, the Kim Young Sam government's initial approach to resolving Kia's problems was firmly in the nationalist tradition. It announced in October 1997 that it would place Kia Motors and Asia Motors under court receivership, and that the state-run Korea Development Bank's loans to Kia would be converted to equity, making the Bank, with 30% of its total equity, Kia's largest shareholder (*Korea Herald*, October 23, 1997). The minister of finance and economy asserted that the government had no intention of allowing Kia to be taken over by a third party but would run the company as a successful state enterprise (*Korea Herald*, October 27, 1997).

The deepening of the economic crisis (with the collapse of the won in the following month), however, and the election of the opposition leader, Kim Dae Jung, as president, led to a reversal of policy. The currency crisis strengthened the hands of the liberalizers, and opened the way for the international financial institutions and bilateral creditors to exert significant external pressure for a reduced role for the state. The government eventually agreed to auction off Kia's assets. The manner in which the new government conducted the auction, however, raised doubts about its willingness to permit the takeover of Korean assets by foreign companies. Kia was eventually sold to the highest bidder, Hyundai, amidst allegations that economic nationalism had prevailed over a more rational solution of selling the troubled automaker to Ford, the only foreign bidder. The takeover served various nationalist purposes: it consolidated Hyundai's role as the dominant Korea producer; and it prevented a powerful foreign producer from gaining a major foothold in the Korean market.

The Kim Dae Jung government, meanwhile, had pressed the chaebol to consolidate their operations by engaging in asset swaps (the "Big Deal" program) and to reduce their debt to equity ratios to below 200% by the end of 1999. For the automobile sector, the principal issue was what was to become of Samsung Motors. With the collapse of the domestic market in Korea following the onset of the financial crisis, Samsung could hardly have faced a less auspicious climate for the start of its operations. The company operated for only 11 months, during which it sold about 30,000 cars. Each car sold was estimated to have lost the company $5,000. The corporation acknowledged that its relatively small output would preclude the development of a viable enterprise and aspired to take over the much larger Kia Motors. But corporate hubris eventually gave way under pressure from the government, and Samsung agreed in September 1998 to exchange its auto operations for Daewoo's consumer electronics plants. The corporations, however, failed to reach agreement over the terms of the deal: it was overtaken by the financial difficulties that pushed Daewoo into receivership in July 1999 and the decision the following month to dismantle the group.

The eventual sale of Samsung Motors to Renault was relatively non-controversial in that no alternative bidder expressed an interest. Renault acquired 70% of the company, on which the Samsung chaebol had lavished more than $5 billion since 1994 to create production and research facilities and dealerships, for a cash payment of only $100 million (Automotive Intelligence News 2000). Renault was a natural partner for the bankrupt Korean company: in March 1999 it had acquired 36.8% of Nissan, from which Samsung had acquired the technology for its plant.

In opening the way for possible foreign purchase of the flagship arm of Korea's third largest corporation, Daewoo, the government faced opposition from a formidable nationalist coalition comprising public opinion, the Federation of Korean Industries (the chaebol's lobby group), the Korean Federation of Small Business, many civic groups, and the opposition Grand National Party. Daewoo's unions, concerned about job security, opposed a sale to a foreign company, as did affiliates of the Korean Auto Industries Cooperation Association. Their fear was that a foreign company would confine Daewoo's future operations to the domestic market (*Korea Herald*, June 27, 2000).

Although Hyundai expressed interest in acquiring Daewoo, key agencies of the state—notably the Ministry of Finance and Economy, the state-owned Korean Development Bank (Daewoo's largest creditor), the Fair Trade Commission, and several research agencies including the Korea Development Institute and the Korea Institute for International Economic Policy—opposed a further reinforcement of Hyundai's domestic market share. Eventually the government turned to Daewoo's old partner, General Motors. Again, the foreign partner was able to acquire Korean assets at fire-sale prices: GM and its partners Suzuki and SAIC (Shanghai Automotive) purchased two-thirds of Daewoo Motor for $400 million (Agence France-Presse 2001). It also received significant tax concessions. For a paltry $25 million, GM acquired the dubious privilege of using the Daewoo Motor brand.

Ssangyong, which Daewoo had controlled for less than 12 months before its own bankruptcy, was not part of the GM purchase: it was managed by creditors until late 2003 when a majority share was put up for auction. After the preferred bidder, China's Blue Star, a conglomerate with no experience in the auto industry, failed to agree on a price (Ssangyong's debt was estimated at $1.14 billion), SAIC acquired a controlling 48.9% share of the company for $500 million (Automotive News 2004; Webb and Chang 2004; China Daily 2004).

The Asian Financial Crisis thus dramatically transformed the landscape of the Korean auto industry (not least the components sector). Three of the country's auto assemblers fell into foreign hands for a total expenditure of less than $1.5 billion (the huge debts that the companies had assumed in the rush for growth in the 1990s in all cases exceeded the value of their assets). The Korean state was clearly ambivalent about the fire sale but had few alternatives if the companies were to be rescued from bankruptcy. Liberalizing elements in the state used the opportunity to push for greater internationalization (Noble and Ravenhill 2000). Foreign acquisitions were permitted, however, only after the state had secured continued domestic ownership of the country's second largest producer, Kia, and, through its merger with Hyundai, the consolidation of a dominant auto manufacturer that enjoyed 70% of the domestic market. The cost was a substantial increase in HMC's debt—which gave rise to the skepticism about the company's future captured in Edward Graham's epigraph to this chapter.

Auto Components

The components sector was long regarded as the Achilles' heel of the Korean auto industry. Many of the quality problems associated with Korean cars in the 1980s and 1990s were attributed to the inferior parts they contained Lautier (2001: 225).

The government initially attempted to foster the growth of an auto parts industry by limiting in-house production by assemblers to only engines and bodies. It reserved the manufacture of power-transmitting equipment, braking systems, and suspensions for component manufacturers, which received subsidized finance and protection under the 1962 Medium and Small Firms' Cooperative Association Law. As part of its emphasis on targeting the auto sector as a strategic export industry at the end of the 1970s, however, the government permitted a wider range of components to be produced in-house and encouraged parts suppliers to affiliate with a single assembly company.

By the early 1990s, the share of in-house components in total production in Korea was around 50%, a high figure by international standards (Chung 1994), testimony to the unwillingness of the chaebol to rely on outsiders for any significant input. Much of the technological learning in the industry's development was captured by the assemblers: Lautier (2001: fn. 11) reports that the assemblers' share of automobile industry value added rose from 18% to 60% between 1970 and 1985.

With the exception of a few companies closely tied to a chaebol (for instance, the Mando group, part of the Halla chaebol), components production outside of the assemblers was dominated by small and medium enterprises. At the onset of the Asian financial crisis, two-thirds of firms supplying directly to assemblers had fewer than 100 employees. They often lacked the technologies needed to ensure consistent quality of product. The feudal organization of the parts industry, in which most producers were tied to a single assembler, combined with a lack of standardization of components across models to preclude the realization of economies of scale (Korean assemblers had failed to keep up with the international best practice of building a range of models on the same platform). The system of separate pyramids for organizing the auto supply chain in Korea also had government support: when the government eventually allowed Samsung to enter car production in the mid-1990s, it instructed the company to establish its own supply chain independent of existing producers. Unlike their Japanese counterparts, few Korean companies had the capacity to design parts independently: production usually was to specifications provided by the assemblers—and the development of new components was relatively slow: in the mid-1990s this took an average of 52 months in Korea, compared with 36 months in Japan (McKinsey Seoul Office 1998). A quarter of a century later, the components sector was still characterized by very low rates of expenditure on research and development in comparison with international competitors: larger South Korean companies invested 1.4% of revenue in R&D, compared with the investment by Japan's Denso of 9% of income and 7.5% by Germany's Bosch (Kim 2018).

FDI in the Korean auto components industry was relatively small in the pre–financial crisis era. Although a number of global first-tier suppliers, e.g., Delco Remy, had established a presence in Korea, they were compelled during the era of military governments to enter into joint ventures with domestic partners. The Asian financial crisis spurred a dramatic restructuring of the industry, facilitated by the availability of Korean assets at fire sale prices. Two hundred local components suppliers went bankrupt in the first 12 months of the crisis (Guillén 2001: 169). Close to 100 foreign companies either increased their presence in or entered the Korean components industry after the onset of the crisis (Korea Automobile Manufacturers Association n.d.). By the turn of the century, all of the global first-tier suppliers in the auto industry had established or consolidated a presence in Korea, attracted both by the size of the domestic car market and by the local industry's prospects for exports (Ravenhill 2005). Approximately 30% of first-tier suppliers are joint ventures or fully foreign-owned companies (interview, KIET).

A second significant outcome from the financial crisis was the spin-off of in-house component production into separate companies as part of chaebol restructuring. Particularly notable was the creation of Hyundai Mobis and the various incarnations of Daewoo Precision (now known as S&T Motiv). In developing its in-house parts production and then spinning it off to form Hyundai Mobis, Hyundai created a parts company with the technological sophistication and size to compete internationally. Hyundai Mobis, which calls itself a 0.5-tier supplier because it is so closely integrated with Hyundai-Kia, specializes in chassis, cockpit, and front-end modules, but also produces individual components such as brakes, wheels, airbags, and electronic equipment.

As an integral part of the Hyundai Automotive chaebol (and its circular patterns of investment/cross-ownership, reflected in Figure 6.2), the company benefits from the conglomerate's deep pockets. It has acted strategically in entering licensing agreements and joint ventures with foreign companies for advanced parts that it could not produce itself, and then using the access it has gained to advanced technology to develop its own products (see, for instance, reports on the development of an anti-lock brake system that would save

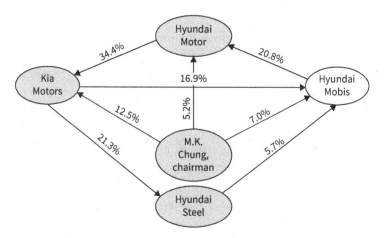

Figure 6.2 Shareholding within the Hyundai Motor group.
Source: Hyundai Motor group (figure no longer available online).

Mobis over $100 million in royalty payments to its previous partner, Bosch (Yonghap English News 2008)).

Mobis was born large—its sales of over $4.5 billion in 2003 placed it in the top 30 global suppliers. It ascended the rankings rapidly—rising to number 10 in 2010, to number 8 in 2012, and to number 7 in 2016, a position it retained in 2019 (data from Automotive News, *Top Suppliers*, various years). Like the components industry in Korea as a whole, the company's success is intimately linked to that of Korea's dominant assemblers, Hyundai and Kia. But Mobis was an early investor in modular approaches and soon gained success in selling to other assemblers, its first major contract in 2004 being to supply Daimler Chrysler's Jeep division with chassis modules. Although Hyundai and Kia still account for approximately half of its total sales, by 2014, Mobis had secured contracts with most of the major global (but notably non-Japanese) assemblers including GM, BMW, VW, Peugeot Citroen, Daimler, and Chrysler.

Three of the other five Korean components suppliers in the world's top 100 are also Hyundai and Kia spin-offs. Hyundai-WIA, 37th on the global suppliers list in 2020 with annual sales of $7.0 billion, was previously known as Kia Heavy Industry. It sells to all of the Korean assemblers and to Dongfeng and SAIC in China. Hyundai Transys, 36th on the 2020 global suppliers list with sales of $7.4 billion, was established in 2019, following the merger of two Hyundai spin-offs, Hyundai Dymos (established 1994) and Hyundai Powertech (spun off in 2001 as a specialist producer of automatic transmissions). It operates five plants in China, and one each co-located with Hyundai-Kia assembly plants in Slovakia, India, the United States, Mexico, and Brazil. Hyundai Kefico, 88th on the global suppliers list with sales of $1.9 billion, began as a joint venture between HMC, Germany's Robert Bosch, and Mitsubish Electric in 1987. In 2005, Mitsubishi sold its shares to Robert Bosch. In 2012, the company, which manufactures engine and transmission control units, became a wholly-owned subsidiary of HMC. It operates plants in China, Mexico, and Vietnam as well as Korea. One hundred percent of its sales are within the Hyundai Motors conglomerate.

Three other Korean producers in the global top 100 component suppliers are not part of the Hyundai empire. The Mando Corporation, ranked 49th in 2020 with annual sales of $4.9 billion, was founded in 1962 by a younger brother of the founder of Hyundai Motor Company, as part of the Halla chaebol. Specializing in brake, steering, and suspension components, Mando sells more than 80% of its output to Hyundai-Kia. Initially it licensed technology from Japan and the United Kingdom. By the time of the Asian financial crisis, it had developed its own technologies, apart from powertrains (interview, Mando Corporation, July 3, 2008). In the wake of the crisis, the Halla Group, the sixth largest of the chaebol, collapsed: Mando was sold to a J.P. Morgan–led consortium for $446 million. In 2005, J.P. Morgan put the company up for sale. Following a failed bid from Hyundai Motor, the company was sold back to the resurrected Halla Group (Hyundai reportedly was able to veto a sale to any of its rivals, a comment that was made to us in interviews (see also Anglebrandt 2008; Tucker 2008a, 2008b). Besides Hyundai and Kia, Mando also supplies General Motors, Fiat Chrysler, Nissan, Volkswagen, BMW, and Suzuki.

Another major components manufacturer that was "lost" to foreign ownership with Halla's collapse was returned to domestic ownership in 2014. Halla Visteon Climate Control (HVCC) was established as a joint venture between Mando and Ford in 1986. Mando sold its stake to the Ford spin-off, Visteon, in 1999. In turn, Visteon filed for bankruptcy 10 years later. In December 2014, it sold its 70% stake in HVCC for $3.6 billion to a consortium comprised of Hahn & Co., a private equity firm, and tire-maker Hankook—apparently in the face of opposition from Hyundai, which relies on HVCC for 70% of its air conditioning systems (the most expensive module that is not produced within the Hyundai empire; interview HCC, July 2008). In 2014, the company acquired the automotive thermal and emissions product line of Cooper Standard Automotive. In July 2015, the company was renamed Hanon Systems. The restructured company, which took over most of Visteon's climate-control business, has more than 40 manufacturing sites globally and annual sales of $6.1 billion, placing it 42nd in the global ranking of auto suppliers. Because of its foreign acquisitions, it is less dependent than the other large Korean components manufacturers on Hyundai-Kia.

The final Korean components manufacturer in the global top 100 is Seoyon E-Hwa, formerly Hanil E-Hwa. It was founded in 1972 to supply seats to the Hyundai Pony. Although seat assemblies remain a major part of its business, it has diversified into producing door trims, consoles, instrument panels, and bumpers. Although it also supplies VW and Audi, Hyundai and Kia remain its principal customers. It has followed them overseas, establishing plants in China, India, Mexico, Slovakia, and the US. In 2019, its global sales totaled $1.7 billion, placing it 94th on the list of top component suppliers.

The emergence of giant Korean components manufacturers has transformed Korea's trade in auto parts. Until the onset of the Asian financial crisis, Korea ran a deficit in auto parts trade, a reflection of the continuing dependence of the assemblers on imported components, especially sophisticated items such as engines and transmissions. With the acquisition of in-house capabilities, then spun off into affiliated companies, the situation was dramatically transformed. Korea has enjoyed a surplus in its auto parts trade every year since 1997 (reaching over $20 billion in 2014) (Figure 6.3). Exports grew

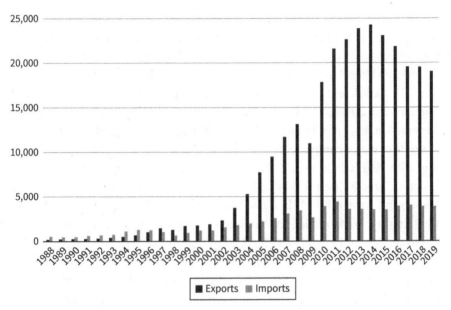

Figure 6.3 Korea Auto Parts Trade ($m).
Source: UN Comtrade. Auto parts defined as HS 8708.

exponentially even though the larger companies established multiple overseas manufacturing subsidiaries to support the foreign assembly plants of Hyundai and Kia. They, however, did fall back in the years after 2013 both because of the decline in demand for Korean cars in China (sales of components to "Asia" fell by 37% between 2014 and 2018), and because of the expansion of international production (http://www.kaica.or.kr/bbs/content.php?co_id=import).

Even these substantial increases in exports, however, have been exceeded by local sales, predominantly for local assembly (OEM production) (Figure 6.4).

The rosy picture of the health of Korea's auto parts industry provided by the production and trade data rests primarily on the performance of large companies and reflects their deep pockets—which have facilitated the reacquisition of assets sold to foreigners during the financial crisis (plus a few significant new overseas purchases). Elsewhere in the sector, the situation of many companies is less healthy. According to interviewees, a marked difference exists depending on whether or not they are suppliers to Hyundai (those primarily supplying the other assemblers have fared much more poorly). Across the sector as a whole, however, companies were in far from robust health. A KAICA survey in 2007 found that the operating profit of 477 auto suppliers averaged 4.4%, substantially below the average of 5.9% for all industries. For SMEs, the average was only 3.4% (data supplied in interview at KIET in July 2008). A decade later,

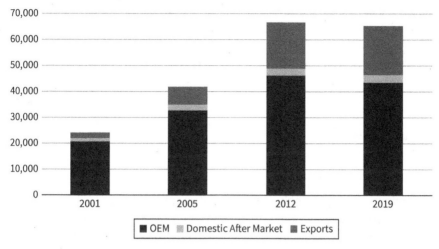

Figure 6.4 Korea Sales Destination of Components 2001-19 ($m).
Source: Korea Auto Industries Coop Association Annual Reports.
Key: OEM: Domestic Assemblers (Original Equipment Manufacturers)

matters had not improved. The government unveiled a $3 billion funding plan for the components industry at the end of 2018. In the second half of that year, the average operating margin for larger suppliers dropped to 1.2% as companies came under increasing competitive pressure from China (Kim 2018).

Surprisingly little consolidation occurred in the industry in the years between 2003 and 2018, contrary to a strong trend in the global industry. Although the number of first-tier suppliers at Kia fell by 16%, a reflection of the integration of its supply chain with that of Hyundai, and Ssangyong also marginally reduced its numbers, the other assemblers moved in the opposite direction. Renault Samsung increased its number of first-tier suppliers by 50% during these years as it developed its domestic supply chain, and GM Korea, despite expectations expressed in interviews we conducted in 2008, also increased the number of its first-tier suppliers by 10% in this period (see Table 6.1).

Table 6.1 Korea: Number of First Tier Suppliers by Company

(Year)	Hyundai	Kia	GM Korea	Ssangyong	Renault Samsung	Daewoo Bus	Tata-Daewoo	Total	(Separate Companies)
2003	355	395	273	243	125	140	184	1,695	(878)
2019	359	343	293	219	197	176	184	1,771	(824)

Source: Korea Auto Industries Coop Association, <http://www.kaica.or.kr/bbs/content.php?co_id=statics> various years. Accessed on 21 October 2020.

Table 6.2 Korea: First Tier Suppliers by Number of Employees (in 2019)

Size	Small	Medium			Large		Total
Number of Employees	< 49	50~99	100~299	300~499	500-999	> 1,000	
	234	151	257	79	68	35	824

Source: Korea Auto Industries Coop Association at <http://www.kaica.or.kr/bbs/content.php?co_id=statics> (accessed 21 October 2020).

Even in 2018, nearly 30% of the country's first-tier suppliers had fewer than 50 employees; close to a half had under 100 employees (Table 6.2).

Although the government regularly announced programs to support small suppliers, implementation remained weak and sporadic, and SMEs continued to lack resources and technology. The insistence of the assemblers in the 1990s that their suppliers should not also manufacture for their competitors limited economies of scale and product standardization. Links with companies further up the supply chain and ultimately with the assemblers themselves were the principal channel through which technology passed. Given the preference of the assemblers to control the more sophisticated technologies in-house, however, the record of technology transfer down the supply chain was relatively poor. The primary interest of assemblers was to obtain components at the lowest cost (and they often were slow in making payments to their subcontractors). In many cases, low prices, lack of standardization, and absence of economies of scale denied SMEs sufficient revenue to engage in research and development activities. In contrast to the relations of trust developed between Toyota and its suppliers, those between Korean assemblers and their lower-tier suppliers were frequently adversarial (Park and Jun 2001; Jang, Han, and Lee 1999). And, again in contrast to Japan, the state did little to provide a framework for more cooperative arrangements between large and small companies.

In this century, the situation for SMEs improved somewhat as the assemblers became more concerned about quality control and consequently more willing to share expertise with their suppliers. In July 2002, Hyundai, Kia, and Mobis, in conjunction with 164 parts suppliers, set up a training center, KAP, which provides technical assistance to suppliers. Besides running seminars, it sends technical experts to spend time with suppliers. Two-thirds of the cost of training is paid for by the government's Small and Medium Enterprise Development Foundation. KAP can also provide funding for up to 30% of the cost of new equipment for companies, e.g., measurement apparatus (interview, KAP, Seoul, July 1, 2008).

It has also become more common for component manufacturers to supply more than one company. But even by 2019, of the total of 1,771 first-tier suppliers across the domestic assembly industry, there were 824 separate companies—indicating that a large number of companies still only supplied one assembler. Little had changed from the previous decade. Interviewees told us that the breach of the feudal structure of the industry at the turn of the century was largely a temporary phenomenon—a response to supply disruptions caused by the difficulties companies faced in the wake of the Asian financial crisis (interview July 2008).

As we have seen throughout the region, component suppliers continue to come under intense pressure to lower prices—and are particularly vulnerable in Korea given the feudal structure of the industry. In 2012 Korea's Fair Trade Commission fined Hyundai Mobis $2.5 million for abusing its market dominance in the years 2008–2011 by demanding price cuts from suppliers. Similarly, a first-tier supplier to Hyundai, Seohan Industries, which followed Hyundai to Alabama, was fined in 2013 for demanding price cuts from subcontractors. We heard in interviews in Korea in 2008 that the primary concern for Hyundai even in dealing with large suppliers was still cost—with technological competence coming second.

SMEs are also increasingly vulnerable to low-cost imports from China. Korea's entry into new preferential trade agreements generated increasing pressure for removal of the non-tariff barriers that have protected its domestic supply industry. In 2014, the government introduced new measures for certification of auto parts that were intended to reduce the costs of replacement parts for foreign cars in the Korean market. If extended to domestic cars, a shake-up in the industry will follow. For instance, Mobis has had exclusive rights to sell all Hyundai and Kia after-market products—a very lucrative business because prices in the after-market are estimated to be between three and five times those for supplying to the assemblers (interview, Korea, July 2008).

Institutions for Upgrading

The Education System

Korea's rapid industrialization was built on a workforce that was highly educated by international standards. Illiteracy declined from 40% of the workforce in 1946 to zero by 1963 (Amsden 1989: 221–222). In 1960, Korea's primary enrollment stood at 96%, compared with the average of 34% for other countries at similar per capita incomes (Ra and Shim 2009: 5). By 1970, half of the workforce in manufacturing had at least secondary education. By the middle of that decade, the share of scientists and engineers in the population and the share of scientists and engineers in R&D in the population in Korea substantially exceeded that of Singapore. State provision of formal education was supplemented by subsidies to firms for enterprise training. In the 1970s, the government borrowed funds from the Asian Development Bank and the World Bank to set up vocational training centers.

As we discussed in Chapter 3, Korea scores exceptionally on nearly all the indicators of science and technology capabilities—ranging from R&D researchers per million population through vocational training through the output of articles in scientific journals. It has the highest tertiary gross enroll-ment ratio of any country in the world. Sixty-five percent of Korean 25–34-year-olds have attained tertiary education, while over 97% of that same age group have finished at least upper secondary education, the highest among OECD countries. Korean high school students regularly rank in the top two countries in the world on the OECD's triennial Program for International Student Assessment.

Korea succeeded in training a workforce with the basic skills necessary for factory work. It was less successful in providing vocational training suited for the needs of specific sectors. In 1975, following disappointment with com-panies' efforts to upgrade skills, the government introduced mandatory workplace training in companies with over 300 employees. Although the in-itial response was strong, with over 80% of the workforce enrolled in the late 1970s, a decade later only 10% were in training (Rowley and Yoo 2013: 68). In the 1990s, the program was converted into a training levy system. Currently, about 27% of South Korean students are enrolled in school-based voca-tional and technical education. Of these students, 43% go on to junior col-lege, and another 25% go on to university (Center on International Education Benchmarking 2017).

At the university level, Korean institutions do surprisingly poorly in inter-national rankings: in the Shanghai Jiao Tong ranking, no Korean university makes the top 100, while just 10 universities are in the top 500. In engineering and a few other specific fields, however, a number of Korean institutions do much better. The Korean Advanced Institute of Science and Technology, Korea University, and Seoul National all rank in the top 75, and Pohang University of Science and Technology in the top 100 in engineering (http://www.shanghairanking.com/). Several universities established departments of automotive engineering in the 1990s, e.g., Kookmin, Hangyang, Inje, and the Seoul National University of Science and Technology.

In the interviews that we conducted in Korea, little concern was expressed about the supply of skilled personnel, a dramatically different situation from our Southeast Asian cases. Some SMEs, however, noted the increasing difficulty of finding workers for "dirty" jobs, and Hyundai had problems in recruiting for its electronics division when it was located outside of the greater Seoul region. After the Asian financial crisis, employment in the private sector gained in prestige, while that of government jobs declined: large corporations such as Hyundai had the pick of recent graduates. With the rise in wage rates on the shop floor, Korea's competitive advantage moved away from low-cost assembly to relatively low-cost engineers.

The current system of vocational training has been criticized by the OECD for failing to meet the specific skills needs of industry (Kis and Park 2012). Its vocational education system is compared (unfavorably) with those of Germany and the Scandinavian countries. For the purposes of our study, however, the more relevant comparison would be with other middle-income countries seeking to develop an automobile industry. In this context, Korea's record in workforce development is impressive (Panth 2013; Rowley and Yoo 2013).

Industry-Specific Institutions

Korea has a rich variety of state institutions providing support for science and technology in particular and for industry more generally. The two most important institutes in the automotive sector are the Korea Automotive Technology Institute (KATECH) and the Korea Automobile Testing & Research Institute (KATRI).

KATECH (http://www.katech.re.kr/eng/open_contents/sub01/0101.html) was founded in 1990 and is the principal government institute providing assistance to the automotive industry. It specializes in automotive components, providing research and development support to firms, and testing facilities. It now operates about a dozen (small) regional R&D centers. In recent years, it has emphasized the development of new power systems. In 2004, it was designated a Management Institute of Future Vehicle Technology Development Project. It established a Hybrid Vehicle Test Center in 2006, and has set up a Green Powertrain System R&D Center, and a Vehicle-IT Fusion Technology Research Center. In 2010, it was designated the secretariat of the Green Car Strategy Forum. Besides testing physical components, KATECH also analyzes and evaluates vehicle software. In addition to laboratories, KATECH has its own test track. It is responsible for providing ISO certification to Korean companies. According to an interviewee, the fees that KATECH charges for testing and certification are very low by international standards. Additional testing and certification is provided by the Korea Testing and Research Institute (KTR) (which covers all industries). In particular, it assesses whether components meet international standards.

About half of KATECH's funding is devoted to projects—and of these, approximately one-half are initiated in response to requests from individual companies (the other half are projects that KATECH decides to pursue on the basis of its surveys of what component companies need). Technologies developed for individual companies are not shared with their competitors—although some general information may be published (interview, KATECH, July 2008). The ownership of any patents developed goes to the company, although they will be registered in the name of the KATECH researcher. KATECH's recent work on hybrid technologies seems potentially of great significance for the future of the components industry in Korea. Besides the direct cooperation in product development, KATECH's most important contributions to companies are the facilities it provides for testing and certification. These functions distinguish the contributions of KATECH from those of the company-led network, KAP, discussed in the previous section.

KATRI (http://www.ts2020.kr/eng/main.do) was established as a car safety testing unit by the Ministry of Construction and Transport in 1987. Over the next decade, it constructed seven indoor testing facilities including a collision test lab, an impact test lab, a noise test lab, and equipment to test body strength, engine power, and vehicle emissions. It also operates its own test track. It is responsible for operating the New Car Assessment Program for the Korean government, which was introduced in Korea in 1999, only three years after its Japanese counterpart (in contrast, there was no equivalent program in ASEAN until the end of 2011). The program was particularly timely, coming at the end of a decade in which Korean cars had acquired an unwelcome reputation for their poor safety record.

Government Policies in Support of the Industry

In the early days, the industry received help from the Ministry of Science and Technology, which was responsible for developing fundamental scientific technology required by industries, and from the Ministry of Trade and Industry (MTI), whose focus was more on applied technology. In June 1990, the MTI expanded its category of high-technology industry to the automotive sector, which made the sector eligible for tax breaks and financial incentives for R&D in power-generation and transmission systems, chassis, body styling, electric and electronics systems, and safety and information systems. Similar tax breaks and R&D incentives for the localization of auto parts had been promised in the 1987 Five Year Plan. This gave priority to items where Japan supplied more than 50% of imports, and to those that had significant technological spill-over potential or good export prospects (Lew 1992: 300–302).

In 2001 the government announced a Special Laws for Promotion of Parts and Materials 10-year plan. The formula was consistent with long-standing state support for the industry. The Ministry of Industry worked with private experts and trade associations to identify 100 components currently dependent on Japanese inputs and to discern what local suppliers would need to replace them. The government and associated research institutes provided financial support for R&D, specialized machinery, testing facilities, and education for workers. The plan was extended for a further 10 years in 2012, with more detailed reviews occurring every three years (Kwon and Kim 2020: 749).

Much of the government support for the industry from the mid-1990s focused on alternative technologies. In 1998, the government initiated a 10-year "G-7 Next Generation Vehicle Research Project." A total of US$323 million was invested, with funding split roughly evenly between government and private sector sources. This included 31 projects for reducing emissions (Korean cars were increasingly facing problems meeting new emissions standards in industrialized countries), 29 projects for safety, and 29 for the development of components for electric vehicles—including the first projects for hydrogen fuel cell vehicles. Hyun reports that the projects generated 1,082 patents (Hyun 2020: 248). In 2004, the government initiated a further 10-year project with a total investment of US$700 million, again split equally between the state and the private sector, to develop technologies for electric and autonomous vehicles.

The Korean government was relatively late in recognizing the potential importance of fuel-efficient cars—as Hyundai-Kia had been. But as these companies gained increasing competence in relevant technologies, the state became a "big follower." Fuel-efficient vehicles became a central component of President Lee Myun-bak's "Green Growth" strategy (Kim and Thurbon 2015). It promised to allocate 400 billion won (US$341 million) in the five years to 2014 to support development of high-performance batteries and other related systems (Phys. Org 2009). In December 2012, the Ministry of Knowledge Economy committed to spend about 70 billion won (US$65 million) on electric-vehicle development by 2014. The government has also provided support in two areas where Korean companies are internationally competitive: lithium-ion batteries and fuel cells.

Both Hyundai and Kia had ambitious plans to market hybrid and electric vehicles internationally—with Hyundai assembling hybrid versions of its Sonata saloon in its Beijing plant from May 2016 (Ahn 2016). By 2016, Hyundai and Kia combined had become the world's fourth largest producers of eco-friendly cars behind Toyota, Honda, and Renault-Nissan. Their total annual sales, however, were only 74,000: in comparison, Toyota sold 1.08 million eco-friendly vehicles (Chosun Ilbo 2016). Both companies had committed, however, to eco-friendly cars, a move strongly backed by the government (Harris 2017).

The Changing Relationship between State Institutions and the Industry

The relationships between the state automotive research institutes and the numerous other government institutes in science and technology (e.g., the Science and Technology Policy Institute) are often obscure to outsiders—as, indeed, in many instances are their relations with the private sector. The importance of the institutes in research activities relative to what are now giant companies undoubtedly has changed fundamentally over time: Hyundai, Mobis, and Mando now have far larger in-house R&D staffs and budgets than the government research institutes, and have their own testing facilities and tracks. Hyundai's Namyang Technology Research Center, for instance, employed 15,000 researchers in 2015 (Hyun 2020: 243), compared with the total of 600 in the state institutes. In 2009, Hyundai Motor and its affiliate Kia Motors announced plans to invest 4.1 trillion won by end of 2013 to develop fuel-efficient cars and cut carbon emissions, 10 times the sum the government promised to invest (Phys. Org 2009). Even in the case of the assemblers and large component makers, however, any statement on the significance of state support has to be qualified because of the lack of knowledge of the full extent of government subsidies for the companies. In addition, the provision of government funds can serve as an important signaling device. And state institutions have the luxury of devoting resources to basic research with a potential long-term payoff.

The automotive institutes are currently most important for medium-sized enterprises (few small companies have the capital or personnel to devote to the development of new products). Their testing and certification facilities continue to play a significant role for companies seeking a broader domestic as well as international market. The Korean automotive institutes are the most effective among those of our various case studies: they are simply in a different league from the recently established and poorly funded institutions found in Southeast Asia.

The Political Origins of Institutions for Upgrading

Few countries are as vulnerable as South Korea. All but the southeastern corner of the country was invaded by North Korean forces during the war of 1950–1953. With the division of the country, much of the industrial infrastructure lay north of the border. The South had minimal natural resources. It faced an erratic North Korean polity that was publicly committed to reunifying the country, by force if necessary (the civil war was ended by an armistice but no peace treaty was signed). During the 1960s, the North had matched the economic growth rates of its southern neighbor. And the North could count on the support of both China and the Soviet Union.

The South's frontline position in the struggle against communism in Asia gave leaders considerable latitude in exerting claims on economic and military assistance from the United States. As Jung-en Woo (1991) documents, Korea's first postwar president, Syngman Rhee, proved adept at using Korea's security situation to generate resources to sustain his rent-seeking regime. In the mid-1950s, aid was equivalent to 14% of the country's GDP (Krueger 1979: 66–68). Between 1945 and the mid-1960s, US economic and military aid to Korea amounted to more than $13 billion (Kim 1997: 39).

Manipulation of the security threat enabled Rhee and, after him, Park to ignore efforts by Washington to force reforms to the exchange rate and trade regimes (Haggard, Kim, and Moon 1991: 452). The decision to support the US war in Vietnam by sending troops in 1965 and 1966 brought payoffs not only in the military sphere through a short-term deepening of the alliance, but also in the economic realm—as other Western countries joined the United States in extending commercial loans to Korea. Seoul is estimated to have received more than $1 billion from the United States in support of its Vietnam excursion. The normalization of relations with Japan in June 1965 similarly brought an infusion of Japanese capital—more than $600 million in grants, preferential loans, and debt write-offs as reparations for Japan's colonization (Lee 2011b). But Park became more vulnerable to US pressure as the Vietnam War sapped Washington's enthusiasm for propping up Asian allies.

Several factors combined to increase the insecurity of the regime in Korea in the last part of the 1960s—an exacerbated threat from the North; reduced commitments on the part of Washington; and increasing economic difficulties. The Park regime initially believed that because of its contribution to the

US war effort in Vietnam, it would be exempted from the Nixon doctrine, proclaimed in July 1969, which asserted that the United States would no longer provide ground forces if an Asian ally faced aggression other than from a nuclear power. But this proved not to be the case. The United States started to withdraw forces from Korea in 1970. Although only a small number of troops was initially involved, the symbolic importance of the move cannot be overstated. It also raised concerns about future US supply of military equipment, on which the Korean armed forces were highly dependent.

The Nixon administration also launched action in the economic realm that had a significant negative impact on Korea's interests. Textile negotiations, concluded in 1971, led to the imposition of a "voluntary export restraint" on Korea, an early portent of future troubles in the US market for Korea's most competitive export industries.

Park responded immediately to Washington's decision on troop withdrawal by announcing his intention to develop a local defense industry. In June 1970, the government announced a Comprehensive Program for Heavy Industries. The "Four Core Projects" in this program were a speciality steels plant, iron casting, integrated machinery, and a large-scale shipyard. But the hope that the Japanese government would provide the funds for these projects was dashed—in November 1971, the Economic Planning Board reported to the president that little progress had been achieved on the Comprehensive Program. It was obvious that the resources required to promote heavy industrialization would have to be generated internally. After intensive planning, Park formally announced the Heavy and Chemical Industry promotion policy in January 1973. The plan was intended not only to provide the industrial basis for an integrated domestic defense industry, but also to generate $10 billion of exports (in the previous year, exports were only $2.5 billion: the $10 billion target was achieved in 1977) (Horikane 2005: 388).

The automobile industry was a logical choice as one of the strategic sectors for the HCI drive. The industry would provide a key market for POSCO's first steel mill, which began production in 1973. The development of vehicle technologies had obvious potential to enhance local defense capabilities. The emphasis on producing a national car derived in part from the desire first to save on scarce foreign exchange and subsequently to generate substantial export earnings in a context of an economy frequently dislocated by fluctuations in the prices of imported raw materials, especially fuel—although these ambitions were not fully realized for a quarter of a century. Finally, the automobile industry was a significant strand of the symbiotic relationship between the state and the chaebol, which provided military regimes with crucial political and financial support until democratization eventually came in 1988.

One System, Four Companies

The Korean auto industry from the turn of the century provides us with the opportunity to observe how domestically and internationally owned companies fared under essentially similar environmental conditions. This field experiment is far from perfect, not least because of the dominant share of the domestic market that Hyundai-Kia has held, coupled with suspicions on the part of the foreign-owned companies that the government in its design of regulations continued to tilt the playing field to favor the domestically owned company. But the environment was sufficiently similar—in, for example, the institutions that support the industry—that we can confidently ascribe a substantial part of variations in performance across the industry to the attributes of companies themselves.

Hyundai-Kia

Although Hyundai-Kia emerged from the Asian financial crisis with a dominant share of the domestic market, it was a company in disarray, facing formidable challenges. Its reputation in American and European markets remained tarnished by the quality problems of the first generation of exports—with the consequence that Hyundai had become dependent on developing country markets for more than half of its export sales. The acquisition of Kia had exacerbated Hyundai's debt problems. Integrating two major auto assemblers into a single entity had rarely proved successful in the modern auto industry: in this instance, Kia *inter alia* had a completely different supply chain, vehicle platforms, and management tradition.

Yet, Hyundai also had some significant strengths in confronting the challenges of the new century. Its expansion in the 1990s had provided it with the foundation for efficient scale production (even though domestic production had slumped during the Asian financial crisis). With the addition of Kia's plants, Hyundai had a total production capacity of over 2 million cars at the turn of the century. It had overseas assembly facilities in China, India, Malaysia, and Turkey, with a total production capacity of 330,000 vehicles (Lansbury, So, and Kwon 2007: 54). It had built up its own design capabilities: the design of the S-coupe in 1990 was done in-house, beating competition from ItalDesign (Chung and Kim 2014: 7). The company also had acquired substantial depth in engineering skills. It produced the first of its own engines in 1991 and, by the time of the Asian financial crisis, had a full range of engines, ranging from the Epislon 0.8 liter to the Sigma 3.0 liter. Meanwhile,

Daimler Chrysler acquired a 9% stakeholding in HMC in September 2002, providing a cash injection that helped ease the company's debt problems.

A principal challenge for Hyundai was to overcome the negative brand image it had acquired from the late 1980s onward. For many observers, a key turning-point was the decision in 1998 to offer a 10-year or 100K mile powertrain warranty. But shrewd PR was also backed by a marked improvement in quality, driven by the new chairman of the company, Chung Mong-Koo. The company also put increased emphasis on design, building on the work of the design centers it had established in Germany (1995), Japan (1995), and the United States (1990).

The emphasis on quality control paid off: in J. D. Power and Associates Initial Quality Survey, Hyundai's ranking improved from 28th in 2002 to 23rd in 2003 to 7th in 2004, at which point the number of problems per 100 vehicles fell below the industry average. In 2006, it was ranked 3rd, topping all of its Japanese competitors. Hyundai successfully transformed its brand image from "cheap"—and often "nasty"—to "good value." Another PR coup came when Hyundai became the first company to offer an "Assurance Plan" in January 2009 during the global financial crisis, in which it offered to buy back cars if customers lost their jobs (Automotive News 2011). The construction of new assembly plants overseas was a key dimension of Hyundai's strategy. Hyundai re-entered North America through constructing a $1 billion plant in Montgomery, Alabama, which inaugurated production in 2005. Like its Japanese competitors, Hyundai chose a non-unionized locale: with the constant rise of wage rates in Korea, the hourly rate paid to workers in Alabama has been below that paid to domestic workers.

Arguably as important for the company's success in the last decade has been its presence in China. In May 2002, HMC initiated a joint automotive project with Beijing Automotive Industry Holding Corp (BAIC). HMC was a latecomer to the Chinese market (Kia's first plant in China, a joint venture with the Yue Da Group in Nanjing, had opened in 1997; by then, Peugeot-Citroen, VW, GM, and Toyota all had joint ventures in China; Honda entered the market in the following year). Hyundai's choice of partner in China was particularly shrewd. In the Chinese auto market, where rivalries among municipalities stoked fierce competition, Beijing had been singularly unsuccessful. BAIC's principal joint venture, Beijing Jeep, was a case study of the many things that could go wrong in a joint venture in China (Mann 1989, 1997; Chin 2010: 66–69). By the turn of the century, Thun (2006: 239) reports, BAIC had been reduced to a holding company. Hyundai, consequently, enjoyed a strong bargaining position. Given the weakness of the components sector in the Beijing region, Hyundai was able to bring its domestic supply chain with it, with most of the firms, including its key supplier, Mobis, being permitted to establish wholly owned subsidiaries (Thun 2006: 238). Hyundai also benefited significantly from local protectionism: municipal authorities designated two of its models, the Elantra and Sonata, as Beijing's official taxi models. In 2010, China displaced Korea as Hyundai's largest market (Automotive News 2010). Hyundai's annual sales in China among joint ventures were second only to those of VW and accounted for more than 6% of the market in 2015 and 2016 before slumping in 2017 following the crisis over Korea's hosting of the US THAAD missile system.

Hyundai's investment in India has also paid off handsomely. Hyundai's wholly owned subsidiary, Hyundai Motors India, was its second overseas investment, made in 1996 in the wake of the Canadian debacle. Hyundai soon challenged the near monopoly of Maruti Suzuki. From 2002, the Indian subsidiary became a significant player in Hyundai's global strategy, exporting small cars to Europe, Africa, the Middle East, and Australia. Hyundai has also targeted other rapidly growing developing markets, building plants in Turkey (1997), Brazil (2012), and Russia (2011). In 2012, Hyundai's overseas output surpassed its domestic production for the first time. By 2016, overseas production at 3.2 million vehicles was more than three times domestic production (1.0 million) (Hyundai 2017). The global financial crisis saw Hyundai make serious inroads into the European market for the first time. With a 6% share of the European market, facilitated by the Free Trade Agreement between the European Union and Korea that entered into force in July 2011, the combined sales of Hyundai and Kia (over 750,000 vehicles) in the European market currently exceed those of all other non-European companies, including all of Hyundai's Japanese competitors.

By 2010, Hyundai was fully realizing the benefits of the takeover of Kia. Its junior partner faced particular challenges at the time of the merger. All its vehicles had depended heavily on imported design and technology, primarily from Mazda. At the turn of the century its vehicle line-up was not only derivative, but narrow and aging. Its international profile was limited because its exports were sold predominantly under the badge of another manufacturer. This may previously have been an advantage—and the new association with Hyundai, given its poor reputation for quality, provided little on which Kia might build. Although a decision was made to run Kia as a separate company, the relations between the interlinked companies involved in Hyundai's motor manufacturing were typically opaque (see Figure 6.2).

Although integration of platforms and engines began in 2004, it was a decade before the two companies fully exploited the potential savings. Integration of the supply chains was particularly challenging. Despite being a much smaller company, Kia had a larger number of suppliers than Hyundai

(395 versus 355 in 2003), in part because it sourced fewer components in-house. Hyundai aimed to reduce its total number of suppliers for the merged entity from more than 750 to 400, of which 50 would be "core" producers, responsible for particular modules, 100 would be "specialty" producers, and the remainder "commodity" producers with which the company would maintain only an arms-length purchasing arrangement (interview with Hyundai-Kia officials, Seoul, September 2003).

Kia was to be differentiated by appealing to younger customers through vehicles with sportier images (Gadacz 2001). Although it struggled even more than Hyundai with perceptions about the questionable quality of its vehicles, the new vehicles introduced after 2003, especially those in the SUV segment, soon became export successes—by 2004, it was exporting three-quarters of its domestic production of over 900,000 vehicles (and, impressively, 72% of these were to the advanced economy markets of Western Europe and the United States) (http://www.annualreportowl.com/Kia/2005/ Annual%20Report?p=63). Kia's formula for success was similar to that of Hyundai: a renewed emphasis on quality control, and on building up design and engineering capabilities. Unusually for a Korean corporation at the time, Kia reached out to secure the best management talent globally: in 2006, it recruited as its chief designer Peter Schreyer, who was previously in the same position at Audi. Like Hyundai, Kia quickly built up its international facilities. In 2005, it had only one overseas plant—in China—with a limited production capacity of 130,000 vehicles. In 2007 it opened plants in Slovakia and a second plant in China; in 2010 its first plant in the United States—in Georgia, in easy reach of Hyundai's Alabama plant; and in December 2019 its first plant in India. The plants from the two companies collaborated, e.g., the Kia plant in the United States manufactured Hyundai Santa Fe SUVs in 2010 when Hyundai's plant was running at full capacity. Similarly, the Kia plant in Slovakia supplies engines for both brands while its Hyundai counterpart provides transmissions. The proximity of the two companies' overseas manufacturing plants has made it possible for Korean transplant suppliers to service them from a single location. Like Hyundai, Kia has also tapped into foreign expertise by opening design centers in the United States and Germany, and R&D centers in Germany, China, India, Japan, and the United States.

Korean Subsidiaries of Foreign Assemblers

The other Korean auto manufacturers that failed in the Asian financial crisis faced similar challenges to Kia. All had been heavily reliant on foreign technology, having built only limited in-house competencies in engineering and design. They had few models to market to domestic consumers—and, with the exception of Ssangyong, they lacked SUVs, the fastest growing segment in the Korean market. They found it difficult to persuade the Korean public that they were domestic automakers (Ward's Auto World 2004). In addition, they faced the complication of finding a niche for themselves within the global strategies of their new multinational owners. Their relatively poor performance in comparison with Kia was in part a reflection of some of the disadvantages encountered when domestic production is in the hands of subsidiaries of multinational corporations. On the other hand, sales through the global network of their parent companies offered the opportunity to market vehicles without attracting the negative brand image of a made-in-Korea vehicle. The principal beneficiary initially was GM Daewoo (renamed GM Korea in 2011), the country's third largest auto manufacturer.

GM Korea (GMK)

After a difficult period when management crises compounded the challenges of piecing together the elements of the Daewoo auto empire that it had acquired, GM Daewoo invested heavily in the early years of this century to establish Korea as the primary global source for its small vehicles.

GM Daewoo initially benefited from producing new models that had been under development by Daewoo before its bankruptcy. With the resumption of sales in the United States in late 2003, exports became crucial for the company's survival—with more than 75% of its sales coming from cars sold in the United States, Europe, Australia, and Japan under the Chevrolet and Suzuki badges. The Korean operation was also given primary responsibility for worldwide design of small vehicles (assisted by GM subsidiaries in Germany and Australia), drawing on the abundance of relatively low cost designers in Korea. Local production depended on other GM subsidiaries for engine design and/or manufacture, but the strategy of using Korea as the principal source of small vehicles initially enjoyed substantial success. By 2008, GM Korea was responsible for fully one-quarter of GM's global production. But it enjoyed limited success in the domestic market, with only a 10% share, leaving it vulnerable to changing global market conditions and to fluctuations in the exchange rate of the won. The global financial crisis consequently had a severe impact on the company: local output fell by 43% from its peak in 2007 (Table 6.3).

GMK overcame the immediate crisis when international sales picked up in 2010, but production has slumped since the peak of 2011. The dependence on exports has continued; by 2019, domestic sales had fallen to only 76,000

Table 6.3 Domestic Auto Production in Korea by Manufacturer

	Hyundai	Kia	GM Korea	Ssangyong	Renault Samsung
2019	1,786,131	1,450,102	409,830	132,994	164,974
2018	1,747,837	1,469,415	444,816	142,138	215,809
2017	1,651,710	1,522,520	519,385	145,345	264,037
2016	1,679,906	1,556,845	579,745	155,600	243,965
2015	1,858,395	1,718,467	614,808	145,633	205,059
2014	1,876,408	1,712,485	629,230	140,259	152,138
2013	1,852,456	1,598,863	782,721	143,516	129,638
2012	1,905,261	1,585,685	785,757	119,142	153,891
2011	1,892,254	1,583,921	810,854	113,249	244,260
2010	1,743,375	1,416,681	744,096	80,067	275,269
2009	1,606,879	1,137,176	532,191	34,703	189,831
2008	1,670,181	1,054,962	819,436	82,405	197,024
2007	1,706,727	1,118,714	942,805	122,857	177,742
2006	1,618,268	1,150,289	779,630	117,123	161,421

Source: Data from KAMA and KAICA Annual Reports. For 2018 and 2019; see <http://www.kaica.or.kr/bbs/content.php?co_id=statics> accessed 21 October 2020.

vehicles of a total production of over 400,000. In an attempt to capitalize on anti-chaebol sentiment and on Koreans' increasing demand for foreign products, the company changed its name from GM Daewoo, and rebranded its cars for the domestic market as Chevrolets. But this move seemed to alienate as many Koreans as it attracted: a small increase in domestic sales was not sufficient to offset a decline in export markets. Export dependence has become increasingly problematic as wage rates in Korea rose in relation to the company's production costs at plants in other developing economies. Labor costs per vehicle produced by GM in Korea were $1,133 compared with an average of $677 across GM's international operations (Automotive News 2013).

Between 2012 and 2018, GM Korea was reported to have suffered cumulated losses of over $3.5 billion. In February 2018, it announced that it would close one of its four assembly operations, the Kunsan plant that produced Chevrolet models. Two months later, it threatened to file for bankruptcy unless its unions made significant concessions. Following a promise of additional investment of $750 million from the Korea Development Bank, GM agreed to a $7.15 billion rescue plan, to develop two new models, and to maintain assembly operations for five years (Shin 2018). Although Korea continues to be a significant design center for GM, many observers doubt that the company has a long-term commitment to manufacturing cars in Korea. In 2019, its production fell by 10% to

409,830, substantially less than half of its 2009 peak (최경애 2020a). In 2019, the company lost over $300 million. The president of GM's international operations Steve Kiefer stated in November 2020, following another prolonged period of labor unrest, that "we're losing confidence that we're going to be able to continue to invest in [Korea]" (quoted in Klayman and Yang 2020).

Renault Samsung Motors (RSM)

In taking over Samsung's nascent auto manufacturing business, Renault acquired a state-of-the-art manufacturing facility, constructed by its Japanese affiliate, Nissan, located close to Busan, Korea's principal port—but little else. The plant had barely begun production when the Asian financial crisis struck, further weakening its fragile supply chain. The company's sole model was a re-badged Nissan: the company lacked in-house design and engineering skills.

RSM initially made gains in the local market by selling its SM5, essentially a re-badged Nissan Maxima, to taxi fleets, which helped to lift the company's profile. Renault committed 120 billion won (approximately US$100 million) each year between 2002 and 2005 to boost research and development at its new Korean subsidiary. But the company continued to depend on its parent for platforms and engines. The lack of its own models has been a persistent problem for Renault. Although the company has always depended heavily on exports, which accounted for one-third of its output in 2007, rising to 60% in 2010, its export markets are determined by its parent. In many export markets—and these initially were developing economies where Nissan and Renault lacked assembly plants—its vehicles are sold either under the Nissan brand (Middle East, Russia, and Latin America) or the Renault badge (Mexico, Egypt, Colombia). Hopes that it would be able to use its Nissan linkages to export to Japan were not realized, given the reluctance of Japanese consumers to purchase Korean-made vehicles (interview, July 2008) (even Hyundai closed its Japanese operations in 2009; Greimel 2009).

Production halved in the years between 2010 and 2013, with declining sales both within Korea and in export markets when the company failed to introduce new models. The company's plant was running at only 60% of its 300,000 annual capacity in 2013. The company was saved in the short term when Renault made the decision in July 2012 to produce the compact SUV Nissan Rogue in its Korean plant for export to the United States. In 2017, more than 120,000 Korean-manufactured Rogues were shipped to the United States. Exports accounted for two-thirds of the local plant's total output of 265,000 vehicles. In December 2018, however, Renault headquarters announced that the Busan plant would cease production of the Rogue in the following year. The decision came in the context of reported management unhappiness at frequent labor disputes at the Korean plant, and a desire by Nissan, following the near breakdown of its alliance with Renault, to bring more production back home.

Meanwhile, the future of the brand in Korea was increasingly called into question. Samsung itself was said to be planning to re-enter car production through the production of electric vehicles (Seo 2016). In 2016, it paid $8 billion to acquire Harman International Industries, a leading US manufacturer of multimedia, navigation, and visual display systems (Harris 2016). As Korean consumers shed their bias against foreign brands, reports circulated that Renault Samsung was considering dropping the Samsung label (RSM pays 1% royalties on all sales to Samsung for use of its brand name; Lee 2016).

Even though the assembly plant remained relatively efficient (ranked 8th among 146 plants worldwide in productivity in the 2016 Harbour Report), the company, like GMK, was relying more on imported vehicles and concentrating its investments on vehicle design (it had been selected as the group's design center for small SUVs (Korea Herald 2016). In 2019, its sales plunged by 34% to a mere 90,591 units (최경애 2020b).

Ssangyong

Ssangyong, the smallest of the three Korean assemblers that fell into foreign hands after the Asian financial crisis, had by far the most precarious position. When GM and its partners refused to include the company in their takeover of Daewoo, creditors scrambled to find a purchaser, eventually settling on SAIC. The match between the two companies was far from obvious, however. SAIC had no experience of operating overseas affiliates. Exactly where the synergies between the companies lay and what role Ssangyong would play in SAIC's future corporate planning were unclear. And although Ssangyong had its own design capabilities, having produced a number of eccentric-looking SUVs in the 1990s, it continued to rely on Daimler-Benz for engines and transmissions for its vehicles.

The partnership proved to be short-lived, dissolving in acrimony in the early days of the global financial crisis when Ssangyong, having made losses for most of the period since the takeover, filed for court receivership. The Korean government subsequently accused SAIC of stealing Ssanyong technology, specifically a hybrid control unit for which the Korean government provided nearly half the research funds between 2004 and 2008 (Park 2011). Ssangyong remained in limbo between February 2009 and November 2010 until Mahindra & Mahindra Ltd., India's largest SUV maker, paid $378 million for 70% of Ssangyong's shares.

The partnership between SUV makers was a more logical one for Ssangyong. Mahindra & Mahindra needed its distribution network—particularly strong in Russia but also enjoying a presence in China and Latin America, and hoped to use Ssangyong to penetrate the US market. Unlike SAIC, Mahindra & Mahindra invested in new models at Ssangyong. The company's output climbed steadily after the takeover, benefiting from the rebound in SUV sales with the decline in gasoline prices. By 2013, its domestic sales exceeded those of Renault Samsung. More than half of Ssangyong's production was exported. The company remains vulnerable because of its concentration on a niche market, albeit one that is currently popular, and its small production volume (annual output of less than 150,000 vehicles). It has lost money each year since 2013. In 2019, its losses quadrupled to $288 million as sales declined by 5.6% to 135,235 vehicles. (최경애 2020c). The cash-rich Mahindra & Mahindra (which also acquired Italian design company Pininfarina in 2015) appears to be willing to continue to provide Ssangyong a lifeline, committing in early 2020 to invest a further $423 million to turn the company around over a three-year period (*Auto Business News*, January 22, 2020).

Car assembly in Korea has become increasingly challenging given the high wage rates and volatile labor environment. The ritual of annual strikes over wage settlements, a legacy of antagonism between management and militant unions from the days of labor repression, imposes significant costs on assemblers through loss of output. Meanwhile, the five Korean assemblers paid workers an average of US$78,000 in 2017, 10% more than the average pay for workers at Toyota and VW (for Hyundai, the figure was close to US$87,000). Labor costs accounted for 12% of sales revenues for Korea's assemblers in that year, compared with 10% at VW and 6% at Toyota. And in China, wages were one-fifth of the level in Korea (Choi 2019). To address high labor costs, Hyundai and Kia have moved the majority of their assembly operations offshore. In 2018, Hyundai assembled 2.83 million vehicles in overseas plants, and Kia a further 1.22—a total that exceeded Korea's entire domestic output in that year (이준승 2019). And in 2019, Hyundai announced a proposed joint venture with the city of Gwangju where workers in a new assembly plant would be paid only slightly more than one-third of the wages of other Hyundai plants, with the city and national governments subsidizing housing and other employee benefits (Roberts 2019a). Both GM and Renault Samsung cited labor costs and conflict with labor unions as reasons for their moving production away from their Korean subsidiaries.

Conclusion

Korea's success in pursuing a strategy of intensive development in the auto industry is unparalleled. Even the most ardent defenders of free markets would find it difficult to deny that the state intervened effectively in the 1970s to change incentive structures in a manner that encouraged investments in a sector that many observers thought to be beyond the country's capabilities at the time. The state used the full panoply of instruments at its disposal— restrictions on trade and foreign investment, subsidized credit, export subsidies, local content requirements, enforced licensing of technology, manipulation of the currency to keep it at "competitive" levels, and labor repression—to foster local competencies. Korea was alone among developing economies in effectively limiting entry to the industry during a critical period of early expansion, providing the foundations for the realization of economies of scale and, ultimately, internationally competitive production (Wade 1990: 311). Moreover, through the establishment of industry-specific research institutes and through the more general enhancement of educational skills, it provided a supportive infrastructure that enabled local firms to thrive in a competitive international industry.

In line with our argument developed in Chapter 3, security issues played a crucial role in transforming policies toward the sector from the rent-seeking import substitution of the 1960s and 1970s to the export-orientation fostered by the Heavy and Chemical Industry drive. To be sure, the auto industry benefited from some very important good fortune when the Reagan administration imposed voluntary export restraints on Japanese auto producers. But, as Stern et al. (1995: 162) note, without the prior growth of the industry, fostered by the HCI drive, Korean producers would not have been well-placed to take advantage of this opportunity.

Successful as industrial policies were in the 1970s, the history of the Korean auto industry belies simplistic characterizations of the Korean state as acting as "Korea, Inc." Policy contestation was very real throughout the period. By the time of the HCI, the Economic Planning Board, which some commentators have portrayed as playing a role equivalent to that of MITI in Japan, was dominated by economists who believed that the Korean auto sector would only thrive as an outpost of major multinational assemblers. The development of the industry would have been very different had it not been for the influence of President Park Chung Hee and the engineers advising him in the Blue House and the Ministry of Commerce and Industry. Had the neoclassical economists of the Economic Planning Board had their way in the early 1980s, Hyundai would have been forced out of auto production. Plans to promote an integrated local industry would have been abandoned in favor of Korean plants becoming merely a branch of global car assemblers, relegated to the role of component production. Even then, however, only Hyundai among the three domestic car companies embraced Park's vision of producing a "citizen's car." Not surprisingly, the promotion of the auto industry in Korea—both before and after the Asian financial crisis, when Hyundai and its Kia partner became the only locally owned assemblers—has been a story of close collaboration between the state and Hyundai.

With democratization in the late 1980s, industrial policy became increasingly politicized (Eichengreen, Perkins, and Sin 2012: 84). Despite this trend, the state acted decisively in the aftermath of the Asian financial crisis to create a domestic company capable of competing on a global scale by ensuring that Kia was taken over by Hyundai rather than falling into foreign hands. In several instances, however, the subordination of economic to political logic had a negative impact on the auto sector. The decision in the 1990s, for instance, to allow Samsung to fulfill its long-standing desire to enter the auto industry at a time of rapid expansion by other assemblers exacerbated problems of excess capacity that were exposed by the Asian financial crisis. And a coherent policy of promoting electric vehicles was undermined in the 2010s when governments saw policy change as a means of differentiating themselves from their predecessors.

There were both continuities and significant changes in state policies over the years. As the Korean economy matured and the country successfully sought membership in the OECD, it was under continuous pressure from international partners to liberalize its economy, which reduced the scope for state intervention. And the balance of power between corporations and the state ensured that policies moved from being directive to facilitating. Even to the present day, however, the state has worked with industry associations, research institutes, and the private sector to target specific component imports that it hoped to see produced domestically. With the growth of the R&D capabilities of the assemblers and some of the major component producers, the work of the automotive institutes was primarily of interest to medium-sized companies. But even the largest companies participated in some of the basic research activities. More agencies were involved, sometimes at the expense of policy coherence. And, as the industry reached the technological frontier, the tasks were more demanding. In Wong's (2011b) terminology, the challenge now was to manage uncertainty rather than the more obvious risks evident in the catch-up years. Korea has bet quite heavily on hydrogen fuel-cell vehicles, which—whatever their inherent merits—at this point look unlikely to be the preferred technology for electric vehicles in the foreseeable future.

The performance of assemblers has differed dramatically over the last quarter of a century despite their being faced with largely the same institutional context, policy environment and incentive structures. Only Hyundai originally chose to develop its own technology. Despite the incentives provided by the state, Daewoo and Kia were content to rely largely on producing variants of cars designed and engineered by their foreign partners, which also supplied the core technologies for local assembly. This divergence in approach and performance continued after the Asian financial crisis, when three assemblers fell into foreign hands. And it underlined how domestic ownership of companies plays an important role in intensive development in the automobile industry in a country with a relatively small domestic market.

The Hyundai-Kia merger created a company of sufficient size to realize economies of scale, not just in assembly, but also in research and development and in the production of components (although much of this was spun off into affiliated companies). The Korean economy has benefited not just from Hyundai and Kia's domestic operations, but also from the export of components to their overseas plants. Their opening of foreign assembly plants to circumvent foreign government pressure and/or tariffs and non-tariff barriers, and to take advantage of lower labor costs, was usually accompanied by a surge in Korean exports of auto parts—and they took many of their first-tier suppliers with them (Kwon and Kim 2018). Although both firms have opened overseas R&D and design centers, like most transnational companies they have kept the vast majority of their high value-added activities at home. The three foreign-owned assemblers, however, have uncertain futures, their local plants finding it difficult to survive in a context of high labor costs.

Korea is unique among our case studies in laying the foundations—in its educational system and in its network of state research institutions—for a domestic industry that has enjoyed unparalleled success among late developing countries in penetrating international markets. In a context where domestic wages are much higher than those in other developing economies, the opportunities for Korean companies increasingly lie at the technological edge. To date, Korean companies have enjoyed remarkable success as "fast followers"—not themselves at the cutting edge of technology, but having the capability to buy it when required and often to quickly reverse engineer it. Expenditures on R&D in the auto sector in Korea (both by assemblers and component manufacturers), however, remain substantially below those in other parts of the world. The contemporary challenge for the Korean industry is to build on its strong foundations to maintain a competitive position within a rapidly evolving industry.

7

Malaysia

How Intensive Development Strategies Fail in the Absence of Appropriate Institutions

> The Malaysian car project failed because it was implemented twenty years too late.
>
> **—Lim (1988: 48)**

> Malaysia's most visible foray into heavy industry was in pursuit of a goal dearest to Dr. Mahathir's heart, a national car.... With Dr. Mahathir in retirement after 2003 and no longer able to protect it against rivals, Malaysia's car simply ran out of competitive gas.
>
> **—Wain (2009: 96–97)**

> They say Proton is my brainchild. Now the child of my brain has been sold. Yes. I am sad. I can cry. But the deed is done. Proton can no longer be national.
>
> **—Former Prime Minister Mahathir Mohamad, quoted in Lye (2017)**

Malaysia is in many ways a key test for our arguments. In its "Look East" policy adopted in the 1980s, the government of Prime Minister Mahathir sought to emulate Japan and Korea by building an integrated automotive industry through the promotion of national champions—in our terminology, it embarked on a quest for intensive development in the auto industry. As we saw in Chapter 3, Malaysia has scored very well on World Bank indicators of governance. The government enjoyed considerable success in fostering technological innovation in the palm oil and rubber sectors. Moreover, the deep pockets of government-linked companies enabled the principal national car company, Proton (the abbreviation for Perusahaan Otomobil Nasional), to access leading-edge technology through its acquisition of the UK sports car company Lotus.

The Political Economy of Automotive Industrialization in East Asia. Richard F. Doner, Gregory W. Noble and John Ravenhill, Oxford University Press (2021). © Oxford University Press. DOI: 10.1093/oso/9780197520253.003.0007

Malaysia's efforts to develop an integrated national car industry nonetheless must be judged an expensive failure. Already facing the handicap of a limited domestic market, the promotion of the industry was compromised when policies toward the sector were subordinated to the government's desire to promote the economic position of the ethnic Malay (*Bumiputera*) community. Moreover, entirely consistent with our principal argument regarding the importance of industry-specific institutions, the failure of Malaysia's auto strategy owed much to institutional weaknesses.

Industry Performance

Malaysia achieved some success in intensive development, at least in vehicle assembly, seen in the capacity that Proton acquired to design and manufacture its own vehicles. Yet intensive development remained very shallow: this domestic capacity to design and manufacture vehicles rested on substantial imports of key components. The government's Third Industrial Master Plan, for example, acknowledged that, a quarter of a century after the launch of the national car project, "critical and high value parts and components, such as engines, transmission systems and vehicle electronics components, are still being imported" (Malaysia 2006: para 13.37, p. 357). Moreover, locally produced vehicles failed to find a market internationally. With a domestic car market of only slightly over 550,000 vehicles, less than half of Korea's and under 3% of China's, the prospects for attaining economies of scale depended upon success in penetrating export markets—but even at their peak in 2010, export sales were less than 35,000 vehicles, and by 2016 had declined to little over 13,000, a similar figure to when Proton began exporting in 1989. Capacity utilization in assembly plants in Malaysia at the end of the first decade of the new millennium was only slightly over 50%, well below the international average of 70%.

The shallowness of intensive development was not offset by extensive development in either assembly or in components. Malaysia's poor performance in autos is evident in comparing its trade performance with that of its (lower-income) neighbors in Southeast Asia. Despite for many years having the largest national market for automobiles in ASEAN (it has since been surpassed by Thailand and Indonesia), Malaysia lags behind its neighbors in the overall volume of exports from the auto sector (vehicles and components alike) (Figure 7.1). Whereas in the early 1990s, Malaysia's ratio of exports to imports of automotive products was the highest of the four Southeast Asian countries, by the end of that decade it was the lowest, surpassed even by low-income Indonesia and Philippines (see also Figure 7.3).

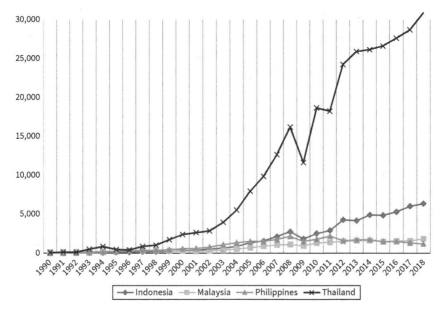

Figure 7.1 Exports of Automotive Products from Southeast Asian Economies ($m).

Source: World Trade Organization, Statistics Database https://data.wto.org

The WTO defines "automotive products" as motor cars and other motor vehicles principally designed for the transport of persons (other than public transport type vehicles) including station wagons and racing cars, motor vehicles for the transport of goods and special purpose motor vehicles, road motor vehicles, n.e.s., parts and accessories of motor vehicles and tractors, internal combustion piston engines for vehicles listed above, electrical equipment, n.e.s., for internal combustion engines and vehicles, and parts thereof (SITC groups 781, 782, 783, 784, and subgroups 7132, 7783).

Political Incentives for Developing Institutions for Upgrading

Although Malaysia at the time of independence faced a significant external threat because of the adoption of the *Konfrontasi* policy by the Soekarno government in Indonesia in January 1963, the military coup that removed Soekarno and replaced him with the less aggressively nationalistic Suharto government, coupled with the formation of ASEAN two years later, effectively removed any immediate external threat to Malaysia. The country's external security was also reinforced by its arrangements with the United Kingdom. The Anglo-Malaysian Defence Agreement of 1963 had legitimated British intervention in support of Malaysia in the *Konfrontasi* dispute. It was replaced in 1971 by the Five Power Defence Agreement that linked Malaysia with Australia, New Zealand, Singapore, and the United Kingdom. Malaysia's relatively benign external security environment enabled it to spend a far smaller proportion of its GDP on the military than did the countries in Northeast Asia: over the period since the late 1980s, its ratio of military expenditure to GDP has averaged about 2.2% annually, having exceeded 3% in only one year (1991).

The primary threat to Malaysian security came from within. Unlike other countries in the region, however, it did not face a serious secessionist threat. Rather, its primary security concern came from tensions between its ethnic communities. These had flared up on several occasions in the 1960s: they came to a head in the aftermath of the 1969 national election, at which non-Malay opposition parties made substantial gains. The riots that followed opposition celebration of the results claimed 196 lives, of whom 145 were Chinese (Crouch 1996: 24). Ethnic tensions were grounded in income inequalities, which had become exacerbated in the post-independence period.

The government's response to the riots marked a radical disjuncture in both the politics and economics of the recently independent country. After 1969, it abandoned an essentially consociational approach, assuring the primacy of the Malay community through manipulating the electoral system and using emergency powers to hinder opposition parties. The systematic over-representation of rural areas ensured that the Malay community's domination of the political system was unassailable so long as it maintained unity.

The government also moved swiftly after the riots to introduce fundamental changes to the economic structure. The New Economic Policy (NEP), introduced in association with the Second Malaysia Plan for 1971–1975, had two principal thrusts: to eradicate poverty "irrespective of race," and to "restructure Malaysian society to reduce and eventually eliminate the identification of race with economic function." The government's proclaimed objective was that within two decades "at least 30% of the total commercial and industrial activities in all categories and scales of operation should have participation by Malays and other indigenous people in terms of ownership and management" (Malaysia 1971: 47).

The principal vehicle that the government used to increase Malay participation in the modern economy was the public enterprise, which was tasked with acting as a trustee for Malay interests as a whole. In the four years after 1969, 67 new public enterprises were established (Mohamed 1995: 63). The government also increasingly used public contracts to generate a dense clientelist network, principally benefiting well-connected Malays.

Despite the oscillation of earnings from commodity exports—which, conforming to our predictions in Chapter 3, did directly produce significant changes in policies, most notably a move to privatization and liberalization in the mid-1980s following a collapse in commodity prices—the Malaysian economy has always enjoyed a substantial cushion provided by its primary product exports. Malaysian governments did not face the same imperative as those in Northeast Asia to move quickly toward exports of manufactures (Edwards 1993; Doner, Ritchie, and Slater 2005). As Hal Hill (2012: 31) noted, Malaysia ironically has suffered because it has experienced crises of *insufficient* severity to prompt radical policy change. The May 1969 clashes and the 1997–1998 financial crisis were relatively short-lived (in part because of effective government responses to both, in part because of the underlying strength of the economy). Governments consequently were able to sacrifice economic efficiency in the pursuit of social objectives. Moreover, revenue from commodities discouraged companies from developing an "innovation culture" (Felker and Jomo 1999: 8).

By the second half of the first decade of the new millennium, however, Malaysia was facing new challenges and sources of vulnerability. As in other Southeast Asian economies, rates of investment failed to recover to the levels experienced before the Asian financial crisis. The phasing out of the exemptions from the WTO's TRIMs agreement, combined with the full implementation of the AEAN Free Trade Agreement and a proliferation of bilateral preferential arrangements, made it increasingly difficult for the Malaysian government to protect favored domestic industries, despite a long record of creativity in sidestepping international obligations. China loomed as an ever-increasing economic threat, squeezing Malaysia's low-end industries: these also suffered from labor shortages, the country's manufacturing sector becoming increasingly dependent on unskilled migrants. Commentators identified Malaysia as a likely victim of the "middle income trap," an economy that would be unable to sustain high rates of economic growth unless it substantially improved its performance in technological innovation and education (Yusuf and Nabeshima 2009; Hill 2012). Even the national car project, which had been largely insulated from pressures for greater efficiency, was no longer sacrosanct: by 2009, the state's investment arm, Khazanah, was signaling strongly that it wished to offload its substantial stake in the company.

Trade and Investment Policies

The post-independence establishment of an automobile industry in Malaysia began as part of an industrialization drive following the dissolution of the federation with Singapore in 1965. A report from the consulting firm Arthur D. Little in 1967 advised that the establishment of an assembly industry was still feasible despite the attenuated market following separation from Singapore. In that year, the government approved six assembly plants: tariffs were raised on assembled cars, and a system of import licensing introduced for the industry. The number of plants—and the variety of models they produced—quickly multiplied. The plants were predominantly established by local automobile distributors (ethnic Chinese capital) in association with foreign manufacturers. By 1969, there were seven plants assembling 10 makes and more than 40 models locally—but the total output was only 64,000 passenger vehicles.

Import substitution, thanks to the high levels of protection, was immediately effective. But the proliferation of plants conflicted with the recommendation of the Arthur D. Little report that there should be no more than three to five assemblers. Although the government in 1969 decreed that no additional makes or models would be approved, the horse had already bolted—an early indication of the government's inability to enforce policies of rationalization in the face of rent-seeking interests. Moreover, the government proved unable to keep the door closed: in 1977 a further five assemblers were licensed to enable *Bumiputera* entrepreneurs to gain access to the industry so that by 1980 there were 11 assemblers. They produced 25 different brands, 122 models, and 212 variants of commercial and passenger vehicles; these had an average local content of only 8% (Abdulsomad 1999: 277–278).

The principal instrument the government employed to promote the domestic industry was the adoption of a local content policy, with the objective of increasing Malaysian content to 35% (by weight) of vehicles by 1982. But even this modest target was "quietly shelved" (Chee Peng Lim 1984: 448) when it caused the price of cars to rise and quality to decline. Government pressures for increased local content relied primarily on "moral suasion." Not surprisingly, the impact was negligible, so that 10 years after the establishment of the assembly industry, local content, measured as a share of the total value of the assembled vehicle, was less than 15%.

A decisive impetus toward increasing local content came not from the government but from an industry organization, the Malaysian Automotive Component Parts Manufacturers' Association (MACPMA), which was created in 1978 by the country's largest auto parts companies, most of which were owned by ethnic Chinese and had equity or licensing links with Japanese companies. MACPMA bypassed the principal coordinating agency for the auto sector, the Motor Vehicle Assembly Committee, and appealed directly to the then minister for trade and industry, Mahathir Mohamad (Doner 1991: 98–99). Increased local content was initially to be achieved through mandatory deletion of CKD components plus higher protection for components manufacturers. A far more ambitious agenda soon superseded this approach, however, with the decision to build a national car.

The establishment of Proton was a key element of the policy of promoting ethnic Malay interests through the creation of the Heavy Industries Corporation of Malaysia (HICOM) in 1980. This approach was explicitly modeled on the Japanese and (especially) the Korean experiences, initially developed when Mahathir was minister for trade and industry and pushed forward as part of the "Look East" policy when he became prime minister in 1981. The heavy industries industrialization policy was conceived in a climate of rising commodity prices in the last part of the 1970s: it pre-dated but was substantially facilitated by the revenue windfall that Malaysia gained from the second oil price shock of 1979–1980 (Bowie and Unger 1997: 82–83).

Industrial planning in Malaysia (including policies toward the auto sector) vacillated between import-substituting and export-oriented approaches, depending on global economic conditions. Following the collapse of commodity prices in the early 1980s, the Fifth Malaysia Plan (1986–1990) emphasized the urgent need to develop non-traditional sources of export revenue. The subsequent plan (Sixth Malaysia Plan, 1991–1995), however, marked a switch back to promoting the domestic industrial base, and reflected an export pessimism born of increased protectionism against Malaysia's traditional exports in European and North American markets, concerns about competition from China and the newly industrialized economies, and fears that the Uruguay Round of GATT negotiations would collapse. By the middle of the decade (the Seventh Malaysia Plan, 1996–2000), the emphasis had switched back again to export-oriented industrialization as the principal means to enhance domestic competitiveness: export pessimism had been replaced by a "global approach to industrialization," encouraged by the successful completion of the Uruguay Round and a buoyant global economy. Although the national car project was not entirely insulated from these externally driven policy about-turns, the government's desire to use it as a means of social engineering resulted in policies of largely unconditional protectionism.

Throughout the vacillations in industrial planning in Malaysia in the last quarter of the 20th century, one thing remained constant: the priority given to promoting Malay economic interests. The ambitious goal of pursuing intensive development in the automotive industry did not mesh well with the desire to use the industry as a means of promoting ethnic Malay participation in manufacturing—and when the two goals clashed, the former was subordinated to the latter. The consequence was that although Mahathir frequently railed against mismanagement and poor performance in Proton, the expectations set for it were modest. As late as August 1994, a decade after Proton's establishment, Mahathir expressed his hope that there would be a genuinely "Malaysian" car within 10 to 15 years (Ghazali 1994). Rather than use external pressures for liberalization as an instrument to place pressure on Proton management to improve competitiveness, the government constantly sought new ways to protect the domestic industry: "Korean and Japanese carmakers were protected for 40 or 50 years," Mahathir told the Malaysian magazine *BusinessWeek*, "Why should we open our own small market after just 20 years?" "Proton cannot survive" without protection, he said. "When you go to Korea you don't see foreign cars. It's the same in Japan. They have ways and means of ensuring that foreign cars do not compete with their cars in their country" (quoted in Permatasari and Amin 2006).

The rationale of the national car project was to provide sufficient protection to enable Proton to reach production levels in the domestic market that would realize economies of scale. The policies developed to establish the national car project paid scant attention to efficiency considerations, however. Mahathir was personally responsible for negotiations with the preferred foreign partner, Mitsubishi (Doner 1991: 107). He set out to prevent existing (ethnic Chinese) interests in the industry from gaining a substantial stake in the national car project. Rather than building on accumulated expertise in the industry, Proton was required to establish a new supplier network, in which Malay-owned companies predominated—a process that Lee Hwok Aun (2004: 228) termed "ethnic by-pass." More than 90% of Proton's own initial workforce of 1,300 were ethnic Malays: the company was told not to hire those non-Malays who had lost their jobs in existing assemblers after Proton's establishment (Jayasankaran 1993: 278).

By choosing to conduct negotiations with only one foreign partner, and by emphasizing the need for their early conclusion, Mahathir considerably weakened the government's bargaining hand. Although the details of the agreement have never been made public, it seems that the commitments made by Mitsubishi (which contributed 30% of the equity of the new company, set up as a subsidiary of HICOM) were modest: to establish a body-stamping plant, which contributed the lion's share of the project's local value added, to train Malaysian personnel (323 were trained in Japan between 1983 and 1986; Jomo 1994: 285), and to change models every five years. But other critical issues, such as increasing local content (which Mitsubishi resisted), the level of royalties, of technology transfers, and of exports, were not specified (Doner 1991: 104; Machado 1994).

Mahathir acknowledged that the national car project was not internationally competitive but nonetheless justified it in terms of the potential benefits from acquiring technology and know-how. The heavy protection Proton received (it was exempted from import tariffs, which were increased threefold for CKDs from other manufacturers), enabled it to quickly lift its domestic market share from 47% in 1986, the year after production began, to 73% in 1988. Three existing assemblers closed down, while others switched to parts production or to vehicles that did not compete with Proton. Some of the larger Chinese firms were compensated by being given a substantial stake in Proton's monopoly distributor, Edaran Otomobil Nasional (EON).

Early projections of the market for Proton proved extremely overoptimistic, however: the domestic market shrank in response to the mid-1980s collapse of commodity prices (down from 96,200 vehicles in 1983 to 38,200 in 1987; Bowie 1991: 136). Despite its success in dominating the local market, Proton's total production in 1986 and 1987 was approximately 25,000 vehicles, less than half the projected volume. Moreover, the depreciation of the local currency following the collapse of commodity prices raised the cost of imported components and that of servicing the debt (mostly raised from Japan) incurred in constructing the Proton plant. Attention turned to utilizing spare capacity for production for export, something apparently not considered when the original negotiations with Mitsubishi took place.

Mitsubishi resisted the new policy direction. As was the experience for other companies heavily dependent on foreign partners, such as Daewoo in its early relationship with GM in Korea (see Chapter 6), the dominant partner did not welcome additional international competition from a new company producing a variant of its own models. Mahathir prevailed in this tussle, however, and in 1988 Proton began exporting, first to other ASEAN countries, then to the United Kingdom, where it took advantage of Malaysia's status as a beneficiary of the UK's Generalized System of Preferences (GSP) scheme. In 1989, more than 10,000 units were sold in the United Kingdom. The substantial rents Proton enjoyed in the protected domestic market were used to subsidize exports (Jayasankaran 1993: 283; Chee Peng Lim 1994: 256; Jomo 2007: 14). Prime Minister Mahathir apparently conceded this point after his (first) retirement: "Initially, we wanted to introduce Proton to foreign markets, and we were prepared to lose money" (Daily Express 2005a). A similar dumping of surplus production in foreign markets was acknowledged as the primary factor in Proton's surge in exports in 1997–1998. Former Proton CEO Tan Sri Tengku Mahaleel Tengku Ariff (Daily Express 2005b) commented that "the record export figure of 27,000 units was not actual export sales but merely shipments with huge subsidies thrown in for the cars. We piled on the shipments just to show an export number to markets in the United Kingdom, Australia and Germany." Ambitious (and, many thought, plainly unrealistic) plans to penetrate the US market collapsed, however, when Proton's partner, Malcolm Bricklin, failed to gain the required US government approvals. In Europe, where Proton was promoted as combining "Japanese technology and

Malaysian style" (Haron 1993), a slogan that consumers found unpersuasive, sales were slow. After the derisory attempt to export to the US market, Proton made no effort to sell in what was then the world's largest market, targeting instead relatively small markets in less developed economies. Tan (2007: 179) quotes Mahathir as stating that Proton would concentrate on selling "not so sophisticated cars with all the gadgets" in developing country markets. Proton increasingly found it difficult to meet the emissions requirements in advanced economies.

The exporting role conceived for Proton was very different from that which the Korean state imposed on its car companies: the Malaysian government saw exporting in terms of utilizing (and dumping) surplus capacity, rather than as a means of forcing the domestic company into internationally competitive levels of efficiency. Insisting on globally competitive production would have threatened the goal of promoting Malay participation in the components industry.

Despite the repeated references by political leaders and Proton management to the need for exports, the company never achieved an export volume sufficient to enable it to approach scale economies (see Figure 7.2). Although Proton at one point was exporting to 50 markets, the majority of sales were in

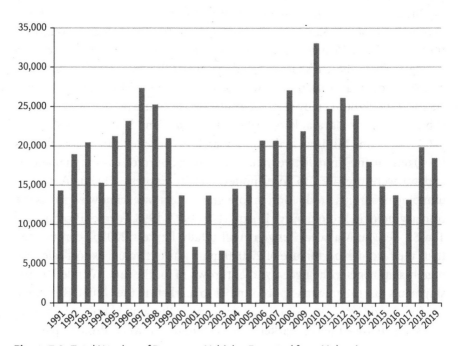

Figure 7.2 Total Number of Passenger Vehicles Exported from Malaysia.
Source: UN Comtrade.

the United Kingdom, where it had offered favorable terms to rental car companies for fleet purchases. But unlike the Korean companies, Proton never was able to overcome a negative image that associated the brand with obsolete technology and quality problems.

With changes in the global and regional trade regimes from the mid-1990s, the government came under increasing pressure to reduce the extraordinary protection Proton had enjoyed in the domestic market. It committed to accelerate implementation of the ASEAN Free Trade Agreement (AFTA), under which all tariffs were to be reduced to 20% by 2002. Rather than use this deadline to exert pressure on Proton to produce more efficiently, however, the government sought ASEAN's approval to continue to exempt the auto industry from tariff cuts until the beginning of 2005, and in 1998 actually increased levels of protection. Tariffs on CBUs ranged from 140% to 300% depending on engine displacement; those on CKDs were in a range from 42% to 80%. In addition, the government maintained an import licensing scheme (Approved Permits), which limited the number of used cars that could be imported in any year (capped in recent years at 10% of the previous year's domestic production). The permits were a classic source of rents for favored clients in the Malay community—they were awarded by the trade ministry at no cost to recipients and could be resold for up to 50,000 ringgit ($13,000) per vehicle.

Facing increasing pressure—domestically from a population that increasingly expressed its frustrations at the high cost of cars, from its ASEAN partners, from potential partners for bilateral trade agreements, especially Japan, and from the WTO over its use of TRIMS—the Malaysian government began in the first decade of the new millennium to reduce levels of protection. Under the terms of the free trade agreement it concluded with Japan in 2005, Malaysia immediately removed tariffs on CKDs imported from Japan, and agreed to phase out tariffs on all cars from Japan over a 10-year period.

The signals that the government sent to Proton continued to be mixed, however: a reflection both of conflicting objectives, and often of divisions within government over how to realize them. International Trade and Industry Minister Datuk Seri Rafidah Aziz promised in 2002 that there would be no discrimination against foreign cars after 2005. But policies remained equivocal. At the end of 2003, the government cut duties on cars imported from ASEAN to 25% (from between 42% and 80%), and those on extra-ASEAN imports to a range of 70% to 190% (from between 140% to 300%). It agreed to further lower tariffs to the ASEAN final target range of 0%–5 % by the beginning of 2008. Simultaneously, however, it imposed new *excise* duties on imported cars and components of between 30% and 100%. Proton continued to enjoy preferential treatment, paying only half of the new excise duty—leading to complaints from other ASEAN countries, especially Thailand, that Malaysia was not complying with the spirit of ASEAN's liberalization efforts. Natsuda, Segawa, and Thorburn (2013: 121) estimated that the effective rate of protection for the *least* protected vehicles in Malaysia in 2011 still stood at the extremely high level of 143%.

Government attempts to promote liberalization led to conflict with Mahathir, who had retired from the prime ministership in 2003 but whose parting gift to Proton was to appoint himself to the company's board of directors. These conflicts came to a head in 2005, marking the last serious stand of the hard-line protectionists against a government determined to push for at least partial liberalization of the auto market. In October of that year, the government announced a National Automotive Policy Framework that was intended to ensure Malaysia's future in the industry by making the country a regional hub. Rather than assisting only the existing designated national car companies, the aim was to attract new investment into auto assembly in Malaysia. All automakers would be eligible to receive assistance, dependent upon their investment commitments, level of value added, extent of technology transfer, levels of foreign exchange earnings, and linkages with local suppliers. The government recommitted itself to comply with the AFTA objective of 5% tariffs by 2008. Approved Permits would be phased out by 2015 (a commitment on which it subsequently reneged: the government announced at the end of 2015 that a reformed system of Approved Permits would be introduced at the beginning of 2017 (Shah 2015); it remained in force at the end of 2020. Proton was to lose its 50% rebate on excise duties but was expected to be the principal beneficiary of the new investment incentives. The government also attempted to encourage rationalization of the industry by suspending the issuance of new manufacturing licenses until overcapacity problems were resolved, and prohibited existing vehicle assemblers from making their excess capacity available to third parties to assemble makes or models that competed with those produced by national car manufacturers.

Despite the overall trend toward liberalization, the government continued to send mixed messages on Proton. In July 2008, the minister for trade and industry, Tan Sri Muyiddin Yassin, stated that Malaysia was not ready to open its market to assemblers from developed countries until Proton had acquired a competitive edge as an export-oriented producer. Because Malaysia was still decades behind developed economies as a car producer, "it needs to be given time and space to catch up" (Bernama.com 2008). Despite liberalization, the Approved Permit system restricted imports of assembled vehicles from outside ASEAN to 10% of the domestic market; imported vehicles were also subject to a 30% tariff plus a 75%–105% excise duty. Auto parts similarly faced a tariff of 30%. The government froze the issuance of new licenses for manufacturing. The ongoing impact of protection of domestic assembly is seen in the share of locally assembled cars in total car registrations in Malaysia: in 2018, fully 94% of cars registered had been manufactured or assembled in Malaysia (calculated from data on domestic car assembly less exports divided by registrations: (522,392 – 19,838)/533,202; http://www.maa.org.my/statistics.html).

Although the reduction in tariffs on intra-ASEAN trade, plus those pending because of the signature of PTAs with China and Japan, improved Malaysia's prospects for serving as a regional hub in the automobile industry, the ongoing protectionism left it in a weaker position than that of neighboring Thailand. The challenge was recognized explicitly by the minister of international trade and industry, Datuk Mustapa Mohamed, who stated that Thailand, although starting late in autos, was now a "giant in the field," implicitly a model that Malaysia should emulate. In a review of the National Automotive Policy conducted in 2009, the government confirmed the direction of gradual liberalization previously adopted. Tariffs on imported vehicles from other ASEAN countries were to be removed effective January 1, 2010. But other tariffs and excise duties would remain at existing levels. The freeze on new manufacturing licenses would be removed, but only for luxury cars, hybrid vehicles, and pickups. With no significant innovations in policy, the government had not made a decisive move to increase Malaysia's attractiveness as a regional hub.

Investment (Dis)Incentives

By limiting the access of foreign assemblers to the domestic market, and by imposing restrictions on foreign investment, the government undermined its objective to make Malaysia a regional hub for foreign auto assemblers and for foreign first-tier components suppliers. With foreign investors limited at best until June 2003 to a 51% share of projects in the auto industry (with uncertainty about gaining any access at all in some areas of the sector), and in assembly facing discriminatory regimes that favored the national car companies, assemblers and many first-tier suppliers chose Thailand (where 100% foreign ownership is permitted) to be their regional hubs. Excess capacity in the auto assembly industry in ASEAN was estimated to be running at 44%

(Malaysia 2006, IMP3, para 13.31) so competition to become a regional hub was intense: Malaysia remained relatively unattractive to foreign investors. Transport equipment attracted only 6.2% of all approved investments in manufacturing in the years 1996–2005. Of the total sums approved for investment in this sector, foreign investors contributed 41%—a much lower share than their average (56%) in all manufacturing investments (Malaysia 2006, IMP3, Table 1.4)

Promoting the Components Industry

The National Automotive Policy provided the components industry with duty-exempt import of raw materials and with generous government incentives for investments, skills upgrading, adoption of technology, participation in trade fairs, and other assistance for exports (through the Malaysian External Trade Development Corporation), and generous tax exemptions as industrial "Pioneers." The requirement that foreign investors seek local partners, especially from the *Bumiputera* community, offered the possibility for joint ventures that domestic companies could utilize to leverage access to advanced technology and upgrading of skills. On the other hand, the guaranteed domestic market reduced incentives for component firms to become more efficient and to upgrade their skills. So long as Proton and the other national car company, Perodua, enjoyed very high levels of protection, they could afford to support vendors that lagged well behind internationally competitive standards. In addition, the government provided finance to the national car companies through the Vendor Development Program to compensate them for purchasing from *Bumiputera* companies.

According to a 2012 report by IHS Automotive, there were 280 first-tier suppliers in Malaysia, and 200 second- and third-tier companies (the comparable figures for Thailand were 709 and 1,100, a reflection of Malaysia's relative unattractiveness as a regional hub for the industry; Gibbs 2014).

The lack of incentives for efficient production and upgrading is reflected in the poor trade performance of the components sector. The value of domestic production doubled in the decade to 2006. But this growth rate failed to keep pace with that of imports, which increased more than fourfold in the same period. The gap between imports and exports widened considerably (Figure 7.3). The rapid growth of imports after 2002 was reflected in a dramatic rise in their share in domestic consumption. By 2005, imports supplied 47% of the domestic market.

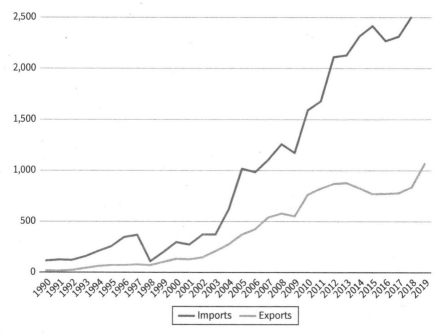

Figure 7.3 Malaysia Imports and Exports of Auto Components ($m).
Source: UN Comtrade data using HS8708 category only.

Product Sophistication and Value Added

Only very limited upgrading in auto components exports has occurred in the years since the national car project was launched. The share of unsophisticated parts in Malaysia's auto exports by 2013 was little changed from the position in 1988: exports of high-tech parts did pick up slightly in the period after 2002, but they still constituted less than 10% of overall auto components exports—an inferior performance to neighboring countries in Southeast Asia, notably Thailand and Indonesia. Malaysia's auto parts exports are dominated by lighting equipment, batteries and battery parts, safety glass, springs, oil and gasoline filters, wire harnesses, brake parts, and bumpers—a reflection of the overall lack of sophistication of the domestic components industry.

As of 2008, the Malaysian Investment Development Authority estimated that there were 690 companies manufacturing over 4,000 automotive components and parts, 70% of which were original equipment manufacturers. But only 45 of these firms were exporting in that year (data cited in Wad and Govindaraju 2011). Malaysia's Third Industrial Master Plan (IMP3) reported a total of 769 firms in the "transport equipment" sector. Most (699) of these were SMEs (Malaysia 2006, IMP3, Table 5.1). Their small size limited their capacity for upgrading: locally owned suppliers were concentrated in the second and third tiers, and in the words of the IMP, "lack capacity and capability in R&D, and are dependent on the design technology from the automotive manufacturers" (Malaysia 2006, IMP3, para 13.40). R&D in the components industry in Malaysia averaged only 0.14% of sales in the period 2000–2005 (Thiruchelvam et al. 2013: 60). Several surveys found that local companies lacked the capabilities to compete effectively with foreign competitors (Rosli and Kari 2008; Wad 2009, 2008). Most of the first-tier suppliers in the country that have the potential to do R&D are foreign owned, but the lack of scale in Malaysia discourages even these firms from conducting R&D locally. One survey found that in the years 2000–2005, foreign companies invested a total of only RM14.3 million (under US$5 million) in R&D in the auto sector in Malaysia (Thiruchelvam et al. 2013: Table 4.2).

For many critics of the components industry, the failure to make the investments required to upgrade was primarily the responsibility of firms themselves. The most common explanation was that the protected environment created by the Vendor Development Program provided too easy an existence for companies. They chose to live off the rents generated rather than to reinvest to become competitive producers. In our interviews, we heard stories of vendors who invested profits in palm plantations rather than improving their capabilities in the auto industry.

Interviewees from SMEs blamed the lack of upgrading in auto components on the low margins that plagued the industry, and the difficulty of attracting and retaining workers, many of whom were migrants who often "job-hopped." Other interviewees suggested that decisions not to attempt to establish operations abroad followed from companies' perceptions that it would be difficult to gain access to the supply chains of foreign producers, especially the Japanese companies that are dominant in the region, and fears that even if they were successful in such an endeavor, their margins would constantly be squeezed.

Institutional Configuration

As we discussed in Chapter 3, Malaysia has generally scored well on the World Bank indicators of governance effectiveness. The government has justifiably received credit for its success over the years in implementing sound macroeconomic policies, which have kept inflation rates low and the exchange rate stable. Malaysia has been among the most open of developing economies in its policies toward trade, investment, and migration (Hill 2012)—albeit not in the automotive sector. The central bank, Bank Negara Malaysia, has enjoyed significant autonomy and played a major role in policy setting that maintained low rates of inflation: the financial system is generally regarded as among the strongest in Southeast Asia (Yap and Teng 2012).

Felker and Jomo (1999: 6) noted at the turn of the century that "few countries have pursued technology development as consistently and self-consciously over the past several years" as Malaysia. The government adopted explicit policies and fostered institutions to promote technology development from the mid-1980s in a conscious attempt to emulate the success of the Northeast Asian Newly Industrializing Economies. But the government failed to establish the effective institutions required to realize the high aspirations for technological development. The two principal institutions founded in the mid-1970s to promote science and technology, the National Council for Scientific Research and Development, and the Ministry of Science, Technology, and Environment "had a low profile within the bureaucracy" in their first decade of operations. Primary responsibility for sectoral industrial policies lay with the Ministry of Trade and Industry (MTI) (Greg Felker with Jomo 1999: 19). With the adoption of a National Science and Technology Plan in 1986, policymaking was increasingly centralized in the office of the prime minister. Despite the new priority given to science and technology, key agencies were understaffed and "lacked reliable information on national technology resources and trends" (Felker 1999: 109). In the interviews we conducted with members of MACPMA in 2011, respondents suggested that effective industrial policy was hampered because officials in the Ministry of International Trade and Industry (the new name for the MTI after 1990) lacked detailed knowledge of the workings of the international automotive industry. Moreover, ethnicity triumphed over expertise: Rasiah (2011b: 730) reported that "the leadership of key meso organizations appears to have been determined by ethnic rather than purely experience-based considerations."

Commentators on Malaysia's science and technology policies frequently noted a disconnect between a policymaking process increasingly centralized in the office of the prime minister and what was happening on the ground. Ambitious aspirations proclaimed at the center "lacked a feel for the real problems and needs of the private sector" (Lall, Boumphrey, and Hitchcock, quoted in Felker 1999: 112). In part, this disconnect reflected the lack of effective input that the private sector had in policymaking. From 1991, peak-level discussions on technology policy occurred in the Malaysian Business Council (MBC), a body whose private-sector representatives were selected by the government. Felker (1999: 104) saw the dominance of the MBC as demonstrating "the continued primacy of informal or clientelist relations between the political and business elites, and the marginalisation of the bureaucracy as a political force in policy-making." A decade later, Rasiah (2011a) observed that the weakness of Malaysia's industrial policies lay not in a lack of institutions, but in the lack of effective links between state institutions and the private sector. These problems remain unresolved: a 2013 report funded by the OECD found that Malaysia's science, technology, and innovation policies were characterized by "weak institutional leadership at all levels" which resulted in "needless duplications and a lack of focus" (Thiruchelvam et al. 2013: 15).

The auto sector was an extreme example of key policy decisions being made in the office of the prime minister rather than in the technical ministries. The history of Malaysia's auto policy is dominated by one person—Mahathir bin Mohamad—for whom Proton was a personal crusade. Efforts to use trade liberalization to force Proton to become more efficient met with blistering attacks, during and after Mahathir's first period in power. His office interfered directly in the appointment of Proton's management. Political interference continued after Mahathir's first resignation: the office of the prime minister torpedoed a deal in 2007 through which VW would have taken management control of Proton's manufacturing subsidiary (interviews and Malaysian Motor Trader 2007).

The government appeared to be suspicious of business associations that asserted any autonomy. The associations themselves were weakened both by ethnic divisions and by the pervasive politics of patronage. Nowhere was this more evident than in the auto parts industry. Most of the members of the principal business association in the auto sector, the Malaysian Automotive Component Parts Manufacturers' Association (MACPMA) were effectively bypassed when the government launched the national car project. The largely Malay-owned companies selected as suppliers to Proton did not join MACPMA but in 1992 set up a rival group, Persatuan Pembekal Proton, the Proton Vendors Association, which was entirely hostage to government policy. The Malaysian Motor Vehicles Assemblers Association (merged with the Malaysian Motor Traders Association in 2000 to form the Malaysian Automotive Association), which represented private assemblers, was similarly weak. Leutert and Sudhoff (1999: 262) note that its various member companies were "usually unwilling to cooperate among themselves." In our own interviews in Malaysia, respondents, particularly from MACPMA, suggested that in the first decade of the new century the associations did become more effective vehicles for pooling information and for engaging with government agencies. They expressed frustration, however, that although consultations with government bodies were frequent, they were often shallow—and many important issues were simply regarded as too politically sensitive for discussion.

The Malaysian government similarly failed in two key areas: education and the establishment of relevant technical institutions to support key sectors. Although Malaysia's record on educational expenditure was superior to that of most of its neighbors in Southeast Asia, it was particularly deficient in two areas—the relatively small share devoted to primary education; and the failure to invest sufficiently in technical education required for key sectors (Hock and Nagaraj 2012; Jimenez, Nguyen, and Patrinos 2012). Three different ministries had responsibility in the 1990s for vocational education. In the mid-1990s, vocational enrollments in Thailand were more than 10 times those in Malaysia (Felker 1999: 134). In 2004, only 14% of secondary school graduates went on to university in Malaysia, compared with 24% in Thailand and 34% in Korea (Thiruchelvam et al. 2013: 29). In 2009, 80% of the workforce in the automotive sector were unskilled (Wad and Govindaraju 2011: 160). A decision in 2020 (Bernama.Com 2020) to retrench 70,000 foreign workers in first-tier and second-tier component suppliers (of a total workforce of 220,000) appeared destined to generate instability in the absence of a trained local workforce.

Although the government in the 1990s established new universities whose focus was on engineering and information systems, the supply of engineers failed to keep up with demand. Leutert and Sudhoff (1999: 261), in a comprehensive survey of auto parts manufacturers, found that there were few links between institutions of higher education and the auto industry. In interviews we conducted a decade later, we heard similar complaints from component producers about the lack of engagement from the university system (see also Thiruchelvam 2013). It was not until 2015 that a full-fledged university devoted to the automotive industry was established (the DRB-HICOM University of Automotive Malaysia; https://www.dhuautomotive.edu.my/).

The inadequacies of the education system are reflected in the relatively small numbers engaged in R&D activities in Malaysia. The ratio of researchers to total population is substantially below those of China, Japan, Korea, and Singapore. In the late 1990s, Malaysia had fewer than half the total number of researchers in Thailand or the Philippines, both countries with substantially lower per capita incomes (Yusuf and Nabeshima 2009: 160–164). Although R&D spending in Malaysia is comparable to that in Brazil and Mexico, countries with similar levels of per capita GDP, it is substantially below that of its competitors in East Asia: China, Japan, Korea, and Singapore. The World Bank ranked Malaysia as 48th on its Knowledge Economy Index in 2012, a fall of three places from 2000, placing the country behind the United Arab

Emirates and Cyprus (World Bank 2012a). Malaysia's total number of ISI-indexed publications in 2010 was only 60% of that of neighboring Singapore despite having six times the island state's population; in 2007 only 158 US patents originated in Malaysia (Thiruchelvam et al. 2013: Table 2.6).

Finally, and perhaps surprisingly given the strength of research institutes in the agricultural sector, the government was slow to set up research institutes specific to the automotive sector. The Standards and Industrial Research Institute of Malaysia, founded in 1974, provides testing procedures for components, including those for the auto industry. But its role has been limited primarily to the localization of low-technology Japanese components. It did not assist in product development (Leutert and Sudhoff 1999: 260). A report by the Japan International Cooperation Agency in the mid-1990s noted that the most urgent need for the industry was the establishment of a Malaysian Automotive Research Test and Information Centre (Leutert and Sudhoff 1999: 260). But the government was slow to heed this call. It was not until 2010 that a Malaysia Automotive Institute (MAI) was established as an independent organization under the auspices of the Ministry of Trade and Industry. In contrast to its counterparts in our cases of successful extensive development in autos, the capacity of the MAI was extremely limited: in 2015, it had only 20 professional staff. Its principal areas of activity were forecasting of automotive trends, arranging training for local parts firms, and helping to publicize international opportunities for local firms. It inherited a long-standing Malaysia-Japan cooperative project under which the Japanese government sent retired Japanese auto experts to provide training to Malaysian SMEs. But for most of its first decade, it lacked any independent technical capacity—and it did not fill the long-standing need to provide testing facilities for locally produced components. At the end of 2018, the MAI was rebranded as the Malaysia Automotive, Robotics & IoT Institute (MARii). A small design center had been added in 2017, and MARii was also given responsibility for managing a National Emission Test Centre, which was established as part of a technology transfer agreement between Daihatsu and Perodua. Although these changes have enhanced the potential contribution that the Institute can make toward upgrading the local industry, its diverse responsibilities underline how under-resourced it continues to be.

Upgrading Competencies

The centrality of the national car project in Malaysia's automotive policies has ensured that Proton has been the dominant force in shaping the sector's technological competencies. In part because of the weakness of domestic institutions discussed in the previous section, technological upgrading at the principal car assembler depended on outsiders—either its partners or the companies that it acquired.

Beginning in August 1988, the Malay management of Proton resigned after criticism from the finance minister, part of a broader purge of Malaysian management in HICOM projects: by early 1990, Mitsubishi Motor personnel had assumed the five top positions in Proton, the irony of which was not lost on critics of the national car project. But the Japanization of Proton's management only exacerbated other tensions, particularly over the government's desire to increase local sourcing of components and to promote exports. By 1993, local content of Proton's flagship model, the Saga, had officially reached only 69% (Leutert and Sudoff [1999: 258] estimate that the actual local content was probably half that claimed). Low levels of localization prompted Mahathir to publicly criticize Mitsubishi for being slow to transfer technology to Proton, for giving preference to its Japanese affiliates in sourcing, and for being unwilling to allow Proton to source internationally other than from Japan, which raised issues not just relevant to local sourcing but to the overall control of Proton's supply chain (Machado 1994). Dependence on Mitsubishi for technology was particularly painful in an era when the yen was appreciating against the ringgit (Proton officials estimated that the company's profits dropped by $1.6 million for every cent the yen appreciated against the ringgit; Sender et al. 1995).

Discontent with Mitsubishi led to a reinstatement of Malaysian management as Proton was gradually privatized, a significant thrust of Malaysian economic policymaking in the early 1990s. The ostensible objective, in line with changing international thinking on development, was to increase the efficiency of often heavily protected state enterprises. As implemented in Malaysia, however, the policy frequently appeared to have as much to do with creating a new source of political patronage and rents as with generating more cost-effective production (Gomez 2002; Gomez and Jomo 1997; Tan 2007). In the case of Proton, the government maintained a controlling interest when its shares were first publicly listed in 1992, but effective control of the company passed to Yahaya Ahmad when Mahathir gave the go-ahead in November 1995 for Ahmad's privately held Mega Consolidated to take a controlling stake in HICOM Holdings (which had a 27.5% shareholding in Proton). The sale occurred without an open tender (Tan 2007: 165).

Yahaya was the first *Bumiputera* to have graduated with a degree in automotive engineering. He was a close friend of former finance minister Tun Daim Zainuddin, the principal architect of the privatization program, and of Deputy PM Anwar Ibrahim, with whom he had gone to school, leading to accusations of political favoritism. But there was no doubting Yahaya's reformist intentions. He put pressure on Mitsubishi to transfer additional technology to Proton, sought alliances with other foreign auto assemblers, cut prices paid to Proton's component suppliers by 30%, and personally negotiated the purchase of the specialist British sports car manufacturer Lotus. The expectation was that the engineering expertise within Lotus would be decisive in assisting Proton to develop its own engines. This reformist chapter was short-lived, however. Yahaya died in a helicopter accident in March 1997, and Proton was afflicted shortly thereafter by the Asian financial crisis of 1997–1998 (Lopez 1997, 1996; McNulty 1996; Ong-Yeoh 1996; Tat 1996).

The acquisition of Lotus did help Proton to develop its own "Campro" engines, which were expected to cut the company's production costs by 20% (Agence France Presse 2002). Significant problems occurred in the development and integration of the new technology, however. The new engine was released two years behind schedule. Interviewees commented that although Lotus had expertise in engine development, as a specialist sports car producer it had no experience of mass production. Tan (2007) reports that Proton was unable itself to develop the variable valve timing technology required by the Campro engines, or its own gearbox, continuing to depend on Mitsubishi for the supply of this key component. Proton had to source the aluminium-casted cylinder heads from its domestic rival, Perodua, and a South Korean company because it lacked the in-house capabilities to produce them (Huey 2004). Shortages of cylinder heads caused delays in fulfilling orders for Proton's new models (Courier-Mail 2005). Problems in manufacturing a sufficient volume of its own engines led to Proton's relying on Renault for the engine for its next model.

Proton's privatization proved to be short-lived. In March 2000, agreement was reached on the sale of HICOM's 25.8% stake in Proton to the state-owned oil company Petronas. With the government's investment arm, Khazanah, owning a further 18%, Proton was effectively back in state ownership, another example of significant policy instability. For many observers, Proton's problems of lack of scale economies and technological backwardness would only be addressed effectively if it found a foreign partner. Once again, though, economic nationalism triumphed over economic rationality. It was unfortunate for Proton that its long-standing partner, Mitsubishi, proved to be the weakest of the major Japanese assemblers in the first decade of the 21st century, a company with its own problems of lack of attractive designs, poor reputation for quality, and absence of cutting-edge technologies. Mitsubishi Motors continued to hold 7.94% of Proton's equity and its parent, Mitsubishi Corporation, had its own shareholding of the same value until February 2004, when Mitsubishi divested itself of both packages of shares. Under Yahaya's stewardship, Proton initiated a tie-up with Citroen—but again the partnership only provided access to dated technology: Proton used the 10-year-old AX platform to develop a new small car. The result was a car that lacked the features offered by imported competitors and which was prone to mechanical problems; it was discontinued after only three years (Tan 2007: 174).

In June 2004, Proton apparently flirted with the possibility of an alliance with Rover, again hardly the most robust of international assemblers. The principal hope for a viable tie-up with a foreign partner, however, was with VW, because the German company was the only significant international assembler not to have a major production platform in Malaysia's principal rival for hub status in the regional auto industry, Thailand. In November 2004, Proton announced a major cooperative arrangement with VW, which would include joint development of a new platform, the supply of engines and transmissions by VW for Proton's new models, and Proton's assembly in Malaysia of VW models (Proton's excess capacity in its modern Tanjung Malim plant being its main attraction to potential partners; Zakariah 2004). VW, however, walked away after lengthy negotiations, stating that the type of close alliance that it envisaged would not be possible unless it obtained management control in key areas of collaboration—but the Malaysian government was not willing to cede this control (Malaysian Motor Trader 2006). The government then set a deadline of the end of March 2007 to find a strategic partner for Proton. Preliminary negotiations were held with GM, PSA Peugeot Citroen, and VW before the government announced that it would resume formal negotiations with VW in mid-2007—the negotiations discussed earlier that were eventually torpedoed by the prime minister's office. Information provided in interviews suggested that the key stumbling block in all of these negotiations was the unwillingness of VW to take on Proton's inefficient network of suppliers—and the government's refusal to abandon *Bumiputera* vendors.

Proton's ongoing reliance on foreign partners was costly on several dimensions. It affected its bottom line because of ongoing royalty payments and the expense of importing components. But equally important was the unwillingness of partners to transfer current technology to a potential competitor, leaving Proton to produce models whose lack of contemporary features made them unattractive to consumers.

The government's desire to rid itself of Proton culminated in its privatization in 2012, when the shares of the state investment arm, Khazanah, were purchased by DRB-HICOM, one of the country's leading conglomerates with diversified interests across construction, manufacturing, and services. Subsequently, Proton's share of the domestic market collapsed as it continued to rely on foreign partners for obsolete technology—its second-generation Perdana sedan, which went on sale to the public in June 2014, was built on the eighth-generation Honda Accord platform, which had been introduced in 2007 and which was superseded in 2013.

Despite the protection Proton continued to enjoy, its executive chairman acknowledged in 2014 that it was making less than $200 net profit on each of the small vehicles it sold. Under private ownership, the direction of the company was largely unchanged but was further compromised by the inability of the parent company to make significant investments in new technology. To many observers' astonishment, the company appointed the 88-year-old former prime minister Mahathir to be chairman of the Board in 2014, not long after he had been unceremoniously removed from his position with Khazanah. His first move was to demand further support from the government: full reimbursement to Proton for the funds it had spent on developing new vehicles plus a RM 1.7 billion grant (more than half the sum at which Proton was valued in the DRB-HICOM takeover). The government made provision of a grant conditional on Proton's finding a strategic partner. Mahathir's demand was substantially more than Geely paid when it acquired Proton in June 2017 (a total of RM 460.3 million, of which only RM 170.3 million was a cash injection, the balance being the supply of an SUV platform to Proton).

Proton's lack of scale constrained its capacity to engage in R&D. Proton was by far the country's largest single investor in R&D; it alone accounted for 76% of all the R&D conducted in the automotive sector in Malaysia (Thiruchelvam et al. 2013: 39). Its ratio of R&D to sales (3.9%) is not much less than the average for automotive assemblers in other parts of the world. Nonetheless, Proton's small production volume and overall revenue ensures that the *absolute* investment it makes in R&D is miniscule compared with most other auto manufacturers—less than 2% of that of Peugeot or Renault, for instance, and less than 1% of that of VW or Toyota (Yusuf and Nabeshima 2009: 165–166).

Government policies and those of Proton itself affected the capacity of component producers to upgrade their capabilities. We have already noted how the government required Proton to set up its own supplier network rather than build on existing domestic capabilities. In the mid-1990s, when Proton decided to develop its own models, the company decentralized the procurement of components with the intention of involving vendors more closely with platform design. In principle, this seems a rational strategy that might have had the positive effect of increasing the design skills of component vendors. In practice, however, the decentralized decision-making implemented under the policy had the unintended and undesirable consequence of producing a proliferation of vendors when Proton appointed different companies to supply the same component for different models. When we conducted interviews at Proton in 2008, we were told that the company had as many as five vendors for the same component—as the company itself acknowledged, many more than needed to ensure security of supply (and a grand total of 246 vendors in that year—up from 151 in 1996). This proliferation of vendors, the opposite from trends in the global industry, occurred at the same time as Proton's market share (and overall production volume) was declining.

Proton's inconsistent policies and problems have caused considerable problems for vendors. Some invested in new plant and equipment in the expectation that sales would continue at historical levels and suffered financial distress as volumes shrunk. Others complained that non-economic factors (i.e., political influence) had driven Proton's decision-making as to which vendors were selected for different models, again creating uncertainty and losses.

A Retreat to Extensive Development?

Proton's problems cast a shadow over the entire automotive industry in Malaysia. The travails of Proton often lead observers to overlook that national car status was given by the government to three other companies. The most important of these is Perusahaan Otomobil Kedua Berhad (Perodua—Second Automobile Manufacturer Limited Corporation), which was established in 1993 in conjunction with the Toyota affiliate, Daihatsu, assembling re-badged Daihatsu models. Unlike Proton, the capital of Perodua was entirely privately held from the beginning: the owners were UMW Corp. (38%; the local assembler of Toyota vehicles), Daihatsu of Japan (20%), MedBumikar Mara (20%), PNB Equity Resource (10%), Mitsui & Co. of Japan (7%), and Daihatsu (Malaysia) (5%). In 2001, a holding company, Perodua Auto Corp., was set up to control the manufacturing operations of Perodua (including its engine manufacturing arm): the shareholders are Daihatsu (40%), Mitsui & Co. (11%), and Perodua (49%). In other words, Perodua's manufacturing operations are controlled by the Japanese partners. The parent Perodua company acts essentially as the domestic distribution arm.

Unlike Proton, Perodua was not forced to establish an independent supplier network from scratch. Over the years, through assembly of small, generally technologically unsophisticated vehicles, Perodua captured market share at Proton's expense: in 2006, Perodua's sales surpassed those of Proton for the first time. It has sustained its lead since then, in 2019 outselling Proton by more than two to one and seizing 43.7% of the domestic market (Proton sold only 100,000 vehicles in that year, a 18% market share; Statista 2020).

Perodua is entirely dependent on Toyota for technology. The local content of its vehicles is substantially below that of Proton's, at between 60% and 70% versus Proton's 90% (Natsuda, Segawa, and Thoburn 2013: Table 5). When the government announced incentives in the 2014 National Automotive Policy for the development of hybrid and electric vehicles, Perodua announced that it would not attempt to exploit these because the investment costs would be too high. Like Proton, it also suffers from lack of economies of scale. Its annual sales have hovered around 220,000 vehicles, which in 2020 were divided among five models. Exports have been negligible (in the first half of 2017, the company exported 1,854 vehicles; Amir 2017; Ministry of International Trade and Industry 2014). The parent company has no interest in Perodua competing with its own vehicles in international markets.

The other two national automakers remain minor players, local assemblers of imported kits. In 1992, Inokom was established as a joint venture with Hyundai (Republic of Korea) and Renault (SA) to manufacture light commercial vehicles. A fourth national car company, NAZA, was formed in 1996, a joint venture with the Korean company Kia that built on a long-standing motor trading company owned by a leading Malay businessman, Tan Sri SM Nasimuddin SM Amin.

In July 2018, to much popular derision, the newly re-elected 93-year-old Prime Minister Mahathir announced that he would launch a new national car project to replace the failed Proton (Lim 2018). The government eventually chose an engineering company, DreamEDGE, to coordinate the project, with Daihatsu providing technical support. The project was supposed to be privately funded but skeptics, who feared that it would degenerate into another rent-seeking exercise, pointed out that the company, which was majority-owned by the government-controlled Malaysian Industry-Government Group for High Technology (located within the Prime Minister's office), would be eligible to apply for government grants—and had already been supplied with an RM 20 million seed fund. In August 2020, the Entrepreneur Development Minister acknowledged that he did not know what had happened to the funds (Jun 2020). The early 2019 deadline for producing a prototype had not been met by the end of 2020 (Lye 2019; Roberts 2019b). Skeptical commentators suggested that at best the project would produce a re-badged Daihatsu.

Electric Vehicles: Coming Late to the Game

In the last decade, Malaysian authorities have increasingly looked over their shoulders to see what they could learn from Thailand's automotive policies.

As we note in Chapter 4, a key focus in Thailand's auto policies in recent years has been the development of Eco Cars. In Malaysia, however, this is another policy area that has been dogged by lack of consistency, rent-seeking, and unproductive links with weak foreign actors.

In the 2011 budget, the government declared that it would exempt hybrid and electric vehicles from import duties (30%) and would refund 50% of the excise duty (which ranged from 80% to 105%). When the 2014 version of the National Automotive Policy was announced, however, the concessions were removed except for locally assembled hybrid and electric vehicles. But at that time, only Honda hybrids were assembled locally, by a company in which Proton's current owner DRB-HICOM BhD had a 34% shareholding. Meanwhile, Proton announced in 2009 that it would mass-produce electric cars for Detroit Electric, a start-up launched by a former chief executive of Lotus Engineering which had taken the name of a long-defunct brand manufactured by the Anderson Electric Car company in Detroit (Reed 2009). Nothing came from this venture. Similarly, Proton's development with Lotus of a hybrid small car in 2007 and an electric version of its Iriz sub-compact in 2015 (with LG, apparently also using technology from Nissan) were not brought into commercial production.

Conclusion

Malaysia's automotive policies were the last remnant of its attempts to emulate the developmental approach of Japan and Korea through the promotion of heavy industries. The sale of Proton, the national champion, to the privately owned Chinese company Geely in 2017 was a vivid reminder that policies are doomed to failure if the appropriate institutional framework and supporting context are not put in place. Successive Malaysian governments were evidently aware of the institutional prerequisites for intensive development in manufacturing—but singularly failed to implement them.

Economists and international organizations such as the World Bank have frequently praised Malaysia's macro-economic policies, which over several decades have facilitated steady economic growth with few problems of inflation or international debt. At the sectoral level, however, Malaysia's policies have varied widely both in their content and their success.

Policies and institutions have been most successful in fostering upgrading in rubber and palm oil, where the Malaysian government at independence inherited sectors that were internationally competitive and featured strong supporting institutions—and were important to ethnic politics. The 2008

National Survey of R&D in Malaysia revealed that agricultural sciences dominated R&D expenditure by public research institutions (Thiruchelvam et al. 2013: 33). The approach in these areas has been one of promoting intensive development—of successfully moving downstream beyond raw materials exports. Rubber, rubber products, and palm oil together account for 10% of Malaysia's exports. In these important export sectors, economic and political rationalities coincided: state support not only facilitated Malaysia's becoming a global leader in these products, but also significantly benefited Malay interests that dominated production.

In the electronics sector, Malaysia adopted an extensive development approach through encouraging subsidiaries of transnational corporations to invest to turn the country into a regional hub for production. The government has provided appropriate supportive policies for an extensive development strategy: generous investment incentives, good infrastructure, and an accommodating labor market. These policies have produced some successes in terms of indicators of extensive development: the electrical and electronics industry is the largest single sector in Malaysian manufacturing, accounting for over a quarter of output, 40% of employment and a similar percentage of the country's merchandise exports (data from Malaysia 2010: 131; Bank Negara Malaysia 2011). Malaysia has failed, however, to build the supportive institutional structure that has facilitated upgrading in the electronics industry in neighboring Singapore. As Felker (1999: 99) noted, "[r]elative to the size and sophistication of Malaysia's manufacturing sector and export profile, the local technological base is remarkably shallow." A decade later, Rasiah (2011a) found that only 1% of the electronics firms in Malaysia engaged in design and R&D activities. To the extent that innovation occurred in the electronics sector, it was through the subsidiaries of transnational corporations accessing their home countries' innovation systems—a classic symptom of extensive development.

In contrast to its policies in these two sectors, the Malaysian government's automotive policies have been an almost unqualified failure. Having set out to pursue a policy of intensive development through building a national champion, the government completely failed to provide the sector with the supporting institutions necessary for success.

Our theoretical framework provides a compelling explanation for Malaysia's failures in promoting intensive development in heavy industry in general and in the automotive sector in particular. One dimension is the country's lack of systemic vulnerability—available revenue and the claims on resources arising from external pressures. Malaysia has pursued sound macro-economic management; the government also benefited from a cushion provided by the substantial revenue from natural resource exports. Government policy was by no means completely immune from falls in export revenue as commodity prices declined. The response was out of the Washington consensus textbook—liberalization and privatization. But economic crises in Malaysia were short-lived: commodity earnings bounced back sufficiently quickly that none of the downturns produced a dramatic break from the past. Through the end of the first decade of the current century, the government failed to invest sufficiently in the institutions required for industrial upgrading. Oil revenues, channeled through the government's sovereign wealth fund, Khazanah, continued to bail out the national car maker. The significance of resource revenues for the national car company is underlined by the experiences when the company was privatized in 1995–2000 and 2012 onward: in these years, it struggled because its private-sector owners were unable to provide the funding needed to develop new models.

The principal source of policy failure was the desire to use the automotive sector for social engineering, which prevented the government from imposing performance requirements on the policy's beneficiaries that might have led to the upgrading required for competitive performance. Key policy decisions came not from the relevant technical ministries but from the office of the prime minister: Proton never escaped from being the personal project of Prime Minister Mahathir.

Moreover, the absence of external threat and the dominance of ethnic politics shaped public perceptions of the car project. Rather than being acclaimed as a *national* champion, Proton from the beginning was viewed as a symbol of Malaysia's ethnic divisions. The contrast with Korea could not be starker. Koreans for many years were willing to support inferior cars produced by domestic companies both because of national pride and because of the key role that the industry was perceived as playing in generating the technology that would contribute to the country's security. With Proton's weaknesses continually exposed by locally assembled foreign brands, the national car company attracted no such loyalty in an environment where external security threats were not a public concern. As Proton continued to drain government revenue, produce poor quality cars, and serve as the direct cause of the relatively high prices that Malaysians paid for automobiles, the government's policies toward the auto sector came under increasing criticism even from the Malay community, which saw them as benefiting only a small group of cronies.

Although Proton enjoyed sufficient protection through policies that restricted imports and foreign investment to enable it to survive despite inefficient production, it was not completely cocooned because the government's desire to satisfy other clients produced competitors within the overall context of a rent-seeking environment. The establishment of the second national car company, Perodua, which enjoyed the same levels of protection as Proton yet was not required to produce its own models or to use *Bumiputera* suppliers, generated significant rents for those involved in what was essentially a re-badging exercise. Meanwhile, the high levels of tariffs sustained various assemblers of foreign vehicle CKDs, especially in niches outside the generally low end of the market occupied by Proton and Perodua. According to the Malaysian Automotive Association (http://www.maa.org.my/listing_map.htm), in 2019 the country housed 21 manufacturing and assembly plants, 15 of which produce passenger vehicles—a prescription for inefficient production given the small size of the domestic market and absence of exports.

In both of the principal national car companies, the splitting of the distribution activities from manufacturing offered new rent-seeking possibilities (including to ethnic Chinese, cut out of Proton's manufacturing chain) that sometimes produced conflict over the sharing of rents in the protected domestic market. The Approved Permit system generated another group of rent-seekers whose interests in expanding the number of imported cars were directly opposed to those of the national automakers (the government's willingness to increase the number of APs led to a clash with Mahathir in 2005). Proton, especially since the turn of the century, thus by no means enjoyed a monopoly—but rather than leading to more efficient production, the increased competition was among various rent-seeking interests benefiting from protection, and simply caused more scale economy problems for Proton as the company's sales collapsed.

Was the failure of Malaysia's auto strategy inevitable? In comparing the experience of Thailand and Malaysia in the auto industry, Richard Baldwin (2011) makes a strong argument that Malaysia's auto strategy was doomed because it persisted with a development model that was impossible to pursue after the extension of global value chains throughout the industry. Certainly, the challenges facing any country seeking to enter the auto industry are formidable, as we detailed in Chapter 2. And Malaysia is handicapped by its small domestic market. But we are not convinced that an intensive strategy in the auto industry was doomed to failure at the time that Malaysia launched its industry. In Malaysia's case, it simply was not pursued—or at least not pursued effectively in that the state failed to put in place appropriate policies and supportive institutions. At the time that Malaysia initiated its national car policy in 1982, the domestic market for autos was 100,000 vehicles, not hugely different from the 145,000 vehicles produced in Korea in that year (see Figure 6.1 in Chapter 6). Korea compensated for its limited domestic market by relying heavily on exports to realize economies of scale. In principle, there was no reason why Malaysia could not have pursued a similar strategy—not least because it had a head start over potential rivals in the entire Southeast Asian market. Rather than an intensive development strategy in autos in Malaysia being doomed for economic reasons, we see the primary cause of its failure in political factors: the lack of a security imperative; the capacity of the state to sustain an inefficient industry because of its revenues from commodity exports; the domestic cleavages that generated a rent-seeking climate in Malaysia to which any domestically owned industry was susceptible; and the resultant reluctance and incapacity to build institutions for technology development and diffusion.

8

China

Revamping Socialist Institutions for a Market Economy

制造业是国民经济的主体，是立国之本、兴国之器、强国之基

Manufacturing is the core of the national economy, the root on which the country is established, the tool for national invigoration, and the foundation for a strong country.

—Opening sentence of *Made in China 2025* **(State Council, May 8, 2015)**

China presents a sharp contrast to the other countries in this study. First and most obvious, it has the largest population and economy, though Thailand, South Korea, and Indonesia are hardly tiny by world standards. Much less widely recognized is a second contrast: among our cases, China trails only Korea in developing independent capabilities to design, engineer, and export vehicles and parts, and to invest abroad and acquire foreign firms. Third, China's institutional challenge is the opposite of that facing our other countries: rather than struggling to devise new institutions to support industrial upgrading, China has had to revamp or, in many cases, scrap and rebuild restrictive and inefficient institutions originally created to support a socialist command economy.

Due to its heft and extended period of rapid growth, China also faces outsize expectations. Most accounts of the country's auto industry fail to put it in comparative perspective, or compare it only to the industries of the most advanced and successful countries, which reached maturity in a far less open global economy. China thus appears to many as a weak giant that has failed to meet the high expectations of its leadership and people, or the anticipations and fears of the global auto industry. The efforts of some smaller Chinese firms to develop their own vehicles, rather than relying on imports or foreign-dominated joint ventures (JVs), have come in for particular derision. "China's own automakers have gone from feared to hapless," proclaimed the *New York*

The Political Economy of Automotive Industrialization in East Asia. Richard F. Doner, Gregory W. Noble and John Ravenhill, Oxford University Press (2021). © Oxford University Press. DOI: 10.1093/oso/9780197520253.003.0008

Times (April 9, 2014: B1), while London's *Financial Times* (March 13, 2014) headlined the claim that "Chinese-brand cars lose traction at home." Brandt and Thun (2016: 4) cite automotive market researchers as asserting that Chinese firms, never noted for quality, are falling further behind. The Chinese people themselves are hardly less critical, routinely assailing the joint ventures with global automakers for relying on easy profits from selling cars designed and engineered by their foreign partners. As for the domestic Chinese brands, Xu Min, a professor of engineering at Shanghai's prestigious Jiaotong University and former head of engineering at the major independent brand Chery, vehemently insisted, "The domestic brands are all doomed! They've been protected in one way or the other, but as the global brands penetrate local markets and go downstream, the locals are doomed" (author interview, Shanghai, August 26, 2013).

These claims are exaggerated and misleading, as we shall see, but they have some foundation. Thirty years after Shanghai Automotive Industry Corporation (since renamed SAIC Motor) and Germany's Volkswagen (VW) created China's first successful automotive joint venture, the Chinese market is still dominated by foreign multinationals, which constrict the ability of their local partners to learn from developing and managing their own models (Nam 2011). The biggest assemblers are inefficient and politicized state-owned enterprises (SOEs). Exports of whole vehicles have stalled, largely because domestic Chinese firms have concentrated on poor and unstable markets such as Russia, Ukraine, and northern Africa. Clearly China is not yet a bigger version of Japan or Korea, which enjoyed decades of protection from imports and foreign investment before establishing competitiveness in the global auto industry.

Yet when we systematically apply the criteria developed in this study for in-dustry deepening, such as R&D spending, ability to design and engineer parts and vehicles, and marketing under independent brands, Chinese firms, both JVs and independent firms, have done remarkably well, and are catching up, not falling back.

This is not to say that the Chinese industry has no problems, but that those problems are in some ways the obverse of those in Southeast Asia and most other developing countries. China engaged in extremely early development of all kinds of institutions to support industrial diffusion, but put them to work in the service of a socialist planned economy and control by the Communist Party. Politically, support institutions reflected acute Chinese perceptions of external threat that created a deep commitment to industrial deepening, and a relative dearth, particularly after growth accelerated in the 1980s, of natural resources that could easily be distributed to supporters. Chinese reformers are struggling to loosen the fetters of state ownership, to break the habit of trying to micro-manage the decisions of company managers, and to develop new institutions and practices better suited to a market economy. Economic, technological, and even institutional progress has been impressive, but a fundamental transformation of the structure of the industry is not yet in sight.

Industry Performance: Both Extensive and Intensive Growth

Extensive Growth: Assembly

After more than two decades of sustained, rapid growth, China has surpassed the United States as the world's largest producer and consumer of passenger vehicles. China's output of 26 million light vehicles in 2019 was more than double that of the United States (OICA 2020). Supporting this huge growth in output has been a rapidly growing industrial capacity and a massive expansion of ports, roads, and railroads.

The Chinese auto industry has a uniquely complex structure. Imports make up about 5% of passenger car sales and are concentrated at the high end. Roughly 55% are produced in assembly plants operated by 50-50 joint ventures between global assemblers and Chinese companies owned by the national, provincial, or municipal governments. Joint venture vehicles are designed and engineered abroad and sold under global brands such as VW or General Motors (GM).

The other 40% are sold under domestic Chinese brands, usually at lower prices. About 6% are produced by the Chinese SOEs separately from, and to some extent in competition with, their joint venture production. With a few exceptions, such as Shanghai Auto's Baojun models, most of these "own brand" products of the Chinese SOEs have been reluctant and unprofitable responses to government pressure to increase "autonomous" production. The other 33% or so come from private companies such as Geely, BYD, and Great Wall, all of which emerged around the end of the previous century without relying on global partners. At first, the private brand models were also licensed from, or more often thinly veiled copies of, global models, but now virtually all are designed and engineered in China. Increasingly the foreign-dominated joint ventures and the domestically owned private firms are engaged in a "fight for the middle" (Brandt and Thun 2010) as the joint ventures expand into rural areas, while the domestics strive to move into big cities with more sophisticated models.

Finally, some Chinese firms have bought existing global brands. The most famous of these Sino-global brands is Volvo, purchased by the leading private firm Geely in 2010. In this chapter, "China" or "Chinese" refers to all vehicles assembled in China. When necessary, we distinguish global brands such as GM and Toyota from domestic or Sino-global brands.

Product quality, once abysmal, has improved dramatically. From 2000 to 2015 initial quality problems in all cars produced in China decreased by 80% (from 514 problems to 105 problems per 100 vehicles). As early as 2012, comparisons of a wide range of "same" models produced in China and the United States found essentially no difference in quality, and international brand luxury vehicles produced in China in 2015 actually scored better than their American counterparts (George 2015: 29, 33). Traditionally, imports displayed noticeably higher quality than cars assembled by the leading joint ventures, with the domestic brands trailing far behind. By 2019, however, the disparity between Chinese brands and the joint ventures had shrunk to only nine—101 initial quality problems vs. 92 (J. D. Power 2019). An editor at *Automotive News Europe* noted with surprise and a little alarm that independent Chinese brands had largely caught up with the Europeans:

> Models such as the Geely X1 small car, the Luxgen U5 and . . . the Changan Eado midsize sedan are on par with products from Europe's volume brands in terms of design, handling, performance, fit and finish and overall quality. . . . But, what should really worry Europe's volume automakers is how *affordable* the Chinese models are. (Ciferri 2018)

Vehicle safety displays a similar trajectory. From the middle of the first decade of the 2000s, YouTube videos of Chinese cars crumpling like tinfoil in international crash tests raced across the Internet (Drive.com.au 2012). By 2017, Chinese models regularly attained 4- and 5-star ratings in foreign crash tests, but they attracted far less attention on YouTube (howsafeisyourcar.com.au 2017).

The Chinese market is highly competitive, offering far more makes and models than are available in any other country (George 2015: 16). Consolidation is gradually proceeding, however. In 2018, the top 10 assemblers accounted for nearly 90% of total output (see Table 8.1). Under pressure from stiff competition and government regulations, dozens of tiny automakers, some of them infamous for producing copycat models, have exited the market in recent years (*Automotive News China*, March 4, 2016). The tremendous boom in output has enabled continuous investment in larger and more efficient factories. Labor productivity in the auto industry (both assembly and

Table 8.1 Leading Chinese Assemblers

Rank	Automaker Name; Headquarters; Date Established; Main Brands	Majority Ownership	2018 Sales (vehicles)
1	**SAIC Motor** (Shanghai; 1955): VW, GM; *MG, Baojun, Roewe*	Provincial SOE	7,012,500
2	**Dongfeng** (Wuhan; 1969): PSA, Nissan, Luxgen, etc.; *Venucia*	Central SOE	3,830,800
3	**FAW** (Changchun; 1953): VW, Toyota, GM; *Besturn, FAW, Red Flag*	Central SOE	3,418,400
4	**Beijing Auto** (1958): Hyundai, Mercedes; *BAIC, Foton, Senova* (Saab)	Provincial SOE	2,402,100
5	**Guangzhou Auto** (GAC) (1997): Honda, Toyota; *Trumpchi; Gonow*	Provincial SOE	2,142,800
6	**Changan** (Chongqing; 1862 [1951]: Suzuki, Ford, PSA; *Changan*	Central (mil.) SOE	2,137,800
7	**Geely** (Taizhou; 1986): *Geely, Kandi*; *Lynk & Co; Volvo, Proton, Lotus*	Private	1,523,100
8	**Great Wall Motors** (Baoding; 1984): *Great Wall, Haval, Wingle*; Mini	Private	1,053,000
9	**Brilliance China** (Shenyang; 1991): BMW; *Brilliance, Jinbei*	Provincial SOE	778,600
10	**Chery** (Wuhu; 1997): *Chery, Qoros*; Jaguar, Land Rover	Mixed: Municipal SOE; since 2019 also private	737,100

Note: Brand name in italics = Chinese-owned; mil. = military-related company. Beijing, Shanghai, and Guangzhou are provincial-level municipalities. Top 10 market share: 88.52%

Source: Author; sales from China Association of Automobile Manufacturers (CAAM).

parts) has expanded rapidly. From 2000 to 2013, value added per worker quadrupled (Development Research Center of the State Council [DRC], Society of Automotive Engineers of China [SAE-CHINA],VW China, 2015: 63). Wages also increased very rapidly (Zhang 2014: 71–80). Gross profits have grown even faster, from 14 billion yuan in 2000 to 620 billion yuan in 2018 (CATARC [China Automotive Technology and Research Center] and CAAM [China Association of Automobile Manufacturers] 2008: 28, and 2019: 431), even as prices of "same vehicles" steadily declined.

The Chinese market is likely to continue growing, albeit at a slower pace. Concerns about congestion, pollution, global warming, and dependence on imported oil all incline the central government and major coastal cities to adopt policies to constrain demand for cars. Nevertheless, incomes are still increasing, bringing cars within the purchasing capacity of a rapidly expanding share of households, especially in central and western China.

Extensive Growth: Parts

Expansion of parts production has been equally impressive. From just under US$100 billion in 2006, output value increased to over US$675 billion in 2017 (IBISWorld 2017: 31). Exports of parts also grew rapidly in the first decade of the 2000s, and the Chinese industry exported more parts than it imported. The greatest strength of Chinese firms lies in relatively low-tech "metal-bending" areas such as bearings, brakes, bumpers, clutches, and electric motors. Chinese suppliers are also gaining ground in automotive interiors and "infotainment" products such as radios and car navigation devices. Engines and even automatic transmissions, once mostly imported or outsourced to foreign suppliers such as Mitsubishi and JATCO, are increasingly built in-house by assemblers (CATARC and CAAM 2015: 421). Limitations of both demand and technological capacity, however, constrain production of engineering plastics, expensive metal alloys, and advanced sensors and software.

The structure of the parts industry remains highly fragmented and diverse in ownership. A 2017 survey counted 4,646 auto parts enterprises operating at 12,872 establishments. The top four supplier groups accounted for barely 10% of total industry output in 2017 (IBISWorld 2016: 31, 16; 2017: 31, 17).

Foreign and private firms dominate the parts industry. Foreign firms, free to establish wholly owned subsidiaries in the parts sector, accounted for 25% of enterprises and 42% of output in 2015. Private domestic firms constituted just under half of all enterprises but accounted for only 30% of output value. Most private parts firms are small, family-run businesses using rudimentary technology. The remaining firms covered a range of ownership types, with state-owned enterprises playing a surprisingly small role (3.6% of total revenue), though state investment dominated some publicly listed firms (IBISWorld 2016: 20–21).

As in the assembly sector, wages in the parts industry have risen at a torrid pace and claim a growing share of revenues despite the rapid increases in productivity (IBISWorld 2016: 31–32: 2017: 31–32). Profitability, nonetheless, remains higher than the global average (Roland Berger 2017: 12).

Intensive Growth

China has aimed at intensive growth since the birth of the modern industry in the 1950s, but only with the surge of demand for passenger cars and a concomitant influx of disruptive new entrants from the mid-1990s did serious progress occur. By the 2010s, government officials, auto executives, and firms from outside the automotive industry explored new possibilities to go beyond intensive growth and "catch up," to leapfrog to positions of global leadership, or at least equal positions at the global technology frontier, in such crucial areas as new powerplants and autonomous driving.

Research, Design, and Engineering

The capacity of Chinese firms, especially those with independent brands, to conceive, design, engineer, produce, brand, and export new vehicles and parts has grown tremendously but still remains behind that of the global leaders. From 2002 to 2015, R&D spending increased nearly tenfold (CATARC and CAAM 2010: 530; 2016: 422). In 2019, among nearly two dozen publicly listed automakers, R&D expenditures as a share of revenue averaged 3.44% (Culture China 2020), still less than the typical global automaker (Hirsh and Jaruzelski 2015: 4) but very high for a developing country, and well above Korea's Hyundai at 2.86% (Hyundai Motor Company 2020: 8, 48) (see Table 8.2). The quality of R&D spending also is improving. The number of R&D personnel has increased rapidly and the share of "core personnel" has grown steadily

Table 8.2   China: Research and Development Efforts

Year	R&D Spending (Billion RMB) [passenger cars]	R&D Intensity (R&D/Sales revenue) [passenger cars]	R&D Personnel	Auto Patents (*Invention* patents awarded)
2001	3.38	1.38%		
2002	5.63	1.65%	53,000	
2003	6.58	1.28%	62,000	
2004	7.51	1.37%	71,000	
2005	9.48	1.70%	89,000	
2006	11.86	1.62%	91,000	8,253
2007	16.29	1.76%	109,000	8,978
2008	20.81	2.01%	124,000	11,037
2009	26.33	1.82%	163,000	13,555
2010	27.06	1.42%	169,000	14,303
2011	27.14	1.28%	187,000	18,758
2012	29.28	1.29%	202,000	23,875
2013	41.60	1.84%	262,000	31,161
2014	47.06	1.94%	266,000	40,077
2015	57.51	2.05%	N/A	43,845

Sources: CATARC and CAAM, various years; R&D personnel, patents, 2006–2013 (DRC et al. 2015: 304, 67). 2001–2005: US$1 = 8.28 RMB; 2005–2015 US$1 = 6~7 RMB. http://baijiahao.baidu.com/s?id=1659212248655202199.

(DRC, SAE-China, and VW China 2015: 64, 304) as has the number of PhDs granted in automotive engineering (197 in 2015) (CATARC and CAAM 2016: 350). Patenting by Chinese auto firms has exploded. The rise of patents awarded to independent brands, particularly private companies led by Geely and Great Wall, is especially striking (CATARC and CAAM 2016: 333–335). The quality of patents by domestic firms still lags, however, and few patents extend to key components (DRC, SAE-China, and VW China 2006: 66-67).

Chinese auto firms have acquired design and engineering capabilities from a wide range of sources. From the 1950s through the 1970s, Chinese automakers copied Soviet and other foreign designs. From the early 1980s, Chinese companies overwhelmingly relied on their joint venture partners. In the late 1990s, independent firms with their own brands, such as Chery, Geely and BYD, began to appear. At first, they copied from a variety of sources, but quickly began outsourcing both design and engineering, particularly for key elements such as engines and external body design. Chinese firms hired a variety of providers, such as Italian design boutiques Italdesign and Pininfarina, and engine and engineering specialists Ricardo (England), FEV (Germany), and AVL (whose storied Austrian founder, Dr. Hans List, taught automotive engineering at the German-funded Tongji University in Shanghai from 1926 to 1932) (AVL 2018). Expatriates from Japan, Korea, and Taiwan also participated. By the mid-2000s, domestic design companies led by IAT and CH-Auto of Beijing, and TJ Innova, a spinoff from Shanghai's Tongji University, played an increasingly important role.

By the 2010s, Chinese assemblers stepped up in-house capabilities, sometimes supplemented by star designers hired from Europe and Japan (CATARC and CAAM 2006: 390–392; 2010: 413). Chinese automakers have also increasingly opened up small overseas outposts for design and occasionally engineering. Changan, for example, has expanded its R&D division to over 6,000 employees, and has opened five R&D centers across China (Chongqing, Shanghai, Beijing, Harbin, and Jiangxi), and four overseas, employing a total of over 300 staff: Turin, Italy (exterior styling), Yokohama, Japan (interior design), Nottingham, UK (advanced powertrain design and development) and Detroit, USA (chassis design and development) (Changan Qiche 2016). Privately owned Great Wall Motor, China's largest SUV maker, is following in Changan's footsteps, increasing R&D spending to US$650 million in 2019 and opening an engineering center in Yokohama, followed by research facilities in North America, Europe, and India (Xianwaibang 2020).

Multinational assemblers and components suppliers are also investing heavily in Chinese research facilities. GM, for example, joined its local partner SAIC Motor in creating a "Pan-Asia Technical Automotive Center" (PATAC).

According to a former PATAC engineer, "Originally it was strictly a concession to the demands of the Chinese government, and GM didn't use it actively for the first couple of years, but now it provides a major advantage over other OEMs [original equipment manufacturers] in adapting products for the Chinese market" (interview, Dr. W. J. Gesang, Air International Thermal Systems, Beijing, November 20, 2006). By the early 2010s, PATAC employed over 3,000, was one of GM's six global engineering and design centers, and designed powertrains and whole vehicles from scratch. GM then erected nearby its own wholly owned Advanced Technology Center, aiming to make it the second largest in GM's global network (Stein 2012; Cheng, 2016). Similarly, leading American parts supplier Delphi has "28 plants, three technical centers and more than 2,900 engineers in China.... Last year, Delphi also moved the global headquarters for its electrical and electronic architecture division to Shanghai from the United States. The division contributes about half of Delphi's revenue globally" (*Automotive News China*, April 29, 2014).

Innovative Activities: New Powerplants, Connected and Self-Driving Vehicles, Automotive Services

Most of the research, design, and development work described previously consists of learning, applying, and slightly modifying process and product technology already well established abroad so as to fit Chinese circumstances. After about 2010, however, Chinese auto firms began to move more actively into new areas still under development even in the leading automaking countries. Government policy was the major stimulant for most of this activity; active consumer demand played almost no role (CATARC, Nissan China, and Dongfeng Motor 2015). The government provided clear signals that applications to expand new assembly facilities would receive quicker and more favorable consideration if they included production of "new energy vehicles" (battery-electric cars, plug-in hybrids, and fuel-cell vehicles). The government subsidized both production and consumption of these new technologies, which it viewed as less mature and thus less dominated by foreign auto firms, as well as contributing to reducing oil consumption and emission of air pollutants and global warming gases. In 2015 central and local governments disbursed over US$3 billion in subsidies for electric vehicles (EVs) and hybrid vehicles, an average of about US$10,000 per vehicle (*Automotive News China*, March 25, 2016).

With this pressure and support from government, Chinese automakers introduced numerous electric and plug-in hybrid vehicles. Especially active were Beijing Auto, Jianghuai, and BYD, which started out as a producer of batteries for consumer electronics and later accepted an investment from

American billionaire Warren Buffett. Some automakers, such as BYD, Geely, and supplier Wanxiang, deepened their involvement in lithium battery production. Many other firms, however, produced warmed-over versions of conventional cars in small numbers just to placate the authorities. With heavy subsidies from the central and local governments, and preferential treatment by traffic authorities in Shanghai, Beijing, and other major cities, electric vehicle sales in China took off. Despite initial shortages and incompatibilities in charging infrastructure, by 2015 China surpassed the United States in sales of battery-electric and plug-in hybrid vehicles. It soon became clear, however, that some of the sales were fraudulent schemes to pocket rich subsidies (Yang 2016), and—less noticed but more important—that nearly half of the demand came from government procurement such as municipal taxi fleets (Ma 2016). The government announced that it would reduce subsidies by 2020, but extended and stiffened an existing carbon credit program (Yang 2019).

Government policy is also exerting, however, an even more powerful *indirect* impetus for upgrading powerplants. By 2020, Chinese emissions and fuel efficiency standards essentially matched those of Europe:

> The stringent China 6 emissions limits that are about to be implemented across the country are matched by equally tough fuel economy requirements for both passenger cars and commercial vehicles. Every year sees a tightening of fuel consumption limits, meaning that vehicles sold in China are now on a par with any in the world in terms of efficiency. (Howard and Zhu 2019; for details, see Continental Automotive 2019)

Meeting those requirements with improved gas or diesel engines alone will be difficult if not impossible. As a result, Chinese manufacturers have begun introducing not only numerous plug-in hybrids but also conventional hybrid vehicles, even though plain hybrids were long excluded from policy support for new energy vehicles on the grounds that the technology is already mature, and that subsidies would only line the pockets of hybrid technology leader Toyota.

Another major area of innovative activity is "connected" or self-driving vehicles. Foreign companies such as Google have established a leading presence in the global race to produce autonomous vehicles, but the Chinese industry talks of the automotive internet or "internet-of-vehicles" (*che lianwang*) as a vital competitive battleground (CATARC and CAAM 2015: 22–24). Some assemblers, such as Changan and Great Wall, rely primarily on internal efforts. Others are allying with software companies or universities and state research institutes (Beijing Auto and Shanghai Auto, for example).

Especially striking is the entry of Chinese software giants such as Tencent, Baidu, and Alibaba, with their formidable technological and financial capabilities. Starting around 2014, a whole slew of electric vehicle startups appeared. The most prominent were founded by IT entrepreneurs who shared a determination to develop autonomous yet connected vehicles, eagerness to take advantage of the hefty subsidies for new energy vehicles, and generous investments from Chinese and American software and venture capital firms. First off the block was Nio, a maker of sports cars and SUVs that attracted investments from Alibaba and Baidu, Singapore's national holding company Temasek, and Silicon Valley's Sequoia Capital. In 2018 Nio's initial public offering (IPO) raised about a billion US dollars (Sun 2020). In July 2020, Li Auto, a producer of more modestly priced extended-range hybrid vehicles, attracted US$1.1 billion with an IPO on Nasdaq. Li Auto had received the backing of China's largest consumer services app Meituan and Bytedance, owner of the controversial video app TikTok (Liao 2020). The next month, yet another Chinese EV start-up succeeded in raising more than a billion US dollars with an American IPO. Xiaopeng (or Xpeng) Auto was founded by two former engineers from Guangzhou Auto, with the backing of former Alibaba executive He Xiaopeng and investments from Alibaba and Taiwan's Foxconn (Lee 2020).

Yet the electric sailing was far from smooth. All these new entrants struggled to attain economies of scale as they competed with each other and existing EV producers such as Chery and BYD for the still-limited EV market just as the central government announced reductions in subsidies and allowed the American EV leader Tesla to build a gigantic, wholly owned "giga-factory" in Shanghai. The rising tensions between China and the United States over trade and technology threatened their American research outposts and cast a long shadow over export plans.

Though the new entrants were private companies, virtually all relied on support from local governments. When NIO ran out of cash, for example, the Hefei municipal government agreed to provide a billion-dollar investment in return for movement of NIO's headquarters and operations from Shanghai to Hefei. Similarly, Xiaopeng Motor enjoys the backing of the Guangzhou City government, while Li Auto "received investments from several entities backed by municipal governments of Changzhou and Xiamen as well as state-run investment bank China International Capital Corporation" (Sun 2020). The local government investments provided vital support as the companies struggled to gain a foothold, but also impeded a shakeout that would have allowed the winners to grab an increasing share of the market and approach an efficient scale of production. Still, given the size of the Chinese market and the support of its government, it seems likely that eventually one or more Chinese EV producers will join Tesla, which is also rapidly expanding its capabilities in China.

Chinese automakers have also shown some success moving into finance, insurance, on-road support, and other "soft" areas that provide the bulk of profits for most dealers in advanced countries. Until recently, progress was slow, because the institutions for automotive registration, credit evaluation, and pricing remained underdeveloped and lacked transparency. Finance and insurance are under the jurisdiction of financial regulators, who are more concerned about avoiding non-performing loans than stimulating the growth of industry. The share of vehicles bought on credit, for example, remained stubbornly low at around 10% for many years, before expanding to 40%–50% by 2018. The government's efforts to strengthen institutions to support industrial coordination and diffusion have long favored production and engineering over automotive services, and determination to limit fraud and over-borrowing has further slowed growth of financial services, but some progress is now being made (S&P Global Ratings 2019).

A Role for Local Capital and Independent Brands

As noted in earlier chapters, some role for local capital is vital if domestic firms are to take advantage of the full range of opportunities for learning global technology and developing independent capabilities, and if capabilities are to defuse down to lower-level suppliers. China lies between Japan and Korea, which resolutely blocked the entry of foreign capital for decades, and Thailand, Mexico, and Brazil, which liberalized until global auto firms attained almost complete dominance. With foreign ownership of assembly plants capped at 50%, Chinese JV partners absorbed a great deal of process technology, but learned little about new product development (Nam 2011).

Dissatisfied with the continuing reliance of Chinese joint ventures on their foreign partners and the low quality of the independent brands that emerged in the late 1990s, the government issued automotive industry policies in 2004 and 2009 effectively requiring the joint ventures to create separate, Chinese brands. With the notable exception of Shanghai GM's Baojun and Wuling brands, the global automakers reluctantly acquiesced to the local brand requirement by slapping Chinese badges on outdated foreign models. Not surprisingly, they failed to excite Chinese consumers. Foreign analysts jibed that "the indigenous brand policy is really dumb because all it does is cannibalize the local Chinese brands" (*Financial Times*, May 4, 2014).

For a time, this critique looked prescient, as the aggregate market share of independent Chinese assemblers shrank under the onslaught of cheaper models from the global brand joint ventures. The independents proved quicker to catch the shift in consumer demand toward SUVs and crossovers, however, and regained some ground: in 2017 Chinese brands accounted for 44% of the total passenger vehicle market (20% of sedans, 61% of SUVs, and 84% of multipurpose vehicles) (CAAM 2018b, 2018a). Industry analyst Mike Dunne captured the new psychology: "Previously the logic was, 'Why invest billions in creating an all-new Chinese product when you can make fat profits—right now—selling Buicks?' "But now the new thinking is, 'Why work hard to sell a Chevy when I can offer our own brand and keep 100% of the revenues?'" (*Financial Times*, September 28, 2017). Chinese-owned firms also retain a dominant role in trucks, buses, and diesel engines, allied fields in which they have become major global players with independent brands. China remains a huge, complicated market with a multitude of ownership arrangements, brands, and models, including a significant role for domestically owned assemblers that are much more likely than foreign automakers to use local parts and materials (see Table 8.3).

Foreign investment in the auto parts sector presents a similarly mixed picture. The spread of global production networks, the size and growth of the Chinese market, the desire of Chinese assemblers to upgrade the quality and sophistication of their offerings by incorporating world class components, China's entry into the WTO, and the lack of restrictions on foreign ownership have combined to boost the share of foreign firms to 43% of overall parts production (IBISWorld 2017: 21). Foreign firms now dominate most of the more sophisticated segments.

Yet the Chinese presence in major parts and materials has not died out, and shows signs of rebounding. Some private Chinese suppliers have prospered amidst the foreign onslaught. Fuyao Glass elbowed aside Japanese competitors to provide over 60% of the glass in new Chinese cars and rank number two in global production of automotive glass (Leaders Magazine 2015), while Wanxiang has rapidly expanded production of universal joints, bearings, and other mechanical parts, and has invested in dozens of American subsidiaries. New joint ventures have sprung up to take advantage of emerging opportunities, sometimes with the Chinese side as majority owner. Examples include joint ventures with Japan's Kobe Steel and Europe's ArcelorMittal to supply lightweight high-tension steel for automotive applications (*The Asahi Shinbun*, August 8, 2014), and joint ventures between Chinese assemblers and foreign financial institutions to provide automotive loans to dealers and households.

In other cases, foreign suppliers have sought to stave off relentless pressure on pricing in both the Chinese and global markets by sloughing off less

Table 8.3 Global and Chinese Automotive Brands

Category	Share of Chinese Market	Producer	Brand Coverage	Examples
Imports	5%	Global automakers	Global	Lexus, Ferrari
Wholly owned foreign subsidiary	(NA: production began December 2019)	Tesla	Global	Tesla
Sino-foreign JV cars	55%	Global automakers + Chinese partners (virtually all SOEs)	Global	VW, GM, Toyota, Nissan, Hyundai, BMW, Benz
Chinese-led JV vehicles		Sino-foreign JVs, but Chinese partner leads	Chinese	Wuling SAIC Baojun
"In-house" domestic brands	40%	SOE auto groups	Chinese	Changan SAIC Roewe Guangqi Trumpchi
Private Chinese autos		Private Chinese automakers	Chinese (but hope to go global)	Geely BYD Great Wall
Sino-global brands	(small)	Global automaker + Chinese owner (usually production both abroad and in China)	Originally global, now Chinese-owned	Volvo Lotus Proton MG
Foreign cars with minority Chinese ownership	NA	Global automakers	Global	Daimler (9%) Peugeot-Citroen (PSA; 15%)

Source: Compiled by author. Passenger cars including sedans, SUVs, MPVs, and crossovers. Market share is approximate as of late 2010s and varies by year.

profitable areas to Chinese partners. The most striking example involved a swap of electronics for interiors between Visteon, formerly the parts division of Ford, and a SAIC subsidiary called Yanfeng Automotive Trim Systems. Yanfeng then established a 70/30 joint venture with Johnson Controls, another leading American supplier. In essence, the American suppliers ceded ground in interiors to SAIC in order to concentrate on electronics. With annual sales of about US$8.5 billion, the resulting joint venture immediately became the largest auto interiors supplier in the world (Yanfeng Automotive Interiors 2015).

As of 2019, seven China-based firms ranked in the *Automotive News* list of "Top 100 global OEM parts suppliers." China trailed only Japan (23), the United States (23), and Germany (20, including three of the top five) and surpassed Korea (6, but only two independent of Hyundai). India and Mexico only managed to place one each; no other developing country hosted a top 100 supplier. Three of the Chinese parts makers were owned by provincial-level governments: Shanghai's Yanfeng Automotive Trim Systems at #15; BHAP, the main parts subsidiary of Beijing Auto, at #61; and Guangxi's Wuling Industry, a partner of Shanghai Auto and GM, at #89. Three others were privately owned: Hong Kong's Johnson Electric at #80; Ningbo's Minth Group (body, trim, and decorative parts) at #86; and Anhui Zhongding, a producer of rubber parts at #92. The central government owned only one: CITIC Dicastal, the world's largest aluminum alloy wheel maker, at #65 (Automotive News 2019).

International Activities: Exports, Outward Investment, Mergers and Acquisitions

Chinese automakers have become increasingly active internationally. Domestic firms, unconstrained by the global networks of mother firms, have led the way. While exports of low- to medium-end parts have expanded rapidly, assembled vehicles have traveled a rockier path. After expanding rapidly in the first decade of the 2000s, exports of motor vehicles, stalled out at about a million units, only about 700,000 of which were passenger cars (CATARC and CAAM 2019: 368). Chinese automakers, like Hyundai 40 years earlier, began exporting before they were ready, and deficiencies in quality, safety, service and stability created a terrible first impression. Domestic brands moved aggressively to poorer markets less well served by the global assemblers, such as the Middle East, but those markets proved volatile and in some cases, such as Russia and Brazil, prone to protectionism.

Multinational assemblers were slower to export from their Chinese facilities despite low costs and rapidly improving quality. The potential harm to their global brand images, limitations on foreign ownership that reduced the potential profits by half, and rapid growth of demand in China all militated against exporting. By 2015, the calculus of the global auto firms, led by GM, began to change. GM had built highly successful joint ventures with SAIC in Shanghai, featuring mainstream GM models, and with Wuling in Liuzhou (Guangxi Province), specializing in inexpensive micro vans and a new and quite successful "independent brand" of inexpensive sedans called Baojun. The mother company, in contrast, struggled in most other developing markets. GM shuttered factories in Thailand and Indonesia, relying instead on exports from Korea, India, and especially China, where an increasing share of the design and engineering was conducted. GM did not limit its expansion of

Chinese exports to low-end models, announcing that it would ship to North America small numbers of high-end crossovers and luxury sedans under the Buick and Cadillac brands. Daimler-Benz and Volvo also began exporting high-end vehicles from China.

Outward foreign direct investment by Chinese firms reveals a similar dynamic of premature ambition leading to disappointment, followed by renewed and sometimes more successful efforts. In Brazil, for example, surging imports of inexpensive Chinese vehicles soon inspired a tariff on imports. All 10 Chinese brands exporting to Brazil then announced plans to jump the tariff barrier by assembling in Brazil, but the drastic weakening of the Brazilian economy combined with the poor image of Chinese brands to prevent all but Chery from carrying through on their plans (Calmon 2015). Russia and Ukraine, too, proved rocky and unstable soil for Chinese investments.

Initial Chinese investments in Western and Korean automakers also proved disappointing, though parts firms have done better. Beijing Auto purchased the rights to two aging platforms and several engines from GM's failing Saab unit, but was unable to do much with them. Similarly, Shanghai Auto took over Korean SUV specialist Ssangyong, but ran into such intense opposition from Ssangyong's unions that it eventually washed its hands of the deal. Automotive mergers often fail, as illustrated by Daimler's unhappy experience with Chrysler, but Chinese firms had the further disadvantage of far less experience with global markets and multinational management, and less enticing brands to sustain the new operations. Parts firms led by Wanxiang and Fuyao Glass have found more success with overseas acquisitions, primarily in North America and Europe, where many suppliers have strong technological capacities and respected brands, but suffer from high costs or lack the scale to compete in a globalizing and consolidating industry.

Chinese assemblers have achieved greater success, however, with some more recent investments. Geely, most ambitious of the private assemblers, purchased Volvo Cars from Ford in 2010. Geely kept the Swedish management team in place, and after some initial culture clashes, Volvo began posting record sales while upholding its reputation for safety, quality, and sophistication. Volvo continued to design larger cars for advanced country markets while helping Geely develop a common platform for smaller vehicles for the Chinese market. The two firms shared some manufacturing plants and co-invested in "Lynk & Co.," an intermediate-level brand focused on connectivity and future electric vehicles (Yang 2017b). Geely also bought 49.9% of Malaysia's ailing former national champion Proton and 51% of its British sports car and engineering subsidiary Lotus Cars. Finally, Geely and its boss Li Shufu invested US$3.3 billion in Volvo Trucks and US$9 billion for a 9.7%

stake in Germany's fabled Daimler, maker of Mercedes Benz cars (Reuters, February 26, 2018).

In 2020, Volvo and Geely announced plans to merge. With sales of 2.2 million units in 2019, the combined group was not far behind the 10th largest global automaker, Mercedes, at 2.6 million units (*Financial Times*, February 17, 2020; Leggett 2019; Focus2move 2020). Political resistance to Chinese acquisitions began to grow, but as long as global competition and industry consolidation produce struggling Western firms, opportunities for investments and even acquisitions by Chinese assemblers and parts firms are likely to reappear.

If the performance of Chinese assemblers and parts firms has disappointed the soaring expectations of both domestic and foreign observers, since about 2000 the ability of Chinese firms to conceive, design, engineer, market, and service vehicles and parts, and to engage in international trade, investment, and acquisitions has made tremendous progress, and ranks second only to Korea among our case countries.

Trade and Investment Policies: Complexity and Layering

The general trend of policy has been a long transformation from state owner-ship and control to liberalized market competition, but from the beginnings of the socialist planned economy in the 1950s and 1960s, policy has been shot through with tensions and contradictions. Five-year and auto industry plans featured spuriously precise numerical goals but typically failed to detail con-crete policies to attain those goals. Initially aggressive plans usually retreated in the face of pressure from industry, particularly foreign assemblers, but the precocious achievements of China's institutions for industrial coordination and diffusion often have been overshadowed by the rigidity of the command and control planning system and intervention by the party at all levels.

The first and most basic tension lay between centralized and local initiatives. The modern industry began in the mid-1950s when Soviet aid helped China construct a truck plant at First Auto Works in the Northeast. Little more than a decade later, the government established Second Automobile Works (later Dongfeng) deep in the hills of central China to protect against a possible Soviet attack. In the meantime, automotive factories sprang up in Shanghai, Nanjing, and other cities as a result of local initiatives, encouraged by the dis-location occasioned by the Great Leap Forward (1958–1961) and the Cultural Revolution (1966–1976), as well as by the Chinese government's propensity for allowing or encouraging local experiments. The government also encouraged pioneers to establish research facilities and to freely transmit their experience and even their blueprints to other factories large and small throughout the country, thus diffusing industrial knowledge at the expense of economies of scale, profitability, and consistent quality control.

From 1964 to the early 2000s, the government sporadically but ineffectually attempted to counterbalance excessive localism by encouraging consolidation into regional industrial "groups" and by trying to bring the production, sales, and trade of the entire industry under the authority of a spin-off from the Ministry of Machinery Building's automotive department called the China National Automotive Industry Corporation (CNAIC) (SAE-China 2003).

With the advent of "reform and opening" in the 1980s, the Chinese government opened the passenger car market to direct foreign investment, hoping that low wages would allow Chinese firms to supplant the sudden flood of imports, and even to export Chinese-assembled vehicles. However, early ventures such as Beijing Jeep and Guangzhou Peugeot failed to take off, victims of an inadequate industrial base, limited demand, and unrealistic expectations on both sides. Licensed production of Japanese compacts such as Suzuki diffused widely, but led to little accumulation of capabilities.

The exception was Shanghai Volkswagen (SVW). Active promotion by the Shanghai municipal government, exacting planning by VW, and occasional pressure from Beijing to increase local content resulted in the methodical development of a high-quality parts supply network (Thun 2006). Almost all of the attention focused on process technology, for VW was slow to introduce new models, and even now conducts relatively little R&D in China. As demand for autos increased rapidly in the 1990s, virtually all of the other global automakers followed VW into the Chinese market.

Deeply influenced by the example of Japan and by interaction with its policymakers and industry representatives, the Chinese government tried to shift emphasis from allocative planning to Japanese-style industrial guidance. In 1987, 1994, 2004, and 2009, the government issued indicative plans to promote the auto industry (Iwahara 1995; Heilmann and Shih 2013), though they featured more grandiose plans and fewer specific policies than their Japanese counterparts. Perhaps the biggest success was a 1997 deal with General Motors, which won permission to build Shanghai's second auto assembly plant in return for a promise to invest over US$1 billion in a factory to build up-to-date Buicks, and to join SAIC in building the PATAC R&D lab. On the other hand, efforts to consolidate production of passenger vehicles in the three biggest firms utterly failed.

More important than industrial planning was Premier Zhu Rongji's prolonged and ultimately spectacularly successful campaign to promote industrial reform by shepherding China into the World Trade Organization (WTO), despite persistent foreign resistance and domestic fears (Lardy 2002). The result for the auto industry was significant liberalization of trade and moderate liberalization of investment (Noble, Ravenhill, and Doner 2005). Tariffs on passenger cars, once over 100%, declined to 25% by the middle of the first decade of the 2000s, while tariffs on parts fell to an average of 10%. The Chinese government insisted on maintaining, even after WTO entry, the 50% cap on foreign ownership of assembly operations and the rule that foreign firms could invest in assembly joint ventures with a maximum of two Chinese partners. The "two partner rule" helped the leading state-owned enterprises, but impeded consolidation and complicated planning for the global automakers. China's approach to liberalization contrasted sharply with those of Thailand and India, which conceded on ownership but retained much higher tariffs on vehicles and parts. Foreign direct investment increased dramatically and contributed both to an upgrading of product quality and an explosion of China's parts exports.

After entering the WTO in 2001, the government continued its efforts at indicative planning and industrial consolidation (Anderson 2012), but still to only modest effect. Continuing de facto controls over new investment have provided some modest leverage, for example in persuading foreign automakers to create new brands in China and to produce "new energy vehicles," but the foreigners have blunted the most controlling initiatives of Chinese planners and, as noted earlier, have managed to comply with government plans in a largely perfunctory fashion. Both foreign multinationals and private firms led by Geely's Chairman Li Shufu repeatedly and publicly called on the government to respect market dynamics, abolish the 50% foreign ownership cap, and provide a level playing field for foreign and private firms (*Financial Times*, March 29, 2015), a stance with which many government officials and industry players actually agreed (DRC 2015). In 2018, under pressure from the United States' Trump administration, the Chinese government announced that it would cut tariffs on passenger vehicles to 15% and on auto parts to a uniform 6%. It also pledged to eliminate restrictions on sole foreign ownership of assembly operations for electric vehicles by 2019 and all passenger vehicles by 2022 (*New York Times*, May 22, 2018). These concessions were insufficient, however, to prevent the outbreak of a sporadic trade war between the United States and China.

Institutional Configuration

Bureaucratic Structures

The structure of policy formation and implementation surrounding the auto industry is complex, divided, and constrained by a ruling party that puts supreme emphasis on political control rather than economic efficiency. Nonetheless, under pressure from market competition and the superior competitiveness of private firms (Lardy 2014), the system has gradually if grudgingly grown better adapted to managing a market economy.

The academic literature has persistently highlighted the difficulty of coordinating China's system of "fragmented authoritarianism" (Lieberthal 2004: 187). Huang (2002) is especially scathing about the failure of the diverse Chinese policymakers to attain their goal of consolidating the auto industry in the 1980s and 1990s, though the extraordinary buoyancy of demand would have frustrated efforts at consolidation almost anywhere. Moreover, it is just as well that coordination failed in China. Consolidation in Korea led to a ferociously aggressive Hyundai Motor; consolidation in the China of the 1980s and 1990s would have entrenched the oligopolistic control of inefficient and politicized state-owned enterprises. The government peevishly resisted new entrants, but their persistence, often with the support of local governments, spurred competition and innovation.

In the years since, a more regularized policymaking process has emerged, though elements of competition remain (Chen and Naughton 2016). Day-to-day promotion and regulation are primarily the responsibility of the Ministry of Industry and Information Technology (MIIT)'s Equipment Industry Department, which is in charge of general machinery, including automobiles and other transport equipment. Peripheral ministerial-level players include the Ministries of Finance (approval of tax incentives and subsidies), Commerce (regulation of auto dealers), Construction, Transportation, and Science and Technology (CATARC and CAAM 2019: 41).

At the local level, provincial and municipal governments remain important players as owners and promoters of most of the auto industry's leading firms. Many local governments have active industrial policies of their own (Thun 2006; Nam 2011). Local regulatory policies, such as restricting the number of new license plates issued each year to reduce congestion, or providing subsidies and traffic preferences to "new energy vehicles," can exert a significant impact on industrial development. For example, for many years virtually all taxis in Shanghai came from Shanghai VW, while more recently Shenzhen has consistently favored the battery-electric vehicles and plug-in hybrids produced by hometown automaker BYD. However, regional protectionism, once a crucial problem created by competing local governments, has greatly eased in recent years under constant pressure from central authorities and increasing market integration and competition (Hubbard 2015).

The State Council, one level above MIIT, establishes overall policy for the auto industry. Three bodies within the State Council are particularly important. The National Development and Reform Commission (NDRC), a descendent of the old state planning commission, is a "super-ministry" in charge of coordinating and setting basic policy directions, and of approving large investments, often in conjunction with the Ministry of Finance and other ministries. Responsibility for the auto industry falls under NDRC's Department of Industry. NDRC is caught between a desire to maintain control and a belief in using market forces. It has consistently but mostly ineffectively tried to use administrative methods to restrain excess capacity. The State-owned Assets Supervision and Administration Commission (SASAC) is the formal owner of three of the six largest firms in the industry: First Auto [FAW], Dongfeng, and Changan; provincial and municipal versions of SASAC own the other "state"-owned automakers. SASAC and its local analogs have an incentive to seek greater efficiency and to ensure business-like operations, including recruitment of external investors who can provide capital and expertise, but their ultimate interest is in maintaining ownership and control. In contrast, the State Council's Development Research Center has equally consistently espoused the cause of active but market-based reform and promotion (DRC, SAE-China, and VW China 2015). At an automotive conference, Liu Shijin, a long-time vice president (vice minister) of DRC, told the authors, "Administrative approval based on production scale and investment is unsuccessful and goes against economic principles. . . . Advocates of price reform are growing, but still in a minority. It's hard to make progress. I talk about it because it needs to be said" (interview, April 17, 2008).

Final coordination, however, comes not from the State Council, but from the top party leadership, particularly in the form of guidance from various "leadership small groups" (Lieberthal 2004: 215–218). Chin (2010) documents the sustained and active role historically played by top leaders, many of them with extensive experience in the automotive industry. Former president Jiang Zemin, for example, served as vice director of the automobile management division of the Ministry of Heavy Industry in 1953, and became chairman of the Chinese branch of the Society of Automotive Engineers when it was established in 1963 (SAE-China, 2003). Some of the coordination work of the leadership small groups may shift to two new "commissions" created by Xi Jinping in 2018: the Central Commission on Comprehensively Deepening

Reform (CCCDR) for long-term macro issues, and the Central Commission on Finance and Economics (CCFE) for more immediate policy concerns (Naughton 2018).

It is certainly true that regulation of the auto industry is more complex and contested in China than in Japan, where the Ministry of Economy, Trade and Industry (METI) has clear preeminence. Even in Japan, however, the Ministries of Finance, Transportation, and Environment have important supporting (or occasionally obstructing) roles to play, just as in China. And despite being far smaller than China or even Japan, South Korea and Taiwan have witnessed productive tensions between market-oriented reform commissions and more protective line ministries (Noble 2011).

The fundamental problem with Chinese industrial policy is not so much convoluted bureaucratic organization as unaccountable political control. State-owned enterprises are key beneficiaries and supporters of communist rule, and promotion and rotation of their top executives is subject to approval by the Communist Party (Lieberthal 2004: 234–238). Corruption is common: in 2013 and 2014, party investigation teams replaced top executives at FAW and Dongfeng; repeated accusations of corruption also plagued Guangzhou Auto (Automotive News China 2016). Even the NDRC has been tainted. More fundamentally, insistence on party leadership by the supreme leader or various "leadership small groups" constrains the regular bureaucratic apparatus of economic policymaking, raises doubts about who is in control, undermines the rule of law, and creates considerable uncertainty about the direction of policy, not least toward reform of state-owned enterprises. Rather than facilitating coordination, then, top-level party intervention often impedes it (Naughton 2016).

Yet despite—or to some extent because of—widespread politicization and uncertainty, and despite the bias of the government and the state-controlled financial system in favor of state-owned enterprises, the less regulated firms are gaining ground and the system of pervasive regulatory approvals is gradually weakening, particularly in autos and other branches of manufacturing (Lardy 2014; Hubbard 2015). Generally speaking, the farther automakers are from central control, the better they have performed. Thus, despite a long head start and preferential support from the center, First Auto and Dongfeng have steadily lost market share to the three major provincially-owned automakers in Beijing, Shanghai, and Guangzhou, while the healthiest and fastest growing firms have been private, even though they lack lucrative joint ventures with global automakers, and have a harder time accessing state banks.

Examination of the career paths of executives in the automobile industry reveals a sharp distinction. Party control of careers at the centrally-owned

SOEs is clear: top leaders have often been moved from one auto SOE to a direct competitor (Automotive News China 2018), or to and from leadership positions in municipal or provincial governments completely unrelated to the auto industry. For example, Miao Wei, the industry minister since 2010, spent the bulk of his career in the auto industry, but from 2005 to 2008 served as party secretary of Dongfeng's headquarters city of Wuhan (Chinavitae. com). Executives at the provincially owned automakers rarely have such experiences, while most of the private firms are still headed by their founders. Similarly, reported spending on R&D as a share of revenues reveals a clear correlation: centrally owned SOEs generally devote the least, followed by the provincial companies, while the private assemblers invest the most (CATARC and CAAM 2018: 394–395).

Centralization of power under Xi Jinping may well sideline these trends for a time (Lardy 2019), it but seems unlikely to fundamentally reverse the economic dynamics, particularly in manufacturing, a highly competitive and relatively open sector. This slow and reluctant yet steady shift away from state planning and control is reminiscent of developments in Taiwan, where the government's share of industrial output peaked in the early 1950s and then steadily declined for the next 60 years.

Intermediaries: Automotive Institute (CATARC), CAAM, and Other Industry Associations

Among the most crucial complements to state institutions for industrial coordination and diffusion are industry associations and industry-specific institutes. As noted in earlier chapters, China's national automotive institute, China Automotive Technology and Research Center (CATARC) was established far earlier than other such institutes in our sample countries, and has come to amass far greater resources.

The historical trajectory of CATARC helps illuminate both its formidable capabilities and the sometimes problematic orientation it has inherited from the socialist planned economy. The Ministry of Heavy Industry established the forerunner of CATARC in 1950, just half a year after the founding of the PRC regime. In 1959 the First Ministry of Machine Building formally placed the office under the jurisdiction of First Auto Works (China FAW Group Corporation R&D Center 2016). When the "reform and opening" of the early 1980s led first to a surge of imported passenger cars and then to an influx of joint ventures, industry leaders saw a need to create an institute capable of supporting the entire industry (Ge 2010; Dong 2014). The State Planning

Commission declined to allocate any funds, and executives at FAW and Dongfeng resisted the idea, but in 1983 leaders interested in autos, such as Li Lanqing (former FAW employee, vice mayor of Tianjin, and later vice premier of China [1998–2003]) and Rao Bin (first factory director of First Auto, prime organizer of Dongfeng, and chairman of CNAIC, often referred to as "the father of the Chinese auto industry"), scrounged up money to build a facility in Tianjin under the auspices of the State Science and Technology Commission. Most of the initial technical staff transferred from First Auto and Dongfeng. CATARC officially opened in 1985. For nearly two decades, CATARC's "ownership" bounced back and forth between various iterations of CNAIC and the Ministry of Machine Building. Only in 2003, when the government placed CATARC under the State Council's SASAC, did it finally achieve a balance of officially sanctioned authority with a degree of stability and autonomy.

In the late 1990s the government stopped funding the center, forcing CATARC's leaders to think like entrepreneurs (Liu 2011). From 1999 to 2009 revenues increased by a factor of eight (Gao and Liu 2014). The bulk of income comes from mandatory certifications, information, factory design, and implementation of government technology projects. The center also organizes conferences and auto shows and carries out factory design, consulting, and quality assurance work for assemblers and parts makers, but in general it does not have a strong market orientation (interview with Dr. Zhang Changling, Policy Research Department, Automotive Industry Development Institute [CATARC], Beijing, September 1, 2014). By 2020 it had a staff of 4,572 and assets of over US$1.6 billion (CATARC 2020). In addition to its work in standards, technology development, drafting of automotive safety and environmental regulations, and industrial policy analysis, the center has diversified by establishing over 20 for-profit companies (CATARC 2020). In 2018 CATARC was formally reorganized as a company—but one still largely focused on carrying out tasks delegated by the government.

CATARC leaders aspire to act simultaneously as a research institute; an independent intermediary between the government, consumers, and the auto industry; and an aggressive, profit-seeking enterprise or even business conglomerate (Wangyi Qiche 2010). From another perspective, CATARC is both umpire and player, contributing to and living off the industry it helps manage. Zhao Hang, who became director in 1999, sometimes spoke boldly, calling for strengthening the rule of law, and reducing the role of policy interventions and CCP oversight: "The party is good at ideology, not at managing [the division of labor of government organizations]. If you don't understand this business, how are you going to divide up the work?" (Gao and Liu 2014). Zhao may have taken boldness a step too far: in early 2016, SASAC suddenly announced that Zhao had been dismissed from his post as director (*mianqu . . . zhuren zhiwu*) and retired, replaced on an interim basis by CATARC's party secretary (*Xinhua*, January 6, 2016).

An even more dynamic process has characterized the main industry associations. Originally spun off from the socialist ministries, they have grown more diverse, competitive, and market oriented. The most prominent group is China Automobile Manufacturers Association (CAAM). In 1987 CAAM was hived out of CNAIC, which as noted earlier was an awkward extension of the Ministry of Machine Building. In principle, CAAM is a voluntary, nonprofit social organization run by and representing member firms, but it also carries out some quasi-official tasks, such as providing permits, organizing annual auto shows, compiling statistics, helping CATARC edit a massive auto industry yearbook, and representing the Chinese industry to other national associations and to the International Organization of Motor Vehicle Manufacturers (OICA). Virtually all large auto firms join. In its first two decades, CAAM was widely seen as a tool of the government and old state-owned enterprises, from which hailed most of its officials, such as Chen Zutao, the Soviet-trained head of CNAIC, and Hu Xinmin, one of the founding cadres of First Auto Works and long-time central bureaucrat (Li 2008).

A turning point came in 2007 with a change of leadership after the abrupt disappearance of CAAM Secretary-General Jiang Lei, who apparently fled to New Zealand in the face of accusations of embezzlement of funds involved in putting on auto shows (Yang 2007). His successor, Dong Yang, came from a traditional background (Ministry of Machine Building, Beijing Auto, SAE-China), but immediately struck a new pose. He pledged to recover the association's prestige and promised, "First, we must clarify that CAAM services (member) firms; it does not represent the government in managing them" (Li 2008). In fact, Dong and CAAM increasingly did act as representatives of the auto industry mainstream, emphasizing market logic and freely criticizing the government in public. Not surprisingly, though, they were far from libertarian ideologues: the association strongly supported the promotion of domestic innovation, repeatedly opposed relaxing the 50% limit on foreign ownership of assembly operations, and supported short-term stimulus measures that even some SOEs criticized as distorting (Guo 2015).

In 1994 a partial alternative and even competitor to CAAM appeared. Rao Da established the China Passenger Car Association (CPCA) in Shanghai, far from the halls of power in Beijing. Rao, son of "the father of the Chinese auto industry" Rao Bin and a market analyst at Shanghai VW, had previously worked at BAIC and Dongfeng. CPCA was a purely private association with no official functions. It focused on analysis of sales data for the passenger car market, so its ambit was considerably narrower than that of CAAM. Rao was active in policy debates, however, and maintained a high profile in the press and a blog on a popular auto internet site. CPCA could be critical of the government, especially about the accuracy of industry data. The official press, in turn, assailed Rao's association as unofficial and even illegal ("it doesn't even have an official chop!"), but admitted that CPCA had forced CAAM to become quicker moving and more open to the public (Zhang 2009). Associations of auto dealers display a strikingly similar evolution toward diversity and competition in a weaker policy area long dominated by manufacturers rather than dealers.

Intermediary associations in the Chinese auto industry are not yet perfectly free to act as they please. CATARC in particular is still a quasi-governmental institution and subject to close supervision by the Chinese Communist Party, a point accentuated by the sudden dismissal of Director Zhao Hang. Nonetheless, both CATARC and the business associations are evolving to meet the demands of a highly competitive industry, and the general trend toward greater representativeness, diversity, and organizational competition is clear.

Upgrading Competencies

State institutions, intermediate associations, and universities have engaged in a wide range of activities to upgrade the competences of local automotive firms. In general, upgrading activities have gradually grown more competitive and transparent.

Standards

Establishing a comprehensive and up-to-date set of industry standards and helping firms, especially smaller companies with few resources, verify compliance with those standards are crucial tasks for auto industries in developing countries, and indeed in all countries. China has long devoted a great deal of attention to standards. In the 1950s, First Auto's Changchun Research Institute took responsibility for acquiring standards from the Soviet Union; unfortunately, they were completely different from those used in Western and Japanese auto industries (Ge 2010). From 1985, CATARC took over the central role in acquiring, developing, and diffusing automotive standards, serving as secretariat of auto-related standards for the national standards committee.

CATARC has been extremely active at both the national and international levels (CATARC and CAAM 2016: 68–73). Nor is the Center content to rely forever on copying and diffusing international (mainly European) automotive standards: China is making a concerted effort to develop new standards, especially in emerging fields such as electric vehicles, and to convince foreign automakers to accept Chinese approaches as international standards (Wangyi Qiche 2010).

Testing and Certification, Crash Testing, and Mandatory Recalls

Testing, verification, and certification have followed a more typical Chinese pattern: the government has invested a good deal of money and effort to develop institutional support, but the institutions have not always been well organized, responsive, or disciplined. As with standards, initial support came from First Auto and CATARC, which remain major providers of testing and certification services. In the 1990s and into the early 2000s, under pressure to prepare for entry to the WTO, the government consolidated and strengthened a formerly chaotic array of certification bodies into the CCC, or 3C (China Compulsory Certification), system. Parts suppliers and assemblers could apply to one of two organizations: China Certification Centre for Automotive Products (CCAP) or China Quality Certification Centre (CQC) (Wang 2015). As auto production mushroomed in the 1990s and early 2000s, additional centers to conduct the actual tests popped up around each of the major auto clusters (CATARC and CAAM 2015: 332). Certification was particularly active in such areas as safety and electric vehicles (FOURIN 2013).

The testing and certification process still revealed many of the old maladies, however. The testing system was bureaucratic and sometimes politicized or corrupt, as demonstrated by the case of China Automotive Engineering Research Institute Company (CAERI). A report on China Central Television (CCTV) revealed that the CAERI center had colluded with automakers and reported fuel efficiency figures 11% higher than the US Environmental Protection Agency (EPA) had found for the same models. The CAERI fraud case came to light just as the State Council was finalizing guidelines to consolidate the national system of testing and verification institutes, reduce bureaucratic intervention, and subject the testing companies to greater market discipline (CATARC and CAAM 2015: 29–31).

A similar dynamic of opaque testing, implausibly positive test results, media muckraking, public outrage, and concerted efforts at reform appears in the case of crash test ratings. Initially, the Chinese subsidiary of an Australian insurance company announced plans to establish a Chinese version of the "new car assessment program" (NCAP) pioneered in the United States and copied in Europe. However, this initiative was abruptly hijacked by CATARC, which proceeded to operate a lax and opaque system in collusion with automakers. Popular criticism and media coverage forced CATARC to adopt rigorous and up-to-date European standards, though it remained less transparent about procedures. A similar "late-but-fast-moving" story applies to reform of the mandatory recall system (Zhongguo qiche zhiliang wang 2014).

Technology Promotion

Development and diffusion of technology, too, has witnessed a struggle between early and vigorous promotion, and difficulty in staving off political intrusion into those promotional efforts.

863 Program Grants

For a developing country, China has devoted significant resources to promotion of basic, applied, and military technology (Cao, Suttmeier, and Simon 2006; Heilmann and Shih 2013). Most relevant to the auto industry is funding provided from the Ministry of Science and Technology's "863 Program" (National High-tech R&D Program, 2001–). The government has been especially supportive of research into "new energy vehicles," where industrial promotion overlaps with important national goals regarding energy security and environmental protection, and in which long-time science and technology minister Wan Gang, a specialist in electric vehicles, took a particular interest. In addition to providing valued financial resources, government support helps to diffuse technology and serves a valuable assessment and signaling function. Companies and individual researchers proudly publicize receipt of "863" grants as evidence of their expertise.

To be sure, "863" and related programs have come in for biting criticisms (Shi and Rao 2010; Cao et al. 2013; Brandt and Thun 2016) for trying to pick winning firms or technologies, or ignoring possible lower-tech winners; favoring big companies and SOEs; relying on biased "insider" evaluation committees and narrow criteria that essentially predetermine the winner; and warping incentives, so that researchers commit fraud and firms rush to file junk patents, or create technologies unrelated to social or market needs.

In cutting-edge fields like semiconductor design or life sciences, the weakness of merit-based funding and the narrowing of technological alternatives in the "863" program may well present serious obstacles to scientific and industrial advancement, but the problems seem less striking in the automobile industry, an incremental, engineering-based enterprise still largely in catch-up mode and thus less concerned with picking winning technologies or products and more focused on how to produce reliable and inexpensive technologies already winnowed out by market competition in more advanced countries. If there is one thing the Chinese auto industry does not lack, it is a plethora of firms and technological approaches.

In particular, in the automobile industry it is not true that the government's technology support has all gone to big SOEs, nor that the government has insisted on pursuing a single "national champion" technology. On the contrary, smaller and private firms developing a range of competing technological approaches have done very well by the "863" programs. Geely won five early "863" awards, including projects for advanced engines and dual clutch (DC) transmissions, and the first use of a large capacitor in a hybrid powertrain (Arashi 2007). During the 11th five-year plan (2006–2010) and the beginning of the 12th, Chery, a small, municipally owned SOE producing under its own brand, won more "863" "new energy" awards than any other automaker, including projects for all three of the major powertrain technologies— hybrids, battery-electric cars, and fuel-cell vehicles (Chen 2011). In 2012, Great Wall Motor, a privately owned producer of SUVs and pickups, won an "863" grant of more than a million US dollars to help develop a small electric car (Baodingshi Kejiju 2013). BYD, a privately owned battery and automaker from Shenzhen, used assistance from "863" to completely redesign its "Qin" plug-in hybrid to great acclaim (MOST [Ministry of Science and Technology] 2015). Nor were parts makers excluded. By 2010, the private Hangzhou firm Wanxiang, the biggest independent Chinese auto supplier and a long-time proponent of electric vehicles, had won seven "863" awards to support its early research into electric vehicle development (Wanxiang Electric Vehicle 2011: 4).

Consortia to Develop Key Technologies

Initially, technology alliances mainly stemmed from government initiatives, but as the industry grew larger and more sophisticated, the government role increasingly became supportive and indirect. The first major development consortium appeared in the mid-1990s as a bid to acquire and indigenize engine electronics. In 1995 the government mobilized 10 major SOE assemblers and parts firms, led by SAIC and fuel injection maker Weifu High-Technology Group, to create a joint subsidiary called Zhong-lian ("China United") Automotive Electronics. Zhong-lian then entered into a 50-50 joint venture with the German parts leader Robert Bosch to make engine control systems, fuel injectors, emissions control equipment, and other key parts. The joint venture remains China's leading engine electronics firm, with over 1,300 R&D personnel and exports of its own technology (UAES [United Automotive Electronic Systems] 2016).

A second state-sponsored consortium focused on the most complex and expensive component of conventional automobiles: automatic transmissions. As China grew wealthier, a wave of imported automatic transmissions began supplanting domestically made manual gearboxes, leading to fears that Chinese automakers were losing control of a key component (CATARC and CAAM 2015: 284–286). In response, in late 2008 the NDRC organized a 12-firm consortium led by FAW and Shanghai Auto to gain technology and avoid duplicative investment by creating a US$200 million, 34/66 joint venture with the American supplier BorgWarner in Dalian to produce three key assemblies (double clutch, torsional vibration, and control modules) (Jiang et al. 2013).

The consortium aimed to commence mass production by 2011 of dual-clutch automatic transmissions, a new technology promising faster shifts and higher efficiency than standard planetary gear automatic transmissions. The resulting modules won acceptance by FAW, SAIC, and Jianghuai for use in multiple vehicles. Others, such as Great Wall Motor and Chery, sought transmissions elsewhere, but still acquired some parts from the consortium, and affirmed the value of what they learned in the consortium. None of the members sold their shares. By 2019, the joint venture had sold over 3 million units to 11 different Chinese automakers (BorgWarner 2019). The alliance with BorgWarner was probably not as significant as the UAES alliance with Bosch more than a decade earlier, but it materially contributed to the capacity of Chinese firms to build a crucial component.

In 2007, as part of the mid- to long-term science plan for 2006–2020, the Ministry of Science and Technology began encouraging a variety of looser industrial innovation alliances among firms, universities, and research institutes. The alliances were explicitly expected to be led by firms and oriented to the market (MOST 2007). The auto industry soon joined in, starting with a weight reduction alliance led by the Chinese branch of the Society of Automotive Engineers (SAE) (Liu 2014; Qiche qinglianghua jishu chuangxin zhanlüe lianmeng 2014). Geely and particularly Great Wall were leading participants. Among the many collective outputs of the long-lived alliance were a set of new industry standards and a joint technology database.

With the remarkable growth of the Chinese auto industry, market pressures and opportunities determine the large bulk of investment. The government retains an important role, however, in strengthening standards and testing, stimulating exploration of next-generation issues, rewarding and signaling excellence, addressing specific bottle-necks, and in encouraging cooperation with universities, research institutes, affiliated industries, and suppliers, especially smaller parts firms that lack direct engagement with global assemblers and first-tier suppliers.

Skills and Training

The development of industrial skills and training in China is a familiar story: high expectations, criticism of weaknesses, yet actually impressive performance backed by elaborate and broadly effective if uneven and ill-coordinated support institutions, particularly an elaborate system of state certification. Education and training for a market economy has deep roots in China. Rawski (2011) notes the high level of literacy and familiarity with complex markets in traditional China. In the early 20th century, work-study programs emerged, followed by a Soviet-style emphasis on vocational training in SOEs after 1949. To be sure, these developments were uneven and were repeatedly interrupted by wars, depressions, and political upheaval, but they left an important base: China's "long boom," Rawski emphasizes, was possible only because it built on an impressive foundation of human capital unmatched in most other developing countries. "Reform and opening" in the early 1980s, and especially SOE reform in the 1990s, led to a massive expansion of both formal and vocational education, including decentralization and social partnerships facilitating the rapid entry of non-state providers (Li, Sheldon, and Sun 2011: 115).

Despite these achievements, many scholars are critical of skills training in contemporary China. Zhu and Warner (2013: 144), for example, conclude that "[a]t the enterprise level, the skills training status quo is less than satisfactory," with too little commitment from top management and too much reliance on on-the-job-training. They point to a continuing bias toward general university education, a gap between what vocational schools provide—often determined by the skills of their staffs—and the needs of enterprises, and a paucity of experienced, high-quality managers (Zhu and Warner 2013: 154–155). American sociologist Zhang (2014) highlights the pervasive impact of insecurity at Chinese automotive assemblers, including widespread reliance on temporary and dispatched workers and term contract employment, which contributed to a wave of damaging strikes beginning around 2010. Beijing University's Song Lei, an expert on industrial sociology, notes that Chinese scholars have undertaken little serious fieldwork on skill formation in factories (interview, September 3, 2014).

Yet skill formation in most countries is imperfect, and insecurity and youth unemployment or underemployment is rising almost everywhere. If we examine the admittedly fragmentary comparative evidence, quite a different picture of China's achievements emerges. The World Bank's China Enterprise Survey (World Bank 2013: 2) reports, "About 85 percent of the workers in Chinese firms have undergone training. This is nearly double the average proportion for all countries." Nor is training limited to assemblers. In a rare comparative survey of work in auto components firms, Steyn (2012) finds that Chinese workers are better educated than their counterparts in India or South Africa, and more likely to receive training domestically, rather than being dispatched to the home country of the mother firm for training. Cho (2006) shows that the actual level of insecurity in Chinese auto firms is no higher than in Japan or Korea, where use of temporary and dispatched workers has also surged.

Even Zhang (2014: 79–80) concedes that the automobile industry (especially the assembly sector) provides high wages and good benefits and is generally viewed in China as prestigious and promising. The industry attracts strong candidates with high educational levels (most blue-collar workers are high school or junior college graduates) and is able to implement rigorous screening and regular evaluations. The result is considerable stress and dissatisfaction, but also a strong incentive to learn and improve. A German manager at Bosch's Suzhou plant puts this drive in comparative perspective: "The quality of human capital is more of a problem in Thailand. Workers there are not as motivated and quick working. There's a program to bring Thai workers to Suzhou for training, but they are not as aggressive as Chinese in seizing new opportunities" (interview, Daniel Pauli, section manager, Chassis Systems Control China, August 27, 2013). Japanese automotive experts visiting the same factory remarked that the span of control (number of machines for which one worker is responsible) was a little narrower than in Japan and the pace a bit more relaxed, but they emphasized that the gap with Japan had significantly narrowed in recent years.

Perhaps most convincing is the detailed comparative fieldwork of Jürgens and Krzywdzinski. They conclude, "Against expectations, automobile companies in China do not pursue 'low road' strategies but have designed intensive internal training programs and long-term career paths for blue-collar workers. . . . At the time of our study, one-third of production workers had already reached the high-level certificate, which was regarded by the management as a rough equivalent to the German *Facharbeiter*. By Chinese and also by international standards, these numbers represent a highly skilled workforce" (Jürgens and Krzywdzinski 2015: 1204, 1216–1217). Blue-collar autoworkers in China, unlike their counterparts in Brazil, Russia, and India, also enjoy some limited opportunities to advance to white-collar technical positions (Jürgens and Krzywdzinski 2016). Nor did this simply reflect the choices of global automakers, for the imprint of national training systems remains deep in both advanced and developing countries. In China, both German and domestic assemblers displayed tight intertwining with formal education institutions and China's state vocational certification system (Japanese assemblers, however, relied on highly developed training systems in the parent company) (Jürgens and Krzywdzinski 2015: 1214, 1221).

Training for engineers is similar: imperfect yet impressive, as one would expect from the comparative data provided earlier on recent Chinese attainments in education and research. Massive expansion in tertiary education in the late 1990s and early 2000s, particularly in engineering, resulted in a plentiful supply of young engineers and designers with ambition and book learning but little practical experience in managing projects, partly because the number of students expanded so rapidly that at first the faculty could not keep up. In interviews, managers from Delphi (US) and Ricardo (UK) separately used the same word to characterize new Chinese (and Indian) engineering graduates: useless. The response of both firms: send them to the home company for six months to a year, after which they were seen as equal to recent American or British graduates. Both also noted that the level of English and sophistication among Chinese engineers was noticeably improving in the early years of this century (interviews, Beijing, April 17, 2008, with Kevin Xiaodong Ye of Delphi and Christian Koehler of Ricardo). The weakness of the formal Chinese educational system in applying theory to practice is another rationale for participating in the national training system.

The Political Origins of Institutions for Upgrading

The central role of external threats and of military officials in economic policymaking is a major theme in the literature on Chinese political economy. Feigenbaum's (2003) influential *China's Techno-Warriors* focuses especially on the 1950s and early 1960s, when the new communist regime became embroiled in border tensions and conflicts with South Korea and India; China also fought brief but bloody border battles with the Soviet Union in 1969 and with Vietnam (perceived as a Soviet proxy) in 1979. Eventually, the United States re-emerged as the main threat. From secret incursions into Tibet, to charging toward the Yalu river during the Korean War, to supporting opposition to China's attempts to consolidate its sweeping, long-held claims in the South China Sea, the United States has also engaged in what the Chinese perceive as a grand plan to contain China's recovery as a great power.

Chinese perceptions of external threats, however, actually long predate the formation of the PRC, and indeed to some extent help account for the communist victory (Johnson 1962). Conflict with northern nomads led to the development of proto-Han nationalism centuries before the Treaty of Westphalia in Europe supposedly issued in the era of the nation-state (Tackett 2017), as well as a martial "cultural realism" among the Chinese leadership (Johnston 1995). Defeat in the Opium and Sino-Japanese wars in the mid- to late 19th century led to an ideology of self-strengthening with a particular focus on developing military technology. Changan Automobile semi-plausibly traces its origins back to the establishment of a munitions factory in Shanghai in 1862 by Li Hongzhang, the central figure in the self-strengthening movement.

In the 20th century, revolution, civil war, and the eight-year war of resistance against Japan intensified those convictions and contributed to the creation in 1932 of the state-run National Resources Commission (NRC) to promote industrial development as a basis for military resistance. The NRC focused primarily on building massive holdings in basic industries such as mining, oil refining, and steel, but also worked on autos and airplanes (Xue 2005: 50, 278, 292). The Chinese civil war ended not with guerrilla warfare but with a clash of massive conventional armies, further highlighting the crucial importance of industrial capacity. After 1949, as Feigenbaum (2003) suggests, the victorious communist forces were obsessed with external threats from the United States and the Soviet Union, and after the "reform and opening" of the 1980s, PRC policymakers became determined to increase "comprehensive national power" by maintaining rapid economic growth, deepening technological capabilities, and sharply expanding military spending (Hu and Men 2004). The American attack on telecommunications maker Huawei and on China's hortatory planning document *Made in China 2025* merely confirmed the perception of threat. Plausible external threats, then, have kept industrial upgrading consistently at the top of the government's agenda for 200 years and more.

This martial preoccupation is clearly reflected in the historical development of the auto industry, from the Soviet-supported creation of the First Auto Works truck plant and military-affiliated Changan's construction of a jeep factory in the 1950s to the formation of the anti-Soviet Dongfeng truck facility in the 1960s, and beyond. Jiang Zemin and many other top leaders had personal experience in the auto industry. They gave the auto industry the first formal industrial policy, and in 1994 named autos one of five "pillar indus-tries." The auto industry has been a major focus of the ideology of "autono-mous development" and "autonomous innovation" (Lu and Feng 2005). As of the first decade of the 2000s, top automotive policymakers still displayed a surprisingly deep suspicion of global automakers and the global economy more generally (Chin 2010). Revelations of American spying against China (among other countries) in the National Security Agency (NSA) documents leaked by Edward Snowden in 2013 spurred the Chinese leadership to an intensified push for technological autonomy (Bloomberg News 2014).

If it is widely accepted that perceptions of external vulnerability have been an important driver of Chinese economic policymaking, the notion that an unfavorable balance of demands and ready resources to meet them might seem harder to credit, given China's rapid growth, its relatively rich resource endowment, and the large trade surpluses it accumulated after joining the WTO in 2001. Surpluses have been far from consistent, however, and since "reform and opening" in the early 1980s, the Chinese leadership has had good cause for concern.

For the first 30 years of the PRC regime, the government controlled the al-location of foreign exchange. Moreover, China was a net exporter of oil until 1993. Automotive production centered on trucks, and imports of automobiles were tightly restricted until the early 1980s, so that FAW and Dongfeng grew up in an era of minimal trade and little concern for import competition. External threats created a concern for building basic industrial capacity, but Chinese firms did not have to worry too much about product quality, con-sumer appeal, or cost efficiency. Not surprisingly, China witnessed a narrow version of upgrading.

With "reform and opening," two big import surges in the 1980s, and fears in the 1990s of withering competition from imports after WTO entry (Noble, Ravenhill, and Doner 2005), that relatively relaxed stance lost viability. The Asian financial crisis of the late 1990s provided an object lesson in the po-tential dangers awaiting China as it liberalized its economy, and the utility of amassing huge stocks of foreign reserves, a message reinforced by the global financial shock set off by the collapse of Lehman Brothers a decade later. Not surprisingly, China displayed redoubled determination to stimulate autono-mous development and autonomous innovation. Moreover, the era of huge current account surpluses lasted only about five years. By 2015, the Chinese leadership found itself fending off fears of accelerating capital flight. Thus, while the exact degree and character of resource dependency has varied over time, at least since the mid-1980s the Chinese leadership has faced recurrent challenges to its ability to defray political demands, and has responded with redoubled attention to industrial upgrading.

Conclusion

Systematic and comparative analysis makes clear what the failure to meet sky-high expectations for China has obscured: the Chinese auto industry has actually made remarkable progress in intensive growth based on industrial upgrading. In a globalized industry dominated by fewer than a dozen multinational assemblers, and characterized by ferocious consolidation, Chinese automakers, particularly independent domestic companies with their own brands, have developed the capacity to conceive, design, engineer, market, and export their own vehicles. They are increasingly active as multinational investors and acquirers of foreign parts and assembly firms. If Geely merges with Volvo, it will mark the birth of a major new global automaker, while BYD, Great Wall, and the independent brand side of Shanghai Auto (SAIC) are emerging as significant players in Asia. China is now the biggest producer of "new energy vehicles," and while it is too early to be sure, Chinese firms from a variety of backgrounds appear to be emerging as a major force in electric vehicles and autonomous driving. China has far outstripped not just Thailand, Malaysia, and the Philippines, but also other large developing countries such as Indonesia, Brazil, India, and Turkey.

One important reason for this unexpectedly impressive performance, we have argued, is the development of a set of institutions to support diffusion of industrial development and upgrading. Institutions such as the automotive testing and research center CATARC, certification centers, universities and research institutes, grants for innovation, and the system of state training certification emerged far earlier, and in a more elaborate and consistent form, than in virtually any other developing country. More acutely than in any of our other case countries, except perhaps South Korea, institution building in China has been motivated by a series of external threats and a lack of easy access to resources with which to procure domestic support.

Building on this impressive base, the prospects of the Chinese auto industry look bright (Noble 2013). China's young and well-educated but inexperienced workforce is gradually maturing and benefiting from the many opportunities the upgrading policies have created for learning by doing. A large, diverse, and ferociously competitive market serves as a spur to efficiency and innovation. Ongoing reforms are gradually improving institutions such as testing centers and crash evaluation programs, partly because autos are high-profile products of great interest to citizens and the news media.

Yet the legacy of the old system of socialist planning and party control has also constrained the emergence of a healthy automotive market. Where Southeast Asian countries have struggled to build new institutions from scratch, China has struggled to reform, or "scrap-and-build," existing institutions. In that process, political considerations have often overridden market logic. The heavy hand of planning and control has often weighed down the light touch of coordination and diffusion. The line between state and private ownership has grown blurrier. Chery, for example, has moved from local state ownership to mixed public-private ownership, and is now less reliant on the municipal government of its home base of Wuhu City in Anhui, but behind the new private players lie other local governments (Zheng and Li 2019). Notwithstanding the superior performance of private firms, SOEs protected by their privileged position as 50% joint venture partners of global automakers remain the dominant players. Despite the planned abolition of the 50% cap, so far the change has been limited to permission for Tesla to establish a wholly owned subsidiary to build electric cars, and BMW's successful campaign to acquire 75% of China Brilliance. In most other cases, the Chinese partners appear reluctant to give up their cash cows.

The government has already ordered the three big centrally owned assemblers—FAW, Dongfeng, and Changan—to step up cooperation and move toward an eventual merger (Yang 2017). Such a union would be hard to accomplish, but even partial movement toward a merger is ominous, for the resulting giant would crowd out healthier firms and exacerbate trade tensions with the United States.

Many serious challenges remain. Concerns about pollution, congestion, and energy security will continue to constrain growth. Slower growth, in turn, means that the long-feared excess capacity may re-emerge with a vengeance, partly because the exit mechanism remains so weak in China. Neither central nor local officials will easily reconcile themselves to the possible bankruptcy of major auto firms, with all the attendant economic, social, and political ramifications.

China has created impressive institutions for industrial coordination and diffusion, but without further reform, the Chinese auto industry will be severely constrained by the Leninist legacy of controls on investment and trade, market-distorting subsidies, and political interference in management. The increasing tension between economics and politics under Xi Jinping is likely to make that reform difficult.

9

Taiwan

Balancing Independent Assembly, MNCs, and Parts Promotion in a Small Market

發動機救國 Engines will save the country.

—**President Chiang Kai-shek (Xie 1993: 8)**

Taiwan's automotive development strongly supports the proposition that capable institutions are crucial to helping firms in developing countries undertake industrial upgrading. Research institutes, testing and certification centers, export promotion agencies, training programs, industry associations, and government-supported corporate alliances have flourished for many years, contributing to the emergence of significant automotive capabilities. Though modest in size and little known abroad, Taiwan's leading auto companies export high-quality cars, design and engineer their own models, invest abroad, and produce and export a wide variety of auto parts and car electronics.

The success of Taiwanese firms is all the more striking in light of Taiwan's small and volatile domestic market, and academic works in the 1980s and 1990s that denigrated automotive policy in Taiwan for failing to emulate the determination and success of Korea (Arnold 1989: 12–13; Chu 1994). Instead of trying to match Korea, the government of Taiwan embarked on a course of gradual liberalization in the 1980s. Yet it never relinquished the goal of fostering the development of domestically owned companies capable of designing, engineering, and marketing their own vehicles, and simultaneously supported the activities of small and medium-sized firms that have achieved striking success in exporting automotive parts, especially bumpers, body panels, and other accessories for the after-sales market. Finally, by the turn of the millennium, it was impossible to understand the Taiwanese automotive

The Political Economy of Automotive Industrialization in East Asia. Richard F. Doner, Gregory W. Noble and John Ravenhill, Oxford University Press (2021). © Oxford University Press. DOI: 10.1093/oso/9780197520253.003.0009

industry without taking into account its electronics industry and the island's increasingly complex trade and investment with China.

The policies and institutions that evolved to promote upgrading of both assembly and parts, in turn, reflected the particular external security challenges facing Taiwan, which made the political system firmly committed to industrialization and upgrading, but also sensitive to the interests of firms from vital diplomatic partners, particularly the United States and Japan. Taiwan balanced cooperation with foreign "mother firms" such as Toyota, support for independent local assembly, and promotion of auto parts.

Industry Performance: Both Extensive and Intensive Growth

Taiwan is unusual in sustaining a balance between assembly of whole vehicles and production of parts. The overall market of fewer than half a million units a year is the smallest in our seven case countries, as is Taiwan's population of about 23 million people. Production and sales of autos grew strongly from the 1970s, but by the mid-1990s peaked and then declined. High population density, an unusually relaxed policy toward registration of motorcycles, and an increasingly mature mass transit system in the capital city of Taipei have all limited demand for cars. Despite gradual liberalization, domestic production comprised 70%–85% of sales until later in the first decade of the 2000s, when imports, led by luxury vehicles, rose to account for nearly half of all sales. Exports of vehicles sputtered until 2006, when they began to rise, accounting for over one-quarter of total production before declining again (Table 9.1).

Since 2006 the value of parts production (Table 9.2) has exceeded that of vehicle assembly. Outward direct investment by both assemblers and parts companies, particularly in mainland China, complements local production, providing valuable economies of scale and scope and encouraging higher value-added activities at home. Taiwan's performance in extensive growth, then, while not as striking as Thailand's, can be considered successful given the limited size of the domestic market. Taiwan's record in intensive growth— in upgrading the sophistication and value of production—is also surprisingly impressive.

Table 9.1 Taiwan: Production, Sales, and Exports of Assembled Vehicles

Year	Production	Imports	Exports	Total Domestic Sales*
1989	328,990		3,575	330,266
1990	362,751		4,249	347,301
1991	403,257		1,292	396,401
1992	436,732		492	422,756
1993	404,524		649	405,967
1994	423,318		1,281	408,901
1995	406,480		3,795	405,834
1996	366,026		3,003	361,238
1997	381,103		3,696	375,712
1998	404,545		3,043	401,640
1999	350,273		1,160	357,835
2000	372,613		1,965	354,729
2001	271,704		2,838	284,386
2002	333,699		3,043	340,866
2003	386,686		6,338	361,878
2004	430,814	61,882	1,052	484,292
2005	446,345	70,157	1,081	514,627
2006	303,229	59,928	8,420	366,316
2007	283,439	55,116	7,689	326,781
2008	182,969	42,744	7,196	229,497
2009	226,356	60,444	9,655	294,423
2010	303,456	74,893	36,914	327,615
2011	343,296	97,090	54,785	378,288
2012	339,038	98,844	70,906	365,871
2013	338,720	115,015	82,427	378,449
2014	379,223	140,205	95,518	423,836
2015	351,085	159,195	83,307	420,775
2016	309,531	174,444	51,463	439,585
2017	291,563	189,712	39,519	444,629
2018	253,241	202,444	23,982	435,131
2019	251,304	214,847	32,482	439,835

Source: Taiwan Transportation Vehicle Manufacturers Association (TTVMA)

https://www.ttvma.org.tw//statistics

https://www.ttvma.org.tw/industry#2

*1989–2003 only includes sales to dealers.

Table 9.2 Taiwan: Value of Assembly and Parts Production (100 million NTD$)

Year	Vehicle Assembly	Parts Production for Domestic Consumption (Conventional)	Parts Exports (Conventional)	Parts Production (Electronic)*
2004	2,197	2,079	1,274	
2005	2,309	2,162	1,280	500
2006	1,601	1,974	1,329	560
2007	1,451	2,036	1,479	710
2008	1,016	1,839	1,526	678
2009	1,185	1,697	1,397	800
2010	1,649	2,107	1,713	918
2011	1,928	2,249	1,848	1,030
2012	1,894	2,263	1,948	1,124
2013	1,885	2,227	1,979	1,339
2014	2,216	2,336	2,077	1,473
2015	2,081	2,342	2,145	1,650
2016	1,906	2,279	2,113	1,820
2017	1,831	2,316	2,149	2,080
2018	1,670	2,257	2,147	2,202
2019	1,674	2,226	2,148	NA
2020				2,786

Source: TTVMA; hundreds of millions of New Taiwan dollars; during this period, the exchange rate was approximately US$ = 30 NTD;

https://www.ttvma.org.tw/statistics;   https://www.ttvma.org.tw/industry#1;   https://www.ttvma.org.tw/industry#2

*Production of electronic parts: (Hwang 2013; Liang 2015; SIPO [Smart Electronics Industry Project Promotion Office] 2018). Production value of electronic and conventional parts is based on separate surveys; coverage partially overlaps. 2017 is an estimate. 2018–2020 are forecasts.

Assembly

The structure of the assembly industry evolved through three stages:

(1) an initial locally owned **monopoly** producer called Yulon (pinyin: *Yulong*) gave way to

(2) a **fragmented group** of over a dozen assemblers, which gradually winnowed out to

(3) a more consolidated industry with **two dominant poles**: Yulon and the Toyota subsidiary Kuozui (*Guorui*).

See Table 9.3.

Table 9.3 Structure of Taiwan's Assembly Industry

Local Assembler	Yulon (Yulon and Luxgen brands)	Yulon–Nissan (Contract Assembly of Nissan Vehicles)	China Motor (Yulon Group Company)	Kuozui (Guorui)	Ford Lio Ho	Honda	Sanyang
Foreign Partner Partner's Ownership Share	Independent (domestically owned)	Nissan 40%	Mitsubishi Motors MMC 14%; Mitsubishi Corp. 5%	Toyota 70% (Toyota 65%, Hino 5%)	Ford 70%	Honda 100%	Hyundai (domestically owned; originally Honda, 13.5%)
Established	1953	2002	1969	1984	1973	2002	1967
Employees	1,500	420	1,760	3,930	1,800	700	2,250 (incl. motorcycles)
Rated production Capacity	30,000	120,000	120,000	160,000	110,000	35,000	50,000
2018 Production	(Counted under Yulon–Nissan)	42,400	47,200	101,600	13,000	35,800	12,300
R&D Center	1981	2007	1999	2000	1999		
Overseas investment	—Dongfeng Yulon (50%) —Nissan Philippines (24.5%) —Derways [Russia] (50%)	—Dongfeng Fengshen (Guangzhou Aeolus) (15%)	—Dongnan (25%) —Fujian Daimler (16%)				—Xiamen King Long (buses) 25% —Motorcycle joint ventures in China, Indonesia, Vietnam

Source: Compiled by authors from TTVMA, company materials, and press accounts.

Kuozui is a joint venture between Toyota (70%) and its local sales partner Hotai (*Hetai*). Kuozui steadily expanded its market share until it accounted for just over half of all sales. The locally owned Yulon group made up the second pole, with just over a quarter of all sales. Yulon assembled Nissan models as well as its own-brand vehicles, while its sister firm China Motors (established and controlled by the same family) assembled Mitsubishi models (mostly commercial vehicles), along with small numbers of own-brand vehicles. A wholly owned subsidiary of Honda occupied a steady fourth position, while Ford Lio Ho and Sanyang, a leading local motorcycle manufacturer engaged in licensed production of Hyundai models, gradually faded.

The local affiliates of Toyota, Ford, and Honda are all majority-owned by their overseas parents. They are primarily devoted to serving the Taiwan market with local assembly of the mainstream models of their parent firms, though on occasion they export modest volumes when the parent firm lacks production capacity. Yulon and China Motors, in contrast, have developed their own vehicles in addition to assembling Japanese models. They have also invested in a half-dozen overseas production joint ventures, mostly in China, but more recently including the Philippines and Russia. Yulon produces and sells SUVs, MPVs, and sedans under its mid-high end "Luxgen" brand in both Taiwan and in a joint venture with Dongfeng, China's third largest automotive group. Yulon is also actively developing next-generation electric and hybrid vehicles. Yulon's local output of 60,000 vehicles in 2014 seems a precarious base from which to develop an independent brand, as well as independent engines and transmissions, but success in parts and profits from assembly and auto finance in the mainland supported the creation of a steady stream of new models.

The major assemblers, led by Yulon, have all established local research, development, and engineering centers. In additional to the usual localization of models for the domestic market, they occasionally help with modifications of interiors or exteriors of models for the culturally similar Chinese market. Local assemblers spend about 2.5% of revenues on R&D (Yu and Wang 2012: 148–151), only about half the level of the global giants, but considerably higher than in most developing countries.

Auto Parts

Taiwan is the only major parts exporter that thrives without a large assembly sector to drive demand for original and replacement parts. Taiwanese firms are the world's largest suppliers of off-brand replacements for parts damaged in collisions, including metal and plastic body parts, bumpers, and rear-view mirrors (Chen, Xiao, and Xie 2013: 2-119). The structure of Taiwan's auto parts industry is surprisingly complete, from plastic, metal, and rubber materials through production equipment such as machine tools, to molds and dies, and more recently semiconductors and software for auto electronics (TAITRA 2013). Since the end of the first decade of the 2000s, production of electric and electronic auto parts has surged.

Geographically, production of both parts and vehicles falls into three distinct industrial clusters in northern, central, and southern Taiwan, corresponding both to the three major population centers of Taipei, Taichung, and Tainan-Kaohsiung, and to the three major science-based industrial parks run by the government. About 60% of automotive employment is in the north (Chen, Xiao, and Xie 2013: 2-139-2-142).

The parts industry consists of roughly 2,300 firms, of which 400 or so are OEM manufacturers supplying parts directly to the assemblers (Chen, Xiao, and Xie 2013: 2-129, 2-42). The vast majority are locally owned, but many have technology agreements with Japanese suppliers. A few have investments from Japanese, or occasionally American or European, suppliers. Particularly in the export-oriented aftermarket sector, most firms design, engineer, and certify their own parts. Many, such as market leader Tong Yang (Dongyang), one of the world's largest manufacturers of plastic bumpers and body sheet metal, and automobile lamp producers Dipo (Dibao) and TYC Brother (Tiweixi), export under their own brands. As TYC's technological capacities have increased, it has been able to renegotiate its technology transfer agreement with the American supplier Visteon to allow TYC to export OEM items (Huang 2013), while TYC's sister company Taiyih (Dayi) Industrial supplies molds for auto lights to the global production network of its Japanese technology supplier and stockholder Koito (Chen and Chen 2012). The larger suppliers generally have multiple overseas production sites and sales companies, particularly in mainland China, with its huge and nearby market. Several dozen have created plants in China to serve the local production of Yulon and China Motor. All in all, Taiwan's accomplishments in all aspects of upgrading—branding, engineering, design, exports, overseas investment—are quite remarkable for an industry operating in such a small and relatively open market.

Trade and Investment Policies and Institutions

Numerous zigs and zags notwithstanding, Taiwan's policies toward the automobile industry fall neatly into two periods (for a finer breakdown by period, see Yu and Wang 2012; Hwang 2013: 5 provides a graphic summary). From the early 1950s to 1984, the government established intermittently aggressive but unrealistic goals of promoting a national industry in the name of industrial development and military strengthening, culminating in two joint ventures with foreign automakers that eventually fell through. Then from 1985, the government embarked on a path of gradual market liberalization, combined with institution building and persistent but low-key promotion of upgrading of both assembly and parts.

In 1953, industrialist Yen Ching-ling (Yan Qingling) established Yulon, Taiwan's first automobile company (Xie 1993; Yulon). After earning a degree in mechanical engineering from Shanghai's prestigious Tongji University (supported by German funds under the Boxer Indemnity), Yan received a master's degree in engineering in Berlin. Upon returning to Shanghai, he began building textile machinery. When the Kuomintang (KMT) lost control of mainland China, Yan moved his family's textile business to Taiwan. With its weak industrial base, modest population size, and low level of income, Taiwan was unpromising soil in which to plant an auto industry; even Yulon's official history calls the idea "incredible" and "a risky experiment." But deeply impressed by his trips to the United States and Europe, and by President Chiang Kai-shek's exhortation that "engines will save the country," Yan viewed the auto industry as key to economic development and national defense (Xie 1993: 8–9).

Yan initially produced textile machinery, diesel engines for boats and irrigation, many of which he exported to Southeast Asia, and auto parts. In 1953, he procured a license to build cars. He rented space from a little-used air force base near Taichung, recruited key personnel from the Air Force Technology Bureau, and "transferred" more than a dozen airplane engines from the Air Force. Yan cobbled together his own auto engines and vehicles before signing assembly contracts with Willys (Jeep) in 1956 and Nissan in 1957. Into the early 1960s, Yulon consistently lost money, staying in business only with credit guarantees and infusions from Yan's textile business. Under the management of his wife, Vivian Shun-wen Wu (who later ran Yulon for a couple of decades after Yan's death in 1981), Tai Yuan Textiles became one of Taiwan's leading textile producers (Xie 1993: 12–13).

As part of the agreement with Nissan, the government mandated rapid increases in local content, and in 1961 it developed the first industrial policy for automobiles, including high tariffs and stiff local contents requirements. Concerned about chronic shortages of foreign exchange, the government banned imports of compact cars, giving Yulon a near monopoly on production of taxis, the most important type of passenger car at the time. The limited scale of production and lack of experience, however, led to widespread complaints about Yulon's high prices and shaky quality, and in 1965 the government relaxed restrictions on imports. Two years later, the government began opening the market to local Taiwanese industrialists, who signed technology licenses with foreign auto giants, including Honda (Sanyang) and Toyota (later replaced by Ford) in alliance with the Lio Ho (*Liuhe*) group. With Mitsubishi, Yan himself created a second joint venture, China Motor Corporation, which focused on small commercial vehicles. Trade policy was highly inconsistent, discouraging major investments (Yu and Wang 2012: 139–141).

As in many other developing countries, inconsistent protection led to a proliferation of assembly joint ventures (peaking at more than a dozen) and car models that precluded attainment of economies of scale or accumulation of industrial experience. Virtually all assemblers and parts firms depended on technology licenses from Japan—even Ford came to depend on its Japanese affiliate Mazda to supply the Taiwan market—and the government fretted at the island's slow progress in industrial deepening.

Technological dependence, an ever-growing trade deficit with Japan, rapidly increasing wages, the oil shock of the mid-1970s, and Taiwan's increasing diplomatic isolation combined to undermine confidence in the previous strategy of labor-intensive, export-led development and stimulated the government to embark on initiatives to deepen industrial development. The first proposal for the auto industry emerged in 1977, as Taiwan recovered from the first oil shock. The government enticed General Motors (GM) to invest in a joint venture called Hua Tung to build heavy trucks. Army generals pushed the project, and engineers in the technocracy supported it over the objections of specialists in economics and finance. As the security situation stabilized and the effects of the second oil shock of 1979 on both Taiwan and GM deepened, the engineers switched sides and supported the economists. The generals lost influence and Taiwan reduced protection of the project. In 1982 GM pulled out its investment with interest. Toyota soon took over the plant (Noble 1987).

The second statist initiative emerged in 1979. The government solicited a foreign partner to join state-owned Taiwan Machinery Manufacturing and China Steel to build a compact car plant with a capacity of 200,000 units. Such a project would have wiped out much of the existing industry, which fought back tenaciously (Arnold 1989). Many economists also doubted the feasibility of the project. Toyota won the bid, but resisted the government's requirement to combine demanding levels of local contents with a high proportion of exports. After Economics Minister Chao Yao-tung (Zhao Yaodong), the founder of state-owned China Steel and foremost advocate of the statist approach, was transferred to another position in 1984, this second joint venture project quickly fell through.

The "big compact car project" did not die without issue, however. Threatened by the new initiative and determined to show that local firms were deepening their skills, in 1981 Yulon announced the creation of a new engineering center, and despite opposition from Nissan, began work on its first independent vehicle, the Yulon "Feeling" (*Feiling* in Chinese) (Zhuang 1998). The Feeling 101, engineered by Yulon but powered by a Nissan engine, appeared in 1986 to initial acclaim, and Yulon managed to export a few thousand units. However, a lack of refinement combined with a revaluation of the New Taiwan dollar in the aftermath of the 1985 Plaza Accord and Yulon's tardiness in completing a follow-up model doomed the "first car designed by Chinese." Still, the Yulon Engineering Center remained.

In 1985, after the failure of the proposed state-foreign joint ventures, the government announced a policy of slow liberalization, hoping to encourage local assemblers to export, and perhaps to merge with one another to create strong, independent assemblers. In practice, partial liberalization resulted in even more fragmentation and firmer subordination to the overseas mother companies. When smaller assemblers Sanyang (Honda) and Yutian (Peugeot) attempted to follow Yulon in charting more independent courses, they fell flat and exited the industry. Even Yulon faltered. Under direction from the government, Taiwanese assemblers had relied primarily on licensing agreements rather than capital investments, and maintained their own brands, but after a protracted "cold war impasse" with Nissan in 1994, Yulon announced that it would abandon its brand, and accept a 25% investment from Nissan (Zhuang 1998: 76). Similarly, Toyota soon acquired a majority stake in its local assembler Kuozui, while Honda established a fully owned subsidiary to replace Sanyang. In 1999 and 2000, Ford Lio Ho and Kuozui created design and technology centers, but otherwise simply accepted the roles of local assemblers for their global parents (Cheng 2007). Taiwan's assembly industry began to look more like that of Japanese-dominated Thailand than independent Korea.

Despite the policy of gradual liberalization, the government of Taiwan did not eliminate all protection and actively increased promotion to help domestic firms meet the new competitive threats. Imports of small cars from Japan and Korea were banned until 1997. Requirements for local content gradually declined from 70% to under 50% before being phased out when Taiwan joined the WTO in early 2002, but actual local content continued to increase, hitting 80%–90% for most mainstream models. Tariffs on vehicles and parts declined only slowly—passenger car tariffs were still 17.5% after the end of post-WTO reductions in 2010.

While protection played a significant role, more important and more characteristic of Taiwan was the wide range of promotional policies. For example, in 1990, the government devised a plan to reward auto companies exporting parts to the Asian production networks of Japanese auto manufacturers with preferential rights to import Japanese cars under a tariff-quota system. From almost nothing in 1990, auto parts exports to Japanese production networks increased to over a billion dollars in 2004 (Huang 2007).

In addition to encouraging exports to Japanese production networks, the Economics Ministry provided numerous tax incentives and R&D subsidies, and a few low-interest loans (see, e.g., Ministry of Economic Affairs 2009a: 19–23). For example, until 2005 (three years after WTO entry), the government provided a three-percentage point deduction in the commodity tax for cars using domestically designed bodies, chassis, and engines. Support was especially generous for emerging areas such as auto electronics, auto safety, electric cars, and intelligent transportation systems.

The government also moved from banning investment in mainland China to supporting it. In 1995, China Motor Corporation (CMC) established a joint venture across the Taiwan Strait to build small commercial vans designed by Mitsubishi and modified by CMC. Then in 2000, after Nissan stumbled into a crisis and was forced to seek investment from France's Renault, Yulon signed an agreement with Dongfeng, one of China's top three auto groups, to form a joint venture called Fengshen ("Aeolus" or "Wind Spirit") to assemble Nissan Bluebirds in Guangzhou. Yulon accounted for about 10% of the overall ownership of Dongfeng-Nissan, with sales of over a million units in 2010 (Liang 2012b, 2012a).

When Nissan and Mitsubishi recovered from their respective crises and became more comfortable in the Chinese market, however, they began elbowing aside their Taiwanese affiliates. In 2003, Nissan and Dongfeng announced the formation of a billion-dollar joint venture in China, implicitly squeezing Yulon out of production. In response, Yulon divided itself into two companies. Nissan took a 40% share in "Yulon Nissan," which specialized in producing, selling, and servicing Nissan vehicles and spare parts, and also assumed a 40% share of Fengshen, effectively reducing Yulon's share to 24% (by 2015 the share was about 15%). The second entity, the locally owned Yulon Auto Manufacturing (Yulong Qiche Zhizao, usually referred to simply as "Yulon") became free to assemble cars for other firms as well as for Nissan, and to develop independent models. In 2009 Yulon began production of its own "Luxgen" brand of MPVs and SUVs in Taiwan and announced a joint venture with Dongfeng to assemble Luxgen vehicles in Hangzhou. In essence, the Yulon group concluded that the only way to control its own fate and ensure further growth was to develop its own brand and design and engineer its own vehicles. This heroic effort—it would be tempting to call it "foolhardy" if Yulon had not managed to maintain growth and profitability—was possible in good measure because of significant support from the larger institutional environment in Taiwan.

In sharp contrast to independence-oriented Yulon, market leader Kuozui at first glance resembled Toyota assembly operations in other countries. However, despite the constraints of working as a minor cog in Toyota's global production chain, limited elements of intensive growth appeared.

Production of passenger cars began in 1989, as did creation of a suppliers' association. An R&D center of about 160 personnel opened in 2002, followed by a "production technology center" in 2005. Toyota's domestic market share steadily expanded, and exports, primarily to the Middle East, began in 2009 (Kuozui; Yokohama 2004). Output ranged at or above rated production capacity. Kuozui maintained positive but rather distant relations with the government and the rest of the industry. Kuozui's managers were particularly grateful for the high-level of Japanese language capability in Taiwan.

Japanese researchers heaped praise on the company's quality and learning ability. In 2006, Japan's leading theorist of manufacturing observed:

> Of all the many overseas Toyota production locations, Kuozui Motors, a Toyota-affiliate established 20 years ago, is said to have absorbed the Toyota Production System most fully, and even in terms of product quality to have surpassed Toyota's production bases in Europe and America and reached the highest levels. Moreover, Kuozui is known not just in terms of ability in "the art of making things" (*monozukuri*) and self-improvement, but in the ability to evolve. That is, it is known for its conspicuously high level of organizational learning ability to carry out creative capability construction (*sōhatsu teki na nōryoku kōchiku*) over the long run. One even hears executives from Toyota headquarters saying, "It is hardly an exaggeration to say that the practical capabilities of Kuozui Motors are virtually equivalent to those in Japan" (*genba no jitsuryoku wa jun-kokunai*). (Fujimoto Takahiro in Li et al. 2006: 172)

The government and industry press hailed Kuozui's outsized role in Toyota's Asian production networks, as the company tweaked styling of models for the "Chinese" markets in Asia (Taiwan, mainland China, Hong Kong, Singapore, and overseas Chinese consumers in other Southeast Asian countries) and dispatched trained workers to guide production and localization in Toyota's Chinese and Southeast Asian facilities (Yokohama 2004; Liang 2003).

However, as Toyota's factories in China and Southeast Asia improved their capabilities, these high expectations for Taiwan gradually faded, and the role of Kuozui declined. Focus reverted to the tweaking of Toyota models for local and export sales, and the R&D center shrank to about 100 staff. Even at their peak, Kuozui's capabilities were limited to production and design of interiors and exteriors; basic engineering stayed with Toyota in Japan (Yokohama 2004: 6). Despite high product quality and costs much lower than those in Japan (roughly 30% lower in 2010), exports played only a supplementary role, smoothing out production for Toyota's home factories and larger subsidiaries (interview, Hikita Ryō, president, Kuozui Motors, June 3, 2010). The case of Kuozui suggests the limits to extensive capabilities and strategic flexibility in a majority-owned subsidiary of a global giant.

Nor was proud Toyota completely aloof from the wider institutional environment in Taiwan. In 2009, it received more than twice as much funding from the Economics Ministry than did any other Taiwan assembler (Ministry of Economic Affairs 2009b: 10, 66–72). Many of its suppliers were deeply embedded in Taiwan's policy networks. Kuozui even invested in a key subsidiary of the rival Yulon group: Kiang Shen (Jiangshen), a maker of frames and chassis parts that had begun as a supplier to Taiwan's military, made regular use of government research institutes and industry-government-academia alliances, and expanded in mainland China to support the assembly ventures of the Yulon Group (Chen and Chen 2012; Chen 2014; Kiang Shen Corporation). Even the impressive local operations of mighty Toyota, then, cannot fully be understood without reference to the broader institutional environment surrounding Taiwan's auto industry.

Institutional Configuration

The overall quality of the institutional environment in Taiwan is unusually solid, as revealed by the comparative indicators reviewed in Chapter 3 (Wade 1990; Noble 1998; Chu 2006; Ministry of Economic Affairs Department of Industrial Technology 2006). The island's compact size may have contributed to the evolution of a strong but relatively well coordinated set of support institutions. Under the Executive Yuan (Cabinet), the Council for Economic Planning and Development (CEPD; since 2014 the "National Development Council") sets overall plans. The Industrial Development Bureau (IDB) and Department of Industrial Technology of the Ministry of Economic Affairs (MOEA) are responsible for industrial affairs; the National Science Council (since 2014 "Ministry of Science and Technology") controls science policy and the science-based industrial parks; and the Ministry of Education governs universities (see Table 9.4).

Historically, Taiwan's president and premier have delegated economic policymaking to technocrats, most of whom boast graduate degrees from leading American or European universities, including K. T. Li (MS in physics from Cambridge) and Yuan T. Lee (Nobel laureate in chemistry). Bureaucratic recruitment is rigorous. The Ministry of Economic Affairs supervises major state-owned enterprises such as Taiwan Electric Power, maintains intimate links with local firms and industry associations, and provides much of the funding for the industrial development and diffusion agencies discussed in the following. CEPD/NDC and the Economics Ministry also control access to preferential capital from government banks and investment funds, though Taiwan has been quite conservative in allocation of capital. In cooperation with the Ministry of Finance, they also can provide tax breaks to encourage investment and research.

Considering the modest size of Taiwan's market and auto industry, and its famously restrained approach to industrial promotion and capital allocation, a remarkably complete set of institutions surrounds the industry, most supported by the Economics Ministry and to a lesser extent by the industry itself. The locations of the institutes mirror the relatively even dispersion of auto suppliers

Table 9.4 Ministerial Framework Surrounding Taiwan's Auto Industry

Unit	Authority and Functions
Cabinet, premier, president, Legislative Yuan (legilature)	Ultimate political and legal authority
Council for Economic Planning and Development (CEPD) [since 2014, National Development Council]	Cabinet subgrouping in charge of overall planning and coordination (neoclassical economic orientation)
Ministry of Economic Affairs (MOEA) —MOEA Industrial Development Bureau (IDB): Key industrial promotion agency in Taiwan —MOEA Department of Industrial Technology (DOIT): Focuses on strengthening links between industry-government-academic/research agencies	Oriented to local industry (combines economic and engineering orientation)
National Science Council (since 2014, Ministry of Science and Technology)	Sets science policy and controls science-based industrial parks (e.g., Hsinchu SBIP)
Ministry of Education	Controls universities
Ministry of Transportation and Communications (MOTC)	In charge of traffic safety and related standards; also, energy, etc.

Source: Compiled by authors.

along the western plains of Taiwan, from Taipei, Taoyuan, and Hsinchu (home of the original flagship science-based industrial park), past Taichung, the center of Taiwan's machinery industry, and on down to Tainan and the southern port of Kaohsiung, heart of Taiwan's traditional industries (see Table 9.5).

Taiwan's acclaimed *Industrial Technology Research Institute* (ITRI) in Hsinchu, with a staff of about 6,000, two-thirds of whom have advanced degrees, is best known for its work in electronics and optics, but its Mechanical Industry Research Laboratory (now Mechanical and Systems Research Laboratory) has worked closely with the auto industry on a range of projects, including engine development and auto electronics. Just under half of ITRI's income comes from government grants for special projects; the rest is from the private sector (ITRI 2013: 62). In 2018, for example, ITRI (1) conducted basic research on deep learning for advanced driver assistance systems; (2) developed power semiconductors for electric vehicle motor drives; (3) unveiled prototypes of midsize autonomous commercial vehicles and buses; and (4) joined with National Yunlin University of Science to spin off an IC design center for vehicle imaging and design called AutoSys Co., Ltd. (ITRI 2018).

The *Metal Industries Research and Development Centre* (MIRDC) was founded in Kaohsiung in 1963 with help from the United Nations and has long

Table 9.5 Taiwan: Auto-Related Institutes and Centers

Institute	Founded	Staff	Activities
Industrial Technology Research Institute (ITRI) (Hsinchu, Taichung, Tainan) (www.itri.org.tw/)	1973	6,000	Mechanical, Chemical and Electronic labs actively support autos
Metal Industries Research and Development Centre (MIRDC) (Kaohsiung) (www.mirdc.org.tw/)	1963	712	Especially strong in casting, forging, welding
National Chungshan Institute of Science and Technology (NCSIST) (Taoyuan) (https://fas.org/nuke/guide/taiwan/agency/csist.htm)	1969	14,000	Work on dual-use (military-civilian) technology since 1994
Automotive Research & Testing Center (ARTC) (Lukang) (www.artc.org.tw/index_en.aspx)	1990	440	Safety and other testing, standards, certification, calibration, technology
Corporate Synergy Development Center (CSD) (Taipei) (https://www.csd.org.tw/en/en-about04.html)	1990 (1984)	300	Technological and marketing support for small suppliers

Source: Compiled by authors.

provided assistance with practical production problems in metal industries, including casting, forging, stamping, and welding (Hsieh 2015). In 1996 it gained authorization from America's Certified Automotive Parts Association (CAPA) to measure and test auto components for export to the United States. Government contracts provided about 40% of its budget of roughly 73 million dollars in 2014, with the balance coming from consulting and service projects (MIRDC). The Centre also has 10 regional offices.

Under the Ministry of Defense, *National Chungshan Institute of Science and Technology* focuses mainly on weapons systems and aerospace, but it also occasionally works with private firms on commercial projects using dual-use technology. Noticeable examples in the auto industry include air bags (based on expertise in explosives) and radar.

The government established the *Automotive Research and Testing Center* (ARTC) in 1990 to help the local industry cope with gradual liberalization. It includes the only international-standard auto test track in Taiwan, as well as extensive equipment for crash testing, certification, calibration, and technology development, including optical and electronics technologies (ARTC 2015).

In 1984, the Economics Ministry established a small group to support "central factory-satellite factory relations," not least in the auto industry. In 1990, the small group branched off as a separate *Corporate Synergy Development Center* dedicated to providing small suppliers with technology and marketing assistance, and brokering relations among assemblers and suppliers.

The *Taiwan External Trade Development Council* (TAITRA, formerly China External Trade Development Council or CETRA), recognized as one of the most effective trade promotion agencies in the developing world (Wade 1990), worked with the Corporate Synergy Development Center and the ARTC to create an Auto Parts Promotion Center. The Center focuses on helping auto firms, especially smaller suppliers, boost exports and break into international automotive procurement networks.

Industry associations play a crucial intermediary role. The *Taiwan Transportation Vehicle Manufacturers Association* (TTVMA) had about 600 members as of 2017, including the major assemblers (9 firms) and automobile parts suppliers (494). The association is located in the same building in central Taipei as a number of other industry associations and government agencies. It has a staff of about 15 and an industry library. It is the source of authoritative industry statistics and information, co-sponsors the major auto shows, and frequently hosts Chinese, Japanese, and other foreign auto delegations. Relations with government and quasi-government agencies are intimate. For all but two years since the mid-1960s, the chairman of the association has been the head of either Yulon or its sister firm China Motors, the de facto national champions. The career of the long-time general manager of China Motors, Lin Xinyi, provides an illuminating example of the central role of the industry association, and the tight interrelations among Taiwan automotive institutions. After leading the association for five years (1994–1999), Lin served as chair of ARTC, and successively won appointment as minister of economic affairs, chair of the Council on Economic Planning and Development (CEPD), and vice premier under the Democratic Progressive Party (DPP) government of President Chen Shui-bian. After leaving government, Lin headed ITRI, Taiwan's premier industrial research agency (2004–2008), and then served as an advisor to China Motors.

In recent years, the *Taiwan Electrical and Electronic Equipment Manufacturers' Association* (TEEMA) has also become actively involved in the automobile industry, and co-sponsors projects and trade shows related to auto electronics. Several of Taiwan's national and regional universities also maintain close relations with the industry.

Although leading firms have created corporate R&D centers, most assemblers and virtually all parts firms remain heavily dependent on government, quasi-governmental institutes, and universities, as well as Japanese parent firms, for research and development. As with Taiwan's electronics industry, critics worry that quasi-governmental agencies such as ITRI and ARTC substitute for work that firms should do themselves. Given the limited size of both the domestic market and its leading players, however, the industry (particularly its smaller members) has little choice but to find help wherever it can. Moreover, unlike the Institute for the Information Industry (III), which often has been criticized for monopolizing government contracts and inhibiting the growth of private software firms (Breznitz 2007), ITRI and related agencies active in support of the manufacturing industry have been seen as effective (Intarakumnerd 2011), and have constantly adjusted their approach to innovation and technology transfer to maintain widespread support from industry.

Upgrading Competencies: Standards, Certification, Technology Diffusion, and Training

As the preceding review suggests, government and quasi-governmental agencies in Taiwan have been involved in a wide range of activities supporting industrial diffusion and cooperation. In comparative perspective, the government's role in diffusing technology and skills to small and medium-size firms is particularly striking.

Technology Support: Two Small and Three Big Examples

LED Lamps

Most of the upgrading work in Taiwan's auto industry involves assemblers, large (at least by Taiwan's standards) auto parts suppliers, and electronics firms seeking to break into the automotive market. The government and its research institutes have not neglected small firms, however, as other cases show. For example, in 2008, the southern branch of ITRI brought together 13 small auto parts firms in Tainan to form a "high-value added auto lamp parts industry cluster alliance." ITRI's "full-service support" included product development, assistance with manufacturing, and joint marketing (though not joint sales). The alliance focused particularly on development of new LED technology in anticipation of implementation of mandatory use of running lights in the European Union from 2011. ARTC provided technology assistance with dispersion of excess heat from the lamps, as well as training for workers (Li 2009). In succeeding years, alliance members won a number of international awards for innovation (Hwang 2013: 23).

Nuts and Bolts

Another example of support for product upgrading by small firms involves nut, bolts, and other metal fasteners, of which Taiwan was long a leading producer. By the early 2000s, Taiwan's exports of automotive fasteners lost ground to competition from China. In response, ITRI transferred new heat treatment technologies to local firms. With financial support from the Economics Ministry's "Plan to show concern for (*guanhuai*) traditional industries in southern Taiwan," the Metal Industries Research Centre (MIRDC) then helped a group of small southern fastener producers form an "R&D alliance for heat treatment of automotive fasteners." The alliance, and associated industrial groupings supported by MIRDC, helped an increasing proportion of small Taiwanese firms pass the complex and evolving inspections and audits required to comply with the American Automotive Industry Action Group's Heat Treatment System Assessment standard. Gaining certification enabled Taiwan's small firms to move into higher value added products less subject to stiff price competition from China (Song 2008; Chuang 2015).

Engines

The auto industry in developing countries typically lacks a domestic capacity to design engines. For decades, Taiwan was no exception. Even Yulon's "independent" Feeling model of the 1980s depended on a Nissan engine, which constrained export efforts. The first initiative to develop a Taiwanese engine came in 1991 with the formation of the Huaqing (literally "Chinese engine") consortium by the Industrial Technology Research Institute and four local firms. The ITRI team, headed by an American-trained Ph.D. with years of experience at NASA and Ford, conducted most of the design and development work, with assistance from Western consultants, particularly the renowned British auto engineering firm Lotus. The group built a 1.2-liter engine for small commercial vehicles, and began work on a 1.6-liter engine for passenger cars.

Originally, the four most independent assemblers—Yulon, China Motors, Sanyang, and Yutian—expressed interest in participating in the project, but financial problems forced the exit of Yutian, Taiwan's would-be Hyundai, leaving three assembly firms and a small maker of oil filters and engine emission controls. According to the project's director, "The Japanese did everything they could to stop us" (author interview with Jet P. H. Su, deputy general-director, Mechanical Industry Research Laboratory, ITRI, August 3, 1995). The participants persevered, however, and in 1995, three assemblers and the government's New Product Development Fund each put up 20% of the stock, while the state-owned Bank of Transportation chipped in 15% and the oil-filter producer 5%, for a total investment of $60 million (Noble 1996).

The "common engine" was fairly successful in engineering terms, and over the next nine years over 130,000 units were sold (CEC n.d.). Commercially, however, it became an orphan. Nissan and Honda prevented Yulon and Sanyang from using the engine. Only Mitsubishi approved use of the common engine, which powered China Motors' small "Weili" commercial vehicle. Yulon bought out the other partners, bringing Huaqing into the Yulon-CMC family. China Motors built a plant to produce the engine next to its Dongnan joint venture in Fuzhou, but by the time the Chinese government issued a permit for production, Mitsubishi had taken a 25% share in Dongnan, and insisted on procuring engines from a Mitsubishi joint venture plant in northeast China (Hu 2006). Huaqing continued to work with ITRI to develop new engines, branched out into 500-cc engines for all-terrain vehicles, and later provided the engines for Yulon's Luxgen initiative.

Automotive Electronics

The share of automotive value arising from electronics and software has steadily risen, and by most estimates already exceeds 30%. Taiwan is one of the premier manufacturers of semiconductors, computers, and electronic devices of all kinds. Yet for many years, the limited size of the domestic market and the rigorous demands for safety, durability, testing, and certification dissuaded most local electronics firms from entering the auto industry. Moreover, the longer product cycles in the auto industry prevented Taiwanese electronics firms from bringing to bear their comparative advantage in responding quickly to market opportunities.

To push the industry along, in 2002 the Economics Ministry's industrial technology division began to provide subsidies for research in auto electronics, hybrid vehicles, and LED lighting. In 2005, the Ministry added a "Plan to develop autonomous technology for the whole vehicle industry," including research subsidies of up to 40%, twice the usual rate. Participants included auto, electronics, semiconductor, software, and navigation device manufacturers. Yulon and IBM Taiwan took on especially important roles (Lin 2006).

The next year, with prodding from the Economics Ministry, Yulon joined with the government's development fund to create Huachuang ("Chinese innovation") or Haitec, a new auto design and electronics firm. Initially, many of Taiwan's top electronics and semiconductor firms expressed interest. In the end, however, most of them declined to invest. Yulon recruited six electronics companies, including the handset maker HTC, LED producer Everlight, and two smaller electronics companies from within the Yulon group. Without a major partner to balance Yulon, the government pulled out to avoid accusations of favoritism, leaving Yulon with more than 80% of Haitec's shares (Shen and Xue 2006) (author interview, Hwang Wen-fang, TTVMA, January 12, 2007). At the same time, TAITRA and the electronics industry association began sponsoring AutoTronics Taipei, the first annual trade show dedicated to automotive electronics.

Thanks in part to these stimuli, electronics firms began to move into auto-related applications (Yoshida 2017a, 2017b). Some of the larger firms that declined to invest in Haitec entered the auto business on their own. Taiwan Semiconductor (TSMC), the world's largest semiconductor fabricator, designated automotive electronics as one of four strategic areas. Others, such as Foxconn (Honghai), the world's largest contract electronics manufacturer, and leading competitor Compal, joined a government-led auto electronics consortium focused on standard setting, technology development, and relations with Taiwan-invested auto operations in Fujian. Many smaller independent firms entered as well, often supplying relatively simple "infotainment" products such as small LCD screens, auto navigation equipment, or "intelligent" lamps and mirrors. Almost all participated in the trade shows and export promotion activities sponsored by TAITRA and the industry associations. Many, such as E-Lead, a major manufacturer of car navigation and entertainment systems, received R&D grants from the government and participated in various government-organized industrial alliances (Guo 2014;

Wei 2011). Eventually, many of these technologies were incorporated in Yulon's Luxgen brand vehicles.

Electric and Autonomous Vehicles
Work on electric vehicles in energy-dependent Taiwan began early, in response to the first oil crisis in the mid-1970s, and never completely died out. With funding from the National Science Council and support from Taiwan Yuasa, the local subsidiary of a leading Japanese battery maker, and Tangrong, a state-owned enterprise producing stainless steel, a team led by Qinghua University professors produced over 200 small commercial vehicles in the 1970s, mostly for the postal service (Wan n.d.). In 1992, the energy division of the Economics Ministry financed a project led by ITRI to develop electric motorcycles and electric-assisted bicycles. The next year ITRI organized a consortium to produce key parts for electric motorcycles. From 1999 to 2002 the government spent nearly US$200 million subsidizing consumer purchases of electric scooters, but after an initial burst of consumer interest, limitations in the power and quality of batteries suppressed sales, and subsidies were dropped for all but electric-assisted bicycles, in which Taiwan became a leader. In the long run, however, the project helped Taiwan become the leading exporter of electric wheelchairs, and eventually a major producer of sophisticated electric motor scooters (O'Kane 2018).

With support from the National Science Council and other agencies, research by universities and auto and motorcycle firms on electric vehicles and parts continued apace. Taiwanese companies supplied many of the first batteries, motors, and motor controllers to such foreign electric vehicle producers as BMW and Tesla (Chou 2013). In 2005, as part of the autonomous technology plan, the Economics Ministry provided funding for the four leading technology support institutes to create a Taiwan Automotive Research Consortium (TARC) which focused especially on automotive electronics, weight reduction, and development of new energy vehicles. In 2008, Yulon's Haitec and Dayeh University of Changhua (site of ARTC) joined the consortium (TARC Secretariat 2008; Liang 2012a). TARC and other public-private institutions are also actively supporting the movement of electronics firms into autonomous (self-driving) vehicles (Liu 2017; Yoshida 2017a).

Skill Development

According to a major comparative study, "Taiwan has made great progress in the fields of education and training and has one of the best records in Asia"

(Zhu and Warner 2013b: 174), and the auto industry has been among the major beneficiaries. During the rapid growth period, Taiwan's educational system funneled an unusually high proportion of students through vocational high schools and junior colleges, most of them private, but the content of the courses was more academically rigorous than in most developing countries. Taiwan was virtually unique in displaying an even higher rate of return to vocational education than to general academic education (Boyd and Lee 1995; Tilak 2003). The government also provided a wide variety of training programs for workers after they left school.

A survey of 237 small and medium-sized suppliers in the auto industry in the early 1990s found that 60% provided training programs (considerably higher than the average of about one-fourth in Taiwanese manufacturing as of the late 1980s), often supported by or in concert with government organs (Tzannatos and Johnes 1997). These programs, too, displayed very high rates of return on investment. A slightly later study revealed that assemblers provided a significant amount of job rotation, training, and benefits, though they were less attentive to quality circles than were most manufacturing companies in Japan (Lin 1997). Kuozui (Toyota) and China Motors (Mitsubishi) were especially well known for their extensive training programs. Interviews at Toyota (Kuozui), Yulon Nissan, Sanyang, and parts suppliers such as Tung Yang discovered a uniformly positive attitude about the quality and stability of workers in Taiwan, which were often compared favorably with incessant job-hopping in China and perceived laxity in Southeast Asia.

As the share of students matriculating to university and the sophistication of work in Taiwan increased, the government expanded the range and technical content of training programs from universities and public training institutes. Technology transfer from public research institutes such as ITRI, the metals research center, and ARTC increasingly included short-term training programs. In the summer of 2015, for example, ARTC offered over a dozen training courses, ranging from basics of automotive structure to specialized coverage of automotive electronics and design of energy-efficient tires (ARTC 2015).

Alternatives to Upgrading?

In automotive circles, Taiwan is better known for parts than for vehicles, and some influential reports suggest that Taiwan, and by extension other developing countries, should focus more firmly on exports of labor-intensive parts for the after-market, the area in which Taiwanese firms have found the greatest success (Cunningham, Lynch, and Thun 2005). By implication, much of the technology support discussed here, such as development of new engines or greater incorporation of electronics, is irrelevant, since Taiwan's small and shrinking market cannot support a viable assembly industry or major first-tier parts suppliers. Nor, the authors contend, does China pose much of a threat to Taiwanese parts exports in the foreseeable future.

This view certainly highlights a crucial characteristic—the continued vitality of Taiwan's parts exporters, whose output value surpasses that of assembled vehicles. More recent events, however, cast doubt on the viability of simply relying on exports of bumpers, sheet metal, and bits of miscellaneous plastic. Export growth of traditional auto parts slowed sharply after 2004. Over the last decade and more, Taiwan has badly trailed Korea, which was initially much weaker in parts, and China, which led the world in growth of auto parts exports. Nor are Taiwanese exporters independent of developments in the mainland. Almost one-third of all Taiwanese parts firms, including virtually all of the major exporters, have investments in the mainland (compiled by author from TTVMA 2009). High-quality niche production in Taiwan is sustained partly by volume gained in China. As the Chinese auto fleet grows and ages, and China becomes the most important destination for after-market auto parts, inevitably Taiwanese firms will face increasingly fierce competition from mainland rivals who will be able to build on their home-court advantage in China to mount a sustained assault on the US and other foreign markets.

Examination of individual suppliers makes clear just how dependent on mainland operations the Taiwanese auto industry already is. Most firms employ more workers—and frequently more designers and engineers (see, e.g., Hsin Chong Machinery Works)—in the mainland than on Taiwan. For example, Hamg Shing (Hangxin Keji), a producer of antennas and car security devices, employs 355 workers in Taiwan and 3,500 in Shenzhen. Asset Industrial (Fuzhen), a maker of dies, jigs, and gauges, first gained fame by participating in the development of Yulon's independent "Feeling" model, and later provided equipment and design services to help Chery (Qirui), one of the mainland's leading independent auto companies, produce its first model (Chen 2006). By 2009, Asset had 40-odd managers and technicians at its Taiwan facility, but over 2,000 employees in four mainland subsidiaries. It dropped out of the industry association and most collective activities in Taiwan, and even abandoned its website and email address in Taiwan, instead relying on its Tianjin subsidiary (author's telephone interview with Mr. Lü, Asset Industrial Co., Zhongli, October 5, 2009).

Perhaps the most telling case is Tong Yang Industry (Dongyang Shiye), Taiwan's biggest parts firm and one of the world's leading producers of bumpers, instrument panels, and sheet metal parts (Liang 2013; Her 2008). With exports reaching 90% of revenues, the contraction of the local market has not proved a major obstacle. Yet Tong Yang, a family-owned and managed firm in the suburbs of Tainan in southern Taiwan, lacks the unique products and managerial and linguistic skills to sustain export drives in the United States, Japan, or Europe. More than two-thirds of its workforce is in the mainland. Originally, the company planned to supply after-market exports from Taiwan, leaving mainland plants to provide OEM parts to Chinese assemblers. As the mainland market grew, however, Tong Yang began to export after-market parts from Nanjing and other mainland plants. Asked about Tong Yang's overseas investments, an executive explained, "There is no comparison between the mainland and other locations. Its size, rate of growth, physical and cultural proximity, and wide array of clients all make it qualitatively different. Our operations in Italy and Thailand are small and limited, and definitely 'second tier.' India is a possibility, but it is still small. Also, in the mainland we can work with our Japanese technology suppliers because of proximity and the use of Chinese characters" (interview with Hsu-tung Chan [Zhang Xudong], director, Administration Office, OEM Business Operations, Tainan, December 28, 2006).

Tong Yang sees its major strategic opportunity for growth as coming through the development of OEM supply relations with independent Chinese automakers. In order to upgrade after-market parts and move into OEM production, Tong Yang has strengthened its research and development efforts. The company established an R&D division in 1989, began close cooperation with ITRI in 1997, and in 2007 built a new facility in Tainan for its R&D staff of about 120. Most of its capabilities come from internal efforts and support by Japanese suppliers, but Tong Yang also makes regular use of the government's training, testing, certification, marketing, and technology development projects (Ministry of Economic Affairs 2009b: 12).

Tong Yang warns that Taiwanese suppliers unable to make a sustained commitment to upgrading will be wiped out by the new wave of competition and investment from the mainland. Sticking to low-end product niches will not always suffice. Asked to identify the single greatest problem facing the domestic auto industry, the business manager of Taiwan's auto industry association replied simply, "Volume!" (interview with Hwang Wen-fang, TTVMA, June 24, 2009). The era in which Taiwanese firms could prosper simply by exporting low-tech plastic and metal replacement parts is passing. Auto electronics and China loom ever larger for Taiwan's small and medium-sized firms, and navigating them requires a great deal of public-private cooperation built on competent institutions.

A changing of the guard

By the mid-2010s, it became increasingly clear that after decades of success at intensive development, Taiwan's approach to automotive industrialization faced fundamental challenges. By 2019, imported vehicles captured half of the domestic market, squeezing the domestic producers, including even mighty Toyota, whose sales were sliced almost in half. Exports of parts stagnated. Yulon's previous uncanny ability to sustain independent development of new models from a tiny production base faced an existential crisis. Matters came to a head in late 2018. Yulon's longtime boss Kenneth Yen, son of the founders and heir to the mission of spearheading independent industrialization in Taiwan, died of cancer, just as the US-China trade conflict hammered car sales in the mainland (*Taipei Times* editorial, December 10, 2019: 6). For the first time in the 24 years since its partial independence from Nissan, Yulon fell into the red. Yen's widow Lilian applied triage to Yulon's operations, and considered disbanding Haitec, the group's prized research and development arm (Chen 2020).

A little over a year later, a more permanent solution, and a fundamental transformation in Taiwan's automotive industry, appeared. Foxconn (Hon Hai Precision Industry) and Yulon announced a $510 million, 51%–49% joint venture to create an "open platform" for developing hybrid and electric vehicles. Foxconn contributed cash and expertise in components and batteries, while Yulon provided Haitec's experience in vehicle development and systems integration.

The joint venture clearly marks the emergence of a new and much more powerful leader in Taiwan's automotive industry. Foxconn dwarfs Yulon: it is the world's largest contract electronics manufacturer, the leading hardware supplier to Apple, and by far Taiwan's largest company, with 2019 revenues of nearly $180 billion. As noted earlier, it has a long history of supplying components for electric vehicles. Foxconn had already outlined plans to focus on three strategic areas: digital medical technology, robots, and electric vehicles. It had also announced talks about forming an electric vehicle alliance with Fiat-Chrysler (*Lianhe Wanbao*, March 6, 2020). From a broader perspective, the transfer of leadership to an automotive electronics firm played more favorably to Taiwan's comparative advantage in electronics.

If Taiwan's old model of balancing independent development, incorporation into global value chains, and promotion of aftermarket auto parts finally ran out of steam, the surge in production of automotive electronics, and the formation of a powerful new leader in electric vehicles, provided telling evidence that Taiwan's elaborate system of institutional support for industrial diffusion and cooperation remained flexible and effective.

The Political Origins of Institutions for Upgrading

The policies and institutions surrounding Taiwan's automotive industry bear the indelible imprint of the external pressures confronting the country's political leadership. As a small island endowed with few natural resources, facing a much larger enemy across the Taiwan Strait, and hoping, at least initially, to recapture the mainland, the impetus to deepen industrialization was powerful (Cole 2006). In the 1950s, Taiwan enjoyed complete military protection by the United States, which also provided generous amounts of military and economic aid. This external aid gave Taiwan the luxury of indulging in import-substituting industrialization, which provided an important base for later development, but also fostered many inefficiencies. When the United States signaled in the late 1950s that it would reduce and then eliminate aid, the government undertook a series of reforms that resulted in a shift toward export-led growth. The vacillation in automobile policy in the 1960s noted earlier reflected the competing imperatives of long-term deepening and short-term efficiency.

Taiwan's security environment deteriorated alarmingly in the 1970s, as the PRC replaced Taiwan in the United Nations (1971), and first Japan (1972) and then the United States (1979) shifted formal diplomatic relations from Taiwan to the PRC. In combination with the oil shocks of 1974–1975 and 1979–1980, these diplomatic setbacks stimulated the Hua Tung heavy trucks joint venture with GM (1977–1982) and the "big compact car plant" negotiations with Toyota (1979–1984) discussed previously. President Ronald Reagan's "six assurances" to Taiwan in August 1982 and the evolution of Taiwan's military strategy over the course of the late 1960s and early 1970s from offense (retake the mainland) to defense (deter PRC invasion) reduced the military threat (Cole 2006).

The relaxation of direct military pressures combined with the collapse of oil prices in the early 1980s to give Taiwan's government room to take a more measured approach to industrial development, resulting in the shift to gradual liberalization of the auto industry after 1985, and a shift in industrial promotion from heavy industry to electronics and energy conservation. Maintaining the support of American and Japanese investors also rose in importance. Politically, the key transitions came with President Chiang Ching-kuo's decision to banish his long-term ally, the hard-line army general Wang Sheng, to Paraguay in September 1983 (O'Neill 2006) and the removal in May 1984 of Chao Yao-tung, founding head of China Steel and chief proponent of the big compact car plant scheme, as economics minister.

If Taiwan faced an existential security threat that motivated its leadership to take industrial deepening seriously, it is important to note that the specifics of that threat differed substantially from those facing South Korea or even China, particularly after the KMT's dream of recapturing the mainland faded in the 1960s. Where South Korea faced a direct land threat from North Korea, and China after 1960 worried about the presence of a far more powerful neighbor in the form of the Soviet Union, Taiwan was protected by a security treaty with the United States until 1979, and even after that by the US navy. At least through the early 2000s, the security threat increasingly took the form of diplomatic isolation or capital flight. Thus, while South Korea under Presidents Park and Chun undertook a hell-bent-for-leather rush to industrialize in the 1970s and early 1980s, Taiwan's government had to give equal consideration to attracting and keeping foreign investors such as Toyota and Ford, and reassuring the local business community that Taiwan would remain stable. As a result, with the notable exception of the "big compact car plant" proposal hatched as the United States shifted diplomatic recognition from Taipei to Beijing, the Taiwan government refrained from the harsh mergers and rationalization measures that transformed the South Korean auto industry in the early to mid-1980s; nor did it encourage the growth of giant conglomerates (as in Korea) or the retention and even expansion of state-owned enterprises (as in China).

China's program of "reform and opening" under Deng Xiaoping from 1979 created a new security dilemma for Taiwan, as the rise of labor-intensive industrialization in China undermined the competitive position of Taiwanese firms. The emergence of China itself as a market, not least for automobiles, also pushed Taiwanese firms to invest in the mainland, even though in the process they contributed to strengthening the political and military threat posed by the mainland to Taiwan. Faced with this dilemma, the government felt even more impelled to promote upgrading of domestic industry as a way to stay one step ahead of China, and retain Taiwan's important position in the global production networks of Western and Japanese firms.

The political capacities of the regime also influenced its response to political threats. Whereas the military-bureaucratic alliance ruling Korea through the late 1980s had to rely on big business as a crucial ally and source of campaign financing, the KMT "party-state" enjoyed both financial resources and an intricate grassroots organization. Far less dependent than the Korean generals on the support of private business, the KMT used state and quasi-state institutes such as ITRI and the automotive institute to support private firms, rather than relying on huge conglomerates (Noble 2011, 1998). Like Korea and China, the government in Taiwan based much of its legitimacy on its reputation for competent economic management. Taiwan, like Malaysia, suffered from significant social tensions (in the case of Taiwan, "sub-ethnic" tensions over relations between Taiwan and China), but unlike in Malaysia, ethnic cleavages did not correspond neatly to disparities in wealth, class, and entrepreneurship. All groups could agree on the importance of effective economic management and market discipline. The importance of economic performance to political image imparted a strong incentive to upgrade industry, particularly after Taiwan lost its comparative advantage in labor-intensive manufactured exports in the 1980s and early 1990s. The regime's abundant political and administrative capacities allowed it to take a measured approach to upgrading.

Once this structure of supportive institutions was firmly in place, it proved surprisingly resilient in the face of democratization (from 1986) and repeated transfers of partisan control between the KMT and the Democratic Progressive Party. It is true that the DPP was more inclined to restrict Taiwanese investment in the mainland, though that proved difficult to enforce, and it showed special concern for traditional industries in its voting base in southern Taiwan. The broad pattern of relying on state institutions to support upgrading efforts by private firms, however, changed little.

If the security threat provided an obvious and compelling impetus for industrialization that changed in form over time but never entirely disappeared, concerns about foreign exchange might seem a more surprising motivation for industrial deepening. After all, in recent decades Taiwan has been famous for its export prowess and huge trade surpluses. Those surpluses, however, have been neither perpetual nor completely reliable, as noted earlier in passing. In the 1950s, Taiwan ran large deficits, made sustainable only by US aid. The transition to export-led growth did lead to surpluses in the 1960s, but the oil shocks of the 1970s served as rude reminders of Taiwan's complete reliance on imported resources, and the pressing need to earn foreign currency to pay for them. Moreover, dependent as it was on the state of Taiwan's manufacturing industry, rather than the availability of oil or other natural resources, continued export prowess was deeply reliant on upgrading. The "rise of China" in the 1990s, which ate into Taiwan's export shares around the world, only reinforced that message.

Conclusion

Despite the constraints imposed by Taiwan's small and shrinking car market, its automotive industry has achieved surprising success in both extensive growth of after-market replacement parts and intensive growth of a range of automotive parts and whole vehicles. Taiwanese firms have developed the capabilities to design, engineer, brand, and export their own vehicles; they have engaged in extensive overseas investments; and they have carried out significant technology development in electronic parts, software, LED lighting, and even next-generation powerplants.

This surprising success cannot be credited solely to supportive trade and industrial policies. From the birth of the auto industry in the 1950s until the mid-1980s, Taiwan's automotive industrial policies were vacillating and inconsistent. Loans from government-owned banks were far more restricted than in Korea. Protection and promotion did lead to significant increases in value added, but they did not add up to a commercially viable strategy. Nor, conversely, can the liberalization that occurred after 1986 claim sole credit. Even after completion of Taiwan's long-drawn liberalization following accession to the WTO in 2002, protection of whole vehicles remained significant.

The consistent element from the 1950s to the present has been active support for industrial development and extension by a range of public and quasi-public institutions, such as the Industrial Technology Research Institute (ITRI) and the Metal Industries Research and Development Centre (MIRDC), aimed at overcoming a range of market failures and imperfections. Indeed, rather than decreasing support for institutions after the decisive shift to liberalization in 1986, the government created the quasi-governmental Automotive Research and Testing Center (ARTC) to help local firms survive in an increasingly competitive environment.

These institutions have not aimed at nurturing a single "national champion" firm or a cozy oligopoly. After four decades of fierce competition involving over a dozen assemblers, two quite different industry leaders have emerged, one (Toyota's subsidiary Kuozui) foreign-owned and focused primarily on extensive growth, and the other (Yulon, including its sister company China Motors and its subsidiary Haitec) domestically owned and remarkably insistent upon pursuing intensive growth. Instead, public and quasi-public institutions have consistently supported collective action to create public and club goods such as testing, certification, standardization, quality control, training, trouble shooting, technology development, and international marketing. Particularly striking is the intense support for tiny parts firms that have few direct ties to the assemblers or even first-tier suppliers. Both ITRI and MIRDC have developed local branch offices in each of Taiwan's three main regions, and depend on consulting contracts for half or more of their revenue.

Behind this impressive provision of institution for industrial support and outreach we can see the political factors highlighted in this book: Taiwan faced intense external threats and suffered from an almost complete lack of natural resources. The lack of overlapping ethnic and class cleaves and the organizational prowess of the ruling party made it possible to ignore or downplay the distributive consequences of most economic and technology policies. By the time Taiwan democratized in the 1990s, the technocratic machinery was firmly in place. Only a slight increase in concern for the lagging traditional industries of the south betrayed overt political influence. It is particularly telling that as Taiwan's military and diplomatic situation changed, its automotive policy changed as well. In particular, after the mid-1980s, Taiwan became more concerned about maintaining diplomatic support and increasing high-tech development than in merely expanding its heavy industrial base. This balance can be seen in the gradual emergence of Toyota's Kuozui and Yulon as dominant assemblers.

Taiwan is an unusual case, largely defined by diminutive size and challenging security and economic relationships with the United States, Japan, and increasingly China. At the same time, it is a remarkably good illustration of the way security threats and political challenges can create incentives to develop institutions and policies conducive to industrial upgrading.

10

Conclusion

Divergent Roads to Automotive Industrialization

Our case countries reveal two divergent approaches to automotive industrialization. Some countries, particularly in Northeast Asia, have attempted to build deeper local capabilities, a process we refer to as *intensive development.* This approach proved remarkably successful in Korea, where Hyundai-Kia developed into one of a half-dozen leading global automakers, and several Korean-owned parts firms, particularly those connected to Hyundai-Kia, broke into the ranks of major global suppliers.

China has also has made considerable progress in intensive development. To be sure, the Chinese industry is still dominated by joint ventures with global assemblers. But in recent years locally owned companies—some of them privately owned—have designed and engineered their own cars and have embarked on extensive overseas activities, including exports, creation of overseas R&D centers, and acquisition of foreign assemblers and parts makers. China also dominates global production of plug-in and pure electric vehicles. While it has attracted little attention abroad, even Taiwan, with its small market and relatively high wages, has attained considerable success in intensive development in specific automotive niches, including after-market parts and auto electronics.

Efforts at intensive development have not always succeeded, however. Consider Malaysia. After more than 30 years of "looking East" to the examples of Japan and Korea, Malaysia developed some capacities for independent automotive development, but the industry failed to compete internationally. After decades of decline, the Malaysian government finally allowed Proton, its longtime national-champion assembler, to be acquired by the private Chinese firm Geely.

In contrast, Indonesia, the Philippines, and Thailand have come to rely almost solely on foreign multinationals, leading to a shallow but potentially "extensive" pattern of development. The shift to extensive development proved a success (on its own terms) in Thailand, which has emerged as a major assembler and exporter of light vehicles, particularly small pickup trucks. Signs of

The Political Economy of Automotive Industrialization in East Asia. Richard F. Doner, Gregory W. Noble and John Ravenhill, Oxford University Press (2021). © Oxford University Press. DOI: 10.1093/oso/9780197520253.003.0010

increased automotive production and export have also begun to emerge from Indonesia. The Philippines, in contrast, has proved an abject failure at automotive industrialization.

These marked divergences in approach and success have occurred even though all the countries began automotive industrialization in the 1950s and 1960s with import-substituting-industrialization (ISI) policies that relied on foreign direct investment into protected national markets. As we detail in Chapter 2, by the mid-1980s, the global revolutions in transportation and communication led to the fragmentation of production through regional and global value chains (Baldwin 2016) and shortening of product cycles (Whittaker et al. 2010), while the creation of the World Trade Organization (WTO) and the rise of bilateral and regional "free trade agreements" complicated the old ISI strategy of constructing complete industrial bases within each national economy. On the other hand, demand for autos in the developing world swelled. Collectively, these changes rendered the old protected national champion model less relevant, while also opening up new opportunities for countries seeking a foothold in an industry that remains the second most important manufacturing sector in the world.

The capacity to take advantage of those opportunities, though, has varied tremendously. Successful pursuit of both intensive and extensive strategies required, at a minimum, capable governments, efficient and appropriate infrastructure, and conducive monetary and fiscal measures. But as we have demonstrated, successful intensive strategies required consistent support for local firms, and linkage institutions for industrial coordination and diffusion. Thus, the specific policies and institutions required depend upon a country's strategy and stage of development, a distinction that is captured only imperfectly by the recent literature acknowledging the enduring role of industrial policy.

Different Strategies, Stages, and Challenges Require Different Institutions and Policies

By the 1990s, if not earlier, the limits to the old industrial policy (Johnson 1982; Amsden 1989) had become increasingly obvious. Policies that imposed barriers to foreign trade and investment, made heavy use of preferential financing, promoted reliance on national champion firms, often state-owned, and aimed at picking winners among industries and products were constrained by the WTO and other international agreements. They also proved vulnerable to rent-seeking at home, and to competition from increasingly efficient and flexible global value chains overseas. Protection and promotion came to be seen as irrelevant if not counterproductive once firms and countries reached world technology frontiers and engaged in foreign investments beyond the reach of their home governments (Callon 1995).

Disappointment with the succeeding Washington Consensus emphasis on market opening (Williamson 2009) in turn led to interest in a new, lighter version of industrial policy, which argued that policy could be useful in helping even advanced countries to maintain and improve their position in global value chains (see, e.g., Cherif and Hasanov 2019). Rodrik (2007) highlighted the role that industrial policy could play in helping firms in developing countries to search for potentially profitable new products and then diagnose and overcome the binding constraints that prevent them from availing themselves of new opportunities. The focus shifted to coordinating rather than governing or piloting (Kuznetsov and Sabel 2011), and to the process of communication, discovery, error detection, and correction, rather than promotion or protection (Sabel and Jordan 2015). In a similar vein, Bonvillian and Van Atta (2011) and Jordan and Koinis (2014) drew on the experience of America's Defense Advanced Research Projects Agency (DARPA) and Advanced Research Projects Agency–Energy (ARPA–E) to make the case for extreme flexibility in the implementation of industrial policy, including sponsoring multiple projects in the same area, and relying largely on project managers with fixed four-year terms rather than on career bureaucrats. Jordan and Koinis (2014: xvi) also briefly noted the importance of securing political support by "[d]efining clear, unambiguous, and easy-to-measure long-range goals whose failure would threaten the survival of political elites." In the most optimistic versions, this new type of industrial policy could succeed even under weak states and despite the presence of rent-seeking industries (Kuznetsov and Sabel 2011; Ang 2016).

Clearly, our analysis of the East Asian experience in promoting industrialization in the auto sector demonstrates many of the same concerns. We have learned much from this literature. Yet it is important to note differences between our approach and the new industrial policy literature, as well as the systems of national innovation school (Nelson 1993). While we acknowledge the significance of innovation broadly understood, our cases suggest that for firms in developing countries, diffusing and applying technology already established elsewhere, but new to the firm, is a more important and pressing task. Active labor market policies that expand the pool of technical personnel and "soft infrastructure" measures that help firms improve their capacity to improve quality by testing and evaluation are particularly relevant for smaller firms, especially those without foreign investment, as these firms typically lack the competencies required to meet the stringent cost, quality, and delivery requirements of global value chains.

Our focus on the stage- and task-specificity of policies has implications for the literature on global value chains. Far from obviating industrial policy, value chains raise the urgency of the policy response. By dividing the market more finely and fragmenting it geographically, global value chains multiply the coordination challenges and learning externalities inherent in industrial development, particularly in developing countries. This is especially true of a complex, tiered industry like autos. Lead firms such as automotive assemblers can help overcome some of these problems through corporate hierarchies, but only partially and only at the top of the supply pyramid, mostly working with other foreign-owned firms. The consequence is that learning opportunities for locals are occluded. The many remaining coordination failures and learning externalities can be addressed by a combination of old and especially new industrial policy. Thus, far from rendering industrial policy obsolete, global value chains change its character, making it less focused on creating national champion firms (or specific products) but, if anything, even more focused on skills and relationships in particular sectors.

Industrial policy in Korea, for example, favored the growth of giant conglomerates such as Hyundai Motors, and for many years largely ignored small and medium-size enterprises (Park 2007). Hyundai looked after its larger suppliers, especially its subsidiaries, but largely ignored the smallest suppliers. As a result, product quality suffered, and both Hyundai and the government were forced in the new millennium to strengthen outreach to the small suppliers.

Further, because acquiring such competencies—the "what" of our story— requires access to a range of extra-firm actors, we focus more on the various types of spillovers and collective action dilemmas facing firms within an industry, and the coordination mechanisms—the "how" of our story—to overcome such dilemmas both within and across industries. Indeed, we look at a broad range of institutions, such as sectoral institutes, standards and testing agencies, beyond industrial *policy* agencies.

The Centrality of Institutions Linking State and Industry

Our main theoretical contribution in this volume is thus not just to document the limitations of the literatures on national systems of innovation or global value chains, or the continued salience of some elements of industrial policy both old and new, but to highlight the institutional challenges characteristic of extensive vs. intensive development. Attention to the coordination problems and specific types of institutions is, as noted in Chapter 3, an important strength of the developmental state literature, especially in its more recent permutations. But we go beyond the developmental state framework in highlighting how that capacity varies depending on the sector, the stage of development, and the nature of the task at hand. Coordinating tax and tariff policy to balance the interests of the assembly and parts sectors, and focusing attention on one sector, as Thailand did with the one-ton pickup truck segment, for example, is very different from providing the industrial testing and consultation institutes that played a vital role in supporting upgrading by small suppliers in Taiwan and, to a lesser extent, Korea.

This perspective is crucial to understanding contemporary industrialization yet remains underexplored. As noted in Chapter 3, a comprehensive review of over a thousand studies of upgrading efforts by developing countries in light industry and agriculture (Pipkin and Fuentes 2017: 549) concludes that in virtually all cases of significant upgrading, a key role is played by "well-established, high-capacity institutions—especially public institutions, but also developmental business associations, universities, and other actors that might support regulation, technical learning and public goods provision."

The capacity of state and public-private institutions is even more crucial for upgrading in the case of capital and technology-intensive industries such as automobiles. The quality of these public-private institutions varies widely across our case countries. We have noted that quasi-public automotive institutes, technical training schools, testing and certification facilities, and industrial extension institutions, most of which rely on both government funds and fees-for-services from auto firms, appeared much earlier in the countries pursuing intensive growth (excepting laggard Malaysia) and continue to command far greater financial resources and specialized expertise than in the "extensive" countries (see Table 3.8 in Chapter 3). These institutes also provide local firms with crucial assistance in meeting international standards and expectations for quality control, in part by developing a more complete set of complementary national standards (which could also serve protectionist purposes). Korea and China have even become significant participants in the formation of international automotive standards.

Industry associations, to take another crucial example, have attracted increasing academic attention as crucial links between policymakers and business executives (Doner and Schneider 2000; Sen 2013). In the Northeast Asian countries, automotive business associations are stable bodies led primarily by locally owned automakers; they attract nearly universal participation by large and medium-sized firms and even many smaller suppliers;

they deploy competent and stable staffs; and they maintain close connections with policymakers, research institutes, and universities. Southeast Asian associations, in contrast, have fewer resources and less continuity, and are typically led almost entirely by representatives of foreign, usually Japanese, automakers (whose interests may not coincide with state priorities for domestic upgrading).

To be sure, tentative signs of institutional deepening have appeared recently, as competition to attract and retain foreign investment has increased in the wake of regional liberalization. In the Philippines, associations reorganized themselves and contributed to the government's CARS program in 2016. In Indonesia, Hicks (2012: 10) reports that while business associations "are still consumed with the struggle to secure a role in the government procurement process . . . anecdotal evidence from KADIN [peak association] insiders, NGOs and some donors suggests that the sector is professionalising—in parts . . . [and that] a new cohort of TAs [trade associations] covering more specific industrial sectors [has appeared]—putting them in a better position to represent sectoral interests in the policy process." So far, however, automotive industry associations are still dominated by representatives of Japanese firms, whose concerns are largely limited to the production operations of assemblers. Overall, the gap between industry associations in the intensive and extensive countries (with Malaysia again the exception) still looms large.

An especially interesting case is industrial training. Providing rigorous and market-relevant occupational training is difficult, and public and private training programs attract heated criticism even in fully developed countries. Yet in comparative perspective, the programs in Korea and Taiwan are unusually effective, as our case chapters document. Zhu and Warner (2013b: 172), for example, argue that "[u]nions, in partnership with employers and government, . . . play a major role in underpinning and advancing training in the Taiwanese vocational education and training system. The system is a clear tripartite success, which might be a model for the rest of Asia." Similarly, "the Chinese occupational certification system combines country-wide transparency and standards that influence the expectations and behavior of employees, and flexible adaptation to the needs of companies." As a result, "[a]gainst expectations, automobile companies in China do not pursue 'low road' (i.e., low skill) strategies but have designed intensive internal training programs and long-term career paths for blue-collar workers" (Jürgens and Krzywdzinski 2015: 1214, 1204). Occupational training in the "extensive" countries is far weaker.

It is crucial to note that these successful linkage institutions for industrial diffusion are not merely administrative attempts to address coordination failures and incremental learning in the abstract, or to reform the government's policymaking process along private sector lines, as advocated by the "new public management" movement (Hood and Dixon 2015), which has exerted little influence in most Asian countries. It is telling, for example, that Sabel and Jordan's (2015: 39–45) otherwise laudatory account of policy reform and "new industrial policy" in Malaysia acknowledges that the practice, derived from the United Kingdom's "delivery units," of forming temporary and flexible Performance Management and Delivery Units (PEMANDU), achieved little success when applied to industry, and that it flatly failed to reform either the education system or the state bureaucracy. Instead of such relatively hollow organizations, the many public-private institutions we have examined in our cases of successful intensive development are concrete and long-lived entities with specialized personnel, budgets, and intimate ties with (and often partial financial reliance on) individual firms.

Institutions for coordination and diffusion are also important at the subnational level. In Korea and Taiwan, as in Japan earlier, the central government has established regional branches of the central ministries and of some industry testing and research institutes to meet the differentiated needs of smaller firms in specific regions. In Malaysia, and especially in China (Thun 2006), state and provincial governments play important roles, often in competition with each other.

National Institutions and Corporate Strategy

While we have focused on national and international determinants of policy approaches, some room has always remained for strategic choice by individual local firms, both in assembly and in the production of components. As noted in Chapter 2, growing demand for autos has opened up new possibilities, but the combination of liberalization and cost-cutting via use of integrated modules and shared platforms has propelled the consolidation of the global auto industry. Consolidation has confronted East Asian firms with a series of strategic choices. Some have succeeded in carving out a viable path, while most have failed. First and foremost, many Asian firms have either gone bankrupt or have been forced to exit, particularly after the financial crashes of 1998 and 2008. For example, Astra, once Indonesia's largest automaker, drastically reduced its production and specialized in sales. Some have tried to diversify, but amassing the capital and management skills necessary can be tricky, as Korea's Kia discovered when failure of a steel subsidiary led to the bankruptcy of the entire group, and the eventual takeover of Kia Motors by Hyundai. Others have sold excess land and have gone into the real estate development business. Many auto parts firms in Taiwan, and a few in China and elsewhere, have adopted, in whole or in part, a niche strategy focusing on after-service and accessory parts, such as bumpers and panels, not controlled by the global assemblers and first-tier parts firms. In Taiwan, Korea, and Thailand, numerous local parts firms have used licensing from Japan to upgrade product quality, sometimes sufficiently to enable them to break into global value chains.

Few have put significant effort into new product innovation, although some suppliers in Northeast Asia have leveraged strong domestic electronics industries to make inroads in semiconductors, software, car navigation, and infotainment equipment. A handful of assemblers have attempted to develop independent design and engineering capabilities, and only Korea's Hyundai has unambiguously succeeded, though some Chinese firms continue to make significant progress. Similarly, with some important exceptions in China and Korea, East Asian firms have generally avoided or have failed at overseas investments. Failures, such as Shanghai Auto's acquisition of Korea's Ssangyong and Sweden's Saab, have outnumbered successes, such as Geely's takeover of Sweden's Volvo and of Malaysia's long-time national champion, Proton. Chinese automakers and parts suppliers have made some important acquisitions and greenfield investments in the United States and Germany, but increasingly face politically inspired opposition to Chinese investment.

The most common strategies have been to cut costs by expanding scale and accessing cheap labor, often in conjunction with participation in global value chains. Virtually all assemblers and parts firms have attempted to expand capacity to reduce costs, but most have failed, either losing out to more aggressive rivals in times of strong demand, or floundering in debt when weakening demand leads to excess capacity. Even in countries with modest labor costs, the quest for ever-cheaper labor is striking. Thailand and Malaysia (until 2019) have relied heavily on foreign workers, many of them undocumented. Taiwan and Korea have formal programs to admit foreign labor, of which the auto industry is one of the more active users. Taiwanese and, to a lesser extent, Korean firms have also moved much of their production to mainland China. Korea's Hyundai, long plagued by militant unions and high labor costs, has increased the ratio of foreign workers to over 40%, and is replacing exports from Korea with local production in China and in the southern United States and Mexico (Jung 2018).

Joining global value chains has been a goal of many local automakers and parts suppliers, just as many experts have recommended. As we have seen, developing the capacity to participate fully in global value chains has proved a demanding task. One crucial question is which chain to join, and here a clear pattern emerges: firms affiliated with the Toyota group have steadily but surely pulled ahead in virtually every East Asian market except Korea. Those associated with Nissan, Honda, and Mitsubishi, an early investor in Southeast Asia, have generally lost ground, as have affiliates of Ford and GM.

The result of these pressures and strategic choices is a two-tiered structure. Leading the industry in most countries are the subsidiaries of Japanese assemblers and first-tier suppliers. With greater resources and more technical support for manufacturing, on average they are more productive and more likely to export, but only within strict boundaries set by the parent firm. They may grow, but they almost never grow big. The other group consists of domestic suppliers, which are generally smaller and less productive, but have greater freedom to innovate and to invest abroad.

The exceptions to this dichotomy are Korea and, to some extent, China. In Korea, Hyundai-Kia and its affiliates control 70% of the market. In China, Sino-foreign assemblers and their affiliates dominate, but locally owned assemblers, which are far more likely to procure significant parts and modules from local suppliers, are struggling to move upstream in a "fight for the middle" (Brandt and Thun 2010), with occasional success. Competent institutions for coordination and diffusion can help strengthen the capacities and widen the options of local firms, both foreign-owned and especially domestic.

How Politics Has Shaped Institution Building—and May in the Future

What political conditions account for the initiation of such institutions, and particularly for sustained investment in them? A key factor differentiating our case countries is the presence or absence of a credible and relatively long-lived threat to the political regime, particularly existential external threats to security, but also in the form of internal insurrection. All of our intensive growth countries (except Malaysia—in other words, all of our successful intensive cases) experienced brutal civil wars, followed by long periods of unresolved conflict and external threats; none of the extensive growth countries did so.

A second factor is relatively easy access to primary goods that could be used to support clientelist regimes. Classic cases involve oil, gas, and minerals, which were abundant in Indonesia, Malaysia, and even in China through the 1980s. Exploitation of fossil fuels and minerals does not require development of domestic industry. The revenues often lead to currency appreciation, complicating efforts to export manufactured goods, and are often volatile, thus undermining the consistency of efforts at industrialization, as Southeast Asian countries discovered to their chagrin in the 1980s. Other resources can have similar effects. Below and in Chapters 3 and 4, we note the importance of land and agriculture in Thailand, and, as seen in Chapter 5, the availability of migrant remittances has contributed to the resource curse syndrome in the Philippines.

Development of agriculture involves a much broader section of society than does mining, and tellingly, in resource-rich cases such as Malaysia and Thailand, more upgrading occurred within agriculture than in industry. Countries with abundant land—notably Thailand. which is considered "resource-rich" (Birdsall et al. 2000: 14)—can afford to ignore or downplay the most difficult challenges of industrial technology development, even though the manufacturing sector offers more opportunities for sustained growth in employment and productivity. The exception that proves the rule is tires and other rubber-based auto parts, which are linked to the agricultural sector (and the associated clientelist politics). In Malaysia and especially in Thailand (see Chapter 4) the existence of another easily exploited resource—low-skilled (often undocumented) foreign laborers—also undermined the effort to upgrade.

Among our case countries, we observed a stark contrast between Northeast Asia (including China after the 1980s), with its relative dearth of resources, and resource-rich Thailand, Indonesia, and the Philippines (Chapter 3). Malaysia again provides a telling intermediate case. Facing some security threats (albeit primarily internal) but also blessed with abundant resources, particularly in the rural areas dominated by ethnic Malays, the government attempted to mimic the intensive development of Japan and Korea, but failed to build the same linkage institutions or apply the same discipline to manufacturers. Also telling is the case of tiny Singapore: while it focused on electronics and petrochemicals rather than automobiles, the combination of external threats and resource paucity led to the kind of sustained commitment to upgrading seen in our Northeast Asian case studies.

Even if modestly successful in immediate economic terms, moreover, extensive growth based on low wages, low costs, and efficient infrastructure suffers from a serious political shortcoming that bears on the capacity to exit the middle-income trap. Lacking upstream-downstream linkages and a workforce that is relatively well trained and productive—and thus well paid—it also lacks domestic political support for the creation and steady improvement of the many institutions for industrial diffusion highlighted in the preceding chapters. Subsidiaries of foreign multinationals and their close affiliates have little incentive to invest in or even support collective institutions since they can access information and skills from the parent company. Smaller, indigenous firms for whom such institutions are most useful typically lack political weight. Countries depending on a strictly extensive strategy thus fail to create the positive feedback loop visible in the intensive—and high-income—countries, where broad political coalitions reinforce upgrading institutions, which in turn reinforce the power and legitimacy of those political coalitions (Doner and Schneider 2016).

Prospects for Political Change

Could economic development or political reform counteract the effects of resource abundance and a permissive security environment to allow for more systematic investment in coordination and diffusion institutions? Our case study chapters have noted some signs of improved economic governance in Southeast Asia since the Asian financial crisis of 1998, and more recently the Asian Development Bank and others have commented on a significant shift in Indonesia and the Philippines from pork barrel spending and other forms of clientelistic budgetary allocations toward more programmatic investments in infrastructure and education (Asian Development Bank 2017; Warburton 2016). Because clientelism in theory is less attractive as a political strategy in wealthy countries as rising incomes reduce voters' attraction to personal (clientelistic) inducements (Stokes et al. 2013), economic liberalization, at least in principle, tends to create pressures to attend to median voters rather than individual political patrons and their clients (Frieden and Rogowski 1996). Constitutional and electoral reforms thus have the potential to strengthen parties and reduce the incentives to engage in clientelistic appeals (Reynolds, Reilly, and Ellis 2008).

Unfortunately, these effects can take a long time to manifest themselves, and may never be complete. Urban political machines in the United States, for example, emerged in the mid-19th century, but despite economic development and the growth of the federal government, managed to last into the 1970s. The definitive decline of clientelism in Japan did not come until after revision to the electoral system of the lower house in 1994 (Noble 2010; Rosenbluth and Thies 2010), long after the country had become wealthy and urban. As for political reform, party systems in the Philippines and Indonesia grew even more fragmented after reform (see, e.g., Berenschot 2018). In Thailand, constitutional reform did succeed for a time in consolidating the party system, but the key result—the emergence of a dominant party supported by the rural poor—was anathema to conservative forces, which succeeded in overthrowing the new constitutional order. In the two decades following the Asian financial crisis, government-business relations changed surprisingly little in East Asia (Noble 2017). Absent significant changes in the perception of external threats or the balance of resources and political demands, then, it is difficult to foresee immediate changes in political willingness to support institutions of industrial coordination and diffusion.

Local Initiatives and Local Ownership Can Support Global Expansion

If we look only at the national level, the implications of the preceding analysis for more recent industrializers in Asia, and elsewhere, might appear bleak. Lacking the severe external threats and limited natural resources that motivated Japan, Korea, China, and Taiwan in the immediate postwar decades, and facing a far more open and globalized production system dominated by incumbent lead firms from Japan, Korea, North America, and Europe, today's developing countries seem ill-equipped to give birth to firms capable of establishing sustainable positions in highly demanding global and regional production networks.

However, national governments are not the only possible initiators and incubators of institutions of industrial diffusion and the political coalitions sustaining them. In China, "local experiments" is virtually a byword. The energetic competition by Foshan and other cities in Guangdong Province to seize the lead in promoting hydrogen fuel cell vehicles provides a vivid recent example (Gao, Guo, and Liu 2018). Even in compact Korea and Taiwan, we have observed the important role played by regional branches of national automotive research institutes and testing and certification centers.

More relevant to other developing countries, however, is the case of Penang, a state of about one and a half million people encompassing Penang Island, a well-known tourist destination off northwestern Malaysia, and a strip of land on the adjacent coast. Once an economic laggard, Penang leapt ahead in the 1970s and 1980s by attracting multinational investments in the semiconductor testing and assembly industry. The Penang Development Corporation (PDC) created and supported precisely the kinds of institutions for industrial diffusion highlighted in this book, enabling the local electronics industry to move upstream into semiconductor design and to attract more sophisticated investments for producing hard disk drives. The best of the local firms grew into global partners of Intel and other leading American electronics companies (Athukorala 2017).

Crucially, PDC was not the creation of the central government or even a local technocracy, but the crowning electoral initiative of an ethnic Chinese party (Gerakan) and state minister (Dr. Lim Chong Eu) who managed for two decades to forge alliances with local firms and carve out a degree of autonomy vis à vis the ruling UMNO coalition and national bureaucracy (Hutchinson 2008). For Penang, the only Malaysian state with an ethnic Chinese majority, the loss of its free port status constituted an existential threat. Lacking control over tariffs, significant fiscal autonomy, or large local firms, the dominant party, Gerakan, could not foster specific local champions. Instead, Gerakand crafted a "sub-national developmental state" that, working closely with the local Chinese Chamber of Commerce, forged links with transnational electronics giants and supported the upgrading of local firms (Hutchinson 2008).

The experience of small electronics and machining firms, also predominantly owned by ethnic Chinese, in the Kelang Valley stood in marked contrast. Located in Selangor, the state encircling the national capital, Kuala Lumpur, Kelang Valley was subordinated to national policies focused on redistribution to Malays rather than enhancement of the capacities and linkages of local firms. The companies made little progress in upgrading because Kelang Valley lacked a political coalition based on small firms, and the ability to carve out a degree of policy autonomy (Rasiah 2001).

To be sure, Penang was not active in autos, and even in electronics it was unable to completely overcome the limitations of Malaysia's national political system discussed in Chapter 7, including the weakness of the educational system and the paucity of links with local universities (Rasiah 2017). Moreover, the national ruling coalition under Mahathir eventually forced out the pioneering state minister and smothered new local initiatives (Hutchinson 2008). Nevertheless, the case of Penang strongly suggests that bottom-up initiatives can in principle play a crucial role in spurring industrial development if local leaders can create a supportive political coalition.

The Penang case also has important implications for the role of local ownership. Penang—like Korea and Taiwan—was able to retain foreign investors, and to convince many of them to invest in local upgrading despite rapidly rising wages, rather than decamping for cheaper production sites, not just because it offered efficient infrastructure or even a well-educated workforce, but because it nurtured an increasingly complete industrial structure, including many small firms founded by former employees of the multinationals (Athukorala 2017). Tellingly, the success of those locally owned firms stemmed not from restrictions on foreign investment, or from preferential finance directed at local firms, which was often lacking in focus and unprofitable (Hutchinson 2008: 227–228), but from provision of information, coordination, and outreach services. Those services, in turn, were provided by institutions for industrial diffusion, such as the Penang Skills Development Center, backed by supportive political coalitions.

Patterns of Automotive Development in Other Countries

We have examined cases from East Asia, a region unusual in the intensity of its Cold War conflict and the speed of its postwar economic development. Does a similar logic of strategic upgrading apply elsewhere? Recent comparative work from a broader array of countries suggests that it might. Han and Thies (2019) find that while the communist threat elicited the highest degree of national mobilization, a strong perception of strategic rivalry was also an important stimulus. As a measure of mobilization, they examine changes in the ratio of tax revenue over GDP, a broader measure than our focus on the degree of effort put into upgrading, but a preliminary examination of a number of other automotive industrializers suggests that the logic of external threats and rivalry leading to upgrading holds quite well.

Consider, for example, Iran (Billingsley 2018). Under the Shah, the level of threat was low. Iran enjoyed the protection of the United States, and engaged in the usual early pattern of reliance on imports plus a crude form of import-substituting industrialization. The Iranian revolution of 1979, fear of American intervention, and the growing rivalry with Saudi Arabia stimulated a commitment to industrial deepening. The Iran-Iraq war of the 1980s precluded immediate implementation, but in the 1990s the government pushed aggressively, directly or indirectly controlling the two leading assemblers, Iran Khodro and SAIPA, and many parts firms, and sponsoring the indigenous production of parts. Iran entered into licensing and assembly agreements with firms from France and Korea. In the early 2000s, production expanded nearly sixfold, making Iran the largest producer in the Middle East. Modest exports of vehicles began to flow to other developing countries. From 2018, the resumption of American sanctions and the threat of further conflict stimulated another round of upgrading: "The Defense Ministry has had to step in to produce parts that were previously imported but now subject to sanctions. Other local firms are also starting to make car parts, with the government offering to support their efforts with soft loans" (Dudley 2019).

A similar logic applies to India, which is locked in a classic strategic rivalry with its larger neighbor, China (Garver 2015). India lost a border war to China in 1962 and has perceived a continuing threat from China and its ally Pakistan. To indigenize the auto industry, the government founded Maruti Udyog in 1981 and the next year formed a joint venture with the Japanese mini-car maker Suzuki, which in turn stimulated creation of several local components firms (Saraf 2016: 18). Economic reform and liberalization began in the late 1980s, and the auto industry took off from the mid-1990s. Foreign assemblers were not allowed to take a majority share in joint ventures until 1997, and by 1998 Indian firms were already able to design and engineer their own vehicles (Miglani 2019: 444–446). Even after complete liberalization of restrictions on foreign investment in 2001, considerable local capital remained in the auto industry, such as Tata Motors and Mahindra & Mahindra, which conducted far more R&D than did the local subsidiaries of MNCs, and took the lead in exports and in acquisition of foreign assemblers, notably Jaguar and Range Rover (Mani 2013, 2011).

Further policy changes to accelerate upgrading took place from 2000, leading to the formation of the Core Group on Automotive Research & Development in 2003 (Nag and De 2020: 303). In the early 2000s the quasi-state Automotive Research Institute of India, founded in 1966, expanded rapidly (ARAI [Automotive Research Association of India]). The National Automotive Testing and R&D Infrastructure Project (NATRIP) began in 2006. The central government and various state governments invested nearly $400 million over the next decade to build a series of seven research and testing facilities servicing firms across the country (Miglani 2019: 452; *The Economic Times*, January 15, 2016). "Promoting SMEs in the auto sector has been central to the industrial policy of India" (Nag and De 2020: 318), in part because "[l]arge firms make little effort to help suppliers downstream develop key capabilities" (Saraf 2016: 22).

If India has been serious, in the face of a perceived threat, about diffusing capabilities for upgrading, it has not been as successful as its rival, China: Growth in labor productivity and total factor productivity have been slower; only 37% of firms provide training to their employees, compared to 90% in China; and "only 47 per cent of auto firms in India have internationally-recognised quality certification, compared to 83 per cent in China" (Saraf 2016: 4, 13–14).

Similar but slightly more ambiguous is the case of Vietnam, which feels threatened by China. The longtime colonial overlord of Vietnam, China invaded northern Vietnam in 1979, destroying three cities as retribution and warning after Vietnam switched allegiance to the Soviet Union (Zhang

2015). According to our argument in Chapter 3, an acute threat from a larger neighbor should stimulate a serious effort at upgrading and a reluctance simply to rely on foreign investors. And, indeed, it did. The Vietnamese government protected and promoted autos as a "spearhead industry" (Hansen 2016). Initially, however, low incomes, a congested capital, and the existence of a huge fleet of motorcycles built up from the American period combined to throttle demand for autos. High tariffs encouraged investments by global assemblers, but the scale of production remained tiny and inefficient. Entry into the WTO in 2007 and the commitment to eliminate tariffs with ASEAN countries by 2018, which could be seen as ways to shore up international support against the Chinese threat, made it impossible to continue using tariff barriers to protect the industry. The government resorted to high taxes instead, but that only choked off demand and undermined efforts at ISI (Hansen 2016; Long, Tan, and Tran 2015). Rather than opening further to foreign investors and embarking on extensive development, the government moved in the opposite direction, encouraging a private real estate developer with impeccable political connections to organize a new and more powerful domestic producer to serve as national champion (Le Hong Hiep 2019: 16). At the launch of production in 2019, the Vietnamese prime minister sat in on the maiden ride of the company's electric vehicle and urged people to "give priority to using Vietnamese goods" (*Financial Times*, June 27, 2019).

In eastern Europe, automotive industrialization strategies have varied in response to the timing and geography of external threats, as well as the dual role of the European Union as a source of both market discipline and support for industrial policy, particularly toward small and medium-sized enterprises. The traditional external threat came from Russia, but it has varied over time and place. The Russian threat declined after the end of the Cold War and remained relatively low until the invasion of Crimea and eastern Ukraine in 2014. Romania, shielded from Russia by Ukraine and Moldova, perceived the smallest threat and displayed the weakest commitment to automotive industrialization, which became enmired in rent-seeking, including capturing EU funds (Medve-Bálint and Šćepanović 2020). Similarly, Ukraine, though much more geographically exposed, was so intertwined with Russia and Russian interests, and its state so weak, that until 2014 its auto industry concentrated on capturing EU funds and other rents (Langbein 2020).

Poland, in contrast, borders the Russian enclave of Kaliningrad, which houses major military bases that pose an existential threat to Poland. That threat stimulated a commitment to defense and civilian industrialization, particularly after 2014 (Terlikowski 2017). Facing Russia and bolstered by funds from the European Union, "the Polish state engaged actively in industrial policy [to nurture] the rise of a supply industry with forward linkages in the automotive value chain, thus decreasing Poland's dependence on lead MNCs" (Markiewicz 2020: 1147). Poland remains fearful of Russia, but increasingly has also grown wary of foreign investment, asserting that "we don't want a Poland that is a colony of the West" (Traub 2016).

Finally, Brazil and Mexico, two of the biggest auto producers in the world, have faced few security threats and possess abundant natural resources— soybeans, iron ore, sugar, and oil in Brazil, and oil, natural gas, and a variety of minerals in Mexico. Accordingly, we would expect them to adopt extensive development strategies relying on investments from MNCs, and that is what we observe.

Brazil lacks a credible external threat or even a plausible strategic rivalry and enjoys a large market to attract foreign multinationals. After the usual initial period of ISI, economic crisis in the 1980s and early 1990s led to opening of the domestic market and increased dependence on MNCs. Global assemblers situated new investments in lower wage regions and accelerated the move to outsourcing and lean production. As in Thailand, tax policy favored a specific model: one-liter cars capable of running in part or entirely on ethanol derived from sugar. Sales boomed and economies of scale kicked in, but unlike the case of Thailand's one-ton pickups, there was no export market for these ethanol cars, and even at home, economic crisis after 2014 depressed sales (Marx, de Mello, and de Lara 2020).

To be sure, Brazil is a large middle-income country with a long history of automotive production, and it has acquired some design and development capabilities, but they are distinctly limited. A study of Fiat's many production subsidiaries found that "only three of its emerging market subsidiaries [in Brazil, India, and Turkey] undertook any R&D. And, only one of them (in Brazil) came close to possessing the characteristics of a competence-creating subsidiary . . . with more product development responsibilities. . . . Furthermore, technology creation requires active scanning and identification of new sources of ideas—a managerial capability that did not emerge from our interviews with CRF, the parent R&D lab" (Athreye, Tuncay-Celikel, and Ujjual 2014: 111). Nor did Brazilian R&D enjoy a significant degree of autonomy or insulation from Brazil's volatile economy: "subsidiary role enhancement in Brazil was driven largely by parent firm investments" (Athreye, Tuncay-Celikel, and Ujjual 2014: 112), which in turn were driven not by performance in R&D but by local market conditions and the sales performance of the Brazilian subsidiary.

The story of extensive development in permissive circumstances is similar in Mexico, with even less local development capacity, at least until recently.

Occasional border tensions notwithstanding, the United States has not invaded Mexico in a century, and the balance of power so favors the United States that one cannot speak of strategic rivalry. Moreover, as noted earlier, Mexico has considerable resources. Early efforts to convince the American auto giants to cooperate with Mexico's ISI plans proved fruitless (Bennett and Sharpe 1985). However, the huge American market, an equally large disparity in wages, a long shared border, and an increasingly besieged American auto industry made Mexico a more attractive target for MNC investments. Political pressures and a drop in oil prices led Mexico to push for the North American Free Trade Agreement (NAFTA), which came into effect in 1994 (Thacker 2000). An impressive initial spurt of growth was followed by a decade of stagnation in the volume and value of Mexican exports (Covarrubias 2020).

After the global financial crisis of 2008, exports of both vehicles and parts expanded strongly. Global automakers and first-tier suppliers were increasingly pleased with the quality of labor and infrastructure, and poured investments into Mexico (Swiecki and Menk 2016). Some observers attribute this to the complete failure of Mexican wages to increase despite a decade of heavy investment and rising productivity, noting "the key role played by the Mexican industrial relations system, a one-sided system that aims to please management and attract foreign investment" (Covarrubias 2020: 324). Others pointed to the spread of local institutions for diffusion and innovation. In northern Mexico, for example, local institutions created by foundations and universities with funding from the federal and state governments helped former Ford engineers make the transition to running their own firms, supplying technology services such as machining and engineering to the well-known Ford plant in Hermosillo (Contreras and Isiordia 2010: 168–174). Swiecki and Menk (2016: 36–39) credit local initiatives in other states, particularly in education and training, with making it possible to absorb so much investment so quickly.

Despite Mexico's impressive rise as an auto producer and the emergence of useful local institutions in the early 2000s, two important caveats must be kept in mind: first, the level of independent procurement remains low: for Japanese affiliates in Mexico, for example, the rate of reliance on procurement from Japanese companies is similar to that in Thailand and Indonesia, and significantly higher than in Brazil or China (JETRO 2019: 4). Second, and crucial for our purposes, is that in Mexico even positive local activities supported by local institutions are overwhelmingly oriented toward supporting MNC production operations—toward extensive rather than intensive development.

In sum, then, these cases, representing some of the most important auto-producing sites in the developing world, are strongly consistent with the argument we have tested in East Asia: countries facing external threats and lacking readily available resources to procure political support are more likely to choose intensive development strategies; absent such threats, a strategy of extensive development via foreign direct investment is more likely. Linkages with domestically owned suppliers of components remain limited. Variations over time in threat intensity and additional factors such as the role of regional institutions like the European Union and ASEAN slightly complicate the story but do not fundamentally alter it.

Country Size and Location Profoundly Shape Strategic Choice

Some large developing countries, such as China, India, Brazil, Turkey, Mexico, and potentially Indonesia and Iran, have populations and per capita incomes sufficient to support major auto industries, even without breaking into international markets, if the necessary skills and supply chains could be developed. Other developing countries could become regional assembly hubs for leading automakers or, as their competitive advantage shifts from low-cost labor to skilled labor, global centers of excellence for specific operations, just as South Korea emerged as GM's center for design and engineering of small cars.

Many other large countries, however, have struggled even to assemble vehicles for MNCs. Economic mismanagement has strangled demand in Russia, Nigeria, and Pakistan. Argentina and Spain attracted many global assemblers, but demand growth has been erratic, and they are losing ground to newer low-wage assembly sites. Macroeconomic stability, protection of property rights, and provision of infrastructure may not be sufficient conditions to develop an automotive industry, but they are still necessary, as these examples and our case studies show.

A few low-wage countries on the periphery of Europe have attained a significant foothold in the industry by allying with global automakers in a pattern of extensive development. Slovakia, the Czech Republic, and Morocco have all prospered by serving western European assemblers. They have succeeded in part by largely ignoring the orthodox advice to avoid "picking winners" and focusing on narrow capabilities. It is not that these countries have insisted upon fostering whole industries, much less national champions, but that global assemblers have insisted on a coordinated package of support measures focused specifically on autos, including building ports with specialized equipment to export cars, laying out industrial parks specifically for production of auto parts, and providing extensive tax breaks and worker training programs (on Morocco, for example; see Stewart 2012; Volkmann 2016). These countries, in other words, look much like Thailand in the 1990s and the first decade of the 2000s. In contrast to Thailand's relative passivity, they all claim they want to attain intensive growth, and have achieved some success, but dependence on FDI remains high, and spillovers and value added are still limited (Pavlínek, Domański, and Guzik 2009).

Countries lacking the advantages of great size, high incomes, or location on the periphery of rich neighbors will find strategic options more limited. With sufficient market size, assembly of a few high-volume, mainstream models is possible. South Africa, for example, could supply its own market and much of sub-Saharan Africa, if incomes in neighboring countries continue to rise. Firms in most countries, however, will struggle to develop expertise in specific parts. The challenge will be to build and sustain the institutions necessary to sustain a competitive advantage even as wages rise.

New Technology: The Continuing Centrality of Institutions for Coordination and Diffusion

We are on the cusp of three major and a couple of minor transportation revolutions (Sperling 2018; Green et al. 2019). These revolutionary trends pose momentous challenges for firms, workers, governments, and consumers. Even in leading automotive countries such as Germany, Japan, and the United States, meeting these challenges will require developing and repurposing institutions for industrial coordination and diffusion.

Automation and Artificial Intelligence (AI)

Among the smaller revolutions are an increasing wave of automation and a shift from manufacturing to digitalization, software, and services more generally. The auto industry is by far the largest consumer of industrial robots, which are all but certain to make even greater inroads, even in low-wage countries. Thailand and other ASEAN countries are at particular risk. In 2016, the International Labour Organization (ILO) forecast that in the automotive industry, "[t]hese trends have a twofold effect on the labour force. Firstly, low-skill workers will find themselves displaced in favour of automation, and indeed, over 60 per cent of salaried workers in Indonesia and over 70 per cent of workers in Thailand face high automation risk. Secondly, manufacturers will increasingly seek higher skilled talent with R&D competencies, ranging from analytical experts to autonomous driving engineers and sustainability integration experts" (Chang, Rynhart, and Huynh 2016: x).

If the general trends are clear, the details are not, and estimates of job losses and gains vary widely (Balliester and Elsheikhi 2018: 11). The head of electrification for Audi of America, for example, forecast that "[t]he size of the global auto industry could [more than] triple over the next 30 years as proven electrification and mobility technologies mature, which is driving current investments in those areas" (Vellequette 2020). Even assuming a large increase in productivity over that period, this estimate implies significant growth in jobs across the auto industry broadly defined, but few of them are likely to involve semi-skilled labor on the factory floor. Similarly, the timing and impact of artificial intelligence (AI) on the auto industry are difficult to project, other than that AI is sure to affect many cognitively sophisticated jobs and that it is likely to be at least somewhat disruptive (Breunig et al. 2017).

Electrification: Hybrid, Battery Electric, and Hydrogen Fuel-Cell Vehicles

Uncertainty also surrounds the transition away from vehicles powered by traditional internal combustion engines (ICEs) to those propelled by electric motors. The move to new powerplants is motivated in part by concerns about pollution and energy use in Asian cities, but it is mainly driven by developments in technology and regulation in advanced countries, which are setting ever more stringent regulations on pollution emissions and fuel efficiency. Technological uncertainty surrounds both choice of powerplant and the speed of the transition from current ICE vehicles. Each of the contending technologies suffers from significant drawbacks or limitations:

- refined ICE: hard to render sufficiently clean and efficient, and still reliant on petroleum;
- "clean diesel": VW's Diesel testing scandal and new findings about damage to health from diesel pollution have destroyed credibility;
- hybrid gas-electric vehicles: flexible and cheap, but inefficient (they carry around both motor and engine/transmission), still use petroleum, and still pollute;
- battery electric vehicles (EVs): expensive and even after building an extensive charging infrastructure, charging still takes time;
- hydrogen fuel cell vehicles: hydrogen fuel, fueling stations, and vehicles are all expensive; an entirely new fueling system will be required.

Since the initial purchase price of alternative powerplants remains significantly more expensive than ICEs, the assumption, and the ongoing reality, is that their diffusion would be more rapid in wealthy countries, and that developing countries could afford to wait. Cost declines have been more rapid than expected, however. In the case of battery electric vehicles, for example, between 2010 and 2019, the real cost of batteries declined 87% (BloombergNEF 2019). Despite these rapid cost declines, sales for all producers other than Tesla remain disappointing. This gap between production (increasingly oriented toward new powerplants) and sales (still dominated by traditional ICEs) is likely to continue longer in developing countries, though once the tipping point in initial purchase costs has been reached, the transition could be quite rapid. Under pressure from regulators and convinced that the long-term trend is toward electrification, automakers are stuck with the burden of investing in both ICE and new powerplant technologies at the same time, despite the weak sales (Mitchell 2020), a burden that is likely to be especially heavy in developing countries.

The switch to new power plants also exacerbates the problems caused by automation: electric cars will contain far fewer mechanical parts, but far more sensors, semiconductors, and software (vindicating the decision of the Singaporean government, for instance, to see electronics as the channel for penetrating the auto industry). As the shift proceeds, the position of holders of intellectual property rights—mostly global assemblers and gigantic first-tier suppliers, along with electronics "lead firms" in advanced countries—will strengthen. Most automotive jobs will be in design, engineering, and services, not production or assembly.

The transition to new powerplants and the increasing sophistication of connected and autonomous vehicles also raises the specter of pressure on traditional automakers from new entrants emerging from electronics and other industries. With the possible exception of Tesla, the new competition seems less likely to involve the emergence of a new global assembler than a shift in alliances and balance of power. Just as large suppliers have steadily increased their share of total value added at the expense of assemblers, so too are electronics firms and suppliers of batteries and fine chemicals and materials likely to increase their share of the pie. Those new players are far more likely to come from Japan, Korea, or North America than from most developing countries. Thailand, for example, will eventually succeed in assembling more "Eco Cars," but may also promote demand for EVs as major energy producers and chains work with the government to expand the number of EV charging stations (Thaiger 2020). Such market expansion will constitute a further step in extensive development because, based on current trends, little of the high-end content will be designed or manufactured in Thailand.

Many auto industry executives in the developing world believe that the advent of electric and fuel-cell vehicles presents an opportunity to leapfrog the existing ICE industry dominated by masters of engine technology such as Toyota and BMW. Electric vehicles are relatively new to all producers, and consumers in developing countries are less wedded to existing cars and more open to trying new technologies (Gombar 2019). This hopeful vision is not entirely fanciful. China, in particular, has witnessed an enormous wave of investors in new electric vehicle start-ups, including such electronics powerhouses as Alibaba and Baidu. Young Chinese firms such as CATL and BYD have pushed past Japanese and Korean competitors to establish a dominant position in the production of EV batteries (Tanaka, Kawakami, and Omoto 2018), and China's combination of huge market, formidable electronics industry, and dearth of regulations on privacy may give it a leg up in data for mapping and other aspects of autonomous transportation.

Recent experience, however, confirms that barriers to new entry in the automobile industry remain extraordinarily high (Ciferri 2020). After surging from 2014 to 2018 on the back of lavish government subsidies to EV consumers, venture capital invested in the Chinese industry dropped precipitously in 2019 as the central government ordered cuts in subsidies, and new entrants such as Nio struggled to sell vehicles amidst enormous excess capacity (Huang 2019). These setbacks mirrored developments elsewhere, such as the failure of plans by renowned British engineer-entrepreneur James Dyson to build revolutionary EVs at a new company in Singapore. The abandonment of these plans after an investment of more than $3 billion indicates that even firms with deep pockets may find the entry barriers prohibitive. So far, only America's Tesla has fundamentally challenged the existing industry order—including in China—and even Tesla's future is not guaranteed.

Given the size of the Chinese and Indian markets and the enthusiasm of their governments, a handful of Chinese or Indian companies may make some impact, but for all the talk of leapfrogging, by most accounts they remain behind in battery and fuel-cell technology. They are more likely to succeed by acquisition or alliance than by frontal assault. For example, after reviving the storied Volvo brand, China's Geely announced that all future Volvo models would feature either hybrid powerplants or pure electric motors, and then declared its intention to merge the two companies (*Financial Times*, February 17, 2020, https://www.ft.com/content/4e37334a-4e45-11ea-95a0-43d18ec715f50)   in the hopes of creating China's first global automaker. Similarly, at a ceremony in Shanghai to mark the opening of Tesla's new "gigafactory," CEO Elon Musk announced plans to "create a China design and engineering center to actually design an original car in China for worldwide consumption" (Lambert 2020). Such a center would depend not only on the experience and resources of Tesla, but also on the formidable absorptive capabilities nurtured in China over the preceding two decades.

Autonomous but Connected Vehicles

The transition to connected or autonomous vehicles involves even more uncertainty about technology choices and timing, as well as a host of legal and regulatory issues, including legal liability in case of accidents, and relations with taxi and public mass transit systems. Also unclear is the effect on demand for new vehicles. A proliferation of "robo-taxis," whether controlled by a central dispatcher, or rented out by individual households à la Uber, could decimate demand for cars. In the meantime, new entrants from the advanced countries are further raising barriers to entry. The clear leader in autonomous driving technology is Waymo, a division of the internet giant Alphabet, the parent firm of Google. Other new players making multi-billion-dollar investments in self-driving technology include semiconductor leaders Intel and Nvidia, and Japan's Softbank. With a few exceptions from China, such as the search specialist Baidu, firms from developing countries are virtually nowhere to be seen in the self-driving race.

Institutional Responses to New Technology

In addition to complicating the timing and focus of investments by automakers, the transition to higher levels of automation, new power plants, and connected and autonomous vehicles will pose serious issues for public policy. First and most pressing is infrastructure: should national or local governments build or subsidize the construction of electric vehicle charging facilities, hydrogen refueling stations, or both? And how should governments manage the interface between new powerplants, connected vehicles, and the rest of the transportation infrastructure? Second, should governments subsidize the purchase of electric or hydrogen vehicles, and if so, how much and how long? Third, what are the implications of these new trends for the traditional auto industry, especially the small suppliers and workers involved in making parts for engines and transmissions, which will be eliminated in the transition to electrification, whether powered by batteries or fuel cells.

Meeting the challenge of these policy issues will require major institutional responses. First and most important is training and education, as workers shift from pounding metal and shaping plastic to designing and upkeeping software and sensors. The change in the character of work likely will also drive a geographic shift, as jobs move from low-wage rural areas to cities with more sophisticated workforces. All this will require major modifications to institutions for training, whether public, private, or mixed. Nor can training simply be left to the market mechanism, if only because the social dislocation caused by stranded workers and regions will be too great to ignore politically.

A second broad area that will require an intense and long-term institutional response revolves around the practicalities of introducing new powerplants and transportation systems: a vast array of product, safety, and environmental standards; testing and certification; verification of how these new technologies will actually work and interact in practice; detailed and continually updated mapping; legal reform to clarify new rights, and ensure safety and privacy; and others. These institutions will require the capacities to gather information, monitor behavior, and coordinate the different actors and sometimes different industries that we have stressed in this book.

The third area concerns research and development. Most R&D, consulting, and diffusion will be carried out by private companies, particularly traditional automakers, operating in response to market signals. But especially given the fact that even large developing country auto firms, such as Hyundai, spend much less on R&D than their developed country peers (UNCTAD 2019: 22), that still leaves a wide range of tasks for governments, universities, public-private alliances, and industry associations. Basic research on high-tech materials and components for next-generation batteries and fuel-cell stacks, radars, sensors, cameras, and other elements of the new transportation infrastructure is being conducted in universities, national laboratories, and consortia around the world.

Japan's national road map for development of hydrogen fuel-cell vehicles and infrastructure, for example, involves all these elements. It is driven not so much by top-down government planning as by governments helping private firms, including automakers, energy companies, and equipment providers, to coordinate their efforts to drive down costs, harmonize standards, devise complex new infrastructures, and convince consumers that expensive and unfamiliar new technology will be safe, clean, and convenient. Japan's campaign to cut the cost of hydrogen fueling stations is a crucial part of this effort. Industrial standards for dealing with hydrogen, a volatile and potentially flammable fuel, are extremely strict. Applied to local fueling stations, industrial standards drive up costs to uncompetitive levels. Relaxing safety standards for the use of hydrogen in public fueling stations has taken years of planning and coordination with fossil fuel companies, suppliers of industrial gases, automakers, and producers of industrial piping, as well as protracted negotiations with skeptical representatives of ordinary drivers and neighboring residential and commercial areas (Noble 2019; ANRE [Agency for Natural Resources and Energy] 2019). Introducing whole new transportation systems is an institution-intensive business

Similar efforts are occurring in China and Korea, the state of California, the United States as a whole, Germany and other European countries, and the European Union. Firms remain the central actors, but particularly in developing countries, their capacity to absorb, utilize, and develop new technology is heavily dependent on the local institutional and political context. And even in the most advanced countries, coordinating their activities with those of other firms, other industries, universities, and national and local governments requires extensive institutional support.

The revolution in transportation is being led neither by states nor markets alone, but by a kind of multilevel governance (Behnke, Broschek, and Sonnicksen 2019). Universities and governments conduct basic research. Private firms, led by the global assemblers and first-tier suppliers, spend the bulk of money in designing, engineering, and producing new vehicles and parts. Often, they pair up in alliances of convenience, such as the agreement between GM and Honda to develop fuel-cell technology. Consortia, standards coalitions, and cross-industry alliances hammer out the details. Industrial policy at the local, state, national, and regional levels can help coordinate and diffuse the activities of leading private firms. Rent-seeking and excessive top-down planning remain concerns, but they have faded with globalization and liberalization. The real problem is combining coordination, flexibility, and continuity. As we have seen in our East Asian cases, understanding the capacity to achieve that combination requires close attention to the specific collective challenges involved, and the political motivations to devise, develop, and support appropriate institutions.

Conclusion

We have proposed an explanation, rooted in institutional capacities and political incentives, for the puzzles of East Asian automotive industrialization. Although all seven countries covered in this study initiated automotive production with import-substitution strategies, they subsequently pursued different approaches with different degrees of success. Some—Thailand,

Indonesia, and the Philippines—pursued "extensive" strategies involving foreign-dominated, assembly-based exports. Thailand is the clear success in this group, with Indonesia showing signs of significant growth and the Philippines a persistent laggard. Others—South Korea, Taiwan, China, and Malaysia—pursued "intensive" strategies aimed at developing deeper technological capacities in and linkages among domestic firms. Malaysia's efforts have largely failed.

Neither of these strategies is easy to carry out. Requirements of successful extensive growth range from basic property rights and macroeconomic stability to crafted investment incentives, targeted fiscal policies, and infrastructure supporting large-scale production by foreign firms. Yet this process of capital mobilization and allocation does not demand the institutions in support of domestic technological deepening required for the successful pursuit of intensive growth strategies. Such upgrading poses significant coordination challenges beyond the capacity of individual firms. These challenges require effective institutions of technological diffusion; creating such institutions does not occur absent significant political support; and such support is itself a function of political elites' concerns with resource constraints in the face of external and domestic pressures.

Returning to a persistent theme in contemporary development debates, our analysis suggests that claims of the death of industrial policy are premature and potentially misleading. To be sure, some of the classic instruments of industrial policy have been limited by global and regional agreements on trade and investment. Nonetheless, some continue to figure prominently in our cases. In China, Malaysia, and Thailand, tariffs (or excise taxes) on imported vehicles remain high and provide significant protection to domestic producers. In 2018, for instance, Malaysia imported a mere 10,898 passenger cars from Thailand, despite its shared border with Southeast Asia's leading vehicle exporter and their joint membership in the ASEAN Free Trade Area. In Korea, fully a quarter of a century after the domestic car market was supposedly fully liberalized, a variety of non-tariff barriers continue to impede imports. In 2018, imported vehicles accounted for only 20% of new car registrations (calculated from data in https://www.kaida.co.kr/en/kaida/bbsView.do?boardS eq=17&articleSeq=52348, and https://www.statista.com/statistics/698032/ south-korea-passenger-cars-domestic-unit-sales/).

Even preferential trade agreements, which have aided the extension of global and regional value chains through their facilitation of vertical intra-industry trade (Chapter 2), can provide new instruments for protection. In the most advanced of regional schemes, the European Union, the single market does dismantle border barriers, but as Markiewicz (2019) argues, deep integration also makes new developmental tools available, not least through generous financing available through the bloc's Structural Funds. Recent preferential agreements have been as much about the sharing of rents as trade liberalization per se. Negotiations for the Trans-Pacific Partnership (TPP), for instance, pitted alternative designs for the automotive value chain against one another—a trans-Pacific design, which would have required a relaxation of North American rules of origin, versus a North American design (Ravenhill 2017). At first it seemed that the trans-Pacific variant would triumph, with lower local content rules introduced as part of TPP. But the Trump Administration's decision to withdraw from the TPP and to negotiate revisions to the North American Free Trade Agreement saw a reassertion of the North American basis for organization, the US-Mexico-Canada Trade Agreement, providing for an increase in local content requirements and unprecedented linkage to local wage costs (https://usmca.com/rules-of-origin-usmca/). We can expect that the regionalization of value chains in the auto industry that we noted in Chapter 2 to be reinforced in the protectionist environment likely to follow the Covid-19 recession.

Traditional industrial policy tools, then, are far from dead, and as we have emphasized, many institutions for coordination and diffusion rely on neither protection nor preferential financing. A second argument for the obsolescence of industrial policy is that the movement of industries toward the technological frontier is a game-changer (Wong 2011b). The contemporary task facing states promoting industrialization is no longer one of countering known risks but of coping with uncertainty. In a world of multiple "unknown unknowns," states are in jeopardy of losing huge amounts of money in backing the contemporary equivalent of the Sony Betamax.

States seeking to support research at the technological frontier undoubtedly face many hazards—but so do private firms. In our discussion of the contemporary challenges facing the Korean auto industry, for instance, we noted that the significant bet on hydrogen fuel-cell technologies made by Hyundai-Kia (and backed by the Korean state) has yet to pay off. As Mazzucato (2013) shows, state support for basic research has been fundamental to innovation in contemporary industrialized economies. Moving beyond the search for breakthrough technologies, our cases, particularly those of China and Korea, illustrate that there is huge scope for the state—through research institutes and universities—to play a significant role, usually working closely in conjunction with private sector actors, in developing the specific products needed for companies to upgrade and to compete internationally in the contemporary automobile industry. For many middle-income automotive aspirants, the challenge is less to push the technological frontier than to identify, absorb, and adapt existing technologies. Such technology absorption requires policies that deepen the pool of mid-level technical personnel and expand MSTQ capacities within and across firms.

A third set of arguments questioning the continuing relevance of industry policies suggests that in a world economy dominated by global value chains, the coordination problems that classic industrial policies were intended to resolve can best be addressed through the activities of lead firms in these value chains (Taglioni and Winkler 2016). But, as we noted earlier, the globalization of the auto industry has intensified the coordination challenges that firms and governments face. Engaging with global value chains seldom addresses these effectively. As shown by Pipkin and Fuentes (2017), upgrading within value chains is both rare and unlikely to occur in the absence of effective institutions

Our argument, then, is that industrial policies have continuing relevance—but we go beyond this conclusion to argue that a policy focus alone tells a very incomplete story. It misses the significance of institutions and how the roles they need to play differ according to the type of industrialization strategy being pursued. And it ignores the political context in which effective institutions develop. We believe this book provides an important step toward filling this gap through its examination of one of the most important manufacturing sectors in the most dynamic region of the global economy.

References

Abdulsomad, Kamaruding (1999), "Promoting Industrial and Technological Development under Contrasting Industrial Policies: The Automobile Industries in Malaysia and Thailand," in K. S. Jomo, Greg Felker, and Rajah Rasiah (eds.), *Industrial Technology Development in Malaysia: Industry and Firm Studies* (London: Routledge), 274–300.

Abimanyu, Anggito (1997), "Recent Economic Events in Indonesia: From Rapid Economic Growth to National Car Policy," in Gavin W. Jones and Terence H. Hull (eds.), *Indonesia Assessment: Population and Human Resources* (Singapore: Institute of Southeast Asian Studies and Research School of Pacific and Asian Studies, Australian National University), 39–58.

Abinales, Patricio N., and Amoroso, Donna J. (2017), *State and Society in the Philippines* (Boulder, CO: Rowman and Littlefield).

Abonyi, George, and Doner, Richard (2013), "Upgrading Thailand's Rubber Industry: Opportunities and Challenges," Bangkok Case study presented to Ministry of Finance, August 16–18.

AFP (2018), "As Elections Loom, Prayut Gets Cosy with Old Political Clans," *Bangkok Post*, May 7, <https://www.bangkokpost.com/news/politics/1460197/as-elections-loom-prayut-gets-cosy-with-old-political-clans>.

Agence France-Presse (2001), "General Motors Gets Daewoo Motor for 400 Million Dollars," *Agence France-Presse*, September 21, <http://global.factiva.com.virtual.anu.edu.au/aa/?ref=afpr000020010921dx9l0020a&pp=1&fcpil=en&napc=S&sa_from=>.

Agence France Presse (2002), "Malaysia's Proton to Roll out Own Engines Next April," *Agence France Presse*, October 17 <https://www.malaysiakini.com/news/12210>.

Agénor, Pierre-Richard, and Canuto, Otaviano (2012), "Middle-Income Growth Traps" (Washington, DC: World Bank), Policy Research Working Paper 6210, <http://dx.doi.org/10.1596/1813-9450-6210>.

Aghion, Philippe, Guriev, Sergei, and Jo, Kangchul (2019), "Chaebols and Firm Dynamics in Korea" (London: European Bank for Reconstruction and Development), Working Paper 227, June. <https://www.ebrd.com/cs/Satellite?c=Content&cid=1395283080000&pagename=EBRD%2FContent%2FDownloadDocument>.

Ahn, Sung-mi (2016), "Hyundai, Kia Eye Green Car Expansion Abroad-프린트화면," *Korea Herald*, June 27, <http://www.koreaherald.com/common_prog/newsprint.php?ud=20160627000763&dt=2>.

Aldaba, Rafaelita M. (2007). "Assessing the Comptetiveness of the Philippine Auto Parts Industry" (Manila: Philippine Institute for Development Studies, Discussion Paper No. 2007-14).

Aldaba, Rafaelita M. (2008). "Globalization and the Need for Strategic Government-Industry Cooperation in the Philippine Automotive Industry" (Manila: Philippine Institute for Development Studies, Discussion Paper No. 2008-21).

Aldaba, Rafaelita M. (2013), "Can the Philippine Auto Industry Survive Smuggling" (Manila: Philippine Institute of Development Studies, Policy Notes).

Aldaba, Rafaelita M. (2014), "The Philippine Manufacturing Industry Roadmap: Agenda for New Industrial Policy, High Productivity Jobs, and Inclusive Growth" (Manila: Philippine Institute for Development Studies, Discussion Paper Series).

Aldaba, Rafaelita M. (2016a), "Overview of the Philippine Auto Industry Roadmap," Presentation at Acacia Hotel, Alabang, Manila, 29 January, <http://www.asean-sme-academy.org/wp-content/uploads/Presentation-1-DTI-Rafaelita-Aldaba.pdf>.

Aldaba, Rafaelita M. (2016b), "CARS to Rev Engine of Manufacturing," *Philippine Daily Inquirer*, January 31. <http://opinion.inquirer.net/92487/cars-to-rev-engine-of-manufacturing>.

Altshuler, Alan A., et al. (1984), *The Future of the Automobile: The Report of MIT's International Automobile Program* (Cambridge, MA: MIT Press).

Aminullah, Erman, and Adnan, Richardi S. (2011), "Resources of Innovation in Indonesian Automotive Industry the Role of University and Public Research Institute (PRI) [*sic*]," in A. Sunami and Patarapong Intarakumnerd (eds.), *A Comparative Study of the Role of University and PRI as External Resources for Firms' Innovation* (ERIA Research Project Report 2010-10; Jakarta: ERIA), 111–168.

Amir, Jamal (2017), "Perodua Sales Grow 2.4% y/y in H1," *IHS Markit*, <https://global-factiva-com.proxy.lib.uwaterloo.ca/hp/printsavews.aspx?pp=Print&hc=Publication>.

Amsden, Alice H. (1989), *Asia's Next Giant: South Korea and Late Industrialization* (New York: Oxford University Press).

Amsden, Alice H. (2001), *The Rise of "the Rest": Challenges to the West from Late-Industrializing Economies* (Oxford; New York: Oxford University Press).

Anderson, G. E. (2012), *Designated Drivers: How China Plans to Dominate the Global Auto Industry* (Singapore: John Wiley & Sons).

Andrews, Matt (2013), *The Limits of Institutional Reform in Development: Changing Rules for Realistic Solutions* (New York: Cambridge University Press).

Ang, Yuen Yuen (2016), *How China Escaped the Poverty Trap* (Ithaca, NY: Cornell University Press).

Anglebrandt, Gary (2008), "Mando Returns to Hyundai Orbit," *Automotive News*, April 28, <http://www.autonews.com/article/20080428/GLOBAL02/304289979/mando-returns-to-hyundai-orbit>.

ANRE (Agency for Natural Resources and Energy, Government of Japan) (2019), "Formulation of a New Strategic Roadmap for Hydrogen and Fuel Cells," <https://www.meti.go.jp/english/press/2019/0312_002.html>.

ARAI (Automotive Research Association of India) "Our Journey", <https://www.araiindia.com/pages/about-us#timeline>.

Arashi (2007), "Jili chengdan de guojia zhongda yanfa xiangmu jinzhan shunli," <http://www.pcauto.com.cn/news/changshang/0705/442161.html>.

Arisitniran, Lamonphet (2019), "Ministry to Establish EV Panel within 3 Months," December 3, <https://www.bangkokpost.com/business/1807169/ministry-to-establish-ev-panel-within-3-months>.

Arnold, Walter (1989), "Bureaucratic Politics, State Capacity, and Taiwan's Automobile Industry Policy," *Modern China* 15(2), 178–214.

ARTC (2015), "ARTC Profile 2015" (Lugang: Automotive Research & Testing Center).

ASEAN Automotive Federation (2019), "ASEAN Auto Federation 2019 Statistics," <http://www.asean-autofed.com/files/AAF_Statistics_ytd_december2019.pdf>.

ASEAN Briefing (2017), "Industry Spotlight: Thailand's Automotive Industry" (updated March 17, 2017), <https://www.aseanbriefing.com/news/2017/03/17/thailand-automotive-industry.html>.

Asia Monitor Resource Center (2015), "Capital Mobility in Automotive Sector in Thailand" (updated November 11, 2015), <https://amrc.org.hk/content/capital-mobility-automotive-sector-thailand>.

Asian Development Bank (2017), *Asian Development Outlook 2017: Transcending the Middle-Income Challenge* (Manila: Asian Development Bank).

Aswicahyono, Haryo (2000), "How Not to Industrialise? Indonesia's Automotive Industry," *Bulletin of Indonesian Economic Studies* 36(1), 209–241.

Aswicahyono, Harry, Christian, David, and Faur, Adinova (2018), "A Case of the Automotive Industry in Indonesia," in Jeremy Goross and P. S. Intal Jr. (eds.), *Reducing Unnecessary Regulatory Burdens in ASEAN: Country Studies* (Jakarta: Economic Research Institute for ASEAN and East Asia), 144–175.

Aswicahyono, Haryo, and Feridhanusetyawan, Tubagus (2004), "The Evolution and Upgrading of Indonesia's Industry" (CSIS Economic Working Paper Series; Jakarta: Centre for Strategic and International Studies).

Aswicahyono, Haryo, Basri, M. Chatib, and Hill, Hal (2000), "How Not to Industrialise? Indonesia's Automotive Industry," *Bulletin of Indonesian Economic Studies* 36(1), 209–241.

Aswicahyono, Haryo, et al. (2011), "Technological Capability of Indonesia's Automotive Industry," in Patarapong Intarakumnerd (ed.), *How to Enhance Innovation Capability with Internal and External Sources* (ERIA Research Project Report 2010-9; Jakarta: ERIA), 41–103.

Athreye, Suma, Tuncay-Celikel, Asli, and Ujjual, Vandana (2014), "Internationalisation of R&D into Emerging Markets: Fiat's R&D in Brazil, Turkey and India," *Long Range Planning* 47(1), 100–114.

Athukorala, Prema-chandra (2017), "Global Production Sharing and Local Entrepreneurship in Developing Countries: Evidence from Penang Export Hub, Malaysia," *Asia & the Pacific Policy Studies* 4(2), 180–194.

Automotive Intelligence News (2000), "Renault/Samsung Motors Deal Closed: Renault Samsung Motors, the New Subsidary of the Renault Group," *Automotive Intelligence News*, September 5, <http://www.autointell-news.com/news-2000-2/September-05-00-p3.htm>.

Automotive News (2010), "Hyundai to Build Third China Plant," *Automotive News*, September 13, <http://www.autonews.com/apps/pbcs.dll/article?AID=/20100913/OEM/100919970/1131&template=printart>.

Automotive News (2011), "Hyundai Ends Bold Plan That Eased Fear of Job Loss," *Automotive News*, April 4, <http://www.autonews.com/apps/pbcs.dll/article?AID=/20110404/RETAIL03/304049978&template=printart>.

Automotive News (2012), "BMW and Hyundai in Engine Cost-Sharing Talks, Report Says," *Automotive News* (updated May 3), <http://edit.autonews.com/apps/pbcs.dll/article?AID=/20120503/COPY01/305039829&template=printart&nocache=1>.

Automotive News (2013), "GM to Reduce Reliance on South Korean Output as Labor Costs Rise, Report Says," *Automotive News*, August 11, <http://www.autonews.com/apps/pbcs.dll/article?AID=/20130811/GLOBAL/130819997&template=printart>.

Automotive News (2015), "China's Blue Star Says Ssangyong Talks 'Deadlocked,'" *Automotive News*, <http://www.autonews.com/article/20040325/REG/403250710>.

Automotive News (2017a), "Top Suppliers," *Automotive News Supplement*, <http://www.magna.com/docs/default-source/2017-press-releases/automotive-news-top-suppliers-6-26-2017.pdf?sfvrsn=2>.

Automotive News (2017b), "Top 100 Global OEM Parts Suppliers," *Automotive News*, June 26 (Supplement), 5–9 <http://www.nxtbook.com/nxtbooks/crain/an5740978765KIYTC_v2/index.php#/0>.

Automotive News (2019), "Automotive News, North America, Europe and the World Top Suppliers," *Crain Communications*, <https://s3-prod.autonews.com/data-protected/062419-2019TopSuppliers-062419.pdf?djoDirectDownload=true>.

Automotive News (2020), "Top Suppliers: North America, Europe and the World," *Automotive News*, <https://www.nxtbook.com/nxtbooks/crain/an8097364512SITPF_supp/index.php#/p/SIntro>.

Automotive News China (2016), "Former FAW chairman pleads guilty to taking bribes," *Automotive News China*, <https://www.autonews.com/china/former-faw-chairman-pleads-guilty-taking-bribes>.

Automotive News China (2018), "FAW, Dongfeng, Changan deny report of 3-way merger," *Automotive News China*, September 24 <http://www.autonewschina.com/en/article.asp?id=17887>,.

Auty, Richard M. (1994), "Industrial Policy Reform in Six Large Newly Industrializing Countries: The Resource Curse Thesis," *World Development* 22(1), 11–26.

Aveline-Dubach, Natcha (2010), "The Role of Industrial Estates in Thailand's Industrialization, New Challenges for the Future," in Patarapong Intarakumnerd and Yveline Lecler (eds.), *Sustainability of Thailand's Competitiveness: The Policy Challenges* (Singapore: Institute of Southeast Asian Studies), 174–208.

AVL (2018), "AVL Technical Center Shanghai," <https://www.avl.com/-/avl-technical-center-shanghai>.

Awawachintachit, Duangjai (2012), "Thailand: Automotive Hub of Asia," September 21, <www.boi.go.th/upload/content/DSC)Duangjai-Automotive_Campus_Netherlands_Sept%202012_77093.pdf>.

Aziz, Afiq (2020), "MARii to Roll Out Covid-19 Immunity Test Kit," *The Malyasian Reserve* 1 October, <https://themalaysianreserve.com/2020/10/01/marii-to-roll-out-covid-19-immunity-test-kit/>.

Baldwin, Richard (2011), "Trade and Industrialisation after Globalisation's 2nd Unbundling: How Building and Joining a Supply Chain Are Different and Why It Matters" (Cambridge, Ma.: National Bureau of Economic Research), Working Paper 17716, December, <http://www.nber.org/papers/w17716.pdf>.

Baldwin, Richard (2016), *The Great Convergence: Information Technology and the New Globalization* (Cambridge, MA: The Belknap Press of Harvard University Press).

Balliester, Thereza, and Elsheikhi, Adam (2018), "The Future of Work: A Literature Review," *ILO Research Department Working Paper* (29).

Bangkok Post (2019a), "BOI Seeks to Spark EV Interest," *Bangkok Post*, December 23. <https://www.bangkokpost.com/auto/news/1822129/boi-seeks-to-spark-ev-interest>.

Bangkok Post (2019b), "The man behind Thai auto policy", *Bangkok Post*, April 27. <https://www.bangkokpost.com/auto/1668000/the-man-behind-thai-auto-policy>.

Bank Negara Malaysia (2011), "The Changing Structure of Malaysia's Exports" (Kuala Lumpur: Bank Negara Malaysia), 32–35.

Baodingshi Kejiju (2013), "Changcheng Qiche gufen youxian gongsi yixiang guojia 863 jihua [Great Wall's national 863 project]," <http://www.cbcu.com.cn/a/caijingdongxiang/hongguanjingji/20130910/2609.html>.

Barajas, Adolfo, et al. (2016), "Transmission Troubles," *Finance & Development* 53(3), 40–43.

Barrientos, Stephanie, Gereffi, Gary, and Rossi, Arianna (2011), "Economic and Social Upgrading in Global Production Networks: A New Paradigm for a Changing World," *International Labour Review* 150(3–4), 319–340.

BBC News (2014), "China's Car Market Matures after Ultra-Fast Growth" (updated April 22), <http://www.bbc.co.uk/news/business-17786962>.

BDO (2015), "Indonesia Investment Climate Q1 2014," <http://www.bdo.co.id/News/Documents/BKINEWS.pdf>.

Becker, Helmut (2006), *High Noon in the Automotive Industry* (Berlin: Springer).

Becker, Markus C., and Zirpoli, Francesco (2005), "Editorial: Special Issue on Knowledge and Task Partitioning in the Auto Industry: Coordination, Governance and Learning in New Product Development," *International Journal of Automotive Technology and Management* 5(2), 137–145.

Behnke, Nathalie, Broschek, Jörg, and Sonnicksen, Jared (2019), *Configurations, Dynamics and Mechanisms of Multilevel Governance* (Cham: Palgrave Macmillan).

Bennett, Andrew (2004), "Case Study Methods: Design, Use, and Comparative Advantages," in Detlef F. Sprinz and Yael Wolinsky-Nahmias (eds.), *Models, Numbers and Cases: Methods for Studying International Relations* (Ann Arbor: University of Michigan Press), 19–55.

Bennett, Douglas C., and Sharpe, Kenneth E. (1985), *Transnational Corporations versus the State: The Political Economy of the Mexican Auto Industry* (Princeton, NJ: Princeton University Press).

Bent, Alan (2015), "1962 Datsun Bluebird 312," <http://www.earlydatsun.com/datsun312.html>.

Berenschot, Ward (2018), "The Political Economy of Clientelism: A Comparative Study of Indonesia's Patronage Democracy," *Comparative Political Studies* 51(12), 1563–1593.

Bernama.com (2008), "Further Liberalisation of Malaysia's Auto Sector will be Gradual, Says Muhyiddin" (updated July 22, 2008), <http://web10.bernama.com/auto/newsDetail.php?id=347693>.

Bernama.com (2020), "MARii Aims Zero Foreign Labour Utilisation by Year-End" (updated January 23, 2020), <http://www.bernama.com/en/business/news.php?id=1808816>.

Billingsley, Andrew (2018), "Iran's Troubled Auto Industry" (Washington, DC: United States Institute of Peace).

Birdsall, Nancy, Thomas Pinckney, and Richard Sabot (2000), "Natural Resources, Human Capital, and Growth," Carnegie Endowment for International Peace, Global Policy Program Working Papers, No. 9, <https://carnegieendowment.org/files/natresources.pdf>.

Bitonio, Benedicto Ernesto R. (2012), "Industrial Relations and Collective Bargaining in the Philippines" (Geneva: International Labour Organization).

Bland, Ben (2012), "Indonesia: Archipelago apprehension," *Financial Times*, 2012/ 08/29/T19:11:24.000Z, <https://www.ft.com/content/d2b5b3b6-f1e2- 11e1-bba3- 00144feabdc0>.

Blank, Nathan (2014), "The Recruitment Industry in the Philippines: Government-Business Relations in the Overseas Employment Program" (Canberra: Australian National University).

Bloomberg News (2014), "China Said to Plan Sweeping Shift From Foreign Technology to Own", *Bloomberg News* (updated December 18), <http://www. bloomberg.com/news/articles/2014-12-17/china-said-to-plan-sweeping-shift-from-foreign-technology-to-own>.

BloombergNEF (2019), "Battery Pack Prices Fall as Market Ramps Up with Market Average at \$156/kWh in 2019" (Shanghai and London, December 3), <https:// about.bnef.com/blog/battery-pack-prices-fall-as-market-ramps-up-with-market-average-at-156-kwh-in-2019/>.

Board of Investments Thailand (2015), "Thailand's Automotive Industry," <www.boi. go.th/upload/content/BOI-brochure%202015-automotive-20150325)70298.pdf>.

Bonvillian, William B., and Van Atta, Richard (2011), "ARPA-E and DARPA: Applying the DARPA Model to Energy Innovation," *The Journal of Technology Transfer* 36(5), 469–513.

BorgWarner (2019), "BorgWarner United Transmission Systems Celebrates 10-Year Anniversary, Significant Production Milestone," <https://www.borgwarner. com/newsroom/press-releases/2019/10/10/borgwarner-united-transmission-systems-celebrates-10-year-anniversary-significant-production-milestone>, October 10.

Bowie, Alasdair (1991), *Crossing the Industrial Divide: State, Society, and the Politics of Economic Transformation in Malaysia* (New York: Columbia University Press).

Bowie, Alasdair, and Unger, Danny (1997), *The Politics of Open Economies: Indonesia, Malaysia, the Philippines, and Thailand* (Cambridge: Cambridge University Press).

Boyd, T. F., and Lee, C. (1995), "Educational Need and Economic Advancement: The Role of Vocational Education in the Republic of China," in Albert H. Yee (ed.), *East Asian Higher Education: Traditions and Transformations* (Oxford: Pergamon), 193–210.

Bradsher, Keith (1996), "G.M. Expected to Put Plant in Thailand, Not Philippines," *New York Times*, May 30, sec. Business, <https://www.nytimes.com/1996/05/30/ business/gm-expected-to-put-plant-in-thailand-not-philippines.html>.

Brandt, Loren, and Thun, Eric (2010), "The Fight for the Middle: Upgrading, Competition, and Industrial Development in China," *World Development* 38(11), 1555–1574.

Brandt, Loren, and Thun, Eric (2016), "Constructing a Ladder for Growth: Policy, Markets, and Industrial Upgrading in China," *World Development* 80, 78–95.

Breunig, Matthias, et al. (2017), "Building Smarter Cars with Smarter Factories: How AI Will Change the Auto Business," (McKinsey) <https://www.mckinsey.com/~/media/McKinsey/Business%20Functions/McKinsey%20Digital/Our%20Insights/Building%20smarter%20cars/Building-smarter-cars-with-smarter-factories.ashx>.

Breznitz, Dan (2007), *Innovation and the State: Political Choice and Strategies for Growth in Israel, Taiwan, and Ireland* (New Haven, CT: Yale University Press).

Brimble, Peter, and Doner, Richard F. (2006), "University-Industry Linkages and Economic Development: The Case of Thailand," *World Development* 35(6), 1021–1036.

Brown, Andrew (2016), "Political Regimes and Employment Relations in Thailand," *Journal of Industrial Relations* 58(2), 199–214.

Bruton, Christopher (2017), "Solving the Skills Shortage," *Bangkok Post* July 21, <https://www.bangkokpost.com/business/1297199/solving-skill-shortages>.

Bureau of Labor Statistics (2011a), "Labor Costs in the Auto Industry," (updated April 27, 2011) <https://www.bls.gov/opub/ted/2011/ted_20110427.htm>.

Bureau of Labor Statistics (2011b), "India's Organized Manufacturing Industry," (updated August 28, 2013) <https://www.bls.gov/fls/india.htm>.

Bureau of Labor Statistics (2015), "Automobiles," (updated October 11) <http://www.bls.gov/spotlight/2011/auto/>.

Burgess, Robert, and Vikram, Haskar (2005), "Migration and Foreign Remittances in the Philippines" (IMF Working Paper), June.

Burki, Shahid Javed, and Perry, Guillermo (1998), *Beyond the Washington Consensus: Institutions Matter* (Washington, DC: World Bank).

CAAM (China Association of Automobile Manufacturers) (2018a), "2017 nian chengyongche fenguobie xiaoshou qingkuang jianxi [Brief analysis by nationality of 2017 passenger car sales]," January 18. <http://www.caam.org.cn/zhengche/20180118/0905214784.html>.

CAAM (China Association of Automobile Manufacturers) (2018b), "The Market Share of Chinese Brand PCs Up Yearly." http://www.caam.org.cn/AutomotivesStatistics/20180115/1305214915.html.

Caijing (2006), "Chuangxin de 'xianjing' [The innovation 'trap']," *Caijing*, 163, 10 July, <http://www.caam.org.cn/zhengche/20180118/0905214784.html>.

Callon, Scott (1995), *Divided Sun: MITI and the Breakdown of Japanese High-Tech Industrial Policy 1975–1993* (Stanford, CA: Stanford University Press).

Calmon, Fernando (2015), "Brazil: The Fiasco of Chinese Brands That Failed to Catch On," *just-auto*, 26 May 2015, <http://www.just-auto.com/news/the-fiasco-of-chinese-brands-that-failed-to-catch-on_id159297.aspx>.

Campbell, James R. (2012), "Transnational Security Threats to Indonesia," in David Fouse (ed.), *Issues for Engagement: Asian Perspectives on Transnational Security Challenges* (Honolulu, Hawaii: Asia-Pacific Center for Security Studies), 48–56.

Canivel, Roy Stephen (2017), "Local Parts Makers Hit Toyota, Mitsubishi for Ignoring Small Firms," *BusinessWorld Online*, January 24, <http://www.bwordonline/com/content.php?section=Corporate&title=local-parts-makers-hit-toyota-mitsubishi-for-ignoring-small-firms&id=139497>.

Cao, Cong, Suttmeier, Richard P., and Simon, Denis F. (2006), "China's 15-Year Science and Technology Plan," *Physics Today* 59(12), 38–43.

Cao, Cong, et al. (2013), "Reforming China's S&T System," *Science* 341(6145), 460–462. doi: DOI: 10.1126/science.1234206

CATARC (China Automotive Technology and Research Center 中国汽车技术研究中心), and CAAM (China Association of Automobile Manufacturers 中国汽车工业协会) (2006), 中国汽车工业年鉴2006版 *(China Automotive Industry Yearbook 2006)*. 天津: 中国汽车工业年鉴 编辑部 (China Automotive Industry Yearbook Editorial Department).

CATARC (China Automotive Technology and Research Center 中国汽车技术研究中心), and CAAM (China Association of Automobile Manufacturers 中国汽车工业协会) (2008), 中国汽车工业年鉴2008版 *(China Automotive Industry Yearbook, 2008)*. Tianjin: 中国汽车工业年鉴编辑部 (China Automotive Industry Yearbook Editorial Board).

CATARC (China Automotive Technology and Research Center 中国汽车技术研究中心), and CAAM (China Association of Automobile Manufacturers 中国汽车工业协会) (2010), 中国汽车工业年鉴 2010版 *(China Automotive Industry Yearbook, 2010)*. Tianjin: 中国汽车工业年鉴 期刊社 (China Automotive Industry Yearbook Periodicals).

CATARC (China Automotive Technology and Research Center 中国汽车技术研究中心), and CAAM (China Association of Automobile Manufacturers 中国汽车工业协会) (2015), 中国汽车工业年鉴 2015版 *(China Automotive Industry Yearbook, 2015)*. Tianjin: 中国汽车工业年鉴 期刊社 (China Automotive Industry Yearbook Periodicals).

CATARC (China Automotive Technology and Research Center 中国汽车技术研究中心), and CAAM (China Association of Automobile Manufacturers 中国汽车工业协会) (2016), 中国汽车工业年鉴 2016版 *(China Automotive Industry Yearbook, 2016)*. Tianjin: 中国汽车工业年鉴 期刊社 (China Automotive Industry Yearbook Periodicals).

CATARC (China Automotive Technology and Research Center 中国汽车技术研究中心), and CAAM (China Association of Automobile Manufacturers 中国汽车工业协会) (2018), 中国汽车工业年鉴 2018版 *(China Automotive Industry Yearbook, 2018)*. Tianjin: 中国汽车工业年鉴 期刊社 (China Automotive Industry Yearbook Periodicals).

CATARC (China Automotive Technology and Reseach Center 中国汽车技术研究中心), and CAAM (China Association of Automobile Manufacturers

中国汽车工业协会) (2019), 中国汽车工业年鉴 *2019*版 *(China Automotive Industry Yearbook, 2019)*. Tianjin: 中国汽车工业年鉴 期刊社 (China Automotive Industry Yearbook Periodicals).

CATARC (China Automotive Technology and Research Center 中国汽车技术研究中心), Nissan China (日产（中国）投资有限公司), and Dongfeng Motor (东风汽车有限公司), eds. 2015. 中国新能源汽车产业发展报告 *(2015) Annual report on new energy vehicle industry in China (2015)*. Beijing: Social Sciences Academic Press (China) 社会科学文献出版社. CATARC (China Automotive Technology and Research Center) (2016), "Zhongguo qiche jishu yanjiu zhongxin," <http://www.catarc.ac.cn/ac2016/content/20151231/15110.html>.

CATARC (China Automotive Technology and Research Center) (2020), "中心简介 (A brief introduction to the Center)," <http://www.catarc.ac.cn/ac_en/content/20071228/7488.html>.

CATARC (China Automotive Technology and Reseach Center. 2020. "中国汽车技术研究中心有限公司 (China Automotive Technology and Research Center Co., Ltd.)," <http://www.catarc.ac.cn/ac2016/content/20151231/15110.html.>

CEC "Company History,"n.d. <http://cectek-e.so-buy.com/front/bin/ptlist.phtml?Category=303679>.

Center on International Education Benchmarking (2017), "South Korea: School-to-Work Transition" (updated 2017), <http://ncee.org/what-we-do/center-on-international-education-benchmarking/top-performing-countries/south-korea-overview/south-korea-school-to-work-transition/>.

Chalassatien, Tavorn (2014), "Finding Skilled Workers for Desperate Auto Industries: The Dilemma of an Industry in Full Flight," *Thailand Automotive Industry Directory* (Bangkok), 113–123.

Chalassatien, Tavorn (2016), "New Era of Collaboration: Auto Academy Gears Up for Competitive, Sustainable Industry," *Thailand Automotive Industry Directory*: 113–123.

Chalmers, Ian (1994), "Domestic Capital in the Evolution of Nationalist Auto Development Policy in Indonesia: From Instrumental to Structural Power" (Perth: Asia Research Centre, Murdoch University), August.

Chalmers, Ian (1998), "Tommy's Toys Trashed," *Inside Indonesia* 56 (Oct–Dec) <https://www.insideindonesia.org/tommys-toys-trashed>.

Chang, Jae-Hee, Rynhart, Gary, and Huynh, Phu (2016), *ASEAN In Transformation-Automotive and Auto Parts: Shifting Gears* (Geneva: International Labour Organization).

Changan Qiche (2016), "Quanqiu Yanfa Tixi [Global research system]," <http://www.changan.com.cn/research/qqyf/>.

Charoenloet, Voravidh (2015), "Industrialization, Globalization and Labour Force Participation in Thailand," *Journal of the Asia Pacific Economy* 20(1), 130–142.

Chao, Jiang, Huang, Mingli, Gold, Eckart, and Xiang, Xiaoning (2013), "Development of a New 6-Speed Dual Clutch Transmission for the China Market." In *Proceedings of the FISITA 2012 World Automotive Congress* edited by FISITA, 261–270. (Heidelberg: Springer).

Chee Peng Lim (1994), Heavy Industrialization: A Second Round of Import Substitution," in K. S. Jomo (ed.), *Japan and Malaysian Development: In the Shadow of the Rising Sun* 244–262 (London: Routledge).

Chen, Liangrong (2006), "Zhongguo qiche chanye: Feiling jingyan dalu kaihua [The Chinese auto industry: the *Feiling* experience blooms in the mainland]," *Tianxia Zazhi* (347), 208–218.

Chen, Ling, and Naughton, Barry (2016), "An Institutionalized Policy-making Mechanism: China's Return to Techno-industrial Policy," *Research Policy* 45(10), 2138–2152. doi: https://doi.org/10.1016/j.respol.2016.09.014.

Chen, Xinrong, and Chen, Huizhen (2012), "Shouhui ECFA Dayi, Jiangshen jiedan wang [Gaining benefits from ECFA, Dayi and Jiangshen win booming orders]," *Gongshang Shibao*, <http://blog.udn.com/chen04088/6557817>.

Chen, Yajie (2020), "Yan Chen Lilian lianshou Honghai, Yulong Jituan de qiche dameng haiyou xuji [Yan Chen Lilian joins hands with Foxconn, and Yulon Group's great automotive dream still has a sequel]," *Caixun*. https://www.wealth.com.tw/home/articles/24250

Chen, Zhijie (2011), "Qirui 8 ge xin nengyuan xiangmu zaici ruxuan 863 jihua [Eight of Chery's new energy vehicle projects selected for 863 plan]," <http://newenergy.in-en.com/html/newenergy-941892.shtml>.

Chen, Zhiyang, Xiao, Ruisheng, and Xie, Lulin (2013), *2013 Qijiche chanye nianjian [Automobile and Motorcycle Industry Yearbook 2013]* (Xinzhu Zhudong: Industrial Technology Research Institute, Industrial Economics & Knowledge Center ITRI IEK).

Chen, Zongqing (2014), "Checai jishu fazhan lianmeng chuang xinju [Alliance for auto materials technology development opens a new era]," *Zhongguo Shibao*, June 19, <http://www.chinatimes.com/newspapers/20140619000325-260208>.

Cheng, Alfred (2016), "通用泛亚研发中心 (GM's Pan Asia Technical Automotive Center)," zhihu.com. <https://zhuanlan.zhihu.com/p/24598153>.

Cheng, Li-lun (2007), "Surviving in the Middle: Embedded Learning and Managed Dependency among Taiwanese Automakers," in Yukihito Sato and Momoko Kawakami (eds.), *Competition and Cooperation among Asian Enterprises in China* (Chiba-shi: Institute of Developing Economies, JETRO), 61–90.

Cherif, Reda, and Hasanov, Fuad (2019), "The Return of the Policy That Shall Not Be Named: Principles of Industrial Policy" (Washington, DC: International Monetary Fund) Working Paper WP/19/74, March, <https://www.imf.org/~/media/Files/Publications/WP/2019/WPIEA2019074.ashx>.

Chin, Gregory T. (2010), *China's Automotive Modernization: The Party-State and Multinational Corporations* (New York: Palgrave Macmillan).

China Daily (2004), "SAIC Takes on Ssangyong Motors," *China Daily*, October 29, <http://www.china.org.cn/english/BAT/110673.htm>.

China FAW Group Corporation R&D Center (2016), "Retrospect," <http://www.rdc.faw.com.cn/jszx-en/zxgk/lshg.jsp>.

Chinavitae.com. "Miao Wei 苗圩."<http://www.chinavitae.com/biography/Miao_Wei/bio>.

Cho, Seong-Jae (2006), "Employment Relations in the Automobile Industries of Japan, Korea and China: Focusing on Nonstandard Workers in Toyota, Hyundai and Shanghai Volkswagen," *Reports by Visiting Researchers*, <http://www.jil.go.jp/profile/documents/Cho.pdf>.

Choi, Byung-Sun (1991), *Economic Policymaking in Korea: Institutional Analysis of Economic Policy Changes in the 1970s and 1980s* (Seoul: Chomyung Press).

Choi, Jin-Wook (2009), "What Holds Indonesia Back? Structural Roots of Corruption and Reform," *2009 Korean Association for Public Administration International Conference* (University of Incheon at Songdo Campus, Korea).

Choi, Kyong-Ae (2019), "(LEAD) (Yonhap Interview) High Wages, Low Productivity Challenging S. Korean Carmakers," (updated April 29, 2019) <https://en.yna.co.kr/view/AEN20190429007551320>.

Chosun Ilbo (2016), "Korean Automakers Edge up in Global Green Car Market," *Chosun Ilbo*, March 9, <http://english.chosun.com/site/data/html_dir/2016/03/09/2016030901198.html>.

Chou, Yuan (2013), "Electric Vehicles: Why Did Taiwan Lose Tesla?," *Common Wealth Magazine* (532) <https://english.cw.com.tw/article/article.action?id=490>.

Chu, Yun-han (1994), "The State and the Development of the Automobile Industry in South Korea and Taiwan," in Joel D. Aberbach, David Dollar, and Kenneth L. Sokoloff (eds.), *The Role of the State in Taiwan's Development* (Armonk, NY: M. E. Sharpe), 125–169.

Chu, Yun-Peng (2006), "The Political Economy of Taiwan's High-Tech Industrialisation: The 'Developmental State' and its Mutinous Mutation," in Yun-Peng Chu and Hal Hill (eds.), *The East Asian High-Tech Drive* (Cheltenham, UK: Edward Elgar), 119–181.

Chuang, Steve (2015), "Taiwan Fastener Makers Focus on Advanced Heat Treatment Standards to Tap Automotive Segment," *CENS*, <http://www.cens.com/cens/html/en/news/news_inner_48220.html>.

Chung, Kyung-Won, and Kim, Yu-Jin (2014), "Hyundai Motor Company: Design Takes the Driver's Seat" (Cambridge, MA: Design Management Institute), DMI Case Study.

Chung, Myeong-Kee (1994), "Transforming the Subcontracting System and Changes of Industrial Organization in the Korean Automobile Industry," *Actes du GERPISA* (14), 83–98. <http://www.univ-evry.fr/labos/gerpisa/actes/14/index.html>.

Ciferri, Luca (2012), "PSA, Renault Say They Can't Build Small Cars Profitably in France," *Automotive News Europe*, February 15, <http://edit.autonews.com/apps/pbcs.dll/article?AID=/20120215/ANE/120219942&template=printartANE&nocache=1>.

Ciferri, Luca (2018), "Why Chinese Cars, Crossovers Should Worry Europe's Brands," *Automotive News Europe*, June 2, <http://europe.autonews.com/article/20180602/BLOG15/180529757/why-chinese-cars-crossovers--should-worry-europes-brands>.

Ciferri, Luca (2020), "Disruptors Get Disrupted as 'Stone Age' Companies Persist," *Automotive News Europe*, January 11, <ttps://europe.autonews.com/blogs/disruptors-get-disrupted-stone-age-companies-persist>.

Clifford, Mark L. (1998), *Troubled Tiger: Businessmen, Bureaucrats, and Generals in South Korea* (revised ed.; Armonk, NY: M. E. Sharpe).

Clugston, Erika (2019), "Baidu Dominates Chinese Autonomous Driving Tests (But Still Trails Far Behind Google-Waymo)," (updated April 10) <https://cleantechnica.com/2019/04/10/baidu-dominates-chinese-autonomous-driving-tests/>.

Cohen, Wesley M., and Levinthal, Daniel A. (1990), "Absorptive Capacity: A New Perspective on Learning and Innovation," *Administrative Science Quarterly* 35(1), 128–152.

Cole, Bernard D. (2006), *Taiwan's Security: History and Prospects* (New York: Routledge).

Continental Automotive (2019), "Worldwide Emission Standards and Related Regulations: Passenger Cars / Light and Medium Duty Vehicles" (updated May), <https://www.continental-automotive.com/en-gl/Passenger-Cars/Technology-Trends/Real-Driving-Emissions>.

Contreras, Oscar F., and Isiordia, Paula (2010), "Local Institutions, Local Networks and the Upgrading Challenge: Mobilising Regional Assets to Supply the Global Auto Industry in Northern Mexico," *International Journal of Automotive Technology and Management* 10(2–3), 161.

Cook, Malcolm (2017), "Unexpected Benefits from a Battle against ISIS," *International New York Times*, November 6, 2017, <https://www.nytimes.com/2017/11/05/opinion/marawi-philippines-maute-duterte.html>.

Courier-Mail, The (2005), "Engine Hold-Up," *The Courier-Mail*, March 23, <https://advance-lexis-com.proxy.lib.uwaterloo.ca/document/?pdmfid=1516831&crid=556b562e-a683-4922-8cea-bbf04d3a439c&pddocfullpath=%2Fshared%2Fdocument%2Fnews%2Furn%3AcontentItem%3A4FS6-KDX0-015G-Y2GJ-

00000-00&pdcontentcomponentid=244788&pdteaserkey=sr3&pditab=allpods&
ecomp=dzx2k&earg=sr3&prid=a107c2a6-300c-40b5-8420-552f0e5c4b2c>.

Covarrubias V., Alex (2020), "The Boom of the Mexican Automotive Industry: From NAFTA to USMCA," in V. Alex Covarrubias and Sigfrido M. Ramírez Perez (eds.), *New Frontiers of the Automobile Industry* (Cham, Switzerland: Springer), 323–348.

Coxhead, Ian, and Li, Muqun (2008), "Propsects for Skills-Based Export Growth in a Labour-Abundant, Resource-Rich Developing Economy," *Bulletin of Indonesian Economic Studies* 44(2), 209–238.

Crouch, Harold (1996), *Government and Society in Malaysia* (St Leonards, NSW: Allen & Unwin).

Culture China（文化世界）(2020), "2020中国车企研发投入排行榜出炉 (The 2020 ranking of research intensity by Chinese automakers appears) <https://www.culturechina.cn/auto/2020/54752.html>

Cunningham, Edward, Lynch, Teresa, and Thun, Eric (2005), "A Tale of Two Sectors: Diverging Paths in Taiwan's Automotive Industry," in Suzanne Berger and Richard K. Lester (eds.), *Global Taiwan: Building Competitive Strengths in a New International Economy* (Armonk, NY: M. E. Sharpe), 97–136.

Current Development of Taiwan Automobile Industry (2013), (Taiwan Transportation Vehicle Manufacturers Association, October 31).

Daily Express (2005a), "Proton to Push for Stronger Export: CEO" (updated April 4), <http://www.dailyexpress.com.my/print.cfm?NewsID=33670>.

Daily Express (2005b), "Proton Losing out to Dumped Imports" (updated 9 June), <http://www.dailyexpress.com.my/news.cfm?NewsID=35029>.

Davidson, Jamie S. (2015), *Indonesia's Changing Political Economy: Governing the Roads* (New York: Cambridge University Press).

Department of Science and Technology, Philippines (2015), "DOST'S Auto Parts Testing Facility," <www.dost.gov.ph/knowledge-resources/news/44-2015-new/741-dost-s-auto-parts-testing-facility>.

Department of Trade and Industry and Board of Investments (n.d.), "Securing the Future of Philippine Industries—Automotive," <http://industry.gov.ph/industry/automotive/>.

Desiderio, Louella (2019), "Philippines Remains Worst Performer in Vehicle Production in ASEAN," *Philstar Global*, <Philstar.com/business/2019/01/16/11885361/Philippines-remains-worst-performer-vehicle-production-asean>.

Doner, Richard F. (1991), *Driving a Bargain: Automobile Industrialization and Japanese Firms in Southeast Asia* (Berkeley: University of California Press).

Doner, Richard F. (2009), *Politics of Uneven Development: Thailand's Economic Growth in Comparative Perspective* (Cambridge: Cambridge University Press).

Doner, Richard F. (2015a), "Success as Trap? Crises and Challenges in Export-Oriented Southeast Asia," in T. J. Pempel and Keiichi Tsunekawa (eds.), *Two Crises,*

Different Outcomes: East Asia and Global Finance (Cornell Studies in Political Economy; Ithaca, NY: Cornell University Press), 163–184.

Doner, Richard F. (2015b), "Employer and Business Associations in ASEAN: Managing Opportunities and Challenges of Regional Integration" (Geneva: International Labour Organization).

Doner, Richard F. (2016), "The Politics of Productivity Improvement: Quality Infrastructure and the Middle-Income Trap," *Thammasat Economic Journal* 34(1), 1–56.

Doner, Richard F., Intarakumnerd, Patarapong, and Ritchie, Bryan (2010), "Higher Education and Thailand's National Innovation System," *The World Bank Regional Study on Higher Education* (Washington, DC: World Bank).

Doner, Richard F., Noble, Gregory W., and Ravenhill, John (2004), "Production Networks in East Asia's Automotive Parts Industry," in Shahid Yusuf, M. Anjum Altaf, and Kaoru Nabeshima (eds.), *Global Production Networking and Technological Change in East Asia* (Washington, DC: World Bank/Oxford University Press), 159–208.

Doner, Richard F., and Ricks, Jake (2017), "Tasks of Development: Beyond Technical Answers," *Institutions, Governance, and Economic Performance in East Asia Workshop* (Auckland, New Zealand).

Doner, Richard F., Ritchie, Bryan, and Slater, Dan (2005), "Systemic Vulnerability and the Origins of Developmental States: Northeast and Southeast Asia in Comparative Perspective," *International Organization* 59(2), 327–361.

Doner, Richard F., and Schneider, Ben Ross (2000), "Business Associations and Economic Development: Why Some Associations Contribute More Than Others," *Business and Politics* 2(3), 261–288.

Doner, Richard F., and Schneider, Ben Ross (2016), "The Middle-Income Trap: More Politics than Economics," *World Politics* 68(4), 608–644.

Dong, Yang (2014), "Tianjin zhongxin wenxianlou de bianqian [The move of the Tianjin Center's document building]," <http://www.caam.org.cn/blog/dongyang/archive/2014/05/29/tjzxwxldbq.aspx>.

DRC [Development Research Center of the State Council], SAE-CHINA [Society of Automotive Engineers of China], and VW China (2015), *Zhongguo Qiche Chanye Fazhan Baogao (2015) [2015 Chinese automobile industry report]* (Beijing: Shehui Kexue Wenxian Chubanshe).

DRC [Development Research Center of the State Council] (国务院发展研究中心), SAE-CHINA [Society of Automotive Engineers of China] (中国汽车工程学会), and VW China (大众汽车集团（中国）) VW China (2015), 中国汽车产业发展报告（2015）*[2015 Chinese automobile industry report].* 北京: 社会科学文献出版社].

Drive.com.au (2012), "Chinese Car Scores Zero in Crash Test," <https://www.youtube.com/watch?v=aTxbbvCf3zY>.

Dudley, Dominic (2019), "Iran's Auto Industry in Crisis Following Arrest of Senior Executives," *Forbes* 20 August, <https://www.forbes.com/sites/dominicdudley/2019/08/20/iran-auto-crisis/#289d92b947bf>.

Dunseith, Bradley (2018),"Thailand's Eastern Economic Corridor—What You Need to Know," *ASEAN Briefing* (updated June 29, 2018), <https://www.aseanbriefing.com/news/2018/06/29/thailand-eastern-economic-corridor.html>.

Dutu, Richard (2015), "Making the Most of Natural Resources in Indonesia" (OECD Economics Department; Paris: OECD), <http://dx.doi.org/10.1787/5js cqqk421s-en>.

Economic Intelligence Center (2015), "Insight: Bridging Thailand's Labor Gap" (Bangkok: Siam Commercial Bank), <https://222.scbeic.com/en/detail/file/product/1251/e22mx3krw/ENG_labor_insight_Q1_2015.pdf>.

Economist Intelligence Unit (2010), "Vietnam: Automotive Report," May 21, <http://viewswire.eiu.com.proxy.library.library.emory.edu/index.asp?layout>.

Edwards, Chris (1993), "State Intervention and Industrialisation in South Korea: Lessons For Malaysia," in K. S. Jomo (ed.), *Industrialising Malaysia: Policy, Performance, Prospects* (London: Routledge), 302–315.

EIBN [EU-Indonesia Business Network] (2015), "EIBN Sector Reports: Automotive," <indonesian.ahk.de/dileadmin/ahk_Publications/EIBNSecRep2015_Auto_FULL.pdg>.

Eichengreen, Barry, Perkins, Dwight H., and Sin, Kwan-ho (2012), *From Miracle to Maturity: The Growth of the Korean Economy* (Harvard East Asia monographs; Cambridge, MA: Harvard University Asia Center, distributed by Harvard University Press).

European Automobile Manufacturers' Association (2010), "Competitiveness and Prospects of the Slovak Automotive Industry in the EU," <http://www.acea.be/images/uploads/pr/SK_Presentation_March20.pdf>.

Evans, Peter (1995), *Embedded Autonomy: States and Industrial Transformation* (Princeton, NJ: Princeton University Press).

Evans, Peter, and Rauch, James E. (1999), "Bureaucracy and Growth: A Cross-National Analysis of the Effects of 'Weberian' State Structures on Economic Growth," *American Sociological Review* 64, 748–765.

Fan, Emma Xiaoqin (2002), "Technological Spillovers from Foreign Direct Investment—A Survey" (Manila: Asian Development Bank), ERD Working Paper Series 33, <https://www.adb.org/sites/default/files/publication/28326/wp033.pdf>.

Fane, George, and Warr, Peter (2008), "Agricultural Protection in Indonesia," *Bulletin of Indonesian Economic Studies* 44(1), 133–150.

Fashoyin, Tayo (2003), "Social Dialogue and Labour Market Performance in the Philippines" (InFocus Programme on Social Dialogue; Geneva: International Labour Office), February.

Federation of Asian Die and Mold Associations (FADMA) (2007), "Federation of Asian Die & Mold Assoications Country Members Report Year 2007," <www.ctma.com/documents/FADMACountryReport-2007.pdf>.

Feigenbaum, Evan A. (2003), *China's Techno-Warriors: National Security and Strategic Competition from the Nuclear to the Information Age* (Stanford, CA: Stanford University Press).

Felker, Greg (1999), "Malaysia's Innovation System: Actors, Interests and Governance," in K. S. Jomo and Greg Felker (eds.), *Technology, Competitiveness, and the State: Malaysia's Industrial Technology Policies* (London: Routledge), 98–147.

Felker, Greg, and Jomo, K. S. (1999), "Introduction," in K. S. Jomo and Greg Felker (eds.), *Technology, Competitiveness, and the State: Malaysia's Industrial Technology Policies* (London: Routledge), 1–37.

Felker, Greg B., and Jomo, K. S. (2003), "New Approahces to Investment Policy in the ASEAN-4," in K. S. Jomo (ed.), *Southeast Asian Paper Tigers? From Miracle to Debacle and Beyond* (London; New York: RoutledgeCurzon), 81–125.

Fellman, Joshua (2013), "Geely Auto Reaches Accord with BNP for Vehicle-Financing Venture," *BloombergBusiness*, <http://www.bloomberg.com/news/articles/2013-12-16/geely-auto-reaches-accord-with-bnp-for-vehicle-financing-venture>.

Focus2move (2020), "Global auto market. The ranking by manufacturer in 2019," <https://focus2move.com/world-car-group-ranking/>, January 15.

FOURIN (2013), "Shin-ene tesuto, Shanghaishi de chūgoku hatsu to naru shin-ene sha senmon no tesuto kikan o setsuritsu, shin-ene sha no kikaku sakutei oyobi tesuto kasoku [First specialized new energy vehicle testing agency established; accelerated standard setting and testing of new energy vehicles]," *Chūgoku Jidōsha Chōsa Geppō* (203), 32–33.

Frieden, J., and Rogowski, R. (1996), "The Impact of the International Economy on National Policies: An Analytical Overview," in Robert O. Keohane and Helen V. Milner (eds.), *Internationalization and Domestic Politics* (Cambridge; New York: Cambridge University Press), 25–47.

Gadacz, Oles (2001), "At Kia, the Push Is for a Separate Identity," *Automotive News*, December 24, <http://www.autonews.com/article/20011224/SEO/112240721&template=printart>.

Gaikindo (2014), "Indonesian Automotive Industry Report on 2013 Auto Market" (Beijing: Presentation to 20th APEC Automotive Dialogue), April 23–25, <http://mddb.apec.org/Documents/2014/AD/AD1/14_ad1_051.pdf>.

Gaikindo (Association of Indonesian Automotive Industry) (2020), "Government Policy on Future Automotive Technology," <Gaikindo.or.id/wp-content/uploads/2019/07/01-Dirjen-LLmate_Seng-Siang-GOVERNMENT-POLICY-ON-FUTURE-AUTOMOTIVE-TECHNOLOGY-GIAS>.

Gamboa, Rey (2019), "Car Program Headed for an Epic Fail?," *PhilStar Global*, November 14, <https://www.philstar.com/business/2019/11/14/1968501/cars-program-headed-epic-fail>.

Gao, Wei, and Liu, Jing (2014), "Zhao Hang: Zhichi yi fa zhi chehangye guanli jian 'qu zhengce' [Zhao Hang: I support using law to manage the auto industry, gradually getting rid of 'policy']" (updated September 6), <http://auto.sina.com.cn/news/2014-09-06/22321329811.shtml>.

Gao, Xiaoping, Guo, Xiaoge, and Liu, Qian (2018), "Guangdong ni dazao qianyi qing ranliao dianchi che chanye lian [Guangdong planning to establish a 100 billion RMB industry for hydrogen fuel cell vehicles]," *Nanfangwang*, September 12, <http://news.southcn.com/gd/content/2018-09/12/content_183280476.htm>.

Garver, John W. (2015), *Protracted Contest: Sino-Indian Rivalry in the Twentieth Century* (Seattle: University of Washington Press).

Ge, Bangning (2010), "Zhu Dezhao: Zhongguo qiche jishu yanjiu zhongxin chuangjian zhi shimo [Zhu Dezhao: The whole story of the creation of CATARC]" (updated December 28), <http://auto.sohu.com/20101228/n278555408.shtml>.

George, Jacob (2015), "Quality Requirements of the Chinese Consumer" (updated November 11), <http://www.umtri.umich.edu/sites/default/files/Jacob.George.JDPower.China_.2015.pdf>.

Gereffi, Gary (2005), "The Global Economy: Organization, Governance and Development," in Neil Smelser and Richard Swedberg (eds.), *Handbook of Economic Sociology* (2nd ed.; Princeton, NJ: Princeton University Press), 160–182.

Gereffi, Gary (2014), "Global Value Chains in a Post-Washington Consensus World," *Review of International Political Economy* 21(1), 9–37.

Ghazali, Azhar (1994), "A Truly Malaysian Car in 10–15 Years," *Business Times*, August 2, <http://global.factiva.com.virtual.anu.edu.au/hp/printsavews.aspx?ppstype=Article&pp=Print&hc=Publication>.

Gibbs, Nick (2014), "A Surge in Suppliers," *Automotive Manufacturing Solutions*, February 21, <http://www.automotivemanufacturingsolutions.com/focus/surge-in-suppliers>.

Gill, Indermit Singh, Kharas, Homi J., and Bhattasali, Deepak (2007), *An East Asian Renaissance: Ideas for Economic Growth* (Washington, DC: World Bank).

Gombar, Vandana (2019), "India Can 'Leapfrog' to an Electric Car Fleet: Q&A" (updated June 25), <https://about.bnef.com/blog/india-can-leapfrog-electric-car-fleet-qa/>.

Gomez, Edmund Terence (2002), *Political Business in East Asia* (Politics in Asia series; London; New York: Routledge).

Gomez, Edmund Terence, and Jomo, K. S. (1997), *Malaysia's Political Economy: Politics, Patronage, and Profits* (Cambridge: Cambridge University Press).

Goodman, Peter S. (2019), "Philippine Peasants Were Promised Land: Staking a Claim Can Be Deadly," *New York Times*, December 27, <https://www.nytimes.com/2019/12/27/business/philippines-duterte-poverty-farmers.html?searchResultPosition=1>.

Graham, Edward M. (2003), *Reforming Korea's Industrial Conglomerates* (Washington, DC: Institute for International Economics).

Grant, Robert M. (1996), "Toward a Knowledge-Based Theory of the Firm," *Strategic Management Journal* 17(S2), 109–122.

Green, Andrew E. (1992), "South Korea's Automobile Industry: Development and Prospects," *Asian Survey* XXXII(5), 411–248.

Green, William H., et al. (2019), "Insights Into Future Mobility: A Report from the Mobility of the Future Study," <http://energy.mit.edu/wp-content/uploads/2019/11/Insights-into-Future-Mobility.pdf>.

Greenwald, Bruce, and Stiglitz, Joseph E. (2012), "Industrial Policies, the Creation of a Learning Society, and Economic Development," *International Economic Association/World Bank Industrial Policy Roundtable* (Washington, DC).

Greimel, Hans (2009), "Hyundai Suffers Rare Setback, Pulls out of Japan," *Automotive News*, November 30, <http://www.autonews.com/apps/pbcs.dll/article?AID=/20091130/GLOBAL/911309989/1117&template=printart>.

Grindle, Merilee Serrill (2004), *Despite the Odds: The Contentious Politics of Education Reform* (Princeton, NJ: Princeton University Press).

Guillén, Mauro F. (2001), *The Limits of Convergence: Globalization and Organizational Change in Argentina, South Korea, and Spain* (Princeton, NJ: Princeton University Press).

Guo, Suhuan (2014), "2014 Qijiche gongye jishu fudao tuiguang jihua chengguo fabiaohui: Changshang relie canyu chengguo fengshuo [Conference announces results of 2014 auto and motorcyle industry technology support and promotion plan: Manufacturers participate enthusiastically, results are rich]," <http://www.artc.org.tw/chinese/03_service/03_02detail.aspx?pid=2697&nPage=1&syear=&skind1=&skind2=&skeyword=>.

Guo, Xiaoge (2015), "Jiu shi? Jinnian xiaoliang huo fuzengzhang [Save the market? This year sales may contract]", *Nanfangwang*, September 17, <http://car.southcn.com.grkpromos.com/7/2015-09/17/content_132986796.htm>.

Haggard, Stephan (2004), "On Governing the Market," *Issues & Studies* 40(1), 1–28.

Haggard, Stephan (2018), *Developmental States* (Cambridge: Cambridge University Press).

Haggard, Stephan, Kim, Byung-Kook, and Moon, Chung-In (1991), "The Transition to Export-Led Growth in South Korea: 1954–1966," *Journal of Asian Studies* 50(4), 850–873.

Haggard, Stephan, and Kim, Euysung (1997), "The Sources of East Asia's Economic Growth," *Access Asia Review* 1(1), 35–70.

Hagon, Toby (2010), "$250m Tax Bill Puts Toyota in the Red," *Sydney Morning Herald*, July 6, <http://www.smh.com.au/business/250m-tax-bill-puts-toyota-in-the-red-20100705-zxl6.html>.

Hall, Peter A., and Soskice, David W. (2001), "An Introduction to Varieties of Capitalism," in Peter A. Hall and David W. Soskice (eds.), *Varieties of Capitalism: The Institutional Foundations of Comparative Advantage* (Oxford: Oxford University Press), 1–68.

Han, Enze, and Thies, Cameron (2019), "External Threats, Internal Challenges, and State Building in East Asia," *Journal of East Asian Studies* 19(3), 339–360.

Hansen, Arve (2016), "Driving Development? The Problems and Promises of the Car in Vietnam," *Journal of Contemporary Asia* 46(4), 551–569.

Haraguchi, Nobuya (2010), "Impact of the Global Economic Crisis on the Thai Automotive Industry: From the Perspective of the Interplay between Shocks and the Industrial Structure" (Working Paper, 07/2009; Vienna: UNIDO, Research and Statistics Branch).

Haron, Sharif (1993), "Proton Left-Hand Drive Market Entry Timely", *Business Times*, November 15.

Harris, Bryan (2016), "Samsung to Pay $8bn for US Car Tech Group Harman," *Financial Times*, November 14, <https://www.ft.com/content/d22bb4e8-aa3b-11e6-809d-c9f98a0cf216>.

Harris, Bryan (2017), "South Korea Seeks to Boost Motorists' Interest in Electric Cars," *Financial Times*, February 12, <https://www.ft.com/content/2df59014-f0f5-11e6-8758-6876151821a6>.

Harwit, Eric (1995), *China's Automobile Industry: Policies, Problems, and Prospects* (Armonk, NY: M. E. Sharpe).

Hasan, Rumy (1997), "The Continuing Importance of Economies of Scale in the Automotive Industry," *European Business Review* 97(1), 38–42.

Hausmann, Ricardo, and Rodrik, Dani (2002), "Economic Development as Self-Discovery" (National Bureau of Economic Research) Working Paper 8952, 2002, <http://www.nber.org/papers/w8952>.

Hayworth, Philip (2017.), "TVET: The Clue to Guide Us through the 'Thailand 4.0' Labyrinth," *Bangkok Post*, November 13, <https://www.bangkokpost.com/business/1359827/tvet-the-clue-to-guide-us-through-the-thailand-4-0-labyrinth>.

Heilmann, Sebastian, and Shih, Lea (2013), "The Rise of Industrial Policy in China, 1978–2012" (Cambridge, MA: Harvard-Yenching Institute Working Paper Series).

Her, Kelly (2008), "In the Driver's Seat," *Taiwan Review* 58(5), <https://taiwantoday.tw/news.php?unit=8,29,32,45&post=12832>.

Hewison, Kevin, and Tularak, Woradul (2013), "Thailand and Precarious Work: An Assessment," *American Behavioral Scientist* 57, 444–467.

Hicken, Allen (2008), "Politics of Economic Recovery in Thailand and the Philippines," in Andrew MacIntyre, T. J. Pempel, and John Ravenhill (eds.), *Crisis as a Catalyst: Asia's Dynamic Political Economy* (Ithaca, NY: Cornell University Press), 206–230.

Hicks, Jacqueline (2012), "A False Start? Indonesian Business Associations as Democratic Actors in the Immediate Post-Soeharto Era," *Indonesian Studies Working Papers*, 15, 12.

Hill, Hal (2012), "Malaysian Economic Development: Looking Backward and Forward," in Hal Hill, Siew Yean Tham, and Zin Ragayah Haji Mat (eds.), *Malaysia's Development Challenges: Graduating from the Middle* (London: Routledge), 1–42.

Hirsh, Evan R., and Jaruzelski, Barry H. (2015), *The 2014 Global Innovation 1000: Automotive Industry Findings* (New York: Strategy&PWC.com).

Hirst, Paul, and Thompson, Grahame (2009), *Globalization in Question* (3rd ed.; Malden, MA: Polity Press).

Hock, Lee Kiong, and Nagaraj, Shyamala (2012), "The Crisis in Education," in Hal Hill, Siew Yean Tham, and Zin Ragayah Haji Mat (eds.), *Malaysia's Development Challenges: Graduating from the Middle* (London: Routledge), 215–232.

Hood, Christopher, and Dixon, Ruth (2015), *A Government That Worked Better and Cost Less?: Evaluating Three Decades of Reform and Change in UK Central Government* (New York: Oxford University Press).

Horikane, Yumi (2005), "The Political Economy of Heavy Industrialization: The Heavy and Chemical Industry (HCI) Push in South Korea in the 1970s," *Modern Asian Studies* 39(2), 369–397.

Howard, Keith, and Zhu, Ping (2019), "China's Ever-Tightening Fuel Consumption Regulations" (updated February 28), <https://360.lubrizol.com/2019/Chinas-Ever-Tightening-Fuel-Consumption-Regulations>.

howsafeisyourcar.com.au (2017), "Five Stars Continue for Chinese Marques" (updated October 30) <http://www.howsafeisyourcar.com.au/News/2017/Five-stars-continue-for-Chinese-marques/>.

Hsieh, Michelle F. (2015), "The Creative Role of the State and Entrepreneurship: The Case of Taiwan," in Edmund Terence Gomez, et al. (eds.), *Government-Linked Companies and Sustainable, Equitable Development* (Routledge Malaysian studies series; London; New York: Routledge, Taylor & Francis Group), 60–82.

Hsin Chong Machinery Works (n.d.), "Corporate Overview: Research and Development," <http://www.hsinchonggroup.com/e/aboutus5.asp>.

Hu, Angang, and Men, Honghua (2004), "The Rising of Modern China: Comprehensive National Power and Grand Strategy (1980–2000)," in *Rising*

China and the East Asian Economy (Seoul: KIEP [Korea Institute for International Economic Policy]), 19–20 March.

Hu, Xuhui (2006), "'Duli pinpai' Shoukuan suoding qingke Yulong qiaojie Dongfeng ['Independent Brand' settles on light bus for first model—Yulong cleverly makes use of Dongfeng]," *21 Shiji Jingji Baodao*, <http://auto.sohu.com/20060803/n244605067.shtml>.

Huang, Echo (2019), "Venture Capital to China's Electric Vehicle Startups Has Dropped Nearly 90%," June 20. <https://qz.com/1648609/vc-cash-to-chinas-electric-car-startups-drops-nearly-90/>.

Huang, Shuhui (2013), "Tiweixi: Kewang chuxian huoli [TYC looks to earn a profit]," *Lianhe Wanbao*, June 21, 2013, <http://udn.com/NEWS/STOCK/STO4/7978338.shtml#ixzz2ZIHEzPxC>

Huang, Wencheng (2007), "Taiwan qiche gongye de fazhan guocheng ji fazhan qiche dianzi de jihuidian [The development of the Taiwan auto industry and opportunities to develop the auto electronics industry]" (Taipei: Zhonghua Qiche), February 9.

Huang, Yasheng (2002), "Between Two Coordination Failures: Automotive Industrial Policy in China with a Comparison to Korea," *Review of International Political Economy* 9(3), 538–573.

Hubbard, Paul (2015), "Where Have China's State Monopolies Gone?" EABER Working Paper Series, Paper No. 115 (Canberra: Crawford School of Economics and Government, ANU College of Asia and the Pacific, Australian National University), November 30, <http://www.eaber.org/sites/default/files/documents/EABER%20Working%20Paper%20115%20Hubbard.pdf>.

Huey, Yap Lih (2004), "Perodua Collaborates with Proton on Campro Engine," *The Edge Malaysia*, June 11.

Hufbauer, Gary Clyde, and Schott, Jeffrey J. (2005), *NAFTA Revisited: Achievements and Challenges* (Washington, DC: Institute for International Economics).

Humphrey, John, and Schmitz, Hubert (2002), "How Does Insertion in Global Value Chains Affect Upgrading in Industrial Clusters?," *Regional Studies* 36(9), 1017–1027.

Hutchcroft, Paul (1991), "Oligarchs and Cronies in the Philippine State: The Politics of Patrimonial Plunder," *World Politics* 43(3), 414–450.

Hutchcroft, Paul (1994), "Booty Capitalism: Business-Government Relations in the Philippines," in Andrew MacIntyre (ed.), *Business and Government in Industrializing Asia* (Ithaca, NY: Cornell University Press), 216–267.

Hutchinson, Francis Edward (2008), "'Developmental' States and Economic Growth at the Sub-National Level: The Case of Penang," *Southeast Asian Affairs 2008* (ISEAS–Yusof Ishak Institute), 223–244.

Hwang, Wen Fang (2013), *Current Development of Taiwan Automobile Industry* (Taipei: Taiwan Transportation Vehicle Manufacturers Association).

Hyun, young-suk (2020), "Catch-up to Lead in Korea's Automobile Industry," in Alex Covarrubias, V. Sigfrido, and M. Ramírez Perez (eds.), *New Frontiers of the Automobile Industry: Exploring Geographies, Technology, and Institutional Challenges* (Cham, Switzerland: Palgrave MacMillan), 229–254.

Hyundai (2017), "Hyundai Motor Reports 2016 Full Year Global Sales" (updated January 5, 2017), <https://www.hyundai.com/worldwide/en/about-hyundai/news-room/news/hyundai-motor-reports-2016-full-year-global-sales-0000006581?pageNo=1>.

Hyundai Motor Company (2015), *Annual Report 2014* (Seoul: Hyundai Motor Company).

Hyundai Motor Company (2020), Hyundai Motor Company and its Subsidiaries: Consolidated Financial Statements as of and for the Years Ended December 31, 2019 and 2018, <https://www.hyundai.com/content/dam/hyundai/ww/en/images/company/ir/financial-statements/hyundai_motor-company-1h-2019-consolidated-final.pdf>.

IBISWorld (2016), "IBISWorld Industry Report: Auto Parts Manufacturing in China," <https://www.ibisworld.com/gosample.aspx?cid=86&rtid=1>.

IBISWorld (2017), "IBISWorld Industry Report: Auto Parts Manufacturing in China," July 2017, <https://www.ibisworld.com/gosample.aspx?cid=86&rtid=101>.

IHS Markit (2015), "Manufacturers Urge Thai Govt to Rethink Eco-Car Strategy, PM Anxious over Scheme" (March 25), <https://ihsmarkit.com/country-industry-forecasting.html?ID=1065998897>.

Indonesian Commercial Newsletter (2004), "Auto Market Expanding in Indonesia," *Indonesian Commercial Newsletter*, January 13.

Indrawanto (2013), "Toward the Establishment of Indonesian Automotive Research and Development Institute (INARD)" (2nd Asian Automotive Institute Summit, Denpasar, Bali, November 25–27, 2013), <http://www.jari.jp/Portals/0/resource/pdf/AAI%20Summit/H25/1.%20INARDO.pdf>.

Industry Commission (1990), "Strategic Trade Theory: The East Asian Experience" (Canberra: Commonwealth of Australia, Industry Commission), November. <https://www.pc.gov.au/research/supporting/east-asian-trade/east-asian-trade.pdf>.

Intarakumnerd, Patarapong (2011), "Two Models of Research Technology Organisations in Asia," *Science, Technology, and Society* 16(1), 11–28.

Intarakumnerd, Patarapong (2018), *Mismanaging Innovation Systems: Thailand and the Middle-Income Trap* (London: Routledge).

Intarakumnerd, Patarapong, and Charoenporn, Peera (2013a), "The Roles of Intermediaries and the Development of Their Capabilities in Sectoral Innovation

Systems: A Case Study of Thailand," *Asian Journal of Technology Innovation* 21(sup2), 99–114.

Intarakumnerd, Patarapong, and Charoenporn, Peera (2013b), "The Roles of Intermediaries in Sectoral Innovation System in Developing Countries: Public Organizations versus Private Organizations," *Asian Journal of Technology Innovation* 21(1), 108–119.

Intarakumnerd, Patarapong, Gerdsri, Nathasit, and Teekasap, Pard (2012), "The Roles of External Knowledge Sources in Thailand's Automotive Industry," *Asian Journal of Technology Innovation* 20(S1), 85–97.

International Labour Organization (2005), "Motor Vehicle Industry Trends Affecting Component Suppliers" (Geneva: ILO Sectoral Activities Programme), Report for Discussion at the Tripartite Meeting on Employment, Social Dialogue, Rights at Work and Industrial Relations in Transport Equipment Manufacturing.

International Monetary Fund (2015), "Malaysia: Selected Issues" (IMF Country Report; Washington DC: IMF) <https://www.elibrary.imf.org/view/IMF002/21226-9781475529852/21226-9781475529852/21226-9781475529852_A002.xml>.

Investments, Indonesia (2018), "Automotive Manufacturing Industry Indonesia," <www.indonesia-investment.com/business/industries-sectors/automotive-industry/item6047?>.

Itoh, Munehiko, et al. (2018), *Automobile Industry Supply Chain in Thailand* (Singapore: Springer Singapore).

ITRI (2013), "ITRI 2013 Annual Report" (Hsinchu: Industrial Technology Research Institute), <https://www.itri.org.tw/eng/Content/Publications/book_abstract.aspx?&SiteID=1&MmmID=617731525164776565&CatID=617756020516072343>.

ITRI (2018), "ITRI 2018 Annual Report" (Hsinchu: Industrial Technology Research Institute), <https://www.itri.org.tw/eng/Content/Publications/book_abstract.aspx?&SiteID=1&MmmID=617731525164776565&CatID=617756020516072343>.

Iwahara, Taku (1995), *Chūgoku jidōsha sangyō nyūmon* [*An introduction to the Chinese automobile industry*] (Tokyo: Tōyō Keizai Shinpōsha).

J. D. Power and Associates (2010), "2009: Initial Quality Results," <http://www.jdpower.com/autos/articles/2009-Initial-Quality-Study-Results/page-2>.

J. D. Power and Associates (2018), "New-Vehicle Initial Quality Improves Again, J. D. Power Finds," <https://www.jdpower.com/business/press-releases/2018-us-initial-quality-study-iqs>.

J. D. Power and Associates (2019), "New-Vehicle Quality in China Drastically Improves, J. D. Power Finds" (updated August 8), <https://canada.jdpower.com/press-release/2019-china-initial-quality-study-en>.

Jacobs, Alan M. (2011), *Governing for the Long Term: Democracy and the Politics of Investment* (Cambridge; New York: Cambridge University Press).

Jang, Desung, Han, Sang do, and Lee, Seung Jin (1999), "Hankuk Jadongcha Bupum-hymbruk-upch Haek-sim Gongkup-Kuenheng-e Hyung-gu [Study of the Core Supply Practices of Korean Automobile Parts Manufacturers]," *Korea Academic Society of Business Administration* 28(2), 281–302.

Jansen, Karel (1997a), *External Finance in Thailand's Development: An Interpretation of Thailand's Growth Boom* (New York: St. Martin's Press).

Jansen, Karel (1997b), "The Macroeconomic Effects of Direct Foreign Investment: The Case of Thailand," *World Development* 23(2), 193–210.

Jayasankaran, S. (1993), "Made-in-Malaysia: The Proton Project," in K. S. Jomo (ed.), *Industrialising Malaysia: Policy, Performance, Prospects* (London: Routledge), 272–285.

Jeenanunta, Chavalit, Kasemsontitum, Boontariga, and Techakanont, Kriengkrai (2012), "Supply Chain Collaboration and Innovation: Case Study on Promoting Capital Goods in Thailand" (Wiring Innovation Networks: How Networks Upgrade Innovation Capacity in East Asia; Bangkok: ERIA Supporting Study Project Report 2011 [March]).

JETRO (2019), "自動車部品の生産は堅調も部材の現地調達難は続く（メキシコ）," (海外ビジネス情報; Tokyo: JETRO), May 8.

Jimenez, Emmanuel, Nguyen, Vy, and Patrinos, Harry Anthony (2012), "Stuck in the Middle? Human Capital Development and Economic Growth in Malaysia and Thailand" (Washington, DC: World Bank) Policy Research Working Paper 6283, November.

Jittapong, Khettiya (2014), "Thai Auto Sector Slams on Brakes as Political Crisis Rumbles on," *Reuters World News*, May.

Johnson, Chalmers (1982), *MITI and the Japanese Miracle: The Growth of Industrial Policy, 1925–1975* (Stanford, CA: Stanford University Press).

Johnson, Chalmers A. (1962), *Peasant Nationalism and Communist Power: The Emergence of Revolutionary China, 1937–1945* (Stanford, CA: Stanford University Press).

Johnston, Alastair Iain (1995), *Cultural Realism: Strategic Culture and Grand Strategy in Chinese History* (Princeton, NJ: Princeton University Press).

Jomo, K. S. (1994), "The Proton Saga: Malaysian Car, Mitsubishi Gain," in K. S. Jomo (ed.), *Japan and Malaysian Development: In the Shadow of the Rising Sun* (London: Routledge), 263–290.

Jomo, K. S. (2007), "Industrialization and Industrial Policy in Malaysia," in K. S. Jomo (ed.), *Malaysian Industrial Policy* (Singapore: NUS Press), 1–35.

Jones, Leroy P. (1975), *Public Enterprise and Economic Development: The Korean Case* (Seoul: Korea Development Institute).

Jordan, Luke Simon, and Koinis, Katerina (2014), *Flexible Implementation: A Key to Asia's Transformation* (Honolulu: East-West Center).

Jun, Soo Wern (2020), "Minister Says Unsure What Happened to RM20m Given to Third National Car Company," *Malay Mail*, 5 August, <https://www.malaymail.com/news/malaysia/2020/08/05/deputy-minister-says-unsure-what-happened-to-rm20m-given-to-third-national/1891145>.

Jung, Suk-yee (2018), "S. Korean Car Exports to U.S. Falling Despite KORUS FTA," *Business Korea*, <http://www.businesskorea.co.kr/news/articleView.html?idxno=22573>.

Jürgens, Ulrich, and Krzywdzinski, Martin (2015), "Competence Development on the Shop Floor and Industrial Upgrading: Case Studies of Auto Makers in China," *The International Journal of Human Resource Management* 26(9): 1204–1225. doi: 10.1080/09585192.2014.934888.

Jürgens, Ulrich, and Krzywdzinski, Martin (2016), *New Worlds of Work: Varieties of Work in Car Factories in the BRIC Countries* (Oxford: Oxford University Press).

Kaldor, Nicholas (1957), "A Model of Economic Growth," *Economic Journal* 67(268), 591–624.

Kang, David C. (2002), *Crony Capitalism: Corruption and Development in South Korea and the Philippines* (Cambridge: Cambridge University Press).

Kaufmann, Daniel, Kraay, Aart, and Mastruzzi, Massimo (2010), "The Worldwide Governance Indicators: Methodology and Analytical Issues" (Washington, DC: World Bank) World Bank Policy Research Working Paper 5430, September, <https://ssrn.com/abstract=1682130>.

Keller, William W., and Samuels, Richard J. (2003), "Innovation and the Asian Economies," in William W. Keller and Richard J. Samuels (eds.), *Crisis and Innovation in Asian Technology* (Cambridge, UK: Cambridge University Press), 1–22.

Kellerman, Martin (2019), *Ensuring Quality to Gain Access to Global Markets: A Reform Toolkit* (Washington, DC: World Bank).

Kendall, Kris (2018), "Semiconductors in Automotive," <https://blog.lamresearch.com/semiconductors-in-automotive/>.

Kenney, Martin, and Florida, Richard (eds.) (2004), *Locating Global Advantage: Industry Dynamics in the International Economy* (Stanford, CA: Stanford University Press).

KFW Entwicklungsbank (2005), "Thailand: Thai-German Institute Ex-Post Evaluation" (Frankfurt am Main: KFW Entwicklungsbank), <https://www.kfw-entwicklungsbank.de/Evaluierung/Ergebnisse-und-Publikationen/PDF-Dokumente-R-Z/Thailand_Thai_German_Institute_2005.pdf>.

Kharas, Homi, and Gill, Indermit (2019), "Out with the Old: Growth Strategies for Middle-Income Countries," *Workshop on "Trapped in the Middle" Developmental Challenges for Middle-Income Countries* (Madrid).

Kiang Shen Corporation (n.d.), "Gongsi gaikuang [Company overview]," <http://www.kian-shen.com/newsshow.asp?id=230>.

Kim, Chuk Kyo, and Lee, Chul Heui (1983), "Anciliary Firm Development in the Korean Automobile Industry," in Konosuke Odaka (ed.), *The Motor Vehicle Industry in Asia: A Study of Ancillary Firm Development* (Singapore: Published for Council for Asian Manpower Studies by Singapore University Press), 286–420.

Kim, Eun Mee (1988), "From Dominance to Symbiosis: State and *Chaebol* in Korea," *Pacific Focus* III(2), 105–121.

Kim, Eun Mee (1997), *Big Business, Strong State: Collusion and Conflict in South Korean Development, 1960–1990* (SUNY series in Korean studies; Albany: State University of New York Press).

Kim, Hyun-Jeong (2000), "The Korean Automobile Industry: Vertical Disintegration and Competitive Success," Ph.D. thesis, Fitzwilliam College, University of Cambridge.

Kim, Jaewon (2018), "South Korean Auto Suppliers Struggle to Survive," *Nikkei Asian Review*, December 19, <https://asia.nikkei.com/Business/Business-trends/South-Korean-auto-suppliers-struggle-to-survive>.

Kim, Jim Yong (2017), "Indonesia's Future Depends on its Investments Now," *The Jakarta Post*, July 27, <www.worldbank.org/en/news/opinion/2017/07/27/indonesia-future-depends-on-its-investments-now.html>.

Kim, Jong-Cheol (2009), "The Rise and Fall of Daewoo: The Making and Unmaking of the High-debt Firm in Korea," Ph.D. thesis, University of California, Berkeley.

Kim, Kyung Mi, and Kwon, Hyeong-Ki (2017), "The State's Role in Globalization: Korea's Experience from a Comparative Perspective," *Politics & Society* 45(4), 505–531.

Kim, Sung-Young, and Thurbon, Elizabeth (2015), "Developmental Environmentalism: Explaining South Korea's Ambitious Pursuit of Green Growth," *Politics and Society* 43(2), 213–240.

Kis, Viktória, and Park, Eunah (2012), "A Skills beyond School Review of Korea" (Paris: Organization for Economic Cooperation and Development), OECD Reviews of Vocational Education and Training, <http://www.oecd.org/korea/SBS%20Korea.pdf>.

Klayman, Ben, and Yang, Heekyong (2020), "Exclusive: GM Warns Labor Unrest Making South Korea Untenable," *Reuters*, 18 November, <https://www.reuters.com/article/us-gm-southkorea-labor-exclusive-idUSKBN27Y0NR>.

Kohpaiboon, Archanun (2006), *Multinational Enterprises and Industrial Transformation: Evidence from Thailand* (Cheltenham, UK: Edward Elgar).

Kohpaiboon, Archanun, and Jongwanich, Juthathip (2013), "International Production Networks, Clusters, and Industrial Upgrading: Evidence from Automotive and Hard Disk Drive Industries in Thailand," *Review of Policy Research* 30(2), 211–239.

Kohpaiboon, Archanun, and Warr, Peter (2017), "Thailand's Manufacturing Corridor" (Manila: Asian Development Bank) ADB Working Paper 519, December.

Kondo, Hiroyuki (2012), *Auto Industry in Thailand and Automotive Human Resource Development* (Bangkok: JETRO, conference paper).

Korea Automobile Manufacturers Association (n.d.), *The Korean Automobile Market: Cooperation and Competition under Globalization* (Seoul: Korea Automobile Manufacturers Association).

Korea Herald (2016), "Renault's Korean Unit to Lead SUV Development," *Korea Herald*, December 22, <http://www.koreaherald.com/view.php?ud=20161222000856>.

Korea Institute of Science and Technology Evaluation and Planning (2014), "2014 Survey of Research and Development in Korea" (Seoul: Korea Institute of Science and Technology Evaluation and Planning), <http://www.kistep.re.kr/getFileDown. jsp?fileIdx=5926&contentIdx=9674&tbIdx=BRD_BOARD>.

Korth, Kim (2003), "Platform Reductions vs. Demands for Specialization," *Automotive Design and Production*.

KPMG (2014), "Indonesia's Automotive Industry: Navigating 2014," <https://www. kpmg.com/ID/en/IssuesAndInsights/Documents/Indonesias-Automotive-Industry-Navigating-2014.pdf>.

Krueger, Anne O. (1979), *The Developmental Role of the Foreign Sector and Aid* (Cambridge, MA: Harvard University Press, Studies in the Modernization of the Republic of Korea).

Krugman, Paul (1994), "Competitiveness: A Dangerous Obsession," *Foreign Affairs* 73, 28–44.

Kuhonta, Erik Martinez (2011), *The Institutional Imperative: The Politics of Equitable Development in Southeast Asia* (Stanford, CA: Stanford University Press).

Kummritz, Victor, Taglioni, Daria, and Winkler, Deborah (2017), "Economic Upgrading through Global Value Chain Participation: Which Policies Increase the Value Added Gains?" (Washington, DC: World Bank) Policy Research Working Paper 8007, March, <http://documents.worldbank.org/curated/en/567861489688859864/pdf/WPS8007.pdf>.

Kuozui (2019), "Company's Milestone," <http://www.kuozui.com.tw/company/history.htm>.

Kurtz, Marcus J., and Schrank, Andrew (2007), "Growth and Governance: Models, Measures, and Mechanisms," *Journal of Politics* 69(2), 538–554.

Kuznetsov, Yevgeny, and Sabel, Charles (2011), "New Open Economy Industrial Policy: Making Choices without Picking Winners," *World Bank PREMnote* (161), 1–9.

Kwon, Hyeong-Ki, and Kim, Kyung Mi (2020), "Varieties of Globalisation and National Economy: Korea's Experience from a Comparative Perspective," *Journal of International Relations and Development* 23, 728–754.

Lall, Sanjaya (1992), "Technological Capabilities and Industrialization," *World Development* 20, 165–186.

Lall, Sanjaya (2000), "Technological Change and Industrialization in the Asian Newly Industrialized Economies: Achievements and Challenges," in Linsu Kim and Richard R. Nelson (eds.), *Technology, Learning, and Innovation: Experiences of Newly Industrializing Economies* (New York: Cambridge University Press), 13–68.

Lall, Sanjaya, and Teubal, Morris (1998), "'Market-Stimulating' Technology Policies in Developing Countries: A Framework with Examples from East Asia," *World Development* 26(8), 1369–1385.

Lambert, Fred (2020), "Tesla Releases New Design Drawing, Announces Design Center to Build 'Chinese-Style' Car," *Electrek*, January 16, <https://electrek.co/2020/01/16/tesla-new-design-drawing-announces-design-center-chinese-style-car/>.

Langbein, Julia (2020), "Shallow Market Integration and Weak Developmental Capacities: Ukraine's Pathway from Periphery to Periphery," *Review of International Political Economy* 27(5), 1126–1146.

Lansbury, Russell D., So, Chung-sok, and Kwon, Su ng-ho (2007), *The Global Korean Motor Industry: The Hyundai Motor Company's Global Strategy* (Routledge advances in Korean studies; London: Routledge).

Lardy, Nicholas R. (2002), *Integrating China into the Global Economy* (Washington, DC: Brookings Institution Press).

Lardy, Nicholas R. (2014), *Markets over Mao: The Rise of Private Business in China* (Washington, DC: Peterson Institute for International Economics).

Lardy, Nicholas R. (2019), *The state strikes back: the end of economic reform in China?* Washington, DC: Peterson Institute for International Economics.

Larkin, Christopher (2017), "The Thai Government's Latest Gamble: Electric Vehicle Policy," *Frontera*, June 6, <https://frontera.net/news/asia/the-thai-governments-latest-gamble-electric-vehicle-policy/>.

Lateef, K. Sarwar (2016), "Evolution of the World Bank's Thinking on Governance" (Washington, DC: World Bank), Background Paper for 2017 World Development Report, January, <https://openknowledge.worldbank.org/bitstream/handle/10986/26197/112916-WP-PUBLIC-WDR17BPEvolutionofWBThinkingonGovernance.pdf?sequence=1&isAllowed=y>.

Lauridsen, Laurids S. (2008), *State, Institutions and Industrial Development: Industrial Deepening and Upgrading Policies in Taiwan and Thailand Compared*, Vol. 2 (Aachen: Shaker Verlag).

Lautier, Marc (2001), "The International Development of the Korean Automobile Industry", in Frédérique Sachwald (ed.), *Going Multinational: The Korean Experience of Direct Investment* (London: Routledge), 207–273.

Le Hong Hiep (2019), *Vietnam's Industrialization Ambitions: The Case of Vingroup and the Automotive Industry* (Singapore: ISEAS—Yusof Ishak Institute).

Leaders Magazine (2015), "The World's Largest Automotive Glass Supplier," *Leaders Magazine* 38(4), 48–49.

Lee, Georgina (2020), "Tesla's Chinese competitor Xpeng completes debut with 41 per cent premium after upsizing IPO to US$1.5 billion" *South China Morning Post*, 28 August <https://www.scmp.com/business/companies/article/3099059/xpengs-us15-billion-ipo-largest-ever-chinese-electric-car-maker >.

Lee Hwok Aun (2004), "The NEP, Vision 2020 and Dr Mahathir," in Bridget Welsh (ed.), *Reflections: The Mahathir Years* (Washington, DC: Southeast Asia Studies Program, The Paul H. Nitze School of Advanced International Studies, Johns Hopkins University), 270–281.

Lee, Ji-yoon (2016), "Samsung Still Retains Automotive Ambition-프린트화면," *Korea Herald*, July 21, <http://www.koreaherald.com/common_prog/newsprint.php?ud=20160721000981&dt=2>.

Lee, Nae-Young (2011a), "The Vietnam War: South Korea's Search for National Security," in Pyŏng-guk Kim and Ezra F. Vogel (eds.), *The Park Chung Hee Era: The Transformation of South Korea* (Cambridge, MA: Harvard University Press), 403–429.

Lee, Nae-Young (2011b), "The Automobile Industry," in Pyŏng-guk Kim and Ezra F. Vogel (eds.), *The Park Chung Hee Era: The Transformation of South Korea* (Cambridge, MA: Harvard University Press), 295–321.

Leggett, Dave (2019), "Geely sales reach 2.178 million units in 2019." *just-auto*, 14 January <https://www.just-auto.com/news/geely-sales-reach-2178-million-units-in-2019_id193036.aspx>.

Leutert, Hans-Georg, and Sudhoff, Ralf (1999), "Technology Capacity Building in the Malaysian Automotive Industry," in K. S. Jomo, Greg Felker, and Rajah Rasiah (eds.), *Industrial Technology Development in Malaysia: Industry and Firm Studies* (London: Routledge), 247–273.

Lew, Seok-Jin (1992), "Bringing Capital Back In: A Case Study of the South Korean Automobile Industrialization," Ph.D. thesis, Yale University.

Lewis, Jeffrey D. (1994), "Indonesia's Industrial and Trade Policy during and after the Oil Boom" (Harvard Institute for International Development), Development Discussion Paper, June.

Li, Qingwen (2008), "Dong Yang changtan dazao shin zhongqixie [Dong Yang chats about creating the new CAAM]," *Zhongguo Qiche Bao* (updated April 8) <http://www.cnautotime.cn/news.php?rid=162&page=1>.

Li, Yiqiong, Sheldon, Peter, and Sun, Jian-Min (2011), "Education, Training and Skills," in Peter Sheldon et al. (eds.), *China's Changing Workplace* (New York: Routledge), 111–128.

Li, Zhaohua, et al. (2006), "Taiwan jidōsha sangyō no nōryoku kōchiku: Kokuzui Kisha no jirei [Capability construction in the Taiwan automobile industry: The case of Kuozui Motors]," *Akamon Management Review* 5(3), 171–209.

Li, Zhengzong (2009), "Zhongxiaoqiyechu tuidong qunju lianmeng gongyanyuan fudao zhixing [Small and Medium Enterprise Administration promotes cluster alliances—ITRI advises and implements]," *Jingji Ribao*, <http://edn.udn.com/article/view.jsp?aid=160273&cid=55#>.

Liang, Quincy (2003), "Kuozui Unveils Toyota's New Global Car in Taiwan," *CENS*, <http://www.cens.com/cens/html/en/news/news_inner_12378.html>.

Liang, Quincy (2012a), "Yulon Sees Higher ROI from Affiliated Dongfeng Nissan in China," *CENS*, July 3, <http://www.cens.com/cens/html/en/news/news_inner_40617.html>.

Liang, Quincy (2012b), "Yulon Nissan Posts 133% YoY Increase in 1st-half Earnings," *CENS*, <http://news.cens.com/cens/html/en/news/news_inner_41303.html>.

Liang, Quincy (2013), "Tong Yang May Become World's No. 1 Plastic Bumper Maker by 2014," *CENS*, <http://www.cens.com/cens/html/en/news/news_inner_43859.html>.

Liang, Quincy (2015), "Strong Global Demand Energizes Growth in Taiwan's Automotive-Electronic Production: ARTC," *CENS*, <http://www.cens.com/cens/html/en/news/news_inner_48295.html>.

Liao, Rita (2020), "China's electric SUV maker Li Auto raises $1.1 billion in US IPO." *Techcrunch*.

Lieberthal, Kenneth (2004), *Governing China: From Revolution to Reform* (2nd ed.; New York: W. W. Norton).

Lim, Anthony (2018), "Malaysia Aspires to Build Another National Car—Tun M," *Paultan.org* (updated June 11, 2018) <https://paultan.org/2018/06/11/malaysia-aspires-to-start-another-national-car-tun-m/>.

Lim, Chee Peng (1988), "The Proton Saga—No Reverse Gear! The Economic Burden of the Malaysian Car Project," in K. S. Jomo (ed.), *Mahathir's Economic Policies* (Kuala Lumpur: Insan, the Institute of Social Analysis), 48–62.

Limpaitoon, Achana (2013), "(Pres. of Thai Automotive Parts Association), Presentation to the 4th Kuala Lumpur International Automotive Conference (KLIAC)" (Kuala Lumpur).

Lin, Justin Yifu (2010), "Industrial Policy Comes Out of the Cold," <https://www.project-syndicate.org/commentary/industrial-policy-comes-out-of-the-cold>.

Lin, Shizhang (1997), "Taiwan jidōsha sangyō no hatten to kokunai shijō [The development of Taiwan's auto industry and the domestic market]," in Yoshinari Maruyama (ed.), *Shinpan Ajia no jidōsha sangyō* [*The Asian automobile industry, new edition*] (Tokyo: Aki Shobō), 231–266.

Lin, Zhengguo (2006), "Quanqiu shangpinlian xia Taiwan qiche dianzi chanye fazhan wangluo jiegou [Taiwanese Auto-tronic Industry Development Network Structure in Global Commodity Chain]," Master's thesis, National Zhongshan University.

Liu, Honglong (2014), "Zhengche qiye xishou gongguan qinglianghua jishu [Auto companies join hands to tackle lightening technology]," <www.cnautonews.com/qclbj/l_hy/201411/t20141105_332125.htm>.

Liu, J. M. (2011), "'C-NCAP zhi fu' Zhao Hang: Zui kunnan shi ye mei tuisuo ['Father of C-NCAP' Zhao Hang never shrank back even at the most trying times]," <http://auto.ifeng.com/news/expreview/20110307/561911.shtml>.

Liu, Philip (2017), "Taiwan Gearing Up for Driverless Cars," *Taiwan Business Topics*, <https://topics.amcham.com.tw/2017/12/taiwan-gearing-driverless-cars/>.

Long, Nguyen Duc Bao, Tan, Khong Sin, and Tran, Ho Lu Lam (2015), "Vietnam Automotive Industry Toward 2018," *International Journal of Business and Management Studies* 4(2), 191–204.

Lopez, Leslie (1996), "Malaysia's Auto Czar Cracks His Whip—Yahaya Pressures Partners and Part Suppliers, but Skepticism Lingers," *Asian Wall Street Journal*, August 12, <https://global-factiva-com.proxy.lib.uwaterloo.ca/ha/default.aspx#./!?&_suid=16060628462850512454369029496>.

Lopez, Leslie (1997), "Yahaya's Death Puts Succession Issue at Top of DRB-Hicom Group Agenda," *Asian Wall Street Journal*, March 5, <http://global.factiva.com.virtual.anu.edu.au/hp/printsavews.aspx?ppstype=Article&pp=Print&hc=Publication>.

Lu, Feng, and Feng, Kaidong (2005), *Fazhan woguo zizhu zhishi chanquan qiche gongye de zhengce xuanze [Policy choices for developing autonomous intellectual property rights for our country's auto industry]* (Beijing: Beijing daxue chubanshe).

Lye, Gerard (2017), "Tun Mahathir Saddened by Proton-Geely Agreement," *PaulTan.Org*, <https://paultan.org/2017/05/25/tun-mahathir-saddened-by-proton-geely-deal/>.

Lye, Gerard (2019), "Ministry Approves RM20 Million in Funding for New National Car Project to Attract the Private Sector," *Paul Tan's Automotive News*, <https://paultan.org/2019/01/08/ministry-approves-rm20-million-in-funding-for-new-national-car-project-to-attract-the-private-sector/>.

Ma, Jie (2016), "China's EV Boom Fueled by Government Fleet Purchases," *BloombergBusiness*, <http://www.bloomberg.com/news/articles/2016-03-01/china-electric-car-boom-driven-by-state-buying-bernstein-says>.

Machado, Kit G. (1994), "Proton and Malaysia's Motor Vehicle Industry: National Industrial Policies and Japanese Regional Production Strategies," in K. S. Jomo (ed.), *Japan and Malaysian Development: In the Shadow of the Rising Sun* (London: Routledge), 291–325.

Mahoney, James, and Goertz, Gary (2006), "A Tale of Two Cultures: Contrasting Quantitative and Qualitative Research," *Political Analysis* 14(03), 227–249.

Maikaew, Piyachart (2017), "Innovation, Alternative Fuel Hold Keys to Eco-Car Ambitions," *Bangkok Post*, January 5, <https://www.bangkokpost.com/business/1174669/innovation-alternative-fuel-hold-key-to-eco-car-ambitions>.

Malaysia (1971), "Second Malaysia Plan, 1971–1975" (Kuala Lumpur: Government Printers).

Malaysia (2006), "Third Industrial Master Plan (IMP3) 2006–20" (Kuala Lumpur: Ministry of International Trade and Industry), August 18.

Malaysia (2010), "Tenth Malaysia Plan 2011–2015" (Prime Minister's Department Economic Planning Unit; Putrajaya: Government of Malaysia).

Malaysian Motor Trader (2006), "A Missed Opportunity with VW. . . ," *Malaysian Motor Trader News*, January 25, <http://www.motortrader.com.my/NUS/articles/0/article_383/page_m.asp>.

Malaysian Motor Trader (2009), "Malaysian Motor: PM Confirms Volkswagen 'Not Interested'" (updated May 31), <http://www.motortrader.com.my/NUS/articles/article_957/page_m.asp>.

Malerba, Franco (2002), "Sectoral Systems of Innovation and Production," *Research Policy* 31(2), 247–264.

Manger, Mark (2005), "Competition and Bilateralism in Trade Policy: The Case of Japan's Free Trade Agreements," *Review of International Political Economy* 12(5), 804–828.

Mangulabnan, Bernard Paul M. (2015), "Documenting Practices in Human Resource Develpment Planning" (Monograph Series; Manila: Institute for Labor Studies).

Mani, Sunil (2011), "The Indian Automotive Industry: Enhancing Innovation Capability with External and Internal Resources," *2011 Atlanta Conference on Science and Innovation Policy* (Atlanta, GA).

Mani, Sunil (2013), "Outward Foreign Direct Investment from India and Knowledge Flows: The Case of Three Automotive Firms," *Asian Journal of Technology Innovation* 21(sup1), 25–38.

Mann, Jim (1989), *Beijing Jeep: The Short, Unhappy Romance of American Business in China* (New York: Simon and Schuster).

Mann, Jim (1997), *Beijing Jeep: A Case Study of Western Business in China* (Boulder, CO: Westview Press).

Mao, Zhuqing, Qu, Di, and Lee, Keun (forthcoming), "Global Value Chains, Industrial Policy, and Industrial Upgrading: Automotive Sectors in Malaysia, Thailand, and China in Comparison with Korea," *European Journal of Development Research*.

Maquito, Max (2008), "Policy Implications," unpublished conference paper presented to Sekiguchi Global Research Association: *Towards a Roadmap for Shared Growth through the Philippine Automotive Industry* (Manila).

Mardon, Russell (1990), "The State and the Effective Control of Foreign Capital: The Case of South Korea," *World Politics* 43(1), 111–137.

MARii (2020), "MARii and DEVhub Join Forces to Establish Strategic Talent Network for Future Industries," 10 September, <http://www.marii.my/post/marii-and-devhub-join-forces-to-establish-strategic-talent-network-for-future-industries>.

Markiewicz, Olga (2020), "Stuck in Second Gear? EU Integration and the Evolution of Poland's Automotive Industry," *Review of International Political Economy*, 27(5) 1147–1169.

Marx, Roberto, de Mello, Adriana Marotti, and de Lara, Felipe Ferreira (2020), "The New Geography of the Automobile Industry: Trends and Challenges in Brazil," *New Frontiers of the Automobile Industry* (Chan, Switzerland: Springer), 349–375.

Mason, Mark (1992), *American Multinationals and Japan: The Political Economy of Japanese Capital Controls, 1899–1980* (Harvard East Asian monographs; Cambridge, MA: Council on East Asian Studies Distributed by Harvard University Press).

Mazzucato, Mariana (2013), *The Entrepreneurial State* (London: Demos).

McCargo, Duncan (2002), "Thailand's January 2001 General Election: Vindicating Reforms," in Duncan McCargo (ed.), *Reforming Thai Politics* (Copenhagen: Nias Pub.), 247–259.

McConnell, Campbell R., and Brue, Stanley L. (2005), *Economics: Principles, Problems, and Policies* (16th ed.; Boston: McGraw-Hill/Irwin).

McDermott, Gerald A. (2007), "The Politics of Institutional Renovation and Economic Upgrading: Recombining the Vines That Bind in Argentina," *Politics & Society* 35(1), 103–144.

McDermott, Gerald, and Pietrobelli, Carlo (2017), "Walking Before You Can Run: The Knowledge, Networks, and Institutions for Emerging Market SMEs," in Torben Pedersen et al. (eds.), *Breaking up the Global Value Chain: Opportunities and Consequences* (1st ed.; Bingley, UK: Emerald), 311–332.

McDermott, Michael C. (1997), "Korean Auto Producers: Asia's Next Major Force in Europe," *Management Decision* 35(7), 497–507.

McKendrick, David (1992), "Obstacles to 'Catch-up': The Case of the Indonesian Aircraft Industry," *Bulletin of Indonesian Economic Studies* 28(1), 39–66.

McKinsey Seoul Office (1998), "Productivity-Led Growth for Korea" (Seoul: McKinsey Global Institute), March.

McMillan, Margaret, and Rodrik, Dani (2011), "Globalization, Structural Change, and Productivity Growth," in Marc Bacchetta and Marion Jansen (eds.), *Making Globalization Socially Sustainable* (Geneva, Switzerland: International Labour Organization; World Trade Organization), 49–84.

McNabb, Mark (2014), "2015 BYD Qin," *TopSpeed*, <http://www.topspeed.com/cars/byd/2015-byd-qin-ar165864.html>.

McNulty, Sheila (1996), "Proton, Yahaya Buy 80% Stake In Lotus Group," *Asian Wall Street Journal*, October 31, <http://global.factiva.com.virtual.anu.edu.au/hp/printsavews.aspx?ppstype=Article&pp=Print&hc=Publication>.

Medalla, Felipe M., Fabella, Raul V., and de Dios, Emmanuel S. (2014), "Beyond the Remittances-Driven Economy" (Manila: UP School of Economics), Discussion Paper.

Medve-Bálint, Gergő, and Šćepanović, Vera (2020), "EU Funds, State Capacity and the Development of Transnational Industrial Policies in Europe's Eastern Periphery," *Review of International Political Economy*, 27(5), 1063–1082.

Miglani, Smita (2019), "The Growth of the Indian Automobile Industry: Analysis of the Roles of Government Policy and Other Enabling Factors," in Kung-Chung Liu and Uday S. Racherla (eds.), *Innovation, Economic Development, and Intellectual Property in India and China: Comparing Six Economic Sectors* (Singapore: Springer Singapore), 439–463.

Mikamo, Shingo (2013), "Business Associations and Politics in the post-EDSA Philippines: Neither Oligarchy nor Civil Society," *Philippine Political Science Journal* 34(1), 6–26.

Ministry of Economic Affairs (2009a), "Jingjibu Gongyeju 98 niandu zhuan'an jihua qimo zhixing chengguo baogao. Jihua mingcheng: Qijiche gongye jishu fudao tuiguang jihua [Ministry of Economic Affairs, Industrial Development Bureau, report on final outcomes of 2009 special projects plan. Plan name: Auto and motorcycle industry technology guidance and diffusion plan], <https://www.moeaidb.gov.tw/external/ctlr?PRO=filepath.DownloadFile&f=executive&t=f&id=3042>.

Ministry of Economic Affairs (2009b), "Auto Electronics Industry Analysis and Investment Opportunities," <http://www.investintaiwan.org.tw/2009TBAC/download/IAR-PAE-en.pdf> (Taipei: Ministry of Economic Affairs, Department of Investment Services).

Ministry of Economic Affairs Department of Industrial Technology (2006), "Tuidong biange: Daoyin chanye jiazhi chuangxin [Promoting change: Leading industrial value creation]," *Jishu Jianbing* 133, 2–17

Ministry of International Trade and Industry, Malaysia (2014), "Perodua to Enhance EEV Technology in Next 5 Years January 21, 2014," (updated January 21) <http://www.miti.gov.my/cms/content.jsp?id=com.tms.cms.article.Article_b2f818f0-c0a8156f-72974691-2ef45eaf&curpage=tt>.

MIRDC (n.d.), "Welcome to MIRDC," <http://www.mirdc.org.tw/English/HomeStyle.aspx?strlink=english/foreword.htm>.

Misawa, Kazufumi (2005), なぜ日本車は世界最強なのか [*Naze Nihonsha wa sekai saikyō na no ka (Why Japanese cars are the strongest in the world)*] (Tokyo: PHP).

Mitchell, Russ (2020), "Car Buyers Shun Electric Vehicles Not Named Tesla. Are Carmakers Driving off a Cliff?," *Los Angeles Times*, January 17, <https://www.latimes.com/business/story/2020-01-17/ev-sales-fizzle>.

Mohamed, Rugayah (1995), "Public Enterprises," in K. S. Jomo (ed.), *Privatizing Malaysia: Rents, Rhetoric, Realities* (Boulder, CO: Westview Press), 63–80.

Montinola, Gabriella (1999), "Parties and Accountability in the Philippines," *Journal of Democracy* 10(11), 126–138.

Moran, Theodore H. (1998), *Foreign Direct Investment and Development: The New Policy Agenda for Developing Countries and Economies in Transition* (Washington, DC: Institute for International Economics).

MOST (Ministry of Science and Technology) (2007), "Shoupi chengli de sida chanye jishu chuangxin zhanlüe lianmeng jianjie [A brief introduction to the establishment of the first four strategic alliances for industrial technology]," <http://www.most.gov.cn/jscxgc/jscxdtxx/200706/t20070619_50541.htm>.

MOST (Ministry of Science and Technology) (2015), "Woguo shuangmo chadian shi hunhe dongli jiaoche jishu qude zhongda jinzhan [Our country's bimodal plug-in hybrid sedan technology attains a major advance]," <http://www.most.gov.cn/kjbgz/201508/t20150805_121013.htm>.

Motor Vehicle Parts Manufacturers Association of the Philippines (MVPMAP) (2013), "Motor Vehicle Parts Manufacturers Association of the Philippines" (2013 Investment and Business Environment Seminar on Philippines; Seoul: ASEAN-Korea Centre), <https://www.aseankorea.org/aseanZone/downloadFile2.asp?boa_filenum=1991>.

Muscat, Robert J. (1994), *The Fifth Tiger: A Study of Thai Development Policy* (Armonk: M. E. Sharpe).

Nag, Biswajit, and De, Debdeep (2020), "The Indian Automobile Industry: Technology Enablers Preparing for the Future," in Alex Covarrubias V and Sigfrido M. Ramírez Perez (eds.), *New Frontiers of the Automobile Industry: Exploring Geographies, Technology, and Institutional Challenges* (Cham: Springer International), 301–321.

Nair, V. V. (2009), "Suzuki, Hyundai's Indian Car Exports Beat China's (Update2)," *Bloomberg.com*, September 7, <http://www.bloomberg.com/apps/news?pid=2067 0001&sid=aO9LxvSmKTzE>.

Nam, Kyung-Min (2011), "Learning through the International Joint Venture: Lessons from the Experience of China's Automotive Sector," *Industrial and Corporate Change* 20(3), 855–907. doi:10.1093/icc/dtr015.

Narula, Rajneesh, and Dunning, John H. (2012), "Multinational Enterprises, Development and Globalization: Some Clarifications and A Research Agenda," in Rajah Raisah and Carlo Pietrobelli (eds.), *Evidence-Based Development Economics: Essays in Honor of Sanjaya Lall* (Kuala Lumpur: University of Malaya Press), 17–46.

Natsuda, Kaoru, Otsuka, Kozo, and Thoburn, John (2015), "Dawn of Industrialization? The Indonesian Automotive Industry," *Bulletin of Indonesian Economic Studies* 51(1), 47–68.

Natsuda, Kaoru, Segawa, Noriyuki, and Thoburn, John (2013), "Liberalization, Industrial Nationalism, and the Malaysian Automotive Industry," *Global Economic Review* 42(2), 113–134.

Natsuda, Kaoru, and Thoburn, John (2013), "Industrial Policy and the Development of the Automotive Industry in Thailand," *Journal of the Asia Pacific Economy* 18(3), 413–437.

Natsuda, Kaoru, and Thoburn, John (2014), "How Much Policy Space Still Exists under the WTO? A Comparative Study of the Automotive Industry in Thailand and Malaysia," *Review of International Political Economy* 21(6), 1346–1377.

Natsuda, Kaoru, and Thoburn, John (2017), "The Automotive Industry in the Philippines: Ready for Take-Off Yet?" (RCAPS Working Paper Series: Ritsumeikan Center for Asia Pacific Studies), March 16, 2017.

Naughton, Barry (2016), "Supply-Side Structural Reform: Policy-makers Look for a Way Out," *China Leadership Monitor* (49), 1–13.

Naughton, Barry (2018), "Xi's System, Xi's Men: After the March 2018 National People's Congress," *China Leadership Monitor* (56), 10, <https://www.hoover.org/research/xis-system-xis-men-after-march-2018-national-peoples-congress>.

NEAC, Government of Malaysia (2010), "New Economic Model for Malaysia, Part 1: Strategic Policy Directions" (Putrajaya, Malaysia: National Economic Advisory Council), March 30, <http://www.mampu.gov.my/pengumuman/07-04-2010-economicmodel_malaysia.pdf>.

Nehru, Vikram (2015), "Indonesia: The Reluctant Giant," in Ashley J. Tellis, Alison Szalwinski, and Michael Wills (eds.), *Strategic Asia 2015–2016: Foundations of National Power in the Asia-Pacific* (Washington, DC: National Bureau of Asian Research): 190–223.

Nelson, Richard R. (ed.), (1993), *National Innovation Systems: A Comparative Analysis* (New York: Oxford University Press).

Niyomsilpa, Sakkarin (2008), "Industry Globalized: The Automotive Sector," in Phongpaichit Pasuk and Christopher John Baker (eds.), *Thai Capital: After the 1997 Crisis* (Bangkok: Silkworm Books), 62–84.

Noble, Gregory W. (1987), "Contending Forces in Taiwan's Economic Policymaking: The Case of Hua Tung Heavy Trucks," *Asian Survey* 27(6), 683–704.

Noble, Gregory W. (1996), "Trojan Horse or Boomerang: Two-Tiered Investment in the Asian Auto Complex" (Berkeley: Berkeley Roundtable on the International Economy [BRIE]), November. <http://brie.berkeley.edu/publications/WP%2090.pdf>.

Noble, Gregory W. (1998), *Collective Action in East Asia: How Ruling Parties Shape Industrial Policy* (Ithaca, NY: Cornell University Press).

Noble, Gregory W. (2001), "Congestion Ahead: Japanese Automakers in Southeast Asia," *Business and Politics* 3(2), 157–184.

Noble, Gregory W. (2006), "The Emergence of the Chinese and Indian Automobile Industries and Implications for Other Developing Countries" (Background paper for Dancing with Giants: China, India, and the Global Economy; Washington, DC: Institute for Policy Studies and the World Bank).

Noble, Gregory W. (2010), "The Decline of Particularism in Japanese Politics," *Journal of East Asian Studies* 10(2), 239–274.

Noble, Gregory W. (2011), "Industrial Policy in Key Developmental Sectors: South Korea versus Japan and Taiwan," in Pyŏng-guk Kim and Ezra F. Vogel (eds.), *The Park Chung Hee Era: The Transformation of South Korea* (Cambridge, MA: Harvard University Press), 603–628.

Noble, Gregory W. (2013), "The Chinese Auto Industry as Challenge, Opportunity and Partner," in Dan Breznitz and John Zysman (eds.), *The Third Globalization: Can Wealthy Nations Stay Rich in the Twenty-First Century?* (New York: Oxford University Press), 57–81.

Noble, Gregory W. (2017), "Government-Business Relations in Democratizing Asia," in Tun-jen Cheng and Yun-han Chu (eds.), *Routledge Handbook of Democratization in East Asia* (New York: Routledge), 427–442.

Noble, Gregory W. (2019), "Dai 8-shō Nihon no 'suiso shakai' gensetsu—kō risuku enerugī seisaku to fuan no riyō [Chapter 8, Japan's 'Hydrogen Society' discourse: high risk energy policies and the manipulation of anxiety]," in Yuji Genda, Shin Arita, and Takashi Iida (eds.), *Kiki taiō no shakai kagaku-ka: Mirai e no tegotae* [*The social sciences of crisis thinking: Responding to the future*] (Tōkyō-to Bunkyō-ku: University of Tokyo Press), 197–227.

Noble, Gregory W., and Ravenhill, John (2000), "The Good, the Bad and the Ugly? Korea, Taiwan and the Asian Financial Crisis," in Gregory W. Noble and John Ravenhill (eds.), *The Asian Financial Crises and the Global Financial Architecture* (Cambridge: Cambridge University Press), 80–107.

Noble, Gregory W., Ravenhill, John, and Doner, Richard F. (2005), "Executioner or Disciplinarian: WTO Accession and the Chinese Auto Industry," *Business and Politics* 7(2), Article 1.

O'Neill, Mark (2006), "Death of a Superspy," *South China Morning Post*, November 13, <http://www.scmp.com/node/571387>.

O'Kane, Sean (2018), "Kymco's New Electric Scooters Could Be the Sign of a Coming Boom", *theverge.com*, <https://www.theverge.com/2018/6/17/17468276/kymco-electric-scooters-taiwan-gogoro>.

OECD, (2016), "PISA 2015 Results in Focus," <https://www.oecd.org/pisa/pisa-2015-results-in-focus.pdf>

Ofreneo, Rene E. (2008), "Arrested Development: Multinationals, TRIMs and the Philippines' Automotive Industry," *Asia Pacific Business Review* 14(1), 65–84.

Ofreneo, Rene E. (2015), "Growth and Employment in De-Industrializing Philippines," *Journal of the Asia Pacific Economy* 20(1), 111–129.

Ofreneo, Rene E. (2016), "Auto and Car Parts Production: Can the Philippines Catch up with Asia?," *Asia Pacific Business Review* 22(1), 48–64.

Ofreneo, Rene E. (2017), "Trapped in the Middle for over Four Decades," *Business Mirror*, May 10, <https://businessmirror.com.ph/trapped-in-the-middle-for-over-four-decades/>.

OICA, (n.d.) "2015 Production Statistics," <http://www.oica.net/category/production-statistics/>.

OICA (2020), "2019 Production Statistics." Organisation Internationale des Constructeurs d'Automobiles, <http://www.oica.net/category/production-statistics/2019-statistics/>.

Ong-Yeoh, David (1996), "Proton, Yahaya Acquire UK's Lotus Group," *Business Times*, October 31, <http://global.factiva.com.virtual.anu.edu.au/hp/printsavews.aspx?ppstype=Article&pp=Print&hc=Publication>.

Pack, Howard (2000), "Research and Development in the Industrial Development Process," in Linsu Kim and Richard R. Nelson (eds.), *Technology, Learning and Innovation* (New York: Cambridge University Press), 69–94.

Panth, Brajesh (2013), "Skills Training and Workforce Development with Reference to Underemployment and Migration," in Rupert Maclean, Jagannathan Shanti, and Jouko Sarvi (eds.), *Skills Development for Inclusive and Sustainable Growth in Developing Asia-Pacific* (Technical and vocational education and training: issues, concerns and prospects; Dordrecht: Springer), 195–212.

Panthong, Kanittha (2012), "Dedicated Testing Centre Sorely Needed," *The Nation*, April 19, sec. Business.

Paopongsakornm, Nipon (1999), *Thailand Automotive Industry (Part I)* (Bangkok: Thailand Development Research Institute).

Park, Chang Wong, and Jun, Han (2001), "Hankuk Jadongcha Sanup HaChung Hyun-kjul-mang Tuk-Sung-eDae-han-Hyun-gu [The Structure of Auto Parts Supply Networks of the Korean Auto Industry]", *Korean Sociological Association* 6, 1–27.

Park, Hun Joo (2007), *Diseased Dirigisme: The Political Sources of Financial Policy toward Small Business in Korea* (Berkeley: Institute of East Asian Studies, University of California).

Park, Si-soo (2011), "Chinese Carmaker SAIC Accused of Tech Theft," *Korea Times*, November 11, <http://www.koreatimes.co.kr/www/common/printpreview.asp?categoryCode=117&newsIdx=55305>.

Pasha, Mochamad, and Setiati, Ira (2011), "Trade Liberalization and International Production Networks: Indonesia's Automotive Industry," *Fighting Irrelevance: The Role of Regional Trade Agreements in International Production Networks in Asia* (New York: United Nations Economic and Social Commission for Asia and the Pacific [ESCAP]), 131–152.

Patel, Parimal, and Pavitt, Keith (1994), "National Innovation Systems: Why They Are Important And How They Might Be Measured And Compared," *Economics of Innovation and New Technology* 3(1), 77–95.

Patunru, Arianto A., and Rahardja, Sjamsu (2015), "Trade Protectionism in Indonesia: Bad Times and Bad Policy" (Sydney: Lowy Institute for International Policy), <https://www.lowyinstitute.org/publications/trade-protectionism-indonesia-bad-times-and-bad-policy>.

Pavlínek, Petr, Domański, Bolesław, and Guzik, Robert (2009), "Industrial Upgrading Through Foreign Direct Investment in Central European Automotive Manufacturing," *European Urban and Regional Studies* 16(1), 43–63.

Pavlinek, Petr (2018), "Global Production Networks, Foreign Direct Investment, and Supplier Linkages in the Integrated Peripheries of the Automotive Industry," *Economic Geography* 94(2), 141–165.

Permatasari, Soraya, and Amin, Haslinda (2010), "Proton Will Collapse Without Partner, Mahathir Says (Update2)" (updated October 12, 2006), <http://www.bloomberg.com/apps/news?pid=20670001&sid=aQWmUWxzKUNU>.

Philippines News Agency (2016), "Auto Sales Increase by 27% in First Half," <http://www.mb.com.ph/auto-sales-increase-by-27-in-first-half>.

Phongpaichit, Pasuk, and Baker, Christopher John (2008), "Conclusion", in Phongpaichit Pasuk and Christopher John Baker (eds.), *Thai Capital: After the 1997 Crisis* (Bangkok: Silkworm Books), 267–277.

Phongpaichit, Pasuk, and Benyaapikul, Pornthep (2014), "Social and Political Aspects of a Middle Income Trap: Thailand's Challenges and Opportunities for Political Reform," *"Middle Income Trap" in Southeast Asia, National Graduate Institute for Policy Studies (GRIPS)* (Tokyo).

Phys.Org (2009), "SKorea Targets World Electric Car Market," *Phys.Org*, October 8, <http://phys.org/print174198541.html>.

Pietrobelli, Carlo, Rasiah, Rajah, and Lall, Sanjaya (2012), *Evidence-Based Development Economics: Essays in honor of Sanjaya Lall* (Kuala Lumpur, Malaysia: University of Malaya Press).

Pipkin, Seth, and Fuentes, Alberto (2017), "Spurred to Upgrade: A Review of Triggers and Consequences of Industrial Upgrading in the Global Value Chain Literature," *World Development* 98, 536–554.

Pongsudhirak, Thitinan (2012), "Between Economic and Political Crises: Thailand's Contested Free Trade Agreements," *The JICA-Reserach Institute Workshop on the Second East Asian Miracle* (Tokyo).

Porter, Michael E. (1998), *The Competitive Advantage of Nations* (New York: Free Press).

Qiche qinglianghua jishu chuangxin zhanlüe lianmeng (2014), "Gongzuo Jianbao [Work Bulletin]," *Gongzuo Jianbao* (12).

Quimba, Francis Mark A., and Rosellon, Maureen Ane D. (2016), "Innovation in the Automotive Sector of the Philippines," <http://dirp3.pids.gov.ph/ris/dps/pidsdps1117.pdf>.

Ra, Young-Sun, and Shim, Kyung Woo (2009), "The Korean Case Study: Past Experience and New Trends in Training Policies" (Washington, DC: World Bank) SP Discussion Paper 0931, December, <http://siteresources.worldbank.org/SOCIALPROTECTION/Resources/SP-Discussion-papers/Labor-Market-DP/0931.pdf>.

Raquiza, Marivic Victoria (2015), "Making the Link between Good Governance, Institutional Reforms, and Poverty Reduction: The Philippine Experience," PhD dissertation, City University of Hong Kong.

Rasiah, Rajah (2001), "Politics, Institutions, and Flexibility: Microelectronics Transnationals and Machine Tool Linkages in Malaysia," in Frederic C. Deyo, Richard F. Doner, and Eric Hershberg (eds.), *Economic Governance and the Challenge of Flexibility in East Asia* (Lanham, MD: Rowman & Littlefield), 165–189.

Rasiah, Rajah (2011a), "Is Malaysia Facing Negative Deindustrialization?," *Pacific Affairs* 84(4), 715–736.

Rasiah, Rajah (2011b), "Industrial Policy and Industrialization," in Rajah Rasiah (ed.), *Malaysian Economy: Unfolding Growth and Social Change* (Kuala Lumpur: Oxford University Press).

Rasiah, Rajah (2017), "The Industrial Policy Experience of the Electronics Industry in Malaysia," in John Page and Finn Tarp (eds.), *The Practice of Industrial Policy* (Oxford: Oxford University Press), 123–144.

Ravenhill, John (1999), "Japanese and U.S. Subsidiaries in East Asia: Host Country Effects," in Dennis Encarnation (ed.), *Japanese Multinationals in Asia: Regional Operations in Comparative Perspective* (New York: Oxford University Press), 261–284.

Ravenhill, John (2003), "From National Champions to Global Partners: Crisis, Globalization, and the Korean Auto Industry," in William W. Keller and Richard J. Samuels (eds.), *Crisis and Innovation in Asian Technology* (Cambridge: Cambridge University Press), 108–136.

Ravenhill, John (2005), "FDI in the Korean Auto Industry," (Paris: Institut français des relations internationales) Les Études de l'IFRI 3, <https://www.researchgate.net/profile/John_Ravenhill/publication/238722504_FDI_IN_THE_KOREAN_AUTO_INDUSTRY/links/004635387414027d03000000/FDI-IN-THE-KOREAN-AUTO-INDUSTRY.pdf>.

Ravenhill, John (2014), "Global Value Chains and Development," *Review of International Political Economy* 21(1), 264–274.

Ravenhill, John (2017), "The Political Economy of a '21st Century' Trade Agreement: The TransPacific Partnership," *New Political Economy* 22(5), 573–594.

Rawski, Thomas G. (2011), "Human Resources and China's Long Economic Boom," *Asia Policy* (12), 33–78.

Raymundo, Roberto B. (2005), "Establishing the Role of the Philippine Automotive Industry in the East Asian Production Network: Identifying Industrial Adjustment Policies That Will Further Enhance Participation in the Network and Responding to the Challenges Posed by China's Emerging Automotive Industry" (Manila: DLSU-Angelo King Institute for Economics and Business Studies).

Reed, John (2009), "Proton to Build Cars for Detroit Electric," *Financial Times*, March 29, <https://www.ft.com/content/4de13962-1c93-11de-977c-00144feabdc0>.

Republic of Turkey (2014), "Turkey's Automotive Industry" (Ankara: Republic of Turkey Prime Ministry Investment Support and Promotion Agency), <http://www.invest.gov.tr/en-US/infocenter/publications/Documents/AUTOMOTIVE.INDUSTRY.pdf>.

Reynolds, Andrew, Reilly, Ben, and Ellis, Andrew (2008), *Electoral System Design: The New International IDEA Handbook* (Stockholm: International Institute for Democracy and Electoral Assistance).

Roberts, Graeme (2019a), "Hyundai Agrees Cheap Labour Plant in Gwangju" (updated February 1, 2019), <https://global.factiva.com/ha/default.aspx#./!?&_suid=15747136672590030677749575522162>.

Roberts, Graeme (2019b), "Minister Details Third Malaysian National Car Project" (updated August 9), <http://global.factiva.com/redir/default.aspx?P=sa&an=JUAUT00020190809ef890008e&cat=a&ep=ASE>.

Rodrik, Dani (2007), *One Economics, Many Recipes: Globalization, Institutions and Economic Growth* (Princeton, NJ: Princeton University Press).

Rogers, Christina (2012), "1 VW Platform, 4 Million Cars: VW's Modular Unit Will Be the Basis for More than 40 Models Worldwide," *Automotive News*, April 9, <http://edit.autonews.com/apps/pbcs.dll/article?AID=/20120409/OEM03/304099975&template=printart&nocache=1>.

Roland_Berger (2017), "Global Automotive Supplier Study 2018," December, <https://www.rolandberger.com/en/Publications/pub_global_automotive_supplier_study_2018.html>.

Roll, Michael (ed.), (2014), *The Politics of Public Sector Performance: Pockets of Effectiveness in Developing Countries* (Routledge research in comparative politics; London: Routledge).

Romer, Paul (1990), "Endogenous Technological Change," *Journal of Political Economy* 98(5), S71–S104.

Rosenbluth, Frances McCall, and Thies, Michael F. (2010), *Japan Transformed: Political Change and Economic Restructuring* (Princeton, NJ: Princeton University Press).

Rosenstein-Rodan, Paul N. (1984), "Natura Facit Saltum: Analysis of the Disequilibrium Process," in Gerald M. Meier and Dudley Seers (eds.), *Pioneers in Development* (New York: Published for the World Bank, Oxford University Press), 207–221.

Rosli, Mohamad, and Kari, Fatimah (2008), "Malaysia's National Automotive Policy and the Performance of Proton's Foreign and Local Vendors," *Asia Pacific Business Review* 14(1), 103–118.

Ross, Michael L. (1999), "The Political Economy of the Resource Curse," *World Politics* 51(2), 297–322.

Rosser, Andrew (2004), "Why Did Indonesia Overcome the Resource Curse?" (Working paper series, Working Paper No. 222; Brighton: Institute of Development Studies).

Rothstein, Bo (2015), "The Chinese Paradox of High Growth and Low Quality of Government: The Cadre Organization Meets Max Weber," *Governance: An International Journal of Policy, Administration, and Institutions* 28(4), 533–548.

Rowley, Chris, and Yoo, Kil-Sang (2013), "Workforce Development in South Korea: A Driving Force in the Korean Miracle," in John Benson, Howard F. Gospel, and Ying Zhu (eds.), *Workforce Development and Skill Formation in Asia* (London: Routledge), 67–88.

S&P Global Ratings (2019), "An Overview of China's Auto Finance Market and Auto Loan Securitization" (updated March 12), <https://structuredfinance.org/wp-content/uploads/2019/06/RatingsDirectAnOverviewOfChinasAutoFinanceMark etAndAutoLoanSecuritizati....pdf>.

Sabel, Charles, and Jordan, Luke (2015), *Doing, Learning, Being: Some Lessons Learned from Malaysia's National Transformation Program* (Washington, DC: World Bank Competitive Industries and Innovation Program [CIIP]).

Sachs, Jeffrey D., and Warner, Andrew M. (1995), "Natural Resource Abundance and Economic Growth" (Working Paper No. 5398; Cambridge, MA: National Bureau for Economic Research).

Saraf, Priyam (2016), *Automotive in South Asia: From Fringe to Global* (Washington, DC: World Bank).

Schneider, Ben Ross (2004), *Business Politics and the State in Twentieth-Century Latin America* (Cambridge; New York: Cambridge University Press).

Schneider, Ben Ross (2010), "Crisis and Institutional Origins: Business Associations in Latin America," in Richard F. Doner (ed.), *Explaining Institutional Innovation: Case Studies from Latin America and East Asia* (New York: Social Science Research Council), 57–68.

Schneider, Ben Ross (2015), *Designing Industrial Policy in Latin America: Business-State Relations and the New Developmentalism* (Latin American political economy; Basingstoke, UK; New York: Palgrave Macmillan).

Schumpeter, J. A. (1983), *The Theory of Economic Development: An Inquiry into Profits, Capital, Credit, Interest, and the Business Cycle, Social Science Classics Series* (New Brunswick, NJ: Transaction Books).

Schwab, Klaus (2010), "The Global Competitiveness Report 2010–2011" (Geneva, Switzerland: World Economic Forum), <https://www.weforum.org/reports/global-competitiveness-report-2010-2011>.

Schwab, Klaus (ed.), (2016), *The Global Competitiveness Report 2016–2017* (Geneva: World Economic Forum).

Seetong, Kanita (2017), "Farmers Demand Removal of Rubber Authority's Board," *The Nation*, November 14, <www.nationalmultimedia.com/detail/national/30331521>.

Segawa, Noriyuki, Natsuda, Kaoru, and Thoburn, John (2014), "Affirmative Action and Economic Liberalisation: The Dilemmas of the Malaysian Automotive Industry," *Asian Studies Review* 38(3), 422–441.

Sen, Kunal (ed.), (2013), *State-Business Relations and Economic Development in Africa and India* (New York: Routledge).

Sender, Henny, et al. (1995), "Economies: The Great Escape," *Far Eastern Economic Review*, March 30.

Seo, Jee-yeon (2016), "Will Samsung Make Car Again?-프린트화면," *Korea Herald*, December 13, <http://www.koreaherald.com/common_prog/newsprint.php?ud=20151213000431&dt=2>.

Sexton, Don (2010), "Hyundai" (New York: Columbia Business School), February 23.

Shah, Hafriz (2015), "Approved Permit (AP) Policy to Remain in Malaysia," (updated December 23 2015) <https://paultan.org/2015/12/23/approved-permit-ap-policy-to-remain-in-malaysia-improvements-to-the-system-to-come-in-2017-miti/>.

Shapira, Philip (1992), "Modernizing Small Manufacturers in Japan: The Role of Local Public Technology Centers," *The Journal of Technology Transfer* 17(1), 40–57.

Shapira, Phillip, et al. (2015), "Institutions for Technology Diffusion" (Manchester, UK: Manchester Institute of Innovation Research, Manchester Business School, University of Manchester), June, <https://strathprints.strath.ac.uk/64641/1/Shapira_etal_2015_Institutions_for_Technology_Diffusion.pdf>.

Shen, Meixing, and Xue, Xiang (2006), "Liu jia IT yezhe kawei rugu huachuang chedian [Six IT firms placed to take shares in Huachuang auto electronics]," *Shibao Zixun*, December 30, <http://tw.stock.yahoo.com/news_content/url/d/a/061230/3/90fx.html>.

Shi, Yigong, and Rao, Yi (2010), "China's Research Culture," *Science* 329(5996), 1128. doi: DOI: 10.1126/science.1196916.

Shin, Ji-hye (2018), "GM, Seoul Agree on $7.15b Rescue Plan," *Korea Herald*, May 10, <http://www.koreaherald.com/view.php?ud=20180510000775>.

Simon, Bernard (2010), "GM Purchasing Head Acts to Mend Fences," *Financial Times*, April 18, <http://www.ft.com/cms/s/c3775986-4b0e-11df-a7ff-00144feab49a,dwp_uuid=b30de674-2ffb-11da-ba9f-00000e2511c8,print=yes.html>.

SIPO (Smart Electronics Industry Project Promotion Office) (2018), "2017 Taiwan's Automotive Electronics Output Value Grows Year by Year," <https://www.sipo.

org.tw/en/industry-overview/industry-state-quo/smart-car-electronics-industry-state-quo.html>.

Siriprachai, Somboon (2012), "Export-Oriented Industrialization Strategy with Land Abundance: Some of Thailand's Shortcomings," *Thammasat Economic Journal*, 16(2), June 1998, pp. 83-138 reprinted in Somboon Siriprachai *Industrialization with a Weak State: Thailand's Development* edited by Pasuk Phongpaichit, Chris Baker, and Kaoru Sugihara (Singapore: NUS Press).

Slater, Dan (2010), *Ordering Power: Contentious Politics and Authoritarian Leviathans in Southeast Asia* (Cambridge: Cambridge University Press).

Slater, Dan (2018), "Party Cartelisation, Indonesian-style," *East Asia Forum*, March 14, <www.eastasiaforum.org/2018/03/14/party-cartelisation-indonesian-style/>.

Smith, Benjamin (2012), "Oil and Politics in Southeast Asia," in Robert E. Looney (ed.), *Handbook of Oil Politics* (New York: Routledge), 206–218.

Smitka, Michael J. (2002), "Adjustment in the Japanese Automotive Industry: A Microcosm of Japanese Cyclical and Structural Change?" (Lexington, VA: Washington and Lee University, Williams School of Commerce) unpublished paper, <http://home.wlu.edu/~smitkam/autoswithgraphs.pdf>.

Soh, Changrok (1997), *From Investment to Innovation: The Korean Political Economy and Changes in Industrial Competitiveness* (Seoul: Global Research Institute, Korea University).

Solis, Mireya (2003), "On the Myth of the Keiretsu Network: Japanese Electronics in North America," *Business and Politics* 5(3), 303–333.

Somchai, Jitsuchon (2013), "Thailand in a Middle-Income Trap," *TDRI Quarterly Review* 27(2), 13–20.

Song, Jiansheng (2008), "Jinshu zhongxin qiang baiyi qiche koujian shangji [MIRDC grabs at 10 billion NTD fastener market opportunity]," *Jingji Ribao*, April 17, 2008.

Song, Jung-a (2019), "Hyundai Motor and Aptiv Seal $4bn Autonomous Car Joint Venture," *Financial Times*, September 23, <https://www.ft.com/content/01721eae-ddf1-11e9-9743-db5a370481bc>.

Song, Jung-a, and White, Edward (2019), "Hyundai Urges Rivals to Buy Its Fuel Cell Tech to Boost Sector," *Financial Times*, June 2, <https://www.ft.com/content/a9362bca-832a-11e9-9935-ad75bb96c849>.

Sperling, Daniel (2018), *Three Revolutions: Steering Automated, Shared, and Electric Vehicles to a Better Future* (Washington, DC: Island Press).

Stahl, C. W. (1986). Overseas workers' remittances in Asian development. *International Migration Review*, 20(4), 899–925.

Statista (2016), "Automobile Manufacturing Industry in China" (Hamburg: Statista), <https://www.statista.com/download/MTU3MDU0NjgyNCMjMjA0MDIxOCMjMTE3MzYjIzEjI3BkZiMjU3R1ZHk=>.

Statista (2019), "Automotive Electronics Cost as a Percentage of Total Car Cost Worldwide from 1950 to 2030," <https://www.statista.com/statistics/277931/automotive-electronics-cost-as-a-share-of-total-car-cost-worldwide/>.

Statista (2020), "Automotive Industry in Malaysia" (New York: Statista), <https://www-statista-com.proxy.lib.uwaterloo.ca/study/59135/automotive-industry-in-malaysia/>.

Stein, Jason (2012), "GM to Bulk Up Engineering in Pan Asia Region," *Automotive News*, April 24 <http://www.autonews.com/article/20120423/GLOBAL03/120429970/gm-to-bulk-up-engineering-resources-in-pan-asia-region-akerson-says>.

Stern, Joseph J., et al. (1995), *Industrialization and the State: The Korean Heavy and Chemical Industry Drive* (Cambridge, MA: Harvard Institute for International Development and Korea Development Institute).

Stewart, Michael (2012), "Moroccan Auto Industry Moving into Top Gear," *Automotive Industries*, <http://www.ai-online.com/Adv/Previous/show_issue.php?id=4367#sthash.MPuJnwLT.dpbs>.

Steyn, Jesper (2012), "Education and Training in Automotive Component Manufacturing," *Innovate* 7 (University of Pretoria Graduate School of Technology Management), 60–61.

Stiglitz, Joseph E., and Lin, Justin Yifu (eds.) (2013), *The Industrial Policy Revolution I: The Role of Government Beyond Ideology* (IEA conference volume, Houndmills, Basingstoke, UK: Palgrave Macmillan).

Stokes, Susan C., et al. (2013), *Brokers, Voters, and Clientelism: The Puzzle of Distributive Politics* (Cambridge: Cambridge University Press).

Strauss, Valerie (2019), "China is No. 1 on PISA—but Here's Why Its Test Scores Are Hard to Believe," *Washington Post*, December 4, <https://www.washingtonpost.com/education/2019/12/04/china-is-no-pisa-heres-why-its-test-scores-are-hard-believe/>.

Sturgeon, Timothy, et al. (2016), "The Philippines in the Automotive Global Value Chain" (Durham, NC: Center on Globalization, Governance, and Competitiveness, Duke University), <https://gvcc.duke.edu/wp-content/uploads/2016_Philippines_Automotive_Global_Value_Chain.pdf>.

Sturgeon, Timothy J., and Lester, Richard K. (2004), "The New Global Supply Base: New Challenges for Local Suppliers in East Asia," in Shahid Yusuf, M. Anjum Altaf, and Kaoru Nabeshima (eds.), *Global Production Networking and Technological Change in East Asia* (New York: Oxford University Press), 35–87.

Sturgeon, Timothy J., and van Biesebroeck, Johannes (2011), "Global Value Chains in the Automotive Industry: An Enhanced Role for Developing Countries?," *International Journal of Technological Learning, Innovation and Development* 4(1–3), 181–205.

Suehiro, Akira (2010), "Industrial Restructuring Policies in Thailand: Japanese or American Approach," in Patarapong Intarakumnerd and Yveline Lecler (eds.),

Sustainability of Thailand's Competitiveness: The Policy Challenges (Singapore: ISEAS), 129–173.

Sun, Nikki (2020), "China's local governments ride to the rescue of EV startups." *Nikkei Asian Review*, August 28, <https://asia.nikkei.com/Business/Business-Spotlight/China-s-local-governments-ride-to-the-rescue-of-EV-startups>.

Sunseth, Bradley (2018), "Thailand's Eastern Economic Corridor—What You need to Know" (updated June 29), <Asianbriefing.com/news/2018/06/29/Thailand-eastern-economic-corridor.html>.

Sutton, John (2004), "The Auto-Component Supply Chain in China and India—A Benchmarking Study" (London: London School of Economics and Political Science), The Toyota Centre, Suntory and Toyota International Centres for Economics and Related Disciplines, Working Paper EI/34.

Swiecki, Bernard, and Menk, Debbie (2016), "The Growing Role of Mexico in the North American Automotive Industry: Trends, Drivers and Forecasts" (Ann Arbor, MI: Center for Automotive Research).

Symaco, Lorraine Pe (2013), "Education in the Knowledge-Based Society: The Case of the Philippines," *Asia-Pacific Journal of Education* 33(2), 183–196.

Tackett, Nicolas (2017), *The Origins of the Chinese Nation: Song China and the Forging of an East Asian World Order* (Cambridge: Cambridge University Press).

TAFTA Propels Automotive Exports (2019), *Bangkok Post*, May 4, <https://www.bangkokpost.com/business/1671664/tafta-propels-automotive-exports>.

Taglioni, Daria, and Winkler, Deborah (2016), *Making Global Value Chains Work for Development* (Washington, DC: World Bank).

TAITRA (2013), *Taiwan Auto Parts and Accessories Industry: Development and Competitive Advantages* (Taipei: Taiwan External Trade Development Council).

Takii, Sadayuki (2004), "Exports, Imports, and Plant Efficiency in Indonesia's Automotive Industry" (2004-22: ICSEAD ASEAN-Auto Project) Working Paper, <file:///F:/USB20FD/Removable%20Disk/auto/indonesia/exports-imports%20 competitiveness%202004%20-%20takii.pdf>.

Tan, Jeff (2007), *Privatization in Malaysia: Regulation, Rent-Seeking, and Policy Failure* (Routledge Malaysian studies series; New York: Routledge).

Tanaka, Akito, Kawakami, Takashi, and Omoto, Yukihiro (2018), "Battery Wars: Japan and South Korea Battle China for Future of EVs," *Nikkei Asian Review*, November 14, <https://asia.nikkei.com/spotlight/cover-story/battery-wars-japan-and-south-korea-battle-china-for-future-of-evs>.

TARC Secretariat (2008), *Taiwan cheliang yanfa lianmeng (TARC) jishu kaifa xiankuang shuoming [An explanation of the current state of technology development at the Taiwan Automotive Research Consortium (TARC)]* (Lugang: ARTC).

Tat, Ho Kay (1996), "Proton Asks Suppliers to Cut Prices of Components by 30%," *The Business Times Singapore*, April 27, <http://global.factiva.com.virtual.anu.edu.au/hp/printsavews.aspx?ppstype=Article&pp=Print&hc=Publication>.

Taylor, Mark Zachary (2016), *The Politics of Innovation: Why Some Countries Are Better than Others at Science and Technology* (New York: Oxford University Press).

Techakanont, Kriengkrai (2011), "Thailand Automotive Parts Industry" (Intermediate Goods Trade in East Asia: Economic Deepening Through FTAs/EPAs, BRC Research Report No. 5; Bangkok: Bangkok Research Center, IDE-JETRO).

Technology Promotion Association (Thailand-Japan) (2019), "Perspective of TPA," <http://www.tpa.or.th/tpanew/default_en.php>.

Temple, Jonathan (1999), "The New Growth Evidence," *Journal of Economic Literature* XXXVII(1), 112–156.

Terlikowski, Marcin (2017), "Defence and Industrial Policy in Poland—Drivers and Influence" (Armament industry European research group [ARES]), July, <https://www.iris-france.org/wp-content/uploads/2017/07/Ares_Defence_Industrial_Policy_in_Poland_July_2017.pdf>.

Thacker, Strom C. (2000), *Big Business, the State, and Free Trade: Constructing Coalitions in Mexico* (Cambridge Univ Press).

Thai German Institute (TGI) (2018), "Thai-German Institute: Its task in Evolving Industrial Sector to Industry 4.0," *Bangkok Post*, January 22 <https://www.pressreader.com/thailand/bangkok-post/20180122/284172221328379>..

Thai Kasikorn Bank "Thailand's Automotive Industry Outlook 2019," <https://kasikornbank.com/international-business/en/Thailand/IndustryBusiness/Pages/201901_Thailand_AutoOutlook19.aspx>.

Thaiger (2020), "Thailand Charges Towards an Electric Car Future," *Thaiger*, March 23, <Thethaiger.com/hot-news/transport/Thailand-charges-twards-an-electric-car-future-with-a-few-speed-bumps>.

Thailand Automotive Institute (TAI) (2012), "Master Plan for Automotive Industry, 2012–2016" (Bangkok: Ministry of Industry).

The Conference Board (2017), "International Comparisons of Hourly Compensation Costs in Manufacturing, 2015—Summary Tables" (updated April 12, 2016) <https://www.conference-board.org/ilcprogram/index.cfm?id=38269>.

The Economist Intelligence Unit (2014), "Auto Production and Exports Reach Record Highs in 2013" (The Economist Intelligence Unit), January 9, <http://www.eiu.com/industry/article/1301403314/auto-production-and-exports-reach-record-highs-in-2013/2014-01-09>.

Thee, Kian Wie (2006), "Policies Affecting Indonesia's Industrial Technology Development," *ASEAN Economic Bulletin* 23(3), 341–359.

Thee, Kian Wie (2007), "The Auto Parts Industry," unpublished background paper for World Bank report on Reviving Growth in Indonesia's Manufacturing Sector.

Thee, Kian Wie (2012), *Indonesia's Economy since Independence* (Singapore: Institute of Southeast Asian Studies).

Thiruchelvam, K., et al. (2013), "Malaysia's Quest for Innovation Progress and Lessons Learned" (Petaling Jaya, Malaysia: Strategic Information and Research Development Centre).

Thorpe, Norman (2005), "Quebec Mistakes Still Haunt Hyundai," *Automotive News*, June 13, <http://www.autonews.com/article/20050613/SUB/506130710/quebec-mistakes-still-haunt-hyundai>.

Thun, Eric (2006), *Changing Lanes in China: Foreign Direct Investment, Local Governments, and Auto Sector Development* (Cambridge: Cambridge University Press).

Tijaja, Julia, and Faisal, Mohammad (2014), "Industrial Policy in Indonesia: A Global Value Chain Perspective" (Manila: Asian Development Bank), Working Paper.

Tilak, Jandhyala B. G. (2003), "Vocational Education and Training in Asia," in John P. Keeves and Ryo Watanabe (eds.), *The International Handbook of Educational Research in the Asia-Pacific Region* (Dordrecht: Kluwer), 673–686.

Times Higher Education (2020), "World University Rankings 2021," <https://www.timeshighereducation.com/world-university-rankings>.

Tjiptoherijanto, Prijono (2010), "Trust in Government: The Indonesian Experience," *International Public Management Review* 11(2), 132–138.

Traub, James (2016), "The Party That Wants to Make Poland Great Again," *New York Times Magazine*, <https://www.nytimes.com/2016/11/06/magazine/the-party-that-wants-to-make-poland-great-again.html?_r=0>.

TTVMA (2009), *List of Taiwanese Businesses Overseas* (Taipei: Taiwan Transportation Vehicle Manufacturers Association).

Tucker, Sundeep (2008a), "Halla Takes the Wheel at Mando Again," *Financial Times*, January 21, <http://www.ft.com/intl/cms/s/0/c4dec7d6-c7f9-11dc-94a6-0000779fd2ac.html>.

Tucker, Sundeep (2008b), "Mando Sale Saga Highlights Renaissance of Korea Inc.," *Financial Times*, January 22, <http://www.ft.com/intl/cms/s/0/12808b48-c88e-11dc-94a6-0000779fd2ac.html>.

Tzannatos, Zafiris, and Johnes, Geraint (1997), "Training and Skills Development in the East Asian Newly Industrialised Countries: A Comparison and Lessons for Developing Countries," *Journal of Vocational Education and Training* 49(3), 431–453.

UAES (United Automotive Electronic Systems) (2016), "UAES," <http://www.uaes.com/servlet/portal/T_index>.

UNCTAD (2013), "Global Value Chains and Development: Investment and Value Added Trade in the Global Economy" (Geneva: UNCTAD), <http://unctad.org/en/PublicationsLibrary/diae2013d1_en.pdf>.

UNCTAD (2014), "ASEAN Investment Report 2013–2014: FDI Development and Regional Value Chains" (Geneva: UNCTAD), <http://unctad.org/en/PublicationsLibrary/unctad_asean_air2014d1.pdf>.

UNCTAD (2015), "Science, Technology & Innovation Policy Review: Thailand" (Geneva: UNCTAD).

UNCTAD (2019), "World Investment Report 2019: Special Economic Zones" (Geneva: UNCTAD), <https://unctad.org/en/PublicationsLibrary/wir2019_en.pdf>.

Unger, Daniel H., and Mahakanjana, Chandra (2016), *Thai Politics: Between Democracy and Its Discontents* (Boulder, CO: Lynne Rienner).

UNICO (1999), "The Follow-up Study on Supporting Industries Development in the Kingdom of Thailand" (JICA Study Team, UNICO International Corporation, International Development Center of Japan).

UNIDO (2016), "Quality Infrastructure: Building Trust for Trade" (Vienna: UNIDO), <www.unido.org/sites/default/files/2016-05/UNIDO_Quality_system_0.pdf>.

US Department of Health and Human Services (2010), "Escalating Health Care Costs" (updated April 13) <http://www.healthreform.gov/reports/inaction/>.

Vellequette, Larry P. (2020), "Audi Exec Says Electrication, Mobility Could Triple Size of Industry by 2050," *Automotive News Europe*, <https://europe.autonews.com/automakers/audi-exec-says-electrification-mobility-could-triple-size-industry-2050>.

Volkmann, Elizia (2016), "French Connection Nurturing Morocco's Auto Industry," *WardsAuto*, <https://www.wardsauto.com/industry/french-connection-nurturing-morocco-s-auto-industry>.

Wad, Peter (2008), "The Development of Automotive Parts Suppliers in Korea and Malaysia: A Global Value Chain Perspective," *Asia Pacific Business Review* 14(1), 47–64.

Wad, Peter (2009), "The Automobile Industry of Southeast Asia: Malaysia and Thailand," *Journal of the Asia Pacific Economy* 14(2), 172–193.

Wad, Peter, and Govindaraju, V. G. R. Chandran (2011), "Automotive Industry in Malaysia: An Assessment of Its Development," *International Journal of Automotive Technology and Management* 11(2), 152–171.

Wade, Robert (1990), *Governing the Market: Economic Theory and the Role of Government in East Asian Industrialization* (Princeton, NJ: Princeton University Press).

Wade, Robert (1992), "East Asia's Economic Success: Conflicting Perspectives, Partial Insights, Shaky Evidence," *World Politics* 44(2), 270–320.

Wade, Robert (2003), "What Development Strategies Are Viable for Developing Countries? The World Trade Organisation and the Shrinking of 'Development Space,'" *Review of International Political Economy* 10(4), 621–644.

Wade, Robert H. (2014), "Industrial Policy—Better, Not Less" (Geneva: United Nations Conference on Trade and Development), September 16, <http://unctad.org/meetings/en/Presentation/tdb61_Rwade_item8_en.pdf>.

Wain, Barry (2009), *Malaysian Maverick: Mahathir Mohamad in Turbulent Times* (Basingstoke, UK: Palgrave Macmillan).

Waldner, David (1999), *State Building and Late Development* (Ithaca, NY: Cornell University Press).

Wan, Qichao (n.d.), "Zhuandong nengyuan xin xiwang [Turning to a new hope for energy] (Taipei: Ministry of Science and Technology), <http://www.most.gov.tw/50th/ct.asp?xItem=16195&ctnode=3177>.

Wang, Paul (2015), "An Overview of Automotive Vehicle and Component Regulations in China," <http://incompliancemag.com/article/an-overview-of-automotive-vehicle-and-component-regulations-in-china/>.

Wang, Yunshi, Teter, Jacob, and Sperling, Daniel (2011), "China's Soaring Vehicle Population: Even Greater than Forecasted?," *Energy Policy* 39(6), 3296–3306.

Wangyi Qiche (2010), "Zhao Hang: Zhongqi zhongxin zhuanqi hou bu neng diou diao shehui zeren [Zhao Hang: Even after corporatization, CATARC cannot abandon social responsibility]," 网易汽车 (updated May 23), <http://auto.163.com/10/0523/18/67D1CASF00084EGE.html>.

Wanxiang Electric Vehicle (2011), "Wanxiang Electric Vehicle," <http://www.wanxiang.com/Wanxiang%20EV_general.pdf>.

Warburton, Eve (2016), "Jokowi and the New Developmentalism," *Bulletin of Indonesian Economic Studies* 52(3), 297–320.

Ward's Auto World (2004), "Local Market Disappoints GMDAT," *Ward's Auto World*, March 1, <https://global-factiva-com.proxy.lib.uwaterloo.ca/hp/printsavews.aspx?pp=Print&hc=Publication>.

Warr, Peter (2011), "Thailand's Development Strategy and Growth Performance" (UNU-WIDER Working Paper, 2011/02: United Nations University), January.

Waverman, Leonard, and Murphy, Steven (1992), "Total Factor Productivity in Automobile Production in Argentina, Mexico, Korea, and Canada: The Impacts of Protection," in Gerald K. Helleiner (ed.), *Trade Policy, Industrialization and Development* (Oxford: Clarendon Press), 279–315.

Webb, Alysha, and Chang, Peter (2004), "SAIC Preferred Bidder for Ssangyong," *Automotive News*, July 26, <http://www.autonews.com/article/20040726/SUB/407260770?template=printart>.

Wei, Shu (2011), "Gongyanyuan chengli daohang dingwei chanye lianmeng [ITRI establishes industrial alliance for navigational positioning]," *Zhongyangshe*, December 12 <https://n.yam.com/Article/20111202060947>.

Whittaker, D. Hugh, Tianbiao Zhu, Timothy Sturgeon, Mon Han Tsai, and Toshie Okita (2010), "Compressed Development," *Studies in Comparative International Development* 45, 439–467.

Whittaker, D. Hugh, Timothy J. Sturgeon, Toshie Okita, and Tianbiao Zhu (2020), *Compressed Development: Time and Timing in Economic and Social Development* (New York: Oxford University Press).

Williamson, John (2009), "A Short History of the Washington Consensus," *Law & Business Review of the Americas* 15, 7.

Womack, James P., Jones, Daniel T., and Roos, Daniel (1991), *The Machine That Changed the World: The Story of Lean Production—How Japan's Secret Weapon in the Global Auto Wars Will Revolutionize Western Industry* (New York: Harper Collins).

Wong, Chan-Yuan (2011a), "Rent-Seeking, Industrial Policies and National Innovation Systems in Southeast Asian Economies," *Technology in Society* 33(3–4), 231–243.

Wong, Joseph (2011), *Betting on Biotech: Innovation and the Limits of Asia's Developmental State* (Ithaca, NY: Cornell University Press).

Woo, Jung-en (1991), *Race to the Swift: State and Finance in Korean Industrialization* (New York: Columbia University Press).

World Bank (2008), "Thailand—Investment Climate Assessment Update" (Report No. 44248-TH: Poverty Reduction and Economic Management Sector Unit, East Asia and Pacific Region), <http://documents.worldbank.org/curated/en/268141468120847586/pdf/442480ESW0P1061C0disclosed071281091.pdf>.

World Bank (2010), *Thailand Economic Monitor* (Bangkok, Thailand: World Bank Office Bangkok).

World Bank (2012b), "Leading with Ideas: Skills for Growth and Equity in Thailand" (Bangkok, Thailand: World Bank).

World Bank (2013), "2012 China Enterprise Survey," <http://www.enterprisesurveys.org/~/media/GIAWB/EnterpriseSurveys/Documents/CountryHighlights/China-2012.pdf>.

World Bank (2014a), "Fundacion Chile Incubator: Chile Case Study (English)", (Washington, DC: World Bank), Working Paper 90122, January, <http://documents.worldbank.org/curated/en/270771468023424195/pdf/901220WP0Box380business-chile0-web0.pdf>.

World Bank (2014b), "Knowledge Economy Index," <http://siteresources.worldbank.org/INTUNIKAM/Resources/2012.pdf>.

World Bank (2017a), "Military Expenditure (% of GDP)," <https://data.worldbank.org/indicator/MS.MIL.XPND.GD.ZS>.

World Bank (2017b), "Research and Development Expenditure (% of GDP)," <https://data.worldbank.org/indicator/GB.XPD.RSDV.GD.ZS>.

World Bank (n.d.), *Worldwide Governance Indicators: Interactive Data Access*, <http://info.worldbank.org/governance/wgi/index.aspx#reports>.

World Bank (2018a), *Quality Infrastructure* (Washington, DC: World Bank) <https://www.worldbank.org/en/topic/competitiveness/brief/qi>.

World Bank (2018b), *Thailand Economic Monitor* (Bangkok, Thailand: World Bank Office Bangkok).

Xianwaibang (2020), "长城汽车在技术研发投入上，真的很抠门吗？(Is Great Wall Motor Really Stingy in Its Investment in Technology Research and Development?)," July 22, 2020. <https://zhuanlan.zhihu.com/p/162768835>.

Xie, Xilin (1993), *Yulong sishi nian [40 years of Yulon]* (Taipei: Yulong Yuekan).

Xue Yi (2005), *Guomin zhengfu ziyuan weiyuanhui yanjiu [Research on the Nationalist Government's National Resources Commission]* (Beijing: Shehui Kexue Wenxian Chubanshe).

Yamamoto, Hajime (2011), "Automotive Industry Outlook," *2nd Asia Pacific Elastomer Science and Technology Conference* (Bangkok: IHS Automotive).

Yamamoto, Hajime (2012), "ASEAN Automotive Market Outlook and Challenges and Opportunities for Suppliers," <http://www.thaiautoparts.or.th/download/Asian_Auto_Market1.pdf>.

Yanfeng Automotive Interiors (2015), "Yanfeng Automotive Interiors Joint Venture Formally Launches: Joint Venture Ranks as World's Largest Automotive Interiors Supplier," <http://www.prnewswire.com/news-releases/yanfeng-automotive-interiors-joint-venture-formally-launches-300108086.htm>.

Yang, Dali L. (2004), *Remaking the Chinese Leviathan: Market Transition and the Politics of Governance in China* (Stanford, CA: Stanford University Press).

Yang, Jian (2016), "The Man Who Could Revolutionize China's 'Green Car' Market," *Automotive News China*, <http://www.autonewschina.com/en/article.asp?id=14309>.

Yang, Jian (2017a), "How China Plans to Create a Giant State-Owned Automaker," *Automotive News China*, <http://www.autonewschina.com/en/article.asp?id=14309>.

Yang, Jian (2017b), "With Volvo Support, Geely's Lynk & CO Has a Good Chance to Gain U.S. Foothold," *Automotive News China*, <http://www.autonewschina.com/en/article.asp?id=16481>.

Yang, Jian (2019), "Why Beijing May Not Rescue Auto Market" (updated July 12), <https://www.autonews.com/china-commentary/why-beijing-may-not-rescue-auto-market>.

Yang, Kairan (2007), "Jiang Lei shenmi lijing ge qiche jituan zhengduo zhongqixie mishuzhang zhiwei [(After) Jiang Lei's mysterious departure all the automotive groups fight for the position of Secretary General of CAAM]," *Jinghua Shibao*, May 24, <http://news.sohu.com/20070524/n250192497.shtml>.

Yap, Michael Meow-Chung, and Teng, Kwek Kian (2012), "Monetary Policy and Financial Sector Development," in Hal Hill, Siew Yean Tham, and Zin Ragayah Haji Mat (eds.), *Malaysia's Development Challenges: Graduating from the Middle* (London: Routledge), 106–130.

Yokohama, Takashi (2004), "Taiwan kaihatsu no shashu o tōnan ajia ya chūgoku de mo katsuyō [Utilizing Taiwan-developed car models in Southeast Asia, China, and so on, too]," *Chūka Minkoku Taiwan Tōshi Tsūshin* 102, 6–7.

Yonghap English News (2008), "Hyundai Mobis Develops Homegrown Brake System," *Yonghap News*, February 26, <http://english.yonhapnews.co.kr/>.

Yoshida, Junko (2017a), "Is Foxconn Ready for Cars?," *EE Times*, <https://www.eetimes.com/author.asp?section_id=36&doc_id=1331640>.

Yoshida, Junko (2017b), "Taiwan Eyes Automotive Market," *EETimes*, <https://www.eetimes.com/document.asp?doc_id=1331628>.

Yoshihara, Kunio (1988), *The Rise of Ersatz Capitalism in South-East Asia* (Singapore; New York: Oxford University Press).

Young, Alwyn (1994), "Lessons from the East Asian NICs: A Contrarian View," *European Economic Review* 38(3–4), 964–973.

Yu, Zongxian, and Wang, Jinli (2012), *Taiwan chanye fazhan hequ hecong* [*The course of Taiwan's industrial development*] (Taipei: Lianjing Chuban).

Yulon (n.d.), "Yulon Group history," <http://www.yulon-group.com/history.php>.

Yusuf, Shahid, and Nabeshima, Kaoru (2009), *Tiger Economies under Threat: A Comparative Analysis of Malaysia's Industrial Prospects and Policy Options* (Washington, DC: World Bank).

Zacks.com (2008), "Auto Industry—Zacks.com" (updated December 12, 2008), <http://www.zacks.com/stock/news/16378/Auto+Industry?print=print>.

Zakariah, Faizal (2004), "Comprehensive Proton and VW Tie-Up," *The Edge Malaysia*, November 2, <http://global.factiva.com.virtual.anu.edu.au/hp/printsavews.aspx?ppstype=Article&pp=Print&hc=Publication>.

Zhang, Lu (2014), *Inside China's Automobile Factories: The Politics of Labor and Worker Resistance* (Cambridge: Cambridge University Press).

Zhang, Xiaoming (2015), *Deng Xiaoping's Long War: The Military Conflict between China and Vietnam, 1979–1991* (Chapel Hill: University of North Carolina Press).

Zhang, Yi (2009), "'Cheng Lian Hui' Zhenxiang: Yige 'sanwu' zuzhi eryi [The truth about 'CPCA,' just a 'three-nothings' organization]," *Xinhua*, <http://news.xinhuanet.com/auto/2009-01/16/content_10666696.htm>.

Zheng, Lichun, and Li, Isabelle (2019), "Exclusive: Local Governments Lurk Behind Chery Automobile's Two Bidders." *Caixin*, <https://www.caixinglobal.com/2019-09-26/exclusive-local-governments-lurk-behind-chery-automobiles-two-bidders-101466762.html>, September 26.

Zhongguo qiche gongcheng xuehui and Shanghai huabao chubanshe (2003), *Zhongguo qiche wushi nian* [*50 Years of the Chinese Automobile Industry*] (Shanghai: Shanghai Huabao Chubanshe).

Zhongguo qiche jishu yanjiu zhongxin, Nissan (Zhongguo) touzi youxian gongsi, and Dongfeng qiche youxian gongsi (eds.) (2015), *Zhongguo Xin Nengyuan Qiche Chanye Fazhan Baogao (2015)* [*Annual report on new energy vehicle industry in China (2015)*] (Beijing: Shehui Kexue Wenxian Chubanshe).

Zhongguo qiche jishu yanjiu zhongxin (CATARC) and Zhongguo qiche gongye xiehui (CAAM) (2006), *Zhongguo qiche gongye nianjian 2006 nian ban* [*China Automotive Industry Yearbook, 2006*] (Tianjin: Zhongguo qiche gongye nianjian bianjibu).

Zhongguo qiche jishu yanjiu zhongxin (CATARC) and Zhongguo qiche gongye xiehui (CAAM) (2010), *Zhongguo qiche gongye nianjian 2010 nian ban* [*China Automotive Industry Yearbook, 2010*] (Tianjin: Zhongguo Qiche Gongye Nianjian Bianjibu).

Zhongguo qiche jishu yanjiu zhongxin (CATARC) and Zhongguo qiche gongye xiehui (CAAM) (2015), *Zhongguo qiche gongye nianjian 2015 nian ban* [*China Automotive Industry Yearbook, 2015*] (Tianjin: Zhongguo Qiche Gongye Nianjian Qikanshe).

Zhongguo qiche jishu yanjiu zhongxin (CATARC) and Zhongguo qiche gongye xiehui (CAAM) (2016), *Zhongguo qiche gongye nianjian 2016 nian ban* [*China Automotive Industry Yearbook, 2016*] (Tianjin: Zhongguo Qiche Gongye Nianjian Qikanshe).

Zhongguo qiche zhiliang wang (2014), "Zhongguo Quexian Qiche Chanpin Zhaohui Zhidu Shishi Shi nian [10 years of implementation of China's recall system for defective automotive products]," <http://www.caam.org.cn/hangye/20141205/1405140286.html>.

Zhou, Lei, "Miandui Zhongqiyan cheqi wufa raodao erxing [For auto companies, there's no getting around CATARC]," <http://tiantianbk.blog.163.com/blog/static/105528337201042404532361/>.

Zhu, Ying, and Warner, Malcolm (2013a), "Workforce Development and Skill Formation in China: A New 'Long March,'" in John Benson, Howard Gospel, and Ying Zhu (eds.), *Workforce Development and Skill Formation in Asia* (New York: Routledge), 142–158.

Zhu, Ying, and Warner, Malcolm (2013b), "Workforce Development and Skill Formation in Taiwan: Social Cohesion and Nation Building in a Developmental State," in John Benson, Howard Gospel, and Ying Zhu (eds.), *Workforce Development and Skill Formation in Asia* (New York: Routledge), 159–177.

Zhuang, Suyu (1998), *Yan Kaitai fan bai wei sheng* [*Yan Kaitai turns defeat into victory*] (Taipei: Tianxia Zazhi).

이준승 (2019), "Hyundai, Kia Moving Global Production Facilities to Emerging Markets" (updated February 6, 2019), <https://en.yna.co.kr/view/AEN20190206001300320>.

최경애 (2020a), "Renault Samsung's Jan. Sales Plunge 55 Pct on Lower Demand" (updated February 3, 2020), <https://en.yna.co.kr/view/AEN20200203006100320>.

최경애 (2020b), "SsangYong Motor Q4 Net Losses Widen on Weaker Demand" (updated February 7, 2020), <https://en.yna.co.kr/view/AEN20200207001300320>.

최경애 (2020c), "GM Korea's Jan. Sales Plunge 47 Pct on Lower Demand" (updated February 3, 2020), <https://en.yna.co.kr/view/AEN20200203005600320>.

Index

For the benefit of digital users, indexed terms that span two pages (e.g., 52–53) may, on occasion, appear on only one of those pages.

Tables and figures are indicated by *t* and *f* following the page number